War over Lemuria

War over Lemuria

Richard Shaver, Ray Palmer and the Strangest Chapter of 1940s Science Fiction

RICHARD TORONTO

McFarland & Company, Inc., Publishers
Jefferson, North Carolina, and London

LIBRARY OF CONGRESS CATALOGUING-IN-PUBLICATION DATA

Toronto, Richard, 1946–
War over Lemuria : Richard Shaver, Ray Palmer and the strangest chapter of 1940s science fiction / Richard Toronto.
p.   cm.

Includes bibliographical references and index.

ISBN 978-0-7864-7307-6
softcover : acid free paper ∞

1. Palmer, Ray, 1910–1977.   2. Shaver, Richard S.   3. Science fiction, American—History and criticism.   4. Novelists, American—20th century—Biography.   5. Periodical editors—United States—Biography.   6. Science fiction—Publishing—United States—History—20th century.   7. Science fiction—Periodicals—History.   I. Title.
PS374.S35T67 2013   813'.0876209—dc23   2013012301

BRITISH LIBRARY CATALOGUING DATA ARE AVAILABLE

© 2013 Richard Toronto. All rights reserved

No part of this book may be reproduced or transmitted in any form or by any means, electronic or mechanical, including photocopying or recording, or by any information storage and retrieval system, without permission in writing from the publisher.

Front cover artwork: The controversy was raging about Richard Shaver's yarns about Lemuria, so his "Quest of Brail" story merited this illustration by Robert Gibson Jones on the December 1945 cover of *Amazing Stories* (author's collection)

Manufactured in the United States of America

McFarland & Company, Inc., Publishers
Box 611, Jefferson, North Carolina 28640
www.mcfarlandpub.com

To Chester S. Geier,
everyone's favorite character.

Acknowledgments

Thanks
To Jim Pobst for working on the honor farm;
To Earl Kemp for getting involved when he had doubts;
To Linda J. Palmer for believing in the book;
To Evelyn A. Bryant for memories of her family;
To Frances and Bill Hamling for saving history;
To Chester S. Geier for his friendship;
To Rich and Lynda Horton for being such good hosts;
To Lora Santiago for her incredible technical support;
To Vaughn Greene for writing hoax letters to Rap;
To Steve Volto Dero (whoever you are);
And to Richard Shaver for sending me on a 40-year walkabout.

Table of Contents

Acknowledgments — vi
Preface — 1
Introduction — 3

Part I. The Life and Times of Raymond Alfred Palmer

1. The Memory Comet — 12
2. Education — 22
3. Trauma — 27
4. Spilling the Atoms — 34
5. Politics — 46
6. The Inner Circle — 52

Part II. Richard Sharpe Shaver

7. Shavertown — 62
8. The Early Years — 68
9. The Wicker School of Fine Art — 81
10. Through the Looking Glass — 88
11. Period of Abandonment — 97
12. Ionia, 1938–1943 — 102

Part III. The Rise and Fall of the Shaver Mystery, 1945–1948

13. Howard Browne — 116
14. Lemuria, My Lemuria — 122
15. Conflict — 128
16. Line in the Sand — 133
17. Science of the Damned — 137
18. Fanfeud from Hell — 144
19. Armistice of 1948 — 165

Part IV. Diaspora

20. Reconstructing Ray Palmer	174
21. The Unexpected Gafiation of William L. Hamling	180
22. The Stigmata of Raymond A. Palmer	184
23. Big Trouble in Little Amherst	207
24. Artful Obsession	218
25. Martian Diary	230
26. The Inner Circle's Last Stand, 1975–1977	237
Chapter Notes	243
Bibliography	251
Index	255

Preface

Richard Shaver began writing this book in 1975 when I suggested we collaborate on a book about his life. I had known him through correspondence for two and a half years before I made my upstart proposal. He replied with a flippant remark about my inability to write a cogent letter, let alone a book, but he put aside his misgivings and typed what would have been the first page of an autobiography, parts of which appear in the book you now hold.

Our relationship was clear-cut from the beginning. He was in his late 60s, I was in my early 20s. He was the Kung Fu Master, I was Grasshopper, and he never failed to let me know what a poor student I was. He gave me barely passing grades on my interpretations of rock books, one of his greatest discoveries. The rock books were cryptic, high tech, pre-Flood relics manufactured by an ancient race, he said, and until I understood them I would never know the meaning of life, the universe, or anything, for that matter.

As for our collaboration, he coached me, saying that if I wrote just one page per day, I would have a 365-page book within a year; longer if I took Sundays off. It sounded easy in theory. Then I realized I knew nothing about him, other than what I read about his part in the notorious Shaver Mystery — then, as now, a nearly forgotten skeleton in the closet of science fiction literature. And as any Kung Fu Master will tell you, meaningful answers come only when you ask the right questions.

While I pondered my dilemma, Shaver fell ill and died on November 5, 1975. Thus began my 40 years in the wilderness in search of Shaver's life, times and eventual banishment from the annals of science fiction.

To facilitate my search, in 1979 I founded *Shavertron*, a fanzine of the old order. I cut and pasted on graph paper and printed it on a Gestetner mimeograph machine at my workplace. *Shavertron* was all about Shaver, Ray Palmer (his editor at *Amazing Stories*) and the controversy surrounding them. *Shavertron* was meant to put me in touch with those who could help me in my search, and to some degree it worked.

I sent the first issue — two sheets of blue paper stapled together — to Shaver's personal mailing list, given to me by his widow, Dottie. Many of Shaver's former fans contacted me; even a few personal friends. In 1984 I met Richard Horton, Thomas Brown and Vincent Gaddis in Oceanside, California.

Gaddis was a stage magician and Fortean author who invented the term "Bermuda Triangle" in one of his books. He also wrote fillers for Ray Palmer's *Amazing Stories*. Brown was running Meade Layne's old Borderland Sciences Research Foundation, and Horton was Shaver's unofficially adopted son. I had finally hit pay dirt.

On visits to the Shavers' Wisconsin farm during the early 1950s, Horton became fast friends with Dick and Dottie. Thus Horton was a living record of the farm, Shaver, and

Ray Palmer. In the years that followed our first meeting, Horton and I casually discussed how one day we would write a book about Shaver's life, but it was not until 2006, on a visit to Horton's Banning, California, home, that we agreed there was enough material to begin work. Sad to say, Rich Horton died while working on his contribution. Now I was two Richards down. Nevertheless, the project continued.

During my research into the lives of Ray Palmer and Richard Shaver, I discovered parts of their lives they would rather forget; secret places they chose not to think about. They experienced physical and emotional pain that eventually guided the course of their lives. This shared experience of trauma connected them in unspoken ways that, as survivors, only they fully understood. It also made them difficult for *others* to understand, and opened them up to criticism from people who had no idea what made them tick. They were anomalies, or, as the critics liked to paint them, freaks of nature.

This book is not the final word on the Shaver Mystery, Richard Shaver, or Ray Palmer. In my pursuit for answers I encountered some dead ends. On the other hand, some doors opened to me unexpectedly.

Another thing. This book does nothing to confirm or deny the reality of Shaver's deros — an evil race of beings living inside the Earth — or the existence of flying saucers and whether Richard Shaver and Ray Palmer invented them. This is a story of ordinary men thrust into extraordinary circumstances. What they did to overcome their circumstances hit science fiction with a one-two punch.

Introduction

"I am a cross-eyed old man. What in hell, nothing comes out of my head but repetitive nonsense. I try to write and nothing happens but moon glow on the knobs of horn — blow horn blow."— Richard Shaver

It is said that time heals old wounds. It can change a point of reference, create a new universe or a new attitude. It brings deference to closed minds that, in the dim past, prevailed. Whether time enough has passed for science fiction fandom to forgive the sins of Richard S. Shaver and Raymond A. Palmer is debatable, for history has accused them of the greatest hoax ever foisted on man and science fiction. They called it the Shaver Mystery.

On learning of Shaver's death in 1975, Palmer confessed that it felt as if he had just lost a brother,[1] and though their relationship was often difficult, they were brothers under the skin. They shared a history of trauma, violence, and transformation. The very act of their survival made them brothers.

The Shaver Mystery was a product of its time. It appeared in March 1945 as World War II was turning against the Axis. Atom bombs were about to drop on Japan. Intrigue, conspiracy, paranoia, and the hope and fear spawned by emerging new science ran rampant. Science fiction fans were claiming their place in popular culture. In the midst of all this raged the great conflict known as the Shaver Mystery, a prism through which the angst of war-torn Earthlings seemed to focus.

On its face the Shaver Mystery was the promotion of a series of science fiction yarns that appeared in *Amazing Stories* and *Fantastic Adventures* magazines between 1945 and 1948, with Palmer as editor. It all began with a strange alphabet called Mantong, Earth's "mother tongue." It was an artifact Shaver "discovered" and developed over time.

Science fiction was already full of odd languages and slang. A.E. Van Vogt's *Slan* novels popularized new slang terms among SF fans. The "universal language" of Esperanto gained popularity in SF circles as early as the 1930s. Fans evolved their own language, and it grew into a sizable glossary of words. "Egoboo," "Beardmutterings," "Fiaggh," and "Fugghead" were colorful and puzzling terms to the non-fan. Language has always been the building block of any new movement, something that SF pulp writer L. Ron Hubbard knew when he fashioned Scientology.

The language key may be why Shaver sent his Mantong alphabet to Palmer. Shaver was not merely selling stories, he had a message for humanity. Nevertheless, Mantong was not what sparked the controversy. The controversy — the *mystery*— came from Shaver's claim that his stories were based on facts acquired from another world. Hardcore SF fans found Shaver's facts hard to swallow, though they were not the hoax everyone suspected.

Shaver's facts were what placed him among other historical figures like William Blake, Pythagoras, Galileo, Luther, and Emanuel Swedenborg, all of whom dispensed similar facts that came from auditory and visual hallucinations. Put succinctly, Shaver heard voices. They were similar to the voices heard by luminaries like Joan of Arc and Philip K. Dick, and they gave Shaver information. They also gave him his mission in life.

Shaver's voices explained that prior to the Deluge of Noah, an advanced civilization flourished under the leadership of three races: the Atlans, Titans, and Nortans. These beings came from somewhere in deep space and lived happily on Earth until the neighborhood went to hell in a handbasket. The sun began to spew radioactive particles that were deadly to their existence. Their bodies — once immortal — began to age. This would never do, and their learned ones sought an immediate solution.

At first, they avoided the sun by retreating underground, constructing vast cavern systems within the Earth's crust. This is where they lived and worked for many years, until finally leaving Earth forever, preferring the security of dark space, as far from our deadly sun as possible.

Shaver's incredible story of Earth's history was just a prequel. There were stragglers that somehow missed out on the migration to space. Some continued to live underground in the caverns constructed by the elders. Others moved back to the sun-drenched surface. These surface dwellers became human beings as we know them today. But underground there was a big problem. Many of the stragglers (Shaver called them abandonderos) turned into evil mutants, poisoned by the contamination of their radiation-filtering systems.

The cave people split into two groups: tero (positive) and dero (negative). Shaver's Mantong alphabet defines a dero as a "detrimental robot," that is, someone whose mind is controlled by the destructive emanations of the sun. Even worse, the deros have access to the Atlans' incredible machines left behind in the caves. These "mech" as Shaver called them, now in the hands of deros, inflict invisible rays on surface folk even today, controlling us in various ways.

Mech can eavesdrop on one's innermost thoughts, transmit physical sensations, healing rays, or instant death. A "telaug" mech can put thoughts into one's mind. Unlike his forebears, who explained voices as the word of God or angels, Shaver explained his voices within the framework of science fiction and emerging science.

In modern psychiatric jargon his telaug is explained as an "influencing machine," a symptom of a popular 20th century psychosis called schizophrenia. Whether it *was* schizophrenia is not known for sure; I have not seen Shaver's medical records.

Palmer discovered Shaver in 1943, less than six months after Shaver's release from Ionia State Hospital for the Criminally Insane. Shaver kept his stay in Ionia secret as long as he could, for it had taken a great toll on him. It was a social stigma, a shameful affair that he felt would damage his career as a prophet and successful pulp fiction writer.

Shaver had been hearing voices since 1934, nearly ten years before he contacted Palmer. The voices gave him information that would become the foundation of the Shaver Mystery. Palmer accepted Shaver's information as if he believed it, and for that he was considered a hoaxer and a charlatan. Critics said he knew it could not have been true, that he was using Shaver to create a controversy. Some of that was true, but there was another dimension to the story. Palmer was a true believer in "the unseen."

History has not been kind to the Shaver Mystery. Palmer, known to fans by his initials (Rap), was considered an intelligent man. So was Shaver. Many considered him a genius in his own right. Both men blurred the line between genius and madness, and were condemned as liars and worse.

Unconsciously or not, Ray Palmer transformed Shaver's stories of a subterranean world of evil deros into a metaphor for the evil that gripped a war-torn surface world. The war destroyed Palmer's brother David and some of his closest friends and writers. He may well have seen the Shaver Mystery as an allegory of Man's descent into Hell, a modern-day *Paradise Lost*.

Shaver and Palmer were complex characters. Even those who knew them admitted that, within each of them, there was a wall beyond which no one could see. Their world had not always been a welcoming place for them, and they adjusted as best they could to their misfortunes.

Of the other players on the stage of the Shaver Mystery, few of them wrote autobiographies. Though Shaver yearned for a collaborator to help him tell his story, only Palmer stepped up to sketch a vague portrait of his life in his 1975 autobiography *Martian Diary*.

In the telling of their story, it is hard to know where fact begins and fantasy ends. Rap's critics would have us believe he was a pathological liar. Even his own grandmother could not believe that he remembered minute details of his infancy. He said he did, but she believed it was impossible. According to Palmer, her attitude was consistent with the rest of his family. They would not believe him. So Palmer came to believe he knew something others did not, which he explained in 1968.

> A hundred times a day I open my mouth to say something, then I clamp it shut again. It has been my misfortune to have learned something about that "unseen" world that exists all about us ... and when you speak of it, you'd better be kidding, because even though they may listen respectfully, or tolerantly, or with feigned interest, or with correct politeness, in the back of their minds they don't believe it can possibly be true, and they are firmly convinced that you are, at the very least, deceiving yourself, if you are not actually psychotic.[2]

And so it went with most people who knew Ray Palmer. They were never quite sure what to think of him. Did he truly believe in *anything*? Though he often tried to express his beliefs, he was never very good at it. His agile mind was in a constant state of flux. Facts were open-ended, never a sure thing for very long. Those around him saw this trait, but were at a loss what to think about it. Bea Mahaffey worked closely with Rap as editor of two of his SF magazines during the early 1950s. In a 1980 interview she explained that, try as she might, she could never quite pin down Rap's belief system — on anything. His explanations were so convoluted they left her bewildered:

> There are so many conflicting stories about the man. Having worked with him for five years, it is difficult for anyone to say they knew the real Ray Palmer, you know only what a person permits you to know. Ray was a complex man. He was a science fiction fan, he really loved science fiction and the field, and when the strife came between Ray and the science fiction fans that were so anti–Palmer it hurt Ray a lot more than he let on, and a lot more than people realized. When he lashed out at fans, it was hurt striking out. He was basically a gentle person who was a pacifist to an extreme.[3]

Rap's daughter Linda Jane also noted the confusion caused by her father's expressions of thought. In a note to the author sent October 10, 2010, she said, "By the way my dad talked, it was pretty much impossible to know if he believed what he was saying or not. I think he got a lot of satisfaction from that. He was always a good talker and a good writer and had a vivid imagination."

The obfuscation shielding Palmer's innermost thoughts was likely a self-taught survival technique he had begun using as a boy. He perfected the skill while growing up with an abusive, alcoholic father, who did not share or understand his son's innermost thoughts and dreams. Keeping them secret was young Palmer's way of dealing with the emotional abuse.

SF fandom was a tough audience in Palmer's day, and may be still. Fans considered themselves superior to the rest of humanity — intelligent, well-read, and opinionated. Jokes and hoaxes played on fellow fans were a common pastime, as were fan feuds which were often exasperating and ridiculous.

Fans sometimes wore propeller beanies, dropped water balloons from hotel windows during SF conventions, and set off firecrackers to create general mayhem. City cops were aware of the antics of local SF club members and kept a wary eye on them. In one case, the FBI got involved. Fans set themselves apart from the uninformed masses, and were critical of anyone perceived as outside their point of reference. Rap began as one of these fans.

Fandom became an historical fact when SF fan Jack Speer partitioned it into numerical *fandoms*, or eras, each with its own personality and focus. Palmer's life as a fan began in Eofandom, the earliest era (1930–1933).

During First Fandom (1933–1936) the driving force was *Fantasy Magazine*, where Rap was contributing editor. Then came the First Interregnum (late 1936–October 1937), Second Fandom (October 1937–October 1938), the Second Transition (from the 1938 Philadelphia convention through the 1940 Chicago Worldcon), Third Fandom (September 1940–early 1944), the Third Interregnum (1944), and Fourth Fandom (late 1944–1947), which saw the rise of the Shaver Mystery.

From Eofandom to the end of Fourth Fandom, the number of truly active SF fans numbered less than 200. Shaver became the whipping boy of those fans, thanks to his role in *Amazing Stories* and the Shaver Mystery. This troubled Shaver to no end, to be so reviled, for he believed sincerely in every word he wrote — except for the ones he knew were fiction.

The Shaver Mystery, as it turned out, reflected changing attitudes about mental health as much as it did attitudes about science fiction. Shaver's stories encouraged a heretofore-unrepresented group of readers to come out of the closet. Fandom called them the Lunatic Fringe because they believed in and supported Richard Shaver. Many of these new fans said they heard the same voices that spoke to Shaver. Thousands of letters from readers poured into Palmer's office confirming that *their* voices were saying the same things described by Shaver.

This was a revelation for Rap, who said the letters were proof that Shaver's claims were true. Rap had tapped into a vast, marginalized group of citizens that did in fact hear voices. In Shaver they saw a fellow traveler, for he was hearing the same voices that influenced their day-to-day lives, for better or worse.

What these letters proved was not that Shaver's deros were raying thoughts into people's minds, but that thousands of people were hearing voices. In that sense, the Shaver Mystery became an unintentional support group for sufferers of auditory hallucination. All of that disappeared when the owner of *Amazing Stories* discontinued the Shaver Mystery.

It took another 40 years before these voice—hearers eventually found mainstream support from Dutch professors Marius Romme and Sondra Escher of Maastricht University. Based on their research into the "hearing voices" phenomenon, a Manchester, England, support group formed the Hearing Voices Network in 1990, following a national conference on auditory hallucinations. Its purpose is to promote understanding and remove the stigma from those who hear voices. Romme and Escher estimate that about 4 percent of the world population hears voices. They contend that a diagnosis of schizophrenia is not predestined for those who hear voices, and believe that a normal life is attainable without drugs or incarceration for those willing to learn the purpose of the voices in their lives.

All this was in the far-off future in 1945, when people like Shaver were sent off to asylums. Fandom criticized these voice-hearers unmercifully, while Palmer lauded them for their bravery in speaking out. He also used their stories to sell magazines, which was, after all, his job as an editor.

One man who claims to have known the *real* Ray Palmer says that he was neither a liar nor a charlatan, but believed in what he published. William Lawrence Hamling, science fiction fan, author, and publisher, says Rap was a savvy editor, and knew how to create interest in a magazine. He was not out to snooker anyone with the Shaver Mystery, according to Hamling. In a 2009 interview at his Palm Springs, California, home, Hamling set the record straight on the Shaver Mystery once and for all: "It was not malicious. Palmer was a believer. He wasn't a phony. I can verify that. He was a top-drawer editor, too, and he had the record to prove it.... Ray had strong convictions. He really and factually believed Shaver, but he didn't promulgate fantasy ideas out of it, he *molded* the Shaver Mystery as a record of an era of hidden truth."

Nevertheless, the inability of others to believe in Palmer appears to have made him a lonely man, as he professed in 1966: "The fact is, at 55 years old, I find myself as alone in this world as a Martian, with actually *no one* to talk to! There is a borderline where ideas seem to become 'insanity.' For years I've had to pretend things to enable me to 'get away' with others."[4]

This may explain the story of Harlan Ellison and the elevator confession. One day during the 1952 Worldcon in Chicago, a teenaged Harlan Ellison caught Rap entering an elevator and rushed inside before the doors closed behind them. Having cornered Rap, Ellison demanded Rap's confession that the entire Shaver Mystery was a hoax. As the story goes, Rap acquiesced.

Ellison claimed that Rap replied, "It was a publicity grabber to obtain circulation." The elevator doors opened and Ellison bolted with the scoop of the decade. Word spread throughout fandom that Rap finally confessed to the so-called Lemurian Hoax. In 1957, Ellison went on the Long John Nebel Radio Show and reaffirmed his version of the story.

Rap responded in a letter to Nebel with his version: that he simply told Ellison what he wanted to hear.

> The science fiction fans (that small group officially known as "fandom") had condemned the Shaver Mystery and me, the first as untrue, and me as a "traitor to science fiction." Harlan Ellison was one of the prime movers in this condemnation. Most of them, I discovered by a few questions, didn't even know what the Mystery was about, and in fact, some had not even read it! Thus, when cornered in the elevator ... Mr. Ellison, who put his question as a challenge ... with the preconceived attitude that if I said it was true I was a liar, and if I were honest, I'd say it was untrue, struck me as the least qualified to put such a question, as he was just a boy of about 17. I replied: "I'll give you the answer you want. It was a publicity stunt to increase circulation."[5]

Ellison eventually went on to work for William Hamling, who knew Ellison well enough to believe that there *was* an elevator confession. Hamling says, "Yes, Harlan would do that. Harlan was mean. Very mean. That is true. He was capable of being a little son of a bitch. Harlan was what my wife always said; 'He is a naughty little boy, and always will be.'"[6]

Regardless of what others thought of him, Rap believed in himself completely. If it were not for Ray Palmer, who *would* believe in Ray Palmer? Well, Bea Mahaffey for one. She said as much in a 1980 interview:

> As a human being Ray was kind, warm, generous, very sensitive, and very easily hurt because he had been hurt so much. [He was] easy to work for because he made you feel you were working *with* him not *for* him. He was a very complex person; he was a lot more talented and gave a lot more to science fiction than people are aware; he developed some very good writers. It was a joy to work with him. It was not a matter of "me boss you slave," because it was *our* magazine we were working on, and I think everyone working in the office all felt the same way. It wasn't just a job you came and punched a time clock.[7]

Martin Gardner, a mathematician on a crusade to expose fringe cults, did not believe in Palmer. Convinced that Rap was one of the greatest flimflam artists of all time, he said he had proof. For example, take Rap's middle initial: Gardner said it was meaningless; it was just the letter A. He claimed Rap continued the scam by naming his son Raymond B. Palmer, which naturally follows A. Gardner refused to believe otherwise when a long-time Rap associate told him the A stood for Alfred. Said Gardner, "I'll accept 'Alfred' when I see a copy of Ray's birth certificate."[8]

This was the kind of criticism that plagued Palmer throughout his life, coming from learned men of letters. Gardner dug even deeper into the absurd when he wrote that Charles Brown, in his Palmer obit, "said the 'A' stood for Arthur. In an effort to verify this, I asked Jerome Clark, a *FATE* editor. He replied that his boss, Curtis Fuller, told him the 'A' stood only for the first letter of the alphabet."[9]

Locus editor Charles Brown did mistakenly write that Rap's middle name was Arthur in his September 1977 obit on Rap. As for Curtis Fuller telling Jerome Clark that Rap's middle name was merely an "A," Fuller should have known better, having worked with Rap for years. *Alfred*, not A, not Arthur, was Ray Palmer's middle name. All this went into Gardner's exposé, proving that Bea Mahaffey was correct in her assessment that conflicting information seems to plague Ray Palmer.

Rap surrounded himself with an inner circle of his closest friends and associates, usually writers, editors, and science fiction fans. This helped buffer him from a hostile world. Howard Browne, along with William L. Hamling and a handful of others, made up Palmer's inner circle at Ziff-Davis Publishing in Chicago.

Browne's name became indelibly linked to the genesis of the Shaver Mystery when he opened Richard Shaver's first letter to *Amazing Stories* in 1943. Browne worked as a Ziff-Davis associate editor for five years under Rap's supervision. Browne went on to become one of Ray Palmer's harshest critics, especially after Rap's death in 1977. In a tell-all memoir, Browne described a Friday afternoon ritual at the Ziff-Davis office, where Rap would personally dole out checks to his writers. Why in person? Browne said he knew why: "It was Palmer's way, perhaps subconsciously, of proving that — physically handicapped or not — he was the Big Man, the guy in charge. Cross him in any way, deny him the proper homage, and your income stopped, sometimes briefly, sometimes for good."[10]

William Hamling, who shared an office with Palmer at Ziff-Davis, hit the ceiling on hearing Browne's story for the first time in 2009: "Not true! He is so full of shit! That is Howard Browne at his worst. That is not true! *Not true*! The fact is, Howard resented that Ray was his boss.... Howard Browne is a liar there. I resent that, by God. And you can quote me. He's a liar."

Proving once again that emotions run high when it comes to Ray Palmer.

As for Shaver, he emerged, phoenix-like, from a decade of physical and emotional purgatory within the Michigan state hospital system. During that time, he fought it, escaped and was brought back. He became a victim of the snake pit of Depression-era mental health attitudes.

On his release, he spoke out against the state prison and asylum systems, writing articles and fictional stories to expose what he considered a racket by fat cats who doled out life sentences to innocent people. Rather than cure him, Shaver's ten-year ordeal drove him deeper within himself. Instead of silencing the voices, his incarceration gave him the key to their origin, their purpose, and his mission to expose a vast conspiracy that spanned centuries. His diploma on graduating from Ionia State Hospital was an ancient alphabet and a degree in Lemurian physics that formed the basis of his science fiction stories.

Readers have debated the truth of Shaver's information from the time his first story "I Remember Lemuria!" appeared in the March 1945 issue of *Amazing Stories*. It sparked discussion on the meaning of visions, dreams, and hallucinations. Students of metaphysics took the Shaver Mystery to heart, much to Shaver's dismay. He believed the voices came from living, breathing people inside the Earth. They were not spirits in any way, shape, or form. His down-to-earth personality added fuel to the debate, for, as unbelievable as his stories were, he was the most believable part of them.

Exactly how Shaver arrived at his vision of Lemuria (aka Mu) is something of a mystery in itself, as it differed from accepted occult lore of the time. Lemuria in Shaver's world was the name for Earth, which he attributed to Lemuria's three root races: the Titans, Atlans and Nortans. But the first recorded use of the name Lemuria seems to have come from Victorian zoologist Philip Sclater. In 1864 he posed the theory of a lost continent to explain the mystery of lemurs living on continents separated by vast expanses of ocean. In Sclater's 19th century, pre-continental drift era land bridges that met untimely ends through cataclysmic disaster explained many zoological anomalies.

Though Lemuria as scientific theory was eventually replaced by the theory of plate tectonics, occultists embraced the Lemurian continent, expounding on its history and inhabitants well into the 20th century. Proponents of Lemurian occult history included Madame Helena Blavatsky, theosophist William Scott-Elliot (*The Lost Lemuria*, 1904), Rudolf Steiner (*Atlantis and Lemuria*, 1911), James Bramwell (*Lost Atlantis*, 1937), Col. James Churchward — who turned Lemuria into a cottage industry (*The Lost Continent of Mu Motherland of Man*, 1926; *The Children of Mu*, 1931; *The Lost Continent of Mu*, 1931; *The Sacred Symbols of Mu*, 1933; *Cosmic Forces of Mu*, 1934; *Second Book of Cosmic Forces of Mu*, 1935), and Frederick Spencer Oliver (*A Dweller on Two Planets*, 1905) who believed survivors of the Lemurian catastrophe were alive and well in a complex of tunnels inside Mt. Shasta in California.

Oliver's image of a brotherhood of white-robed Lemurians residing in the bowels of Mt. Shasta was a template for Stanton A. Goblentz's "Enchantress of Lemuria" which appeared on the cover of *Amazing Stories*' September 1941 issue. Goblentz wrote of a scientist who used penetrating television rays to locate a vast man-made tunnel system 15 miles below the surface of Earth. The scientist found an entrance to the cavern world through the use of his invention and, after many days of subterranean wandering, met the descendants of the Lemurian race, which chose to live underground than return to the uncertainty of a cataclysmically challenged surface world. These Lemurians spoke their own root language and had fantastic high-tech machinery at their disposal, affording them a pleasant underground existence.

"Enchantress of Lemuria" appeared a full three years before Shaver became Palmer's top writer at *Amazing*, so Rap was aware of the Lemurian legend long before he rewrote Shaver's first manuscript and renamed it "I Remember Lemuria." As far as the Shaver Mystery is concerned, the question that remains is, how much of the Lemuria legend came from Richard Shaver and how much came from Ray Palmer?

This book barely scratches the surface of a phenomenon spanning several fields of study: space travel, life extension, mental health, history, geology, metaphysics, ancient astronauts, radionics, physics, astronomy, and SF fandom. A third of the original manuscript ended up on the cutting room floor to reduce its size. If nothing else, it is hoped that what remains will put a human face on two science fiction legends that, until now, history has deigned to present as caricatures.

Part I
The Life and Times of Raymond Alfred Palmer

1

The Memory Comet

"Who am I? That seems to me to be an important question...."— Ray Palmer

Ray Palmer's story begins in the black void of space, where all things of great significance to Earth come from. Wayward asteroids, the Big Bang, and most science fiction yarns begin or end somewhere in outer space, as do portents seen in the sky, like Halley's Comet. In Palmer's case, the appearance of Halley's Comet in 1910 is what got the ball rolling, for that was the year of his birth. He claimed the comet as his own, as had Mark Twain before him. Twain, however, was born and died under the glow of Halley's Comet, completing its 76-year cycle. Palmer hoped to repeat Twain's performance but missed his departure date by nine years. For him, the return year would have been 1986.

He was born Raymond Alfred Palmer on August 1, 1910, the same year Mark Twain shed his mortal coil. For the astrologers among you, this particular Raymond A. Palmer was born at 5 P.M. in Milwaukee, Wisconsin, to Roy and Helen Palmer. They were living with Raymond's paternal grandparents at the time, in a modest two-story clapboard house at 3009 St. Paul Street.

Barely married a year, the couple had no reason to believe there was anything more to this blessed event than the birth of their first child. They underestimated the Universe of Infinite Possibilities. The stars at Raymond's birth foretold a tumultuous future for a little-known literary genre known as science fiction, for one day it would come to pass that Raymond Palmer would become editor of *Amazing Stories* and beget the Great Conflict known as the Shaver Mystery.

Halley's Comet often evokes a kind of mystical revelation in those lucky enough to see it, and Palmer was one of those who fell under its spell. He gave the comet an entire page in his autobiography, *Martian Diary*. Whether the title of his memoir came from an ingrained sense of alienation, or the belief that he actually *was* from Mars, only Palmer knew for sure.

He explained that his boyhood was marked by the appearance of superhuman traits, not the least of which was his ability to recall minute details about his early life. One of his favorite memories was his sighting of Halley's Comet from a window in the Palmer family home. This memory was indeed impressive, if not problematic, for the comet had moved beyond Earth's orbit three months prior to his birth. Nevertheless, throughout his career Palmer recounted the story of his comet sighting. Though his story was entertaining, it was astronomically challenged. Never let it be said that Palmer let facts get in the way of a cherished memory. He addressed the comet issue in his 1975 autobiography:

> I have mentioned that I have a memory of my paternal grandmother taking me in her arms, walking to the window, drawing aside a curtain and saying: "Look at the pretty comet." I remember the comet vividly; how its tail stretched across three-quarters of the sky....
>
> It is quite embarrassing to write such a thing and have one of your readers write in with positive proof that you are a liar. It is a fact that the comet of 1910, Halley's Comet, passed beyond the range of vision of the naked eye in mid–June. It is quite obvious that a baby born in August could not have seen the comet. I hadn't been born yet! So how could it be?[1]

The solution was simple: Palmer, like science fiction writer and Scientology founder L. Ron Hubbard, became a convert to pre-birth memory. He had sighted the comet *before* he was born. This ability to access the vast memory banks of his mind did not come naturally. It developed over time as the result of an unexpected series of unfortunate events. A tragic accident at an early age confined him to bed and hospital wards for long periods of time. During these convalescing periods he began to expand his mind, and his memory:

"[While] hospitalized for several years. I used to practice remembering. I would begin by remembering what happened yesterday, then a week ago, a year ago and proceed back into time as far as I could go. Eventually I could remember detailed events of specific days at a very early age. I was astonished at what I could remember. And it always checked out."[2] (His father and grandmother believed none of it. Tossing it off as vivid imagination, they viewed his memory exercises as a "very bad trait, a weakness, even a sort of sickness."[3])

Palmer wrote, "What I am trying to say here is that it has always been that way in my family — I remember very many things vividly, but strangely, members of the family who should be quite conversant with the actual events fail to remember at all, and indeed, emphatically deny that my memories can possibly be true."[4]

This blatant disbelief coming from those around him would haunt Palmer throughout his life. But problems with his family went beyond mere distrust in his memory. His father, a hard-drinking Irish fireman, failed to see the potential in his son. His mother believed in him but subordinated her feelings to her husband's. This is how Palmer learned to believe in himself, in his memories and his superpowers. His pre-birth comet memory became so compelling that as an adult he returned to his birthplace to confirm it. Standing on the front porch of 3009 St. Paul Avenue, he convinced the new owner to let him see the place so deeply etched into his memory.

"In the living room, which faced north, I saw the very window, recognized the woodwork, and proved conclusively to myself that I could certainly have seen the comet in precisely the place in the sky where it actually was visible in May of 1910."[5]

Family

> "...that 'nickname' ... was hung on me 45 years ago by a trio of science fiction fans named Forrie Ackerman,[6] Aubrey Clements and Julius Schwartz (my initials — written as a word — Rap)...."— Ray Palmer

Ray Palmer was born of Irish and German parents, both native Wisconsinites. Their marriage took place in Milwaukee on December 15, 1909. His father, Roy Clarence Palmer, was young, poor and living with his parents, Phineas and Henrietta Palmer, at the time of his marriage. He worked as a timekeeper for the Grant Marble Company. Helen Steber Palmer, Raymond's German mother, was born in 1877, making her a year older than her husband. The couple continued to live with Roy's parents until the following year, when he became a city fireman, a job he held for many years thereafter. With the extra income, the family moved to an apartment on 29th Street.

As family legend has it, the Palmer surname appeared on their ancestor's arrival in America, their original name being Prickett. Grandfather Phineas Palmer told Ray the story of their surname, over his grandmother's objections. The Pricketts, he said, had the same problem as other Irish Protestants: They were "Orangemen" in a predominantly Catholic town.

He recounted the fateful Christmas Eve when "the Pricketts were chased out of Ireland ... by the Catholics."[7] As the sun rose on Christmas Day, the Prickett family packed their bags for America. On arriving in the New World, they swapped their Irish surname for something a little more English, inexplicably converting to Catholicism in the process.

Helen Martha Steber was the daughter of German immigrants Herman Steber and Alvina Krohn. Alvina never learned to speak English. This was not a problem in their mostly German-speaking Milwaukee neighborhood. Like most of the Germans settling in the American Midwest, they were Lutherans.

Milwaukee's nickname at that time was "The Workingman's City" and it was a natural destination for the likes of the Palmers and Stebers. It was a city of immigrants. The Germans were a ubiquitous and influential population. The re-settling of German immigrant workers along the factory-lined west bank of the Milwaukee River was a common practice, and it forever branded that section as "German Milwaukee." "Yankees," as the Germans called them, lived on the east bank.

The 1910 United States census ranked "The Workingman's City" twelfth in population and third as an industrial mecca. Only Buffalo and Detroit had more workers employed in manufacturing. Thanks to its deep Germanic roots, Milwaukee boasted three large beer companies: Pabst, Schlitz, and Blatz. These familiar names were painted on the sides of countless delivery trucks, and would figure into Ray Palmer's life in a big way.

The Steber surname became one of Rap's well-known pen names: R.A. Steber, who wrote for *Amazing Stories* from the time Rap took over as editor in 1938. As a German American, Rap bent over backward during World War II to prove his loyalty to America, though that did little to curb the FBI's interest in him or in Ziff-Davis Publishing, the owner of *Amazing Stories*.

Roy and Helen Palmer were financially strapped throughout their marriage, due in part to Roy's heavy drinking. Ray Palmer rarely talked about his father, but the family knew of their uneven relationship. The rancor escalated whenever Ray sided with his abused mother, whom he idealized as the epitome of womanhood. He learned of her suffering when she confided in him during times of breastfeeding. His mother was unaware that the infant at her breast was cataloging every word she spoke. All this was detailed in his memoir. His photographic memory, he said, recorded things too painful to reveal. He vowed never to speak of his mother's confessions, though in *Martian Diary* he said they changed his life forever, shaping him into the man he would become:

> Naturally those sounds were unintelligible to an infant, but ... as I strove intently to remember, I could recreate the sounds in my mind — and I understood her words! It was then that I learned for the first time in my life how to hate. You see, I was the only one to whom my mother could confide her troubles, in the privacy of my nursery. Coupled with the accident that crippled me, made me a hunchback, I became a lone wolf, a bitterly determined stubborn man dedicated to defying injustice and meanness wherever I found it.... Anyone who did evil to another could never be a friend of mine.[8]

And so Palmer endured an abusive father and a mother he could not rescue; this was his challenge as a boy. The Great Manipulator — his term for whatever it is that guides the universe — had taught him to resist all forms of authority. It is unfortunate that Palmer's ironclad memory failed to prevent significant events of his life from being lost to history. This was certainly an effort on his part as he rarely, if ever, discussed his early childhood, even with his own children. Memories were often too painful to recall.

Nevertheless, at the age of five, life was not all that bad, for that was when Rap got a room of his own on the family sun porch. He played with friends in the neighborhood streets, where many poor children spent their free time in "The Workingman's City."

At the tender age of seven Palmer met his destiny in the worldly guise of a beer truck. Whether it was Schlitz, Blatz, or Pabst is unknown. The incident is essential to the Ray Palmer mythos, but one he did not relish in the telling. More than the direction of his own life, it may well have altered the course of science fiction as we know it, for it changed Palmer's worldview drastically, endowing him with unorthodox beliefs that would guide his career.

A Grim Fairy Tale

> *"I jousted with a truck in the middle of the street. The truck won; and landing on my head, folded me up to a permanent height of 4'8". I'm still folded."*—Ray Palmer

The *legend* of Ray Palmer began during his second year of grade school, when he was injured by a truck. As with most of his life stories, it was prone to variation. Whether it actually *was* a beer truck as some recall, a milk truck as his son believes, or a butcher truck as Rap once described it, all agree it was a truck, and the end result was the same.

While playing in the street near the truck, Ray Palmer's leg became lodged in the wooden spokes of its rear wheel. As the truck began to move, it took young Ray with it. The force of the moving truck yanked him up and slammed him down into the pavement. This went on for agonizing seconds until the driver heard the boy's screams and slammed on the brakes.

The aftermath is somewhat muddled, but it appears that on dislodging the child from the wheel, the distraught truck driver, with information from neighborhood children, found his parents. Speaking with father Roy, he offered to drive the injured boy to the nearest hospital, as the Palmer family had no car. What happened next would haunt Ray Palmer's life as much as the accident itself: After looking the boy over, his father declined the offer. "He'll be all right," he said. "It's only a bruise."[9]

Thus began a chain of events that would cripple Ray Palmer for life. Whether his father truly believed his son would be all right is hard to fathom. More than likely, the offer was rejected because there was no money for a doctor. An X-ray would have revealed a fractured spine, but no X-ray was taken and no doctor consulted. Instead, his father laid him out in the family dining room. That was where Ray Palmer began his life of pain. His distraught mother made him as comfortable as she could, but what happened following the accident was blotted out by family guilt and pain.

Frances Ferris Yerxa Hamling, 92,[10] a close Palmer family friend and confidant to Ray Palmer's wife Marjorie, knows some of that story. In a 2008 interview, she recalled that a Milwaukee social worker paid a visit to the Palmer household after learning of the boy's plight. Social agency visits were not uncommon among poor families at the time, especially when children were at risk.

> He was run over by a beer truck. "The family was very poor, and Catholic. His father was a drunkard. They played in the street all the time. Somebody saw him being run over and they picked him up and carried him to their little meager house. They put him on a cot in the dining room. And there he was, he was dying, and some social worker came to investigate and found him near death.
>
> His father and mother didn't know how to take care of him. His father didn't care. We didn't have any agencies to take care of health issues in those years. There was no Social Security and no hospitalization. No hospital wanted him because they were penniless, so he was put in a TB sanitarium.
>
> While he was there, with his bones all broken (his heart was on the wrong side of his chest — everything [was] all scrambled up in him), he contracted TB of the bone. Seemed like he would have died from that, but he was able to recover. I think it was the TB of the bone that ruined his spine.[11]

The sanitarium she spoke of may have been the tuberculosis ward of the Milwaukee Children's Free Hospital. Opened in 1907, it offered free care to indigent cases. Wherever it was, recovery came slowly. His early exposure to tuberculosis would haunt Palmer throughout his youth, and reemerge some years later, forcing him to convalesce in yet another TB sanitarium.

What is certain is that Palmer did not receive the medical care he needed for a successful recovery. Spinal deterioration continued in the years following the accident until, at age nine, he could no longer walk or stand. It was painfully obvious he would not recover without medical intervention.

Somehow, his parents managed to engage the services of Milwaukee orthopedic surgeon Dr. Frederick J. Gaenslen. It could be that a social agency arranged the surgery as a charity case. Dr. Gaenslen was a staff member at Columbia Hospital, the Children's Hospital, Mount Sinai and Milwaukee Hospital, the Milwaukee County Hospital, the Bradley Memorial Hospital at Madison, and the Methodist Hospital at Madison, and he consulted at Wisconsin State General Hospital at Madison. It was through one of these medical institutions that nine-year-old Ray Palmer came to his attention.

Dr. Gaenslen, Spinal Pioneer

"A great many of the miracles we see around us today were the science fiction of yesterday." — Ray Palmer

Ray Palmer's infallible memory was on the fritz whenever he recalled Frederick J. Gaenslen. He remembered him as Dr. *Herman P.* Gaenslen, writing about him on several occasions by that name. He claimed the operation was Dr. Gaenslen's very first spinal graft — the first in the nation, in fact. Whether true or not, in Palmer's eyes it made his surgery unique. Sad to say, it was.

The desired outcome of a spinal graft is a bridge of solid bone between two vertebrae. Fragments of the patient's bone are implanted, and if conditions are right, they grow over the broken disks to create a solid bridge that holds the spine erect. All it takes is plenty of rest and time to grow. It was simple, effective surgery, but in 1919, it was somewhat experimental. Bone fragments were taken from the patient's hip to start the grafting process.

The harvested area of bone can add even more post-operative pain, lasting weeks or even months.

All seemed to be going well for young Ray Palmer, as his operation appeared to be a success. But the Grim Reaper came knocking. Operating rooms in 1919 were not germ-free. An infection set in and damage was done. The graft loosened. Pain caused the boy to slump down in his bed until his spine bent. Stitches loosened and his spine broke through the open wound. Any attempt to straighten the spine would have meant certain death, the doctor said. And so it was that Palmer was given (as he used to tell it) 24 hours to live. The doctor brushed the gaping wound with a heavy coat of iodine, and strapped him down immobile, leaving him with no hope of survival.

Palmer recounted this part of his life in broad, simple strokes: the accident; the operation; years of convalescence. These were the basics of his public recollections. What went on month after month during those years of recovery is a mystery. Presumably they were months of relentless pain, stays in hospital wards, family stress, and pity from friends. These were his memories. At some point he dropped them all into a dark hole and buried them where his infallible memory could not find them.

Morphine was the preferred painkiller of the era, and presumably his doctors used it to quell the constant pain the boy endured. It would have been cruel and negligent to allow the boy to agonize for weeks and months in his condition. How the morphine affected his memories and his perception of the world is something that should be considered, but about which nothing is known. Morphine users often experience waking dreams, hallucinations, and nightmares. It is likely that Palmer experienced these too. These uncontrollable side effects may well have been the reason he avoided even an aspirin in later life, choosing to endure the pain instead.

By his own account, Palmer was accident-prone. He once summed up his life succinctly: "Falls off roofs, off ladders."[12] He attributed one accident to steeple jacking as a roofer and "was supposed to have broken several fingers while bowling. Baseball also cost him fractured digits. The last traceable smashup occurred in 1940 in Los Angeles, a motor vehicle mishap that caused only bruises."[13]

An accident in 1950 temporarily paralyzed him from the waist down. Yes, Ray Palmer was indeed prone to physical challenges. He spent the better part of his childhood face down in a canvas and steel pipe contraption called a Bradford frame, a device he considered nothing less than medieval torture. "I was ... able only to move the lower part of my legs, my arms and my head," he said.[14] As he healed, doctors sawed or chiseled off any protruding vertebrae, leaving his back horribly disfigured.[15]

At the same time Palmer faced a gloomy future of pain and deformity, Dr. Gaenslen went on to fame and fortune performing truly successful spinal grafts. (His reputation was such that a medical test and a Milwaukee elementary school were named after him). Not surprisingly, Palmer's growth was stunted after the failed operation. While other children attended school, Rap lived a solitary life in and out of the torture bed, reading books. He lived and dreamed in that bed. It became his portal to an infinite mindscape.

"At intervals totaling more than five years," he said, "I got my education from a tutor sent by the Milwaukee School Board, and from reading books delivered weekly by the Milwaukee Public Library."[16]

He read hundreds of books, home schooling himself in math, archeology, history, mythology, and physics. Rap's future wife Marjorie remarked that, "He probably read the entire Milwaukee library, being able to read over 15 books a day. He was an incredibly fast reader."[17]

First he read the library's fiction, then went on to physics, chemistry, astronomy, botany, biology, philosophy, history, archaeology, exploration, and the classics of mythology. He acquired a superficial knowledge of nearly everything, he said, but studied some subjects more intensely. "Thus it was that I found myself skipping grades in grade school, even completing my high school courses in three rather than four years. I became a 'self-educated' man...."[18]

Truth be told, he never completed high school. His public school education, or lack of it, was something he kept to himself. To counterbalance his rigorous in-home education, he became a voracious reader of science fiction. SF gave him hope, just as writing it shaped his future.

Milk Baby Wunderkind

"My picture appeared on Gridley milk bottle caps for a year."—Ray Palmer

Through a stroke of good fortune, Ray Palmer's constitution was nourished by a wellspring of unadulterated ego. This was surprising for a man who confessed to a deep-seated inferiority complex. Ego comforted him in ways that his circumstances did not. The inferiority complex disappeared, he said, after his marriage to Marjorie Wilson in 1942. Writers have commented on his drive and ambition, which Rap never denied. He credited these personality traits to his astrological alignment with Leo the lion.

He did resemble the traditional Leo personality. Leos are said to think big. They thrive on adversity and do not let setbacks get in the way of success. Their personal ambition, schemes, and idealism often clash with those around them. A Leo's greatest physical challenge is eerily correct in his case, for Leo rules the spine.[19]

Rap showed much promise as an emerging Milwaukee personality long before the beer truck incident. His portrait as a cherub-faced toddler appeared on Gridley Dairy milk bottle caps for one year. This was his prize after winning the Gridley Dairy Healthy Baby Contest, which he sometimes referred to as the Gridley Dairy *Perfect* Baby Contest. The attention he received as the winner of that contest ranked right up there with Halley's Comet. "Perhaps that is where I got my sense of superiority," he said. "I have been inordinately proud and even insufferably vain ever since."[20]

And what a precocious toddler he was. In 1915 we find him on his hands and knees on the kitchen floor reading Milwaukee newspapers at the age of five. "I followed World War I with interest. But what I was more interested in reading was the books of science and the books of ancient history."[21]

Ray nurtured a keen interest in ancient Egyptian history, Thothmes III and the Biblical Moses being two of his favorite historical characters. His infatuation with Moses came from the ancient Hebrew's knack for miracles, though young Rap sensed someone pulling strings behind the curtain. As a self-described materialist, he did not accept the notion of miracles. There had to be a mechanism, a process, a trick to it. "I wanted to know how Moses *really* did the things written about in Exodus," he said.[22]

Whether these were the thoughts of five-year-old Ray Palmer in 1915, or the 56-year-old Ray Palmer who was writing about them in 1966, is unknown. Nonetheless, it reflects his fascination with ancient history and supernatural events that continued throughout his life. It also revealed an underlying distrust of experts. He came to believe that history was fraught with error, and doubted the Bible: "Why was it that the Bible was 'the word of God,' and therefore without error — accepted without question, when so obviously even in minor matters it ran quite contrary to easily demonstrable fact. It seemed obvious to me that a very great deal of human knowledge was not that at all, but prejudicial rationalization."[23]

While other toddlers outgrew the habit of relentless questioning and rebelliousness, these traits remained with Palmer for the rest of his life. His early reading ability and his unquenchable curiosity helped him survive years of isolation. These periods of convalescence coincided with the development of his alleged superpowers: the infallible memory, the ability to fulfill his dreams through willpower, even the art of prophecy. At home, in sanitariums and in hospitals he whiled away endless hours pushing the boundaries of his mind.

In bed he practiced something he called mental healing. This was not faith healing, he said, he was too practical for that. As doctors came and went, predicting his imminent demise, Ray used his expanding mental powers to prove them wrong. "All during my life, beginning most specifically at age nine ... I have had this confidence that I could 'do things' I wanted to do ... through sheer determination."[24]

He eventually confessed to another amazing faculty: acute hearing. He first noticed it when he overheard a doctor in an adjoining room informing his mother of his impending doom. "It was quite disconcerting to hear the words that condemn you to death," he said. "I remember my mother sitting beside me, weeping. And suddenly I knew that I wasn't going to die; quite the contrary, I knew that I would live a long time, even to see Halley's Comet again.... I promised her faithfully that I would not die."[25]

This brings us to another of his self-confessed powers: the art of prophecy. Occasionally, his predictions came true, as with his prophecy that he would not die. In that he was only partially correct. He did not see the return of the comet in 1986.

Survival

> *"What is it that makes men think? Is it a textbook, full of thoughts already thought? No, it's something interesting, full of enticing tidbits of entertainment, which lead toward questions, not answers!"*— Ray Palmer

The years following young Ray's accident were stressful for the Palmer household, but Ray took the brunt of it. Not only did he find himself locked in a life-and-death struggle, but he was also forced to come to terms with a world that had turned against him. Suddenly, the boy in his mirror was someone else. In an instant, his fun-loving childhood became a life of pain, suffering, and social isolation.

Ray lived in a cocoon for seven years. His metamorphosis took him to an alternate universe that was far less welcoming than it was for the Gridley Healthy Baby. Before venturing out into this new world, he would need a new set of coping skills. How his family helped him adjust to his new life as a "cripple" is not known, but Ray hinted that what little encouragement he got, came from his mother.

His record as a Milwaukee public school student was sketchy. Ill health and emotional stress kept him at home. The failed spinal graft and the onset of tuberculosis made his disability so pronounced there was no way to hide it. He became hunchbacked and pigeon-chested. He was very short, and would stay that way. At his peak he was four feet, eight inches tall.

With his strong will and keen mind he determined to make his deformity invisible to those that mattered. Fellow Ziff-Davis editor Howard Browne took note of his success. "[His appearance] made meeting the man for the first time a jarring experience, but anyone spending any time at all with him soon became unaware of his deformity."[26] Fantasy writer Robert Bloch also noted this phenomenon. "[A]s we move down the street together I listen to him speak, and find myself forgetting the dwarf stature and hunched back. By the time we arrive at his sister's home ... I've almost completely ignored his physical attributes."[27] Like an Indian fakir, Rap made his physical deformity disappear simply by using his mind.

Itinerant Fireman

"Best place for skeleton is in family closet."— Charlie Chan

Roy Clarence Palmer was a stone that gathered no moss. He ran away from home at age 15, ended up in San Francisco, but returned home — or was dragged back — to his family in Wisconsin. What was behind this wanderlust, no one knows. It continued throughout his life, though much less flamboyantly as an adult. His constant lack of money forced him to stay one step ahead of his landlords, giving him by default a nomadic lifestyle. He changed domiciles as often as a hermit crab.

Becoming a city fireman in 1911, the boost to his salary was enough to free him from his parents' home. From St. Paul Street he moved to 28 29th Street. In 1912 he became a chemical pipe man on Engine 7 and moved to 32 29th Street, probably another flat in the same building. He switched fire engines and domiciles again in 1913 when he became a pipe man on engine 28 and moved to 80 30th Street.

For reasons unknown, Alfred G. Wright's Milwaukee City Directory failed to list Roy and Helen Palmer in its 1914 edition, but by 1915 they were back, living at their former address at 28 29th Street. A 1916 listing gave a fateful address: 3015 Mt. Vernon Avenue. This was Ray Palmer's home at the time of the accident. The family lived two blocks from Phineas and Henrietta Palmer, who were now at 3215 Mt. Vernon Avenue.

The accident occurred in 1917, the same year Roy Palmer appeared on city directory page 1197 as a fireman on Engine 9. Helen gave birth to Raymond's sister Evelyn that year. The aftermath of his son's crippling accident and the birth of a second child were costly. Roy sublet a room to Charles Dewey, age 53. Maybe it was his son's fragile condition or pleas from Helen that made Roy remain at 3015 Mt. Vernon for five years. Helen gave birth to their third child, a son, David, in 1918.

Family finances were worrisome, as was Helen's health. In 1920, grandparents Phineas and Henrietta found themselves with wall-to-wall Palmers when Roy moved into to his parents' Mt. Vernon Avenue home, with Helen Evelyn, David, and sickly Ray in tow.

The previous five years had been stressful for the auburn-haired Helen Steber Palmer. Her health continued to fade, and respiratory problems made her weak. Not only was she caring for her injured son, she now had two younger children in need of her attention. The stress, coupled with a lack of medical care and her husband's abuse and alcoholism had taken its toll.

Nevertheless, the Irish fireman uprooted his family again in 1921. This time they settled at 1165 35th Street, an address that foreshadowed more woe for the Palmers.

Death

"I found out that my mother had not been very happy."— Ray Palmer

The stage was set for yet another Palmer family tragedy. Helen Palmer suffered from peritonitis. The Wisconsin winter of 1922 added complications of bronchial pneumonia. And so it was that on January 26, 1923, Dr. George R. Frey of Mt. Sinai Hospital signed Helen Palmer's death certificate. Her obituary appeared in the *Milwaukee Journal* on page nine, next to the ad for Pluto Water, "America's Physic — When Nature Won't, Pluto Will":

> Palmer, Helen, beloved wife of Roy C. Palmer, and mother of Raymond, David, and Evelyn Palmer, and daughter of Herman and Alvina Steber, and sister of Emma Thomas and Elsie Kunstman, died Friday, Jan. 26 at 6:40 A.M. age 37 years, 11 months 4 days....

Family and friends gathered at the Palmer residence the following Monday, January 29, at 1:30 P.M. In short order they trekked one mile down North 35th Street to the brooding Church of the Reformation, a massive Lutheran fortress at the corner of 35th and West Garfield. Internment followed at Forest Home Cemetery.

The family was now without its temperate side. Roy Palmer, the hard-drinking, hot-tempered fireman, was all it had. The elder Palmers — Phineas and Henrietta — moved into Roy's 35th Street home so that grandmother Palmer could attend to the children. Grandfather Phineas found a job as a machinist, and was able to supplement the family income.

Roy wasted little time courting a new mate, Mathilda, in the months that followed. They married in 1924. Unlike Helen, Roy's senior by a year, "Hilda" was 14 years his junior. Roy managed to contain his nomadic spirit for the next four years at the 35th Street address. In 1928 the couple added one final member to the Palmer household — Robert — and subsequently moved to 2223 Center.

2

Education

"Hi! I'm Rap and I haven't got much education (and lie about what I do have)."—
Ray Palmer

Ray Palmer's teen years got a casual mention from Harry Warner, Jr., the scribe of 20th century SF fandom, who described them as a series of tribulations punctuated by a love of science fiction: "He had another two-year stay in bed, beginning when he was thirteen years of age, and recovered just in time to buy the first issue of *Amazing Stories* from the newsstands. He began building a prozine collection, hiding it under floorboards in the attic because of parental disapproval."[1]

Roy Palmer took Ray's paper route money to pay for family expenses, but Ray cleverly managed to continue buying pulp magazines by secretly taking on a second paper route.

The timing of his alleged relapse into ill health is questionable. About a year after Helen's death, Roy thought it was high time for Ray to test the waters of the Milwaukee public school system. Attendance records are sparse, but a sketchy paper trail does exist.

His health had improved to a point when, at age 13, he enrolled at Washington High School, two miles from his 35th Street home. He attended as an underclassman from February 1924 until June 1925. This would have covered his seventh and eighth grade years. He disappeared from student rosters after June 1925. This may have been the relapse into ill health that Warner mentioned.

Records in the Milwaukee Archdiocesan Archives confirm his enrollment in the ninth grade at St. Anne's Catholic School in February 1926. He attended a full school year of 184 days at St. Anne's. Like other Milwaukee parish schools in 1926, St. Anne's offered only K through ninth grades; no high school, so the transfer from public to parochial school is a mystery. Ray's father, staunchly Catholic and now without his mother's Lutheran influence, may have felt that Catholic school would instill virtues of discipline and spiritual guidance. St. Anne's also offered bookkeeping classes, which interested Roy Palmer much more than his son's spiritual salvation.

To earn a high school diploma, Ray would have re-enrolled in the Milwaukee public school system. That did not happen. Instead, on completing the ninth grade at age 16, he dropped out. He explained in his autobiography, "When I graduated high school, the good sisters of St. Ann's [*sic*] Catholic School sent me to a sheet metal concern ... on Milwaukee's south side. Although my ambition was to be a writer, my father had insisted bookkeeping was far more practical, and it was as a bookkeeper that I was graduated.... It paid $15 a week. It was 1928. I got the job."[2]

Though Rap would have us believe he graduated high school in 1928 at the age of 18, the record says otherwise. Ray's schooling ended at age 16 when he went to work for the

P.J. Lavies Company. Since his father was known to take his paper route money as room and board, it comes as no surprise that he would rather see his son supporting the family as a bookkeeper, even without the benefit of a high school diploma.

A Writer's Life

"Never play the other guy's game."—Ray Palmer

Ray Palmer made his first appearance in the Milwaukee City Directory in 1929 as a bookkeeper. City directories in those days were published at the beginning of each year, reflecting the previous year's information. What this meant was that his appearance coincided with his 18th birthday. By 1929 he had been working for the P.J. Lavies Company nearly two years.

Besides the name Raymond A. Palmer appearing in the city directory, something else important happened that year. Wall Street collapsed. At that moment we find Ray still living with father Roy and stepmother Mathilda at 2226 Vine and, like a responsible son, still contributing to the family's upkeep. The address was short-lived.

The nomadic fireman relocated to 1431 38th Street. This is where we find first evidence of Ray's science fiction fan activities. He and a friend, Walter Dennis, started a fan club here. This was the return address on Rap's prize-winning letter to Hugo Gernsback's[3] "What I Have Done to Further Science Fiction" contest in *Science Wonder Quarterly*.

Gernsback's $100 first prize — a princely sum in Depression dollars — was plowed back into books to stock their club library. Said the iconic Gernsback, "We believe that the club under the leadership of such a man as Mr. Palmer is becoming a great force in the spreading of SF among the masses of people. The final proof of Mr. Palmer's right to the first prize is evidenced by the last paragraph in his letter in which he states that he intends to devote his prize to the further enlargement of a library for his club."[4]

This turned out to be another year of mourning for the Palmer family. Phineas Palmer died on December 15, 1929, at the age of 69. In 1930, death took another crack at Rap, too: His health took a sudden downturn. This time it was Pott's disease, TB of the bone, and it was serious. His spinal disc tissue was dying, being broken down by caseation. His spine would likely collapse.

Muirdale

"God has to nearly kill us sometimes, to teach us lessons."—John Muir

Ray Palmer climbed aboard the Wells-Farwell streetcar bound for Wauwatosa. It would take him to the end of the line, a fact that was probably not lost on him. Destination: Muirdale Sanatorium. His family assumed the worst — that it would be his final journey. TB sanatoriums were the norm until penicillin eliminated the need for them. TB patients were routinely plucked from their homes and quarantined to keep the disease from spreading. Muirdale was large enough to house 300 patients in all phases of the disease. Rates were $10 per week or $5 per week, depending on the patient's ability to pay.

Muirdale was named for naturalist John Muir, which seemed fitting. Like Rap, Muir

Muirdale Sanatorium, Wauwatosa, Wisconsin. Doctors expected Rap to die here in 1930. Instead, he spent nearly a year recovering from Pott's Disease and was released.

had been the victim of an accident that changed his life: In 1867, he was working in a carriage factory when a tool slipped and struck him in the eye. His treatment was a six-week stay in a darkened room where he lay wondering if he would ever see again. When his sight returned, he declared, "God has to nearly kill us sometimes, to teach us lessons."

But Muir never had tuberculosis, due no doubt to the abundance of crisp, fresh air he breathed while hiking through America's future national park system. But he did spend part of his childhood in Wisconsin, and that was enough for Muirdale's founders to call it Muirdale. It featured cottages scattered about the grounds where patients lived — and presumably died.

Ray's prognosis came shortly after his admission. The doctor said Muirdale was where he would die — for *sure* this time. Though it sounded hopeless, it turned into one of Rap's favorite stories: "[The] very blunt German doctor in charge assured me [my death] was only a matter of six months away. However, I knew better, and bet him five dollars I would be cured in that same six months."[5]

It was a rerun of the time another doctor informed his mother he would die within 24 hours. A damning prognosis like this would have disheartened the average patient, but Rap was not an average patient. The doctor told him that TB had nearly destroyed what was left of the spinal graft bridging his broken vertebrae. "It was also destroying as many as six of the vertebrae themselves," Rap explained. "The doctor showed me the X-rays.... When the destruction had proceeded far enough, he told me there would be a sudden collapse, I would be instantly paralyzed and would die immediately."[6]

Being an inquisitive sort, Rap asked what it would take for a recovery. The doctor was incredulous that his patient would delude himself with such false hope. "Ach! Recovery is an impossibility! You need new vertebrae. We can perform spinal grafts, but ... in your case another spinal graft is useless; the area involved is too great. Also, your tuberculosis is merely arrested, not cured." The doctor feared surgery would reactivate the TB and the old graft would become infected. Rap studied the X-rays closely, then asked the doctor, "So what is needed is a massive bone formation to enclose the entire area of damaged vertebrae, so that movement of the spinal cord cannot occur?"

"Yah wohl! But you are speaking of miracles!"[7]

Another Miracle

> *"Unlike most children, I got most of my education strapped to a torture bed."*—Ray Palmer

Ray Palmer's challenges were significant; overcoming them was crucial to his survival. It was no surprise that Muirdale took on a kind of mythical status, not unlike his pre-birth comet memory.

Though he held back the full story of his subsequent miracle recovery, he did give hints of it in his memoir. After all, *Martian Diary* was only the first installment in a monumental series of works that would become his legacy. There was plenty of time to reveal more detail in future volumes. "It is an incredible story that requires much more basic foundation ... before it can be treated adequately," he said.[8]

It boiled down to a thinking process he called mental healing. Having viewed his X-rays, Rap merely "thought up" enough calcium to surround and protect his spinal cord. It was easy, he said, and it worked. "One must hold a mental picture in mind, and while it is impossible to hold it there every instant, we can visualize it over and over again every time we think of it."[9]

He knew that bone is made of calcium, so he whiled away the months at Muirdale with a single thought in mind: *calcium*. This is how he created new bone cells. "We must think of it being removed from the food we eat, think of it being carried by the bloodstream to the desired area, think of it being deposited, cell by cell, gradually enlarging the mass, first as a soft substance that molds itself like putty in the desired place, then hardening, as it would in Nature, into strong cartilage-like substance and finally into bone."[10]

Though Rap saw no value in faith healing, a little semantic juggling gave him a new phrase: mental healing. Confidence was something Rap had plenty of. He said, "In visualizing such a process going on in your body, you must be ... certain that it is actually happening, because this is the way it happens naturally, under the direction of that mysterious 'creative mind' that obviously constructs everything...."[11]

Whether he knew it or not, Rap was tapping into Buddhist (and Rosicrucian) belief that human beings have an ability to actualize thought. Through focus and concentration, thought becomes matter. For the better part of a year, he held his mental picture of a bony mass growing around his ruined spine, and remained as rigid as possible to help his new spinal bridge grow.

Months passed, and because Rap failed to die as predicted, the incredulous German doctor ordered a new set of X-rays. As is often the case in Rap's storytelling, the scenes that followed were appropriately dramatic. "I was brought down to the conference room where I found a dozen doctors waiting to examine me. A miracle, they said. The damaged vertebrae have been wholly enclosed in a solid mass of bone and new cartilage. Impossible, but the

X-rays are incontrovertible evidence!"[12] Rap tried to explain it was not a miracle at all, simply the scientific application of mind power. "They were willing to believe in a miracle, but not in pre-destination," he said.

Doctors came and went throughout Ray Palmer's life, each predicting his imminent demise. Over and over he used strength of will to prove them wrong. He won the bet with the German doctor but never saw the five bucks, he said. One could say that Ray's constant struggle with Death is what produced a mystic's temperament in him.

3

Trauma

"Physical Reality is consistent with universal laws. When the laws do not operate, there is no reality."—Mr. Spock

Ray Palmer's ongoing struggle to stay alive produced unavoidable consequences. Day-to-day life is predicated on the notion that everything bad that happens in the world happens to someone else, and that we—you, me, and Uncle Joe—float through life in a protective bubble while disaster rains down on countless others on the six o'clock news. Human nature wires us to think this way, and yet tragedy strikes ordinary folks every day. It then becomes impossible to maintain the illusion of a benevolent world. It becomes what is known as post-traumatic stress syndrome.

Rap was a trauma survivor. At the time of his first accident, little was known of the effects of trauma on the human psyche. Doctors knew it existed. The term "shell-shocked" was popularized during World War I to describe soldiers who were psychologically immobilized by the horrors of the battlefield. In 1917, trauma survivors got little to no help with their condition, or worse, were seen as crybabies. And so it was that young Ray had to plow through one disaster after another with little help or understanding from people around him. His father may well have considered him dead weight.

The radical change in his physical appearance and the intrusion of unwanted stares from others added insult to injury. He was collateral damage in a world that had turned against him. For a trauma victim to become a trauma survivor, resilience, coping style, and a strong urge to control their world are essential.[1] Rap's ability to shape his own destiny was something he often bragged about. "I have had this confidence that I could 'do things' I wanted to do ... through sheer determination," he said.[2]

His mother became the catalyst for a vision of survival at age nine, when he realized he would not die as the doctor predicted. This type of precognition is not uncommon for trauma survivors. Rap's near-death story is quite similar to a case study of a stabbing victim in Dr. Judith Herman's book *Trauma and Recovery*:

> After they stabbed me and left me for dead, I suddenly had a very powerful image of my father. I realized I couldn't die yet because it would cause him too much grief.... Once I resolved to live, an amazing thing happened. I actually visualized the knot around my wrists, even though my hands were tied behind my back. I untied myself and crawled into the hallway. The neighbors found me just in time.... I felt that I had been given a second chance at life.[3]

Ray's image of his grief-stricken mother crying at the news of his imminent death triggered his prophetic recovery at a crucial moment. In another instance, his ability to visualize his spine and save his life at Muirdale reads like a trauma survivor's diary.

Recovery from a traumatic event happens only through relationships with others. Those who fail to understand the victim inhibit the process. One challenge that Ray faced was the pity of others, and he could not bear it. "We destroy not only ourselves, but those we most intend to help, with wrong attitudes," he wrote. "And it's possible the most evil attitude extant, in terms of the actual harm it does, is pity. 'Poor Ray Palmer, such a pity he's a cripple,' or 'Isn't it awful, I'm glad I'm not like that,' is probably the usual reaction of anyone who sees our hunchbacked, pigeon-chested editor limping along."[4]

Rap set out to neutralize the pity by outdoing the competition. He proved to himself and others that his disability would never slow him down. He left the safety of his bookkeeping job to go steeple jacking for the same company, installing aluminum roofs and rain gutters. He took up bowling; he was a catcher on a softball team, and he began to jog, eventually clocking himself at 4:55 minutes for the mile. "This has all been due to a determination that I would not allow my handicap to earn me anyone's sympathy, or any special consideration," he said.[5]

Recurring nightmares haunt trauma victims, and Rap had his share. Dreaming becomes an important part of recovery. In dreams the victim experiences the traumatic event repeatedly, as if a different ending can be worked out. Rap's vivid dream life became central to his mystical worldview. He believed he could see things happening on the other side of the world through dreams. He claimed he learned of his brother's death in a dream during World War II. He believed his dreams foretold future events. "One in particular was a recurring dream, which always was identical ... except ... for one interesting fact — each dream was a bit longer than the last, and although I always began at the beginning, I always made it just a little way further into the dream."[6]

His fellow editors at Ziff-Davis suspected that, unconsciously, he was guided by emotions stemming from his accident, but Rap denied it. As a staunch believer in self-determination, he felt he was immune. But Rap's challenges were so severe at such an early age, they may well have blurred the line between fact and fantasy. During his long recovery, magical thinking reconstructed previous assumptions about his world and how he fit into it. This new paradigm became a tool that helped him plot the science fiction stories he would one day write. Plotting became a skill that brought him acclaim, and he used it in both his real life and his fictional stories.

He called his positive thinking process many things: determination, mental healing, and extrapolating on a fact. It gave rise to his belief that directed imagination was not only essential to *his* survival, but also to *human* survival. It became the foundation of his philosophy, and he brought his magical thinking to bear on all aspects of his life and work. He hinted at this thinking process in an open letter to friend and fellow writer Otto Binder in 1961:

> Didn't you always start out with a fact, and then expand it into a future concept or a possible outgrowth, or an *extrapolation* (as Editor Campbell liked to call it when he went to science fiction conventions)? But wasn't the *most important* thing to all of us the *fiction* that followed our fact? And didn't we all *believe* with all our hearts that our extrapolations would one day turn out to be gospel truth?"[7]

In Rap's world, fantasy could become fact, and fact could become a fantasy imbued with inspirational qualities. What stale facts needed, he said, was a good dose of fantasy. "[I]t became a fantasy rather than a fact; and unlike a fact, it had life and spirit and an intriguing personality."[8]

His goal of shaping the future through science fiction was often the topic during coffee breaks. He and his cadre of writers would crowd into a booth at a local coffee shop on

Wabash Avenue to exchange ideas. Rap's philosophy that all things are possible at any given moment in an infinite universe gave rise to a character trait that confused friends and foes alike. His factual world was not always "real," and his fantasy world was as real as his mind could make it. In this he was considered something of a trickster. The Great Manipulator, as he called it, had played a huge trick on him as a boy, and that fact was never lost on him.

First Fandom

> *"In the Beginning there was Hugo Gernsback, and he begat Amazing Stories."—Frederik Pohl*

Ray Palmer never forgot his first sale. Few writers do. It marks the beginning of a legacy. Rap's first published science fiction yarn began as an English assignment at St. Anne's Catholic School in 1925. He called it "The Time Ray of Jandra." It was a 16,000-word time travel jungle fantasy. His teacher loved it; so much so, he said, that she gave him an "A" and read his manuscript to the class. "I was rather pleased they were not bored, and the reaction encouraged me to submit the story to a publisher."[9]

The publisher was Hugo Gernsback, creator of the first all–science fiction magazine, *Amazing Stories*. Young Ray Palmer bought the first issue as soon as it hit his local newsstand. On reading it, he had an epiphany. He found that his English assignment was, in fact, science fiction. He mailed "The Time Ray of Jandra" to Gernsback, who responded with a $40 acceptance check. Rap was hooked. From that point forward he dreamed of becoming the editor of *Amazing Stories*. At least, this is how he told the story as years went on.

Rap's earliest recollection of his fannish past drifted even farther back than the first issue of *Amazing Stories*, all the way to 1924 when SF yarns appeared occasionally in *The Electrical Experimenter*. When "Time Ray of Jandra" finally saw print in the June 1930 issue of *Science Wonder Stories*, Rap's life as an SF fan took off.

Gernsback believed that every young SF fan "was a potential scientist, and that the aim of every fan should not be a collection of fantastic fiction, but a home laboratory where fictional dreams might attain reality."[10] To that end, Rap and a group of fervent science fiction fans founded the Science Correspondence Club. Its driving force, as stated on the club newsletter, was the "furtherance of science and its dissemination among the laymen of the world and the final betterment of humanity."[11]

This was May 1930, when ill health forced Rap to check into Muirdale. Members of the club included P. Schuyler Miller, Frank B. Eason, Aubrey McDermott, Robert A. Wait, and Walter Dennis.[12] (Dennis went on to become a newspaper reporter. Comic book history has it that *Superman* creator Jerry Siegel based Clark Kent's physical appearance on a photo of square-jawed Dennis wearing horn-rimmed glasses and a double-breasted suit.)

Dennis helped publish their club newsletter *The Comet*, filling in for Rap while he recovered in Muirdale. SF historians have called *The Comet* the first SF fanzine, which was indeed a milestone for fandom. Unlike SF fanzines that followed, *The Comet* (the name was later changed to *Cosmology*) had a scholarly tone, featuring articles like "The Psychology of Anger," "What Can Be Observed with a Small Telescope," and "Chemistry and the Atomic Theory." Willy Ley contributed articles on German rocketry.[13] It was serious stuff, and very different from what fans would embrace in later fanzines, which were much more fan-oriented.

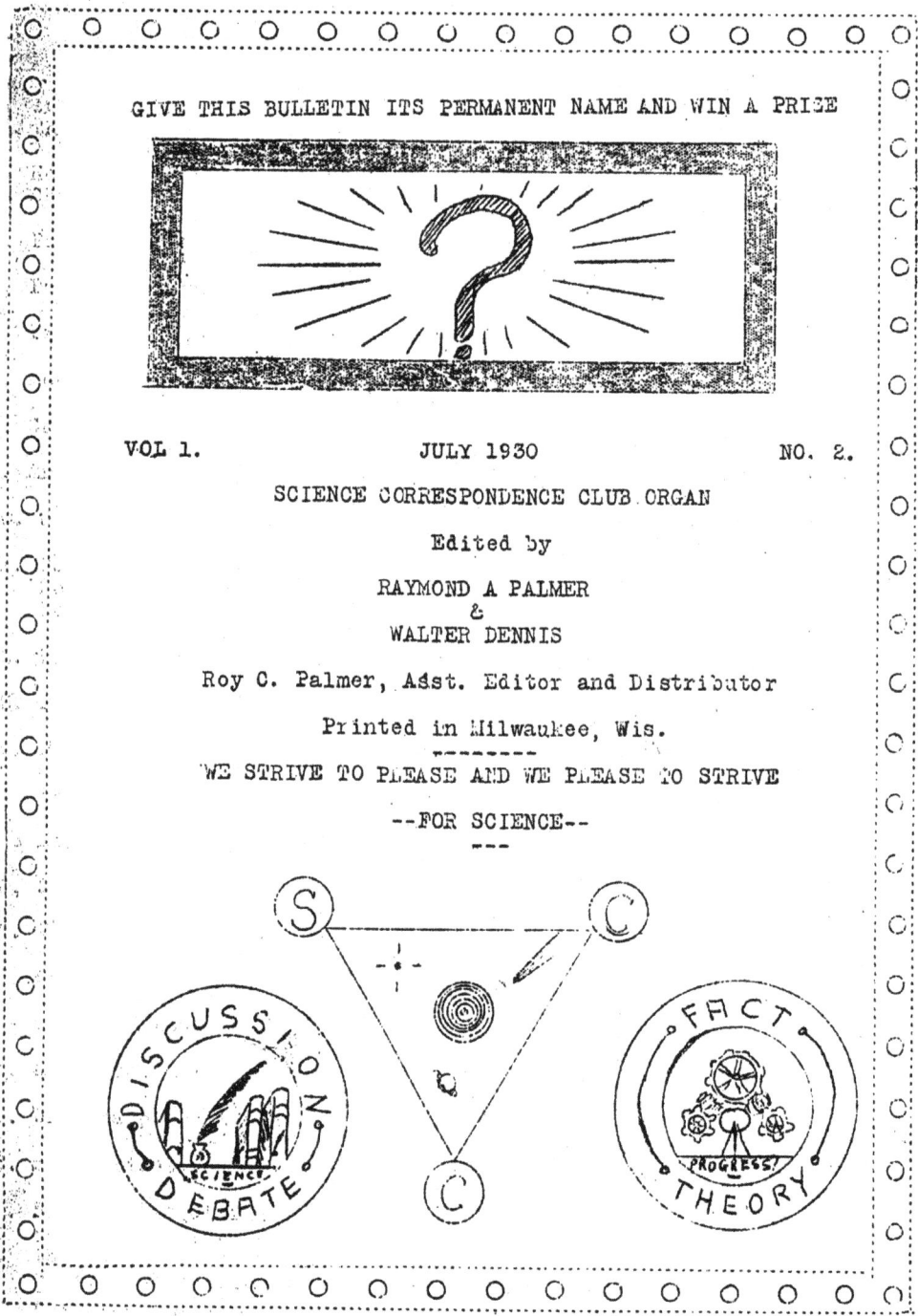

The second issue of Ray Palmer's Science Correspondence Club newsletter still had no name by July 1930. Rap was in Muirdale Sanatorium at the time, which explains why his father was listed as assistant editor with mailing duties. The newsletter, eventually named *The Comet*, is considered by historians to be the first science fiction fanzine (Jim Pobst Archive).

Rap's discharge from Muirdale came in 1931, as *Cosmology* was approaching its 12th issue. The club had changed its name to the International Scientific Association (ISA), and as often happens in fan-run organizations, things began to unravel. *Cosmology*'s publishing schedule became erratic, due to a lack of funds.

In January 1932, Rap transferred his editorial post to Aubrey McDermott and Clifton Amsbury. The club teetered on the brink of collapse. In one final gasp for life, the club published its 17th issue, not as the usual mimeographed newsletter but as a professionally printed fanzine, full of stories by published authors. The club was reorganized from the ground up. Rap, one of its most enthusiastic members, was elected president *and* treasurer. He hyped the upcoming printed edition in *Science Fiction Digest* for October 1932: "The International Scientific Assn. reports that its monthly paper, the *Cosmology*, will come out quarterly hereafter and will be a real printed mag this time. Dues have been reduced to $1.00 per year. Now, what about that for progress? No Depression seems to be able to lick those guys...." None of this was enough to reverse the club's dwindling membership. After three years and 17 issues, Rap disbanded the club. As with many of Rap's projects, it did not completely vanish, but went dormant in the hope it might resurrect itself. Nevertheless, the ISA was no failure. It set a record for fan club longevity, and with 17 issues *Cosmology* ranked among the longest-running club publications at that time. According to historian Sam Moskowitz, the death of the ISA coincided with a growing new trend among fans and fanzines that became more "about science fiction itself rather than the minute details of science involved in it."[14]

Milwaukee Fictioneers

> "*Clearly, Stanley G. Weinbaum is the best author of the year....*"—Julius Schwartz, Fantasy Magazine, 1935

Perhaps the greatest influence on Ray Palmer's writing career came from his association with the Milwaukee Fictioneers, a group of professional pulp fiction writers that met throughout the 1930s. He joined the Fictioneers after his release from Muirdale, probably during its first year, 1932.

Founded by Lawrence A. Keating, a cowboy-turned-writer from La Grange, Illinois, the group had but one officer: its self-appointed president for life, L. A. Keating. There were no dues and no minutes were ever recorded, so there was no need for a secretary-treasurer. Rap promoted the group tirelessly to potential new members like 18-year-old Robert Bloch, who would eventually hit the big time with his novel *Psycho*. Late in life, Bloch documented his time as a Fictioneer in his autobiography, leaving to posterity the only detailed account of their activities.

Every Fictioneer had a day job, even the well-off members. Rap was the roofer-tinsmith-bookkeeper. Morry Zenoff and Al Nelson were journalists. Larry Sternig was a literary agent. Leo Schmidt, Bernie Wirth, and Dudley Brooks were local university professors. Gus Marx and Arthur Tofte wrote advertising copy. Roger Sherman Hoar, aka Ralph Milne Farley, was a corporate attorney. Bloch was just a kid.

Then there was Stanley G. Weinbaum, a chemical engineering grad who decided to take a stab at fiction writing. Rap invited Weinbaum to attend a Fictioneers meeting the same day they met. He was unanimously accepted that very night, in 1934, about a year before Bloch.

The Fictioneers gathered every other Thursday night, round-robin style, at a member's home. The host served coffee and dessert (no alcohol allowed). Meetings were informal, though one rule forbade members from reading their work to the group. Instead, they focused on problem-solving: helping each other with story ideas and plotting problems. Bloch said it was a forerunner of the writers' workshop. "Most certainly it was a mutual-aid society; there was never any feeling of competition in the open-floor comments and criticism offered."[15]

Fictioneer Weinbaum's career skyrocketed as quickly as his health plummeted. He died a victim of cancer at the age of 33, but not before winning the admiration of friends and fans. *A Martian Odyssey*, his first attempt at science fiction, was an instant hit, the most talked-about SF yarn of 1934. Shortly thereafter he began selling everything he wrote. Bloch noted that Weinbaum's fiction "transformed conventional 'bug eyed monsters' into characters. Where they were usually portrayed as threats, he gave them traits; instead of confining extraterrestrials to actions, he allowed them reactions."[16]

This may not seem earth-shattering now, but in the early 1930s it was revolutionary. Isaac Asimov proclaimed *A Martian Odyssey* one of three SF stories that ultimately changed the course of science fiction. Even H.P. Lovecraft lifted his voice in praise of Weinbaum: "Here, I rejoiced, was somebody who could think of another planet in terms of something besides anthropomorphic kings and beautiful princesses and battles of spaceships and rayguns and attacks from the hairy sub-men of the 'dark side' or 'polar cap' region...."[17]

Of those who saw in Weinbaum the dawning of a new age for science fiction, none saw it more clearly than Ray Palmer. During the short span of a year, he would become Weinbaum's biggest supporter. According to Rap, Weinbaum was a modest man who "would not admit that he was good." When fans showered Weinbaum with praise, his reply was "[T]he secret of writing successful science fiction [is to] take one of Lawrence Keating's western story plots and place it on a planet!"[18] For Rap, Weinbaum's friendship was like a religious experience: "How can one write with mere words of the man who would have written each letter of his name in flaming symbols on the stars themselves? How can any language, no matter how flowery, describe the passing of such a one as he?"[19]

The adulation was real. Rap sincerely believed that Weinbaum's death was a blow to the evolution of science fiction, though he vowed to make up for it as best he could. He dedicated his life's work to Weinbaum "in the hope that I can approach the greatness that was his and hereby merit the right to someday rejoin him...."[20]

Rap was a moth transfixed on the flame that was Stanley Weinbaum. The day he first met Weinbaum, he became an instant fan. "Here, I knew instantly, was a mind, keen, discerning, searching, with a driving urge to know, to understand and to interpret the mysteries before it."[21]

Science Fiction Digest

"There has never been a fanzine since which came so close to representing the combined attention and interests of all fandom."— Harry Warner, Jr.

The wave of First Fandom began to crest, and in September 1932 Rap joined the editorial staff of a fanzine that would come to represent the era, a legend among fandom: *Science Fiction Digest*.

SFD was the brainchild of a group of avid letterhacks, fanzine editors, aspiring writers, and generally obsessed fans. They came from the east and west coasts to create a new focal point for fandom. Julius "Julie" Schwarz, Mort Weisinger, Conrad "Conny" Ruppert, Forrest J (no period) "Forrie" Ackerman, Maurice Z. Ingher and Ray Palmer founded an informal corporation in which each member owned an equal share. The corporation, in turn, produced *SFD*. The first issue appeared in September 1932 with Ingher as editor.

Sam Moskowitz lauded *SFD*'s editorial staff in his book *The Immortal Storm*: "For all-around quality, *Science Fiction Digest* has never been surpassed in the history of fandom," he said. Its columnists were known far and wide. "The Science Fiction Eye" by Julius Unger was aimed at the SF collector; "The Ether Vibrates," by Mortimer Weisinger, was full of newsy fan gossip; Ray's "Spilling the Atoms" was a chatty mélange of contests and current SF events; Ackerman's "The Scientifilms" featured reviews of SF and fantasy films; Julius Schwartz's "Science Fiction Scrap Book" offered fantasy book reviews; and "The Service Department" featured bibliographical data. The group managed to lure big-name authors to contribute stories on a regular basis.

SFD was a watershed moment for SF fandom, and as he wrote his column, Rap honed his editorial style. "Spilling the Atoms" was also his editorial debut as *Rap*—his initials written as his trademark. He claimed his new handle was a gift from Ackerman, Clements, and Schwartz. Forever after, Ray Palmer signed his editorials "Rap."

4

Spilling the Atoms

"Each month ... this column will endeavor to present the real dope on science fiction, its authors, its editors, and its readers."— Ray Palmer

Ray Palmer's reputation as a fan and card-carrying member of the Milwaukee Fictioneers added weight to his eventual appearance in *SFD*, where he became an associate editor. He gave the back-story to his column "Spilling the Atoms" in a cryptic reply to a curious reader: "Naturally, at an early age I fell on my head (all science fiction writers do that) but I went one step further — or a lot of them — and rolled completely from the attic to the cellar (and became a spiller of atoms)."[1]

His first column amounted to one long paragraph of gossip, behind-the-scenes shenanigans, previews and who's who in fandom. Anything was fair game. He used the term "sft'ist" when writing about fans of "scientifiction," a word coined by Hugo Gernsback.

In time, Rap began theorizing, predicting, browbeating, creating contests, and generally "gosh-by-gollying" his way to the heart of fandom until he emerged fully formed as *Rap*. He started a contest in his very first column and kept them coming. For his second column, the contest was about the slang of the future. The prize for the best slang words submitted was a copy of *Beyond the Dark Nebula* by Harl Vincent.

In a blatant display of nepotism the winner was Forrest J Ackerman, *SFD*'s movie reviewer. He won Rap over with futuristic phrases like "Go oil a robot" (go jump in the lake); "Give-in" (girl); "She's 87" (she's hot stuff); and "Millicent" (money).

Rap began to receive fan mail which he often published. At *Amazing Stories* he included fan letters in nearly every issue. One of his readers' earliest brickbats appeared in *SFD* number 7: "No doubt with a density as great as yours you would reach the interior of the Earth without the least difficulty. With Lake Michigan so near, why don't you use it! But I like your column anyway, that's the kind of an stf fan I am. Sincerely yours, Felix Gerard."

One suspicious reader took him to task for his editorial moniker in the April 1933 issue: "Dear Sir, I know who you are! Your feeble attempt at a pun in signing this column 'Rap' is so glaringly evident it hurts. You are R.A. Penny, author of 'Emperors of Space.'"

Rap's enthusiasm was part of his personality. It helped boost reader interest in his promotions. Simple contests grew into elaborate plans, and in 1933 he came up with the best one yet, so good that it became the stuff of SF legend. He called it COSMOS, and it excited fans and pros alike. Rap explained his plan in "Spilling the Atoms":

> Some months before *Liberty* came out with its six-author story, written for the movies, I conceived the idea of writing a science fiction novel with ten contributors. Accordingly, the plot of COSMOS was evolved and a tentative "feeler" sent to some of the more prominent stf authors. The instantaneous and enthusiastic response was so encouraging that plans were made to go ahead.

Masthead for Rap's column in *Fantasy Magazine*.

Rap mailed the COSMOS plot to each author expressing interest. Many were the biggest names in science fiction, and Rap included himself among them. The lineup, according to Sam Moskowitz: A. Merritt, Dr. E.E. Smith, Ralph Milne Farley, Dr. David H. Keller, Otis Adelbert Kline, Arthur J. Burks, E. Hoffman Price, P. Schuyler Miller, Rae Winters, John W. Campbell, Jr., Edmond Hamilton, Francis Flagg, Bob Olsen, J. Harvey Haggard, Lloyd A. Eshback, Abner J. Gelula, Eando Binder — and Ray Palmer.

COSMOS gave Rap street cred as one of the heavy hitters of SF fandom. He had become a Big Name Fan. By the time COSMOS ended its run in early 1934, *SFD* had been renamed *Fantasy Magazine*. Rap's column got an illustrated masthead, drawn by art editor Clay Ferguson. According to Rap, Ferguson captured his likeness admirably.

Rap's success at *Fantasy Magazine* tempered the ongoing turmoil within his family. Trouble was brewing in 1934, when Roy and Hilda Palmer's name mysteriously vanished from Wright's City Directory. They were still missing in 1935, until Roy re-appeared in 1936, *sans* Hilda. This missing time was undoubtedly due to the collapse of their marriage. They separated some time in 1933, which likely sent Roy to the bottle with a vengeance. It was a dark time in the Palmer household, and it strained the already tenuous thread between Roy and his eldest son.

Finally it snapped. One evening Rap returned home from his job at the P.J. Lavies Company and found the house empty. The memory of that day was passed down to Rap's family, including his daughter Linda Jane Palmer:

> Dad came home ... and everything was gone, including his father. I speculate that may have been the cause of their rift but it is only a guess. I didn't know much about Grandpa Roy except that he was irresponsible and did not take good care of his family. I'm not surprised that he was an alcoholic, although I never saw that. I have no idea if he quit drinking but he never drank around us.[2]

Big Name Fans

> "I'll never spill any of your private disclosures. I'm glad to have found someone who has the same viewpoint as myself. Maybe we oughta get married? Heh heh."— Ray Palmer

Forrest J Ackerman became one of Rap's best pen friends. It would take 15 years before they met in person. Ackerman lived in Los Angeles, Rap in Milwaukee. They "met" as editors at *SFD*, corresponding on editorial matters, but a friendship grew as their correspondence continued. Rap wrote his letters on P.J. Lavies Company stationery, which was always handy and free at the office.

Ackerman amassed the world's largest private SF and fantasy film memorabilia collection, housing it in his "Ackermansion." Besides earning the title of Science Fiction Fan #1, he was editor of *Famous Monsters of Filmland* and *Vampirella* magazines, as well as film reviewer for Rap's *Other Worlds*. A dedicated nudist, Ackerman earned his living as a Hollywood literary agent. He spoke fluent Esperanto and promoted the proto-language tirelessly. One of his better-known clients, L. Ron Hubbard, eventually left Ackerman to found a religion called Scientology.

Ackerman collected movie memorabilia on a modest scale during the years he corresponded with Ray. He began by contacting Hollywood PR offices, requesting studio portraits of movie stars. He made pocket change by selling duplicate photos to fellow movie buffs like Rap, who became a steady customer.

Ackerman also frequented movie premieres where he asked stars for autographs. He peddled those too. Selling the glitter of Hollywood to fans whose only encounter with the silver screen was at the Majestic Theater on Main Street became a sideline for Ackerman. In time he was offering movie stars' home addresses, which he sold to one of Rap's female friends who fawned over Ralph Bellamy. For only six cents, Rap got Bellamy's address: 1919 Canyon Drive, Hollywood, California.

Rap's tab with Ackerman grew compulsively. Always strapped for cash, Rap tried to rein in his purchases. "I didn't think my bill was so high," he groaned in one letter. "Better go easy until I clean it up altogether. Just send me the very prettiest femmes until I give you the high sign again.... For Pete's sake, don't send me any more photos until I get paid up. The money I owe you keeps me awake nites [*sic*] now!"[3]

Strapped for cash, Rap often resorted to chain letters. He sent one to Ackerman. Against his better judgment, Ackerman acquiesced, adding his name to a strictly SF fan letter. While Ackerman spent his free time in Los Angeles movie palaces, Rap was becoming a regular at Milwaukee's Riverside Theater, where chorus girls stomped the floorboards in unison every Friday night. His obsession with the Riverside was such that he began writing letters to his favorite dancers. He sent one chorus girl named Peggy a 5000-word opus. He got plenty of ribbing from the boys at P.J. Lavies Company for his Friday night jaunts. After threatening Ackerman to eternal damnation if he squawked, Rap confided his infatuation: "She's going to be in town again next week, with the Follies De Paree. So we are going to get together. She got lonesome and decided writing to me would be swell fun while she was on the road. So she hauled the letter I wrote her some time ago out of her trunk ... and answered."[4]

He even tried to produce a show, a comedy night. The Riverside ran amateur nights on Mondays, and he came up with the bright idea of putting on a comedy revue written and produced by local amateurs. He dashed off his proposal to the theater manager and got a reply. "He wrote rite back and said, 'Hell yes, it *is* a good idea!' So I went down thar. Now I've got to write a one-act comedy.... Yeah, you guessed it, I just want to meet the blonde, and don't care how much work it takes. Heh heh."[5] Rap's laugh fest never panned out, but he persisted with his chorus girl rave.

After nearly depleting the supply of P.J. Lavies letterhead, Rap hit a home run. Peggy suggested a meeting, but it was a long time coming, with postponement after postponement.

October 8, 1935. "My chorus cutie's show hasn't come to Milwaukee yet, being postponed, but very soon now, and I've got a date with her. She's going to introduce me to five of the others and throw a little party. The whole gang gets a kick out of my letters.... I'm going to get a big kick out of meeting them."

October 31, 1935. "My gal hain't writ lately, probably working up a nice long letter. She's traveling about yet, and no Milwaukee on the schedule as yet. Dang it! But she's sure to come, since Milw. is her home. And I'll bet she wants to meet me the minute she gets in town. She'll be curious to see the guy who writes her 5000-word letters as if they were so much little-do."

And so it was that after months of anticipation, Rap's chorus line cutie rolled into town. Rap had always been stingy when it came to handing out photos of himself, preferring to keep his likeness a mystery until the last minute. With words, he was king, but in person, there were issues. He kept Peggy in the dark like everyone else, including Ackerman, who practically had to beg him for a portrait. This began to weigh heavily on Rap as his date with Peggy drew nigh.

December 10, 1935. "Tonight I am keeping my first date with the 'Follies De Paree' cutie," he told Ackerman. "She's going to be disappointed with me, I know, if she's expecting to see a handsome writing man. But I guess I'll be able to handle the situation okay.... She seems to think I'm America's Number One Public Author now, and I'm afraid I'm going to have a time of it convincing her I'm just an ordinary punk."

Peggy was good on her word and introduced Rap to the rest of the chorus girls. Apparently they took him in as the Milwaukee mascot of the Follies De Paree. As late as March 1936, Rap was still seeing the Riverside girls, especially Peggy. "Peggy and I are getting along splendidly," he wrote Ackerman. "Look out for little Ray. He's treading a dangerous path!"

The path ended abruptly, for this was his last mention of Peggy and the Follies De Paree. Rap's circumstances changed dramatically. In the first week of March 1936 he told Ackerman he had quit his day job, hoping to strike it rich as a full-time writer. He began working on salary for Associated Authors, making about $150 per month, he said.

Rap was as prolific as he was enthusiastic. By his own calculation, from December 1934 to December 1935 he had written nearly 150,000 words of all types of pulp fiction. His list of published efforts included:

"The Time Tragedy," December, *Thrilling Wonder Stories*
"The Wiper Spook," January, *True Gang Life*
"The Train Wreckers," February, *True Gang Life*
"Alibi Bait," April, *True Gang Life*
"Aces Back to Back," July, *True Gang Life*
"The Ocelot Murders," October, *Murder Mysteries*
"The Blush of Death," November, *Murder Mysteries*
"Shark," December, *Murder Mysteries*
"Three from the Test Tube," December, *Thrilling Wonder Stories*
"Symphony of Death," December, *Amazing Stories*

He was also selling to the *Scarlet Adventuress* while trying to break into *Astounding Science Fiction*. He worked on a series of sexy detective shorts for *Spicy Detective* with fellow Fictioneer Lawrence Keating. If he thought it would sell, Rap wrote it.

Last Hurrah

> *"Is it possible that somewhere, somehow, the total sum of all knowledge exists?"*— Ray Palmer

When Stanley Weinbaum died of cancer on December 14, 1935, his literary agent Julius Schwartz got the news in a telegram from Rap: "WEINBAUM DIED THIS MORNING," the message read. Though he had never met Weinbaum, Schwartz wept at the news.[6]

Schwartz agreed that Rap should eulogize Weinbaum in *Fantasy Magazine*. "Of the members of *Fantasy*'s editorial staff no one is more fitted to write a dedication to Stanley G. Weinbaum than Raymond A. Palmer, who was fortunate in living in the same city, and who was honored in having Weinbaum as a friend."[7]

The Fictioneers drew up plans for the greatest publishing effort fandom had ever known: The Stanley G. Weinbaum memorial volume *Dawn of Flame*. It elevated pulp fiction to leather-bound glory, and was the first anthology for any SF author. Nothing like it had come before. Rap explained his mission in a June 16, 1936, letter to Ackerman:

> I am going ahead with publication of Stan's book, and collecting the money is my next step.... We are publishing 250 copies immediately, and printing 250 more, unbound, in case our orders run over 250, which may easily happen, since I have 125 now. We can make expenses now, and anything further will mean profit for Conny.

Rap wrote the foreword and shouldered the lion's share of work as treasurer and publicity agent. He produced six copies before Weinbaum's widow, Margaret, declared Rap's foreword far too personal. She asked that it be removed. Lawrence Keating wrote a replacement, thereby creating an instant rarity: Only six of Weinbaum's closest friends had a first edition copy with Rap's banished foreword, thus making it impossible for the average collector to obtain anything but a second edition.

Offered at the heady sum of $2.50, sales among Depression era fans were, sad to say, sparse. So Rap rolled out an installment plan for fans too poor to pay in full. He was willing to mail a copy to anyone who plunked down 50 cents and agreed to a weekly installment plan. Still, sales were disappointing. Only about 250 copies sold; many were never bound. Moskowitz claimed it became one of the rarest and most difficult-to-obtain of all fantasy volumes.

Fandom's dismal response to *Dawn of Flame* was one of Rap's great disappointments. Harry Warner, Jr., claimed it turned Rap against fandom: "Palmer charged then that the fan readership of *Fantasy* magazine had failed to support the volume and that the non-fan purchasers of *Astounding* had done the job with support from *Thrilling Wonder Stories* readers."[8] As Warner saw it, it set Rap on a collision course with fandom, which was something of an exaggeration. Rap did feel a sense of gratitude to Weinbaum, who freed him from the science-burdened SF of the past, to embrace the new SF of the human element. In *Fantasy Magazine*'s January 1936 issue, Rap noted that Weinbaum's genius "was the knack of instilling reality into his stories, almost to the extent that his readers found themselves believing them, accepting them as sheer truth, rather than as scientific fantasy." Rap had taken the first step that would lead him to the Shaver Mystery.

Catastrophe Incarnate

"During the past few years there has been a slow, but steady, decline in science fiction interest."— Hugo Gernsback, 1936

Things were going well for Ray Palmer the writer, though he lamented in *Fantasy Magazine* that eking out a living as a science fiction writer was difficult. Still, he had his column, he had the Fictioneers, and he was pounding his typewriter at a fevered pitch.

Then the rumors began. When Ackerman asked Rap why he was delinquent in paying his corporate share at *Fantasy Magazine*, Rap had to explain. The magazine, he said, was about to lose its benefactor and printer, Conrad Ruppert. "Don't know if Julie and Conny have discussed it with you, but it seems they plan to discontinue *Fantasy Mag*, perhaps in September, unless new means are found to make it pay.... I've had the money, have had it for months, but have held off because of Conny's decision."[9]

From its inception, Ruppert printed *Fantasy Magazine* (*Science Fiction Digest*) as a labor of love. When financial pressures at his shop forced Ruppert off the editorial board, things looked grim for managing editor Julius Schwartz. Fanzines have never known substantial support, no matter how brilliant. Low overhead was the key to any fanzine's survival, even *Fantasy Magazine*, with the largest circulation of any of its peers.

Schwartz scraped together enough cash to hire a printer, but suffered yet another blow when his partner and fellow editor Mort Weisinger accepted a job as editor of *Thrilling Wonder Stories*. As Moskowitz saw it, "The full weight of responsibility for carrying on *Fantasy Magazine* now rested entirely upon his shoulders, and all around him was the ill-disguised envy and bitterness of the second and third fandoms, who, incapable of emulating his magazine successfully, would not be overly sorry to see it destroyed."[10]

Moskowitz sketched a colorful image. First fandom was like a lost hunter in the woods, surrounded by hungry wolves. The threat, of course, was the growing influence of second and third fandoms; the unlucky prey was a weak and fading first fandom, symbolized by the staff of *Fantasy Magazine*.

In a move reminiscent of Rap's last-ditch attempt to save *Cosmology*, Schwartz prepared *Fantasy Magazine*'s last stand: its fourth-year anniversary issue. It was a glorious effort, jam-packed with stories by big-name authors, including Ray Palmer. It even featured a never-before-published story by Stanley Weinbaum. Schwartz mailed two thousand copies to potential subscribers, lowering the 15 cents cover price to 10 cents, then sat back and waited. The cavalry never arrived. *Fantasy Magazine*, the greatest of all fan publications, was history.

Meanwhile, fan clubs across the country were locked in bitter power struggles, rising and falling like feudal city-states. Moskowitz recorded this time as the beginning of a Reign of Terror aimed at eliminating what was left of first fandom. Anarchy reigned supreme, replacing BNFs (Big Name Fans) with teenage amateurs. Ray and his fellow editors at *Fantasy Magazine* "gazed out upon the welter of juvenile publications and organizations that surrounded them on every side.... And so, with spiteful swiftness, the door slammed shut on the old guard...."[11]

Moskowitz called it catastrophe incarnate. "Never had such a gold mine of talent departed simultaneously from the field. Survival of fandom in any mature sense of the word had devolved...."[12]

Having lost his high profile, Rap focused on his writing, working for Associated

Authors. He considered himself a full-time writer now. Schwartz became a literary agent specializing in SF authors; Weisinger was editing *Thrilling Wonder Stories*; Forrest J Ackerman became a Hollywood literary agent, but continued his fan activities and collecting.

The gathering clouds of 1937 got darker still for Ray. In June 1937 a fire destroyed the office building where his father worked as a fire department administrator. It was cruel irony that a fire should separate a fireman from his job, but Roy Palmer suddenly found himself unemployed. Rap stepped up to support the family, returning to his old job at the P.J. Lavies Company. He explained the situation to Ackerman in a letter dated June 26, 1936: "[A] little bad luck has made me short, and perhaps for some time. I am supporting a family of seven for an indefinite period, simply because the head of the family is out of work due to a fire at his place of employment.... He may be off a month or so ... am back to work full-time ... due to the above circumstance. A big family is no 'sitting around' matter."

Rap continued his Fictioneer meetings, and was renting an apartment at 1406 West Washington Street. There is no telling how long he supported the family, but it appears that eight months later, Rap had still not returned to full-time writing.

Then the other shoe dropped. Mr. P.J. Lavies fell ill and shut down the business. Rap was at loose ends with no job. His writing career was floundering. He complained to Ackerman: "Prospects of many things, among them losing my present job, going in business for myself, going in for full-time writing, etc. All is confusion at present, largely because of reported near death of my boss."[13]

Less than a year later, Ray Palmer left Milwaukee, disappearing from the pages of Wright's City Directory forever.

Life Is Blueprint Made by Ray Palmer

"There is no such thing as correct thinking, per se; nor is there such a thing as fact, in an absolute sense."— Ray Palmer

The circumstances that changed Ray Palmer from fan to professional editor were far from ordinary. So said Ray Palmer. His recounting of history gathered momentum as time went on, and like most of his life stories, variations exist. Rap's version was often the most entertaining, if not confusing. But the Ray Palmer mythos is best when told by Ray Palmer himself, no matter how embellished or incorrect. As Harry Warner, Jr., begrudgingly admitted, "Palmer is the kind of person around whom legends cling."

In any case, 1937 was shaping up as a dismal year for Rap. So dismal in fact, that he claimed he did something very unusual: He up and quit his full-time job. This was in the depth of the Great Depression, at a time when a steady paycheck was a glory to behold. Rap explained the reasons behind this mysterious behavior in *Martian Diary*: "I gave up my job, went to my rented room, and simply waited.... I was waiting to be called to the editorship of *Amazing Stories* magazine, which was published in New York and had an editor who had no intention of relinquishing his job. In short, I predestined it!"[14]

This made for exciting reading, and tied in with Rap's precognitive ability, but his timeline was way off. He did quit his job at the P.J. Lavies Company, but that was back in March 1936, at his first try at full-time writing. He was not called to work at Ziff-Davis Publishing until February 1938. That would mean he spent two years waiting in his rented room with nothing to do but mock up a mental picture of his new job.

Missing from his storyline was his father's subsequent unemployment, when Rap returned to P.J. Lavies to support the family in June 1936. Conspicuously absent is the part about Mr. Lavies' ill health causing Rap's unexpected layoff in March 1937. In his memoir, he said it was through "pure force of will I had created the conditions I wanted."[15]

Rap's revisionism gave a more profound, metaphysical explanation, in keeping with other, similar stories of his life, but peripheral events swirling around him at the time reveal a far different story. First and foremost to these events is one Roger Sherman Hoar — the man behind the pen name Ralph Milne Farley. Harvard-educated, he was the progeny of the stately New England Hoars, grandson of former U.S. Attorney General Ebenezer Rockwood Hoar. The other side of his family claimed founding father and signer of the Declaration of Independence, Roger Sherman.

Roger Sherman Hoar was an engineer, attorney, mathematician, and former Massachusetts senator. But it was Hoar's alter ego — pulp writer Ralph Milne Farley — who joined the Milwaukee Fictioneers. Farley claimed Edgar Rice Burroughs as a personal friend, and of course, Ray Palmer.

The planets began to line up in Rap's favor as we find the venerable *Amazing Stories*, then owned by Teck Publications of New York, teetering on the brink of bankruptcy. Its editor, Dr. T. O'Conor Sloane — who stated emphatically that man would never achieve space flight — was punching his time card at Teck Publications with less and less enthusiasm as each day passed.

Sloane had been with *Amazing Stories* from the very beginning. He was Hugo Gernsback's managing editor, but was promoted to editor in 1929 when Gernsback filed for bankruptcy and lost the magazine. As editor of the leading science fiction pulp of the era, Sloane published the first works of John W. Campbell, Jr., Clifford Simak, and E.E. "Doc" Smith.

By 1937 *Amazing*'s circulation was plummeting at a giddy pace. It had an anemic 19,000 readers at the time Teck sold it to Ziff-Davis Publishing. Ziff-Davis was only interested in Teck's lucrative sister publication, *Radio News*. Teck agreed to the sale of *Radio News* on one condition, that Ziff-Davis take *Amazing Stories* with it.

Both magazines were relocated to Ziff-Davis headquarters in Chicago, where William B. Ziff and Bernard G. Davis would determine the fate of *Amazing Stories*. They were skeptical it could be salvaged, but determined to give it the college try.

Shortly after *Amazing*'s move to Chicago in February 1938, we find Ralph Milne Farley paying a visit to the new Ziff-Davis headquarters. As Rap tells it, Farley was feeling out the new owners as a potential market for his fiction. Davis, he said, was quick to inform Farley, "We don't need stories, we need an editor!" At which point Davis offered him the job. Robert Bloch tells a slightly different version of this story, saying that Davis called Farley specifically to offer him the job.

In any case, both versions share the same ending, told by Bloch. "After politely refusing the seventy-five-dollar-a-week job,"[16] Hoar informed Davis that he knew someone who would be perfect — a friend, a true SF fan, a former editor at *Fantasy* magazine and an avid pulp writer — Ray Palmer.

In truth, Rap was barely getting by as a freelancer, and had recently been laid off his job with the P.J. Lavies Company. But Davis knew nothing of that and gratefully accepted Farley's advice. The version told by Harry Warner, Jr., added further detail: "Davis asked Palmer to write a letter outlining his qualifications. Instead, at Farley's suggestion, Palmer applied in person at the editorial office in Chicago."[17]

In *Martian Diary*, Rap gives us *his* version: "'I know just the man for you,' said Mr.

Hoar, and recommended me. The advantages in having a personal friend at the helm of *Amazing Stories* were not lost upon him. He promised I would be in Mr. Davis' office at 10 A.M. the next morning. That night I received a call from Mr. Hoar, and the next morning went to Chicago to begin work in my new job."[18]

The Ray Palmer mythos works best with a deeper meaning to any story, so Rap added a few flourishes. In a roundabout way, his memoir revealed the inner workings of Ray Palmer's universe:

> I had decided that this was precisely what I wanted to happen. And I fixed in my mind that this was my "destination." I knew it could be done. If I could do what I had already done in winning a $5.00 bet, I knew that I could do anything I wanted. I could make it happen.... The events of my own life had already taught me never to reject anything as impossible, and especially not to deride such things.[19]

And so it was that his job at *Amazing Stories* joined the ranks of other miracle events, like his escape from certain death at age seven, nine, and again at 20. It took its place among cosmic mysteries that, quite possibly, only Rap understood. Still, the events did happen, though not in the order he remembered them.

Amazing Resurrection

"All I needed was a typewriter. Santa Claus brought that."— Ray Palmer

Thanks to a vast, arcane knowledge acquired during an unusual childhood, Ray Palmer charted his life's course early on. The boy who doctors said would never live to see his tenth birthday had now become editor of *Amazing Stories* at age 27.

Details of his first day as editor, February 14, 1938, are sketchy, for here, too, there are dueling versions of what happened. Those who knew him, like Robert Bloch, had a fair knowledge of what was going on. Bloch was an insider—a Fictioneer. Piecing it together from several sources, what follows is a reconstruction of that day, beginning with Rap's version.

He arrived bright and early at Mr. Davis' Chicago office. Davis briefed him on their desperate situation. *Amazing Stories* was about to go under. "I was informed by Mr. Davis that the magazine was a dud, that they intended only to publish one issue to assure themselves it was indeed dead, then discontinue. It was up to me."[20]

Rap's initial euphoria gave way to the reality of his predicament, which hit him with a dull thud. Bloch gave his version of what came next in his autobiography *Once Around the Bloch*. Rap's challenge, said Bloch, was the slush pile of stories he inherited from his predecessor, which "would amaze nobody. Faced with his employer's ultimatum that the magazine must appear without skipping an issue, Ray sold himself some of his own material, purchased what little was available at the moment from various writers he knew, and cried out to the Fictioneers for help."[21]

Another problem was the cover art for his first two issues. A Ziff-Davis editor, probably from *Popular Photography* (another ZD-owned magazine) convinced Mr. Davis to use photographic illustrations. The two cover photos depicted live models in odd scenes and costumes, having nothing to do with the magazine's content. This challenge was nothing new to Rap. During his *Fantasy Magazine* days he often held contests where he encouraged writers to write stories around illustrations.

As a Fictioneer in good standing, Bloch got the honor of writing a story around one of these photo illustrations; he wrote the cover story for Rap's second issue. It was Bloch's first, and far from last, yarn in *Amazing*. In retrospect, it gave no solace to Bloch. "Ray sealed my doom by dumping a copy of one cover on me, and I sealed his by dumping a story on him.... It remains an example (along with several hundred other efforts) of my worst work."[22]

Rap disagreed. In describing Bloch's yarn *"Secret of the Observatory,"* he showered it with praise: "Robert Bloch, author of this month's feature story, and the subject of our ... direct-color cover photo, has written a story that clicks in more ways than one. The story is about future photography and possibilities in future espionage and intrigue. And if we aren't bad guessers, he'll be breaking into our pages again in the near future. He's done a fine job on his first attempt."[23]

Harry Warner, Jr., added a few more details to Rap's first day. Naming his source as an "unidentified timekeeper," he acquired a log of Rap's first day at *Amazing*. "Palmer arrived at 10:22 A.M., began to go through the pile of manuscripts on hand at 10:41 A.M., received complete charge of the magazine at 5:11 P.M., and got home at 9 P.M., having gone without food and drink for 27 hours."[24]

Warner had a juicier tidbit to add. He quoted Rap himself, who confirmed Warner's image of Rap as the Rasputin of first fandom. "'Here at last,' Palmer said, 'I had it in my power to do to my old hobby what I had always had the driving desire to do to it. I had in my hands the power to change, to destroy, to create, to remake, at my own discretion.'"[25]

Fans watched Rap's transformation from fan to pro with keen interest. Mr. Spilling the Atoms made good after all. It was a bittersweet moment for first fandom. In short order, Rap transformed *Amazing* from a stodgy wasteland of dull science fiction into a lively, entertaining pulp magazine. That was a big disappointment to fandom's intelligentsia. They yearned for "mature" SF. Regardless of Rap's critics, Sam Moskowitz gave him credit for increasing the popularity of the genre:

> Though occasional stories of superior merit did appear, Palmer concentrated on stories that veteran fans considered "written down" and far too elementary and stereotyped in concept. But despite disappointing the old guard, the magazine's circulation rose in substantial jumps with every issue. Thus science fiction, for the first time in years, began to expand rather than diminish its audience. Moreover, Palmer, probably remembering his own fan days, was liberal in publishing free notices of various fan events and publications.[26]

Rap's plan was to recreate the kind of magazine that gave him adrenalin-pumping thrills as a teenager, a time when he became a diehard fan. His approach paid off. He tapped into the same sense of wonder that still thumped in the hearts of young readers — the kind of kids that would plunk down two bits on *Amazing Stories* every month to keep the thrills coming.

Rap added humor and science quizzes and quirky history fillers. He knew enough to include plenty of fan letters in the popular "Discussions" letter column, too. Letters from young kids like Philip K. Dick and Ray Bradbury appeared in "Discussions." Demand for *Amazing* was such that by the following year, Rap convinced Mr. Davis to launch a sister publication called *Fantastic Adventures*, geared to fantasy fiction fans.

Claiming he got his figures from Rap, Harry Warner, Jr., said Rap's first issue sold 45,000 copies. The second soared to 75,000, then held steady at around 90,000. But Rap had different figures. "My first issue sold 75,000 copies, the second 93,000 and within a year the circulation was 185,000 and I was editor of seven additional magazines."[27]

1940

> *"Put aside a quarter for a heck of a lot more entertainment and pleasure any quarter ever bought you before!"*— Ray Palmer

Ray Palmer began his third year at *Amazing* with characteristic enthusiasm. The previous year had introduced one of *Amazing*'s most popular literary characters, Adam Link — Eando Binder's thinking, feeling robot — in "I, Robot." In 1940 he continued the series with "Adam Link in Business."

Rap sensed that 1940 would be a watershed year for science fiction: "[I]t seems significant that where some years ago, science fiction writers graduated into other fields; today writers in other fields are graduating to science fiction. It makes us feel pretty good."[28]

What also made Rap feel good was the fact that he was buying stories from editors he used to peddle his own stories to, like F. Orlin Tremaine of *Astounding*, who sold Rap a yarn for Ziff-Davis' *South Sea Stories*' February 1940 issue. Things were indeed looking up.

His weekly visits to the Riverside Theater were replaced by his newly organized Ziff-Davis bowling team, which worked out well because Rap enjoyed bowling almost as much as he did the shows at the Riverside. Decked out in his team's green and gold satin bowling shirt with *Amazing Stories* stitched across the back, Rap took on all comers. He bragged to his readers, "We apply *science* to our bowling. Your editor got a 278 the other day."

On a more serious note, Rap was beginning to have doubts about atomic power long before the bomb was dropped. He explained that U-235 is 30 million times more powerful that dynamite, and wondered aloud what would happen to the *Queen Mary* if it was struck by a bomb made of U-235. "Your editor wonders whether we want that kind of atomic power or not!"

Aside from the usual heckles of fandom, life had been good to Rap. "[T]hey try to keep your editor on his toes by telling him how odorous he is. But how they love him in spite of it all," he said. On August 1, 1940, he would turn 30. Though this did not seem ominous to the casual observer, it might have been to Ray. Zero years in anyone's life are milestones, time for contemplation, change, and rejuvenation. A zero year is a time when all the years that came before it are plumbed for depth of meaning.

Most of Rap's cherished dreams had already come true, from his humble beginnings as an SF fan, moving on to Big Name Fan, to freelance author, and finally his job as a professional editor. Ten years earlier, he stood toe to toe with Death and won. But now it was 1940, and deep within his core he knew something was missing. Rap's desire was for companionship, a wife and family, but his celebrated willpower had failed to lure a soul mate. His accomplishments with the fairer sex were dismal due to his inferiority complex and his physical appearance. To those around him he appeared to be an ascetic, said William L. Hamling. "He didn't mix well with anybody else. Women were almost, you know.... But he was not a queer guy. He was completely heterosexual. You might have thought he'd gone that way, but he never did."[29]

In 1940 Rap lived in Berwyn, a Chicago suburb. Berwyn was also home to teenager Florence MacMillan, who turned out to be the girl of his dreams, more or less. How he met her and how long they knew each other before Rap proposed is a mystery. He left out the history of his impromptu marriage to Florence MacMillan when writing his life story; not so much because of what happened when they met as what happened after.

Florence was a Chicago native born January 22, 1921. Her father, Ora D. MacMillan, was a steel company rep. He and his wife were Canadian immigrants.

On Thursday, August 1, 1940 (Rap's 30th birthday), Rap and Florence — age 19 — applied for a marriage license. The marriage took place in a flash at the Oak Park, Illinois, First Presbyterian Church on Saturday, August 3. No mention of the wedding found its way into Rap's editorials, though he often spoke of his friends' marriages and engagements with unbridled enthusiasm.

Nothing is known about the circumstances that led up to the annulment that followed a few weeks later. A dark cloud of secrecy descended over the incident, though word had gotten around the office. It was best to keep quiet about it, as Hamling did, until he finally acknowledged it in 2009. Said Hamling, "The 'marriage' deal is fact — but it amounted to nothing more than a drunken weekend. Forget it!"[30]

Most of Rap's associates did, though Howard Browne, one of Rap's fellow editors, said that he knew of a couple of women who had taken Rap to the cleaners for a sizable chunk of cash. Even the marriage annulment papers were swallowed up in time, as Rap would have wanted. It was a bittersweet year for Ray, having won and lost his first wife. The marriage produced no children and Florence went on to remarry. Rap did his best to forget and move on.

5

Politics

"I like to think I run my own little world."—Ray Palmer

East Coast science fiction, lorded over by the Futurians' science fiction club, was organized by Bolshevik SF fan Donald Wollheim. Frederik Pohl, Isaac Asimov, John Michel, and Robert Lowndes were some of the better-known Futurians. They made no bones about their leftist leanings, just as Ray and his Midwest writers aligned themselves with Mom and apple pie. They were the yin and the yang; one, cerebral and leftist, the other, visceral, shot through and through with two-fisted American action. Rap was a registered Republican, embracing the conservative values of his era. He was an old-school conservative, and if alive today would likely be a Libertarian.

A great divide separated East and Midwest SF. Bill Hamling still remembers the Futurians with disdain. "They were *Communists*! Strictly Commies. They wouldn't like a guy like Ray Palmer. Freddie Pohl! Shit…! That whole crowd back east! We not only frowned on them, we spit on them. There was no meeting of the minds. No way, José."[1]

Feuding between New York and Chicago factions flared in 1940 when Chicago became the site of the Second World Science Fiction Convention (The Chicon). The Futurians planned to disrupt the convention to vent their displeasure that it was being held on Ray's turf.

The plan was exposed, and Futurians were summarily banned from the convention. Sam Moskowitz was instrumental in the ban. He characterized the Futurians as Marxists and Bohemians and worse; most of them were still living with their *parents*, he said. Ironically, this was true of the majority of attendees.

The Futurians were not discouraged. They printed an anti–Ray Palmer brochure titled "An Amazing Story" that denounced Rap as a fascist and panderer to juvenile tastes in SF. The brochure was to be handed to all attendees as they filed in. Futurians ignored the fact that Rap donated thousands of dollars in original cover and interior art to the convention's fundraising auction. Rap also plugged the convention in *Amazing*, encouraging his readers to attend. On Sunday, September 1, Rap delivered a speech, "What Science Fiction Really Is," to approximately 123 fans. Fan Bob Tucker tallied the official member list that day at 128, but that was after Rap had signed his name five times, using various pen names.[2]

Moskowitz's expulsion of the Futurians opened a chasm that further alienated Midwest and East Coast fans. *Amazing Stories* rarely, if ever, got a kind word from East Coast fandom. This ancient conflict echoes to this day within the historic record whenever the name Ray Palmer or *Amazing Stories* is mentioned.

New Editorial Policy

"When the action begins to slow down, drop a body through the skylight."— Ray Palmer

With Ray Palmer holding the reins, *Amazing Stories* fans buckled up for a wild ride. And when readers began to question where Rap was taking them, he laid out his editorial manifesto. It mirrored his policy in *Fantasy Magazine*, and reflected the influence of Stanley Weinbaum. He once told aspiring writer Frank M. Robinson: "[You can] make a story better by taking out all the 'fine writing.'" Robinson agreed, adding, "Depending on your interpretation of 'fine writing,' he had a point."[3] Rap often spoke about the kind of writing he looked for in a writer, usually in "The Observatory," his regular editorial column in *Amazing*:

- December 1938. "Science fiction has become just a trifle too mechanical. That is, there is not enough variety. Too many scientific machines and not enough other scientific factors."
- January 1939. "Aha! You will say (some very few of you). We are not ordinary 'pulp' readers. We don't read for slam-bang action with ray guns, heroes rescuing fair damsels from the ferocious people of Venus.... Here I must partially disagree. In the majority, you want action and thrills."
- May 1939. "We've concentrated more on stories and other content improvements than on mechanical things which don't really add anything to science fiction."
- June 1939. "Our writers are quite proud of their part in pointing the way toward future betterment and true scientific Americanism ideals; purposes are naturally reflected in everything they write."
- August 1939. "We want plot. We want a 'story' [in which] the science can be removed ... and still leave a story. If we can't drop the science without leaving a pointless husk, then we don't accept the story. Further, we want fast action ... dramatic tempo ... suspense, situation, complications, fast dialogue, a minimum of scientific and entirely descriptive matter which tend to slow up the continuity of action ... and a reasonable degree of active atmosphere which tends to vitalize the scene for the readers ... of people we can all understand — this entails good characterization."

Editorial policy at *Amazing Stories* became a rip-roaring good time from the minute Rap took over until his departure eleven years later. For that, his "Discussions" letter column received its fair share of brickbats from a vocal fan minority. One letter signed RM complained in May 1941 of Rap's "insipid love angles" and characters who speak "a particularly obnoxious form of obsolete high school slang in 80 percent of the stories."

Another fan, S. Gibson, accused Rap in December 1942 of publishing "cheap adventure having very little science fiction. [The stories] look like the kind that were turned down by every other magazine on the market and came to you as a last resort.... [T]his work is the corniest I have ever had the misfortune to buy.... [The stories have] unnecessary ... cowboys and injuns trimmings."

A favorite activity at the time was the fan poll, meant to determine favorite authors, pulps, and stories. Art Widner, a Massachusetts fan, released the results of his Widner Poll in 1940. Of the top ten science fiction pulps voted on by fans, not one belonged to Ziff-Davis. When a gloating reader pointed this out to Rap, he summarily dismissed it, saying that although Widner's poll may have represented a dozen fans, Ziff-Davis circulation figures showed its magazines represented several hundred thousand readers from all walks of life, all over the world.

This was true. Active fans were but a handful compared to *Amazing*'s total readership. Rap often called SF fandom an insignificant drop in the bucket. This, in turn, infuriated organized fandom, which had completed two world SF conventions by 1940, each attended by something less than 130 fans. Club fanzines ebbed and flowed at a frenetic pace. But fandom was making lists of its friends and foes, and Rap was edging his way to the top of the hit list. Unanimously, fandom sided with John W. Campbell, Jr., at *Astounding Science Fiction*.

Campbell vs. Palmer

"Pulp magazines are not intended to present enduring literature."— Ray Palmer

Fandom would forever compare Ray Palmer and John W. Campbell, Jr. It still does. Fandom defers to Campbell as the guru of highbrow science fiction. For that, fans welcomed Campbell into the First Fandom Hall of Fame with open arms, something they have yet to do with Rap. The two men shared similar backgrounds, up to a point.

Like Rap, Campbell was born in 1910 and grew up in an emotionally troubled family. Instead of the hard-drinking, authoritarian Roy Palmer, Campbell's father was an aloof, unaffectionate electrical engineer. Both men began writing SF in their teens, their first published work appearing in 1930—Rap's in *Thrilling Wonder Stories*, Campbell's in *Amazing Stories*.

Campbell, however, graduated from high school and enrolled at MIT; in 1932 he earned his physics degree from Duke University. This was the year Rap was employed as a bookkeeper and sheet metal worker, having earned his degree in the School of Hard Knocks. Campbell's physics degree placed him head and shoulders above Rap in the eyes of fandom's intelligentsia. While Campbell rubbed elbows with scientists and writers with lofty degrees, Rap spent his time at the bowling alley with high school–educated, self-taught writers. Both men went from fan to pro at about the same age. F. Orlin Tremaine hired Campbell to edit *Astounding Stories* in late 1937, though Campbell would not assume full authority of the magazine until May 1938. Ray became editor at *Amazing Stories* on February 14, 1938.

From there the two men took two vastly different editorial paths, building a fan base with their own distinctive styles. Though Palmer far outsold Campbell at the newsstands, he earned the wrath of Campbell's fans in the bargain. Old feuds die hard, and Bill Hamling was not immune to them. He still resents Campbell's fans more than 60 years later: "They idolized John Campbell and *Astounding*, and they hated *Amazing Stories* because they considered it too crass and marketable. We had a circulation around the 200,000 mark, which was a helluva lot of copies in those days. *Astounding* never had that kind of circulation, believe me, no matter how good and erudite John Campbell thought he was."[4]

Fandom believed SF would only be taken seriously if it contained serious science, or at the very least, intelligent *theories* about science. The thorn in their side, of course, was Ray and *Amazing Stories*. He was single-handedly destroying SF as thoughtful literature. But Rap was publishing a magazine for the sailor in the Pacific, the infantryman fighting the Axis in Europe, and the kid on the street where he grew up. These readers preferred escapism and entertainment, not cerebral stimulation, and this was the market that raked in big dividends for Ziff-Davis.

Nevertheless, Rap's fragile relationship with fandom troubled him greatly. He seemed at a loss how to fix it. As an editor, he alternately loved and loathed his fannish brethren, many of whom were intent on his destruction. Their brickbats appeared in "Discussions." One letter, from a Raymond Washington of Live Oak, Florida, became a template for future letters that haunted Rap throughout his career. It appeared in *Amazing Stories*, September 1943.

> Fandom has its radicals and communists and emotionally unstable, perhaps more so than conventional organizations.... Yes, respected editor, fandom is a minority. After all, what are a hundred and fifty fans to a half million readers? A fan pays 25¢ for *Amazing Stories*, but a reader pays the same, so obviously an attempt must be made to please the majority, or close shop.
> According to many of the fans, the Ziff-Davis science fiction publications concentrate on action, with a definite appeal to juveniles, and delight in presenting hack-work for the passing entertainment value the hordes of readers derive. The fans want more adult fiction, more good writing, and intellectual appeal, and less blood and thunder.... In any average group found anywhere in any town, the trend is toward stupidity. The majority is stupid. In a fan gathering, the majority is intelligent, and stupidity is conspicuous. People do not organize to think. *Fans* think! Normalcy is not desirable because of the trend downward.

The letter captured the essence of the Rap insurgency, and Rap's response exemplified his ongoing attitude toward SF elitists, a subject he would return to again and again.

> Your placing of the "fans" in the only "thinking" capacity in any average group in any town, is a thoughtless statement we're sure you really don't mean. Also, we disagree that "normalcy" is not desired. We are fighting today to return this world to normalcy. Our part in that fight is entertainment to hold up morale. We publish over two million words a year. Not all of that can be "deathless" literature. If it were, the term "worthwhile literature" would become meaningless because of its very plentitude. What then would you consider "worthwhile?" Not all of us can be geniuses. If we were, we'd all be "average." Some scientists say that none of us really "think" in the pure sense of the word. After all, it's a hard job, and we must relax sometimes. *Amazing Stories* believes its job is to provide that relaxation.— Rap

Historian Harry Warner, Jr., sided with the insurgency. Fandom lauded Warner's 1960 book *All Our Yesterdays* as a scholarly record of early 20th century fandom. The chapter titled "Fans Turned Pros" included a few pages on Rap, who, according to Warner, used and abused fandom. "Palmer attracted more attention among fans than most prozine editors ... because of his curious habit of swinging unpredictably between wheedling and alienating them."[5]

Warner was apparently one of those fans who felt wheedled and alienated. His most acerbic attack on Rap came in 1957, when he became incensed over a subscription solicitation from Rap's Amherst Publishing house. Warner dashed off a scathing screed to a local fanzine. Then, for reasons beyond comprehension, Rap picked up Warner's attack and reprinted it as a guest editorial in one of his magazines. This riled Warner further, as Rap failed to ask permission to publish it. But Rap may have sensed a seed of truth in Warner's rant, excerpts of which follow.

> Science fiction in pulp magazines was never a particularly beautiful winged creature. But [Ray Palmer] dragged it down in the late 1930s when he assumed command of *Amazing Stories*. He accepted the scolding of fandom and continued to engage in a series of commercialized massacres of the literary flights of science fiction, through the long series of new titles, new policies, new sensations, and new inanities that have characterized his magazines for nearly two decades. And each time he scored a direct hit on some healthy section of science fiction's life, he inevitably hauled the bloody corpse up to fandom, and proudly laid it there to await a reaction, knowing

in advance what fandom would say, acting hurt and injured himself when his latest kill was not acclaimed.

One chapter of his scriptures was based on the theory that fans were not representative of science fiction readers as a whole, and to follow their likings would be commercial suicide. That was exactly the theory that John W. Campbell, Jr., expressed in print so frequently in those days. The difference between the two men was that Campbell failed to let his theorizing guide his editorial policy. Events proved the truth: that the quality prozines like *Astounding* and *Galaxy*, which the active fans like the best, are the ones that survive the commercial storms in the pulp market.[6]

Ray's response was as mysterious as it was magnanimous. "We are deeply indebted to Mr. Warner for his kindness, and above all, for his accuracy of reporting, which is a lost art these days."[7]

Sarcasm or capitulation? Warner's attack may have triggered a few melancholic memories of his age-old fan feud. This was the same year, 1957, when Rap threw in the towel, leaving the SF field forever. Did Rap sense he was becoming a dinosaur? Possibly. At 47, he was middle-aged, having spent the last seven of those years in constant physical pain.

Bea Mahaffey, Rap's editor at *Other Worlds Science Stories,* recalled in a 1980 interview, "As a human being Ray was ... very sensitive, and very easily hurt because he had been hurt so much.... He was a very complex person; he was a lot more talented and gave a lot more to science fiction than people are aware. He developed some very good writers."[8]

The War Years

"V for Victory! That's the battle cry of this issue of Amazing Stories!"— Ray Palmer

Ray believed science fiction had the ability to foreshadow Mankind's future. He also believed *Amazing Stories* was leading the way, and the Second World War was his first big chance to demonstrate SF's prophetic ability. When the Japanese bombed Pearl Harbor on December 7, 1941, Rap quickly connected the dots.

"Dozens of our writers have foretold this attack. But none of them dreamed of its treachery. In this we see the true awfulness of the shame that has come upon the Japs, a shame that not even science fiction writers will be able to erase. Nor even imagine...."[9]

From Pearl Harbor to VJ Day, Rap engaged the enemy head-on from Ziff-Davis headquarters in Chicago. *Amazing* was featuring stories of war as early as 1940, when Alfred R. Steber set his sights on the Japanese in the July 1940 issue. He destroyed the entire island of Japan in "When the Gods Make War." In the same issue, Eando Binder's "Adam Link Fights a War" focused on a Japanese invasion, and Robert Moore Williams wrote "Fifth Column of Mars."

Rap would never be drafted due to his physical handicap. This became a hard fact of life for him when his brother David signed up as an Army infantryman. Rap hinted that he was about to be drafted in 1942, though details were sparse and mostly imagined. "[Y]our editor is wondering if he will be editing an army edition of *Amazing Stories* before very long. It seems Uncle Sam is very much interested in us, and our only gripe is that it's going to be tough on us to be able to throw only exclamation marks at the Japs. We'd rather they were bullets! That's the bad part of being an editor! Nobody believes he's good for anything else."[10]

Pearl Harbor was still smoldering when Rap's writers began shipping out to points unknown. He kept a running tally of their comings and goings, and began to publish issues with big wartime appeal. One of his best friends and writers, David Wright O'Brien, was a waist gunner on a B-29, and wrote SF for Rap between bombing runs. Two years earlier, Rap and Hamling celebrated O'Brien's wedding in Evanston.

On December 14, 1944, O'Brien was killed when his B-29 was shot down over Germany. In the months that followed, Rap doled out O'Brien's unpublished manuscripts one by one, dreading the day when there would be no more. But war worries or no, Rap never missed a chance to promote science fiction. The war, as it turned out, was his greatest proof that science fiction was what America needed most in its time of need:

> How long will it take for us to realize that science fiction's voice has been too weak, too much blanketed beneath the scorn of the man in the street? Our writers have written stories which denounced the shortsighted defense policy by showing how science can make any defense vulnerable.... Come on, America ... wake up! Get those gadgets off pulp paper and onto assembly lines. We've got a fight on our hands![11]

Rap announced plans for his first Victory Issue, one of many of its kind that appeared during the war. He assured readers that "it's strictly not a stunt, but something you'll read two years from now and gasp with amazement, because of the things it contained which came true."[12]

Amazing's 17th anniversary issue was dedicated to winning the war; it featured what Rap called "the greatest of all interplanetary war stories," Nelson S. Bond's "That Worlds May Live."

Using the nom de plume Frank Patton, Rap wrote "A Patriot Never Dies" for the August 1943 issue. It bristled with virile action lines like, "The muffled purr of the silenced hi-ex atomic bullets was sweet music in Martin's ears as he bent his tensed body over the vibrating machine gun and fed a seemingly endless belt of cartridges into its maw." Even Rap's non-war issues looked like war issues. Battleships, super tanks, atomic machine guns, and spaceships attacking Earth's armed forces appeared on cover after cover.

Wanting to do more than simply promote patriotic enthusiasm in *Amazing*, Rap pitched in on the home front, too. Noting that thoughtless drivers were exceeding the government-mandated 35-MPH speed limit, he decided to do something about it.

"When you are passed by one of these unpatriotic, or at least unthinking drivers, just press down on your horn button three short and one long — and watch 'em tramp down on the brakes with a red face! Here's one way for us to regulate that wasteful speeding without the necessity of a flock of policemen. V for victory!"[13]

6

The Inner Circle

"He always had trouble with neckties ... but he was an excellent bowler."—Howard Browne on Rap

Ziff-Davis Publishing in 1940 was located at 608 South Dearborn, its offices sprawled across the 22nd floor of a modern 1930s skyscraper south of the Loop, three city blocks from Lake Michigan. William B. Ziff then moved his company to 540 North Michigan Avenue in 1941, and a few years later to 185 South Wabash Avenue, in the heart of the Loop.

The Loop is an area of downtown Chicago surrounded by an elevated railway system. The Loop is where Ziff-Davis associate editor Howard Browne set his hard-boiled detective novels starring Paul Pine, who worked out of a rented Wabash Avenue office. The din of traffic and people and railcars squealing across the elevated tracks above gave the Loop its character. That, and a thick haze Chicagoans called air.

This was Rap's world. It was a noisy, gritty place where he established his informal club of Midwest writers and editors. He stood at the center of an inner circle—a kind of Rat Pack before Sinatra. Howard Browne was one of the first to join its ranks.

Born in Omaha, Nebraska, Browne began his writing career on his high school newspaper. He spent two years at the University of Nebraska before accepting a job as a sports writer on an Omaha newspaper. But his career was eclectic and heading nowhere. In 1926 he hitchhiked to Chicago where he worked at a series of jobs, as an order picker in a steel foundry, as a waiter at a TB sanitarium, as a State Street department store shipping clerk. He was a butter and egg salesman, a night clerk in a small hotel, machine operator for a furniture manufacturer, and finally a department store collections agent.[1] He joined the Ziff-Davis fiction group in 1942.

Then there was William L. Hamling, born in Chicago, June 14, 1921. His father was a railroad man. As a teenager, Hamling was a go-getter and self-promoter at Chicago's Lane Technical High School. He made a name for himself among Lane's 9,000 students as a writer and active SF fan.

As editor-in-chief of the *Lane Tech Prep*, at that time the largest slick prep magazine in the world,[2] Hamling found himself chronically late for class. His excuses centered on dire emergencies with the school magazine or important meetings with editorial and printing staff. As his friend Chester S. Geier recalled, "The teachers heard him out in bemused wonder, docile, impressed beyond any possibility of objection. Bill Hamling was BMOC—Big Man on Campus.... He wrote a *Weird Tales* sort of story, 'The Finger,' for the school magazine, ballyhooed it for months with signs in the halls, and when the issue with the story appeared, it was a sell-out."[3]

Geier, Henry Bott, Hamling, and "three other chaps"[4] started a short-lived afterschool

SF club. In March 1940, Hamling debuted *Stardust,* an SF fanzine that lasted for a handful of issues. The *Stardust* team consisted of Geier, Neil DeJack, Howard Funk, Harry Warner, Jr., and editor-in-chief W. Lawrence Hamling. It was indeed an impressive first fanzine, with content supplied by the likes of L. Sprague DeCamp, Robert Moore Williams, Charles D. Hornig, Ralph Milne Farley, and of course Chester Geier and Henry Bott. One issue included an exclusive interview with Ray Palmer. Lane Tech High writers appearing in *Stardust* accompanied Hamling throughout his publishing career.

While other high school SF fans were cranking out newsletters on mimeograph machines, *Stardust* appeared as a typeset semi-prozine envied by one and all. How did Hamling do it? Like everyone else, he was just a high school kid living at home. Hamling explained the mystery 70 years later in an interview: "*Stardust* was strictly a fan magazine, but I had friends in the printing business. A couple of guys named Quaver; Tom and his brother. They printed the first issue of *Stardust*—you won't believe this—for $10. It was just for fandom; localized fandom. But $10! Hell, you give more than that for a tip at any restaurant."[5] As his publishing prowess surged in the years to come, Hamling would eat at restaurants where $10 was the down payment on a glass of water.

Hamling had no problem making a name for himself among Chicago fandom. In 1939 he and fellow fan Mark Reinsberg collaborated on a space yarn titled "Dead Victory." Hamling hustled it over to Rap, who bought it, changed the title to "War with Jupiter" and became Hamling's mentor in the bargain. He became Rap's biggest supporter.

"It was a 9,500-word novelette, and he cut it back to 5,600 words and sent me a check, the first check I ever got, for $56. It was better than a million! I'll never forget that. I took the check out of the envelope and it was a great day—the beginning of my literary life."[6]

"War with Jupiter" had the added bonus of bringing Rap his staunchest ally, and Hamling determined to become a member of Rap's innermost circle. Even now, Hamling defends Ray Palmer from the barbs of an ungrateful fandom which, according to Hamling, never understood him. "Fandom never adjusted to him because Ray was kind of a radical, you know. People like me were also in that category, you might say, for one reason or another."[7]

On graduating high school, Hamling and Geier formed a partnership, sharing an office where they began working as full-time pulp writers. Hamling was the conduit to Rap and Ziff-Davis, where most of their stories sold. The two young writers gradually became members of a fascinating group of characters. As time went on, Hamling became indispensable to Rap, who sponsored him as an assistant editor at Ziff-Davis. Hamling remembered those far-off days from the mid-century quietude of his Palm Springs mansion in 2009:

> As events are happening you're not tagging them. Later you say, "Do you remember three years ago, when the inner circle, blah blah blah?" The real inner circle, that would be me, Howard Browne, well, and Chester Geier; he had a unique role in it, because he was deaf. The fact is, Chet never played [poker] with Ray, but he was always included in our group. Berkeley Livingston[8] would be along for the ride. He'd play poker and have money on the table, but was not like the active ones on the bowling team from the fiction group. [The inner circle was essentially] the three of us [Rap, Hamling, Browne], because we were the editors at Ziff-Davis. Berkeley was never involved at Ziff-Davis other than being published.[9]

Though Hamling did not recall Geier as part of the bowling team, Geier bowled on at least one occasion. Geier remembered the time and place. The team that night was comprised of Geier, Hamling, Rap, Browne, and Ziff-Davis writers Rog Phillips and Berkeley Livingston. They met at Rap's favorite restaurant for waffles and sandwiches after the game. Geier set the scene, with Hamling front and center.

Hamling was a James Cagney type, brash, bold, cocky, aggressive, impertinent, even arrogant. He was good-humored and bawdy enough most of the time, so that his other characteristics did not become obnoxious, but I suppose they remained noticeable.

I saw Hamling interfacing with Palmer and Browne and while I did not hear what was said I had the impression that often Hamling was argumentative, challenging, truculent, and derisive in their discussion.... Hamling felt himself on equal terms with anyone, and probably would have elbowed General Douglas MacArthur in the ribs and asked, "How's your sex life, you old bastard?"[10]

Freddy Funk and the Ferris Wheel

> *"As long as the writin' machine will work and my index fingers hold out—I'll go on trying to convince some editor that I'm the flaxen-haired youth of his editorial dreams."*—Leroy Yerxa

As the U.S. Navy was mopping up after the attack on Pearl Harbor, a young man named Leroy Yerxa was about to become one of Ray Palmer's steadiest and most prolific writers. He became one of Rap's closest friends in the bargain.

He was known to readers as Elroy Arno and several other Ziff-Davis house names[11]; it was a rare wartime issue of *Amazing Stories* or *Fantastic Adventures* that did not include a Leroy Yerxa yarn. His Freddy Funk series was a hit, beginning with "Freddy Funk's Madcap Mermaid" in 1943. That year was the peak of Yerxa's productivity, when Rap bought 30 Yerxa stories, an incredible output for any pulp writer.

Yerxa, born in 1915, one of six children, was a heavyset self-described "scale punisher," who jokingly blamed his size on his Yankee grandmother's "baked beans, Johnny cake, biscuits, and donuts."[12] His family moved frequently, and to make up for his piecemeal public education, Yerxa became a voracious reader at public libraries. His writing career began at Cooley High School on the northwest side of Detroit, where he became editor of the school newspaper.

When his father, a textile worker, lost his job, the family moved to Eaton Rapids, Michigan, a small mill town on the Grand River, south of Lansing. There he found work at the Horner Woolen Mill. Leroy enrolled at Eaton Rapids High School where he met pretty farm girl Frances Ferris, descendant of George Washington Gale Ferris, Jr., inventor of the amusement park ride bearing his name. Leroy and Frances married soon after graduation. Four children followed in quick succession.

Yerxa scrambled to support his growing family. He knew he could write, and he wanted to sell to the slicks for big money, so they left Eaton Rapids behind and moved to Chicago. Time passed, and with few sales, Yerxa was floundering. He heard about a local meeting of SF writers scheduled to take place near his home north of the Loop. Out of sheer desperation, he attended. There he met an SF fan who listened to his plight and suggested he forget about the slicks and write science fiction. The unnamed fan mentioned that an editor named Ray Palmer was seeking new writers, and that his office was on nearby Michigan Avenue.

Yerxa boned up by reading a few science fiction pulps, then sat down at his shaky typewriter stand to peck out his first SF story. He lived close enough to Michigan Avenue to deliver the manuscript in person, so he hopped aboard the elevated. To his everlasting joy, he and Ray hit it off, and Yerxa made his first sale. Glowing with his good fortune, Yerxa returned home with the news.

Meanwhile, Ray's association with Yerxa was about to change his life forever. As it happened, Frances Yerxa had a good friend at Eaton Rapids High School named Marjorie Wilson who, like the Yerxas, had moved to Chicago after high school graduation. Wilson would become a key figure in both the Yerxas' and Rap's lives.

In a November 2008 interview, Frances revealed a story that few people outside of Rap's inner circle have heard. She began her recollection at the point when Leroy returned from his first visit with Ray Palmer.

Leroy and Ray and Frances and Marjorie

"Can you imagine a job as soft as ours? Sitting here reading hundreds of swell stories and playing God in selecting the ones you'll read?"—Ray Palmer

Frances recalled,

Leroy thought [Ray] was absolutely amazing, which he was. He came home and told me all about it. [He and Ray] became such good friends over the time he was submitting stories to him.

I knew Marjorie Wilson from French class in our junior-senior year. That's how I met her. She was smart. She graduated magna cum laude. Our circumstances were somewhat the same. She was born and raised on a farm in Michigan, and it was in the middle of the Depression. A lot of farmers, or most of them, lost their farms. That happened with her family too.

After graduation, we were living in Chicago and my husband was writing full-time at home, and Marjorie had been working at The Cradle, which at that time was a very famous orphanage. The reason it was famous was the rumor that brilliant Northwestern University professors sired the babies. Whenever the movie industry people wanted to adopt a baby they'd come here to adopt because they thought they'd get something close to a genius. Marjorie said that wasn't true, that they had babies from all walks of life.[13]

Sometimes I'd take the North Shore train and go up and spend the day with her if she had a day off. We kind of rekindled our friendship. About that time they closed The Cradle, and Marjorie was out of a job. She really knew how to take care of babies, so she had the idea that if we rented a duplex, my husband and I and the four kids could live in the apartment on the second floor, and she could live in the one downstairs and we would turn it into a day nursery.

Day nurseries were needed at that time in Chicago because the war was on and the men were away fighting ... and the mothers had to go to work to pay rent and take care of their children. They needed day nurseries to take care of their babies. So that's what we did. We had to have a big limousine with a driver and another person to stay in the limo to mind the babies while we went up the back stairs of the apartments to get babies and carry them down. Turned out to be an awful hard job.

About that time, my husband had invited Ray Palmer to come have dinner with us. I was so excited to have him come because I had never met him before; I had just heard about him. He came at 6 o'clock, about the time Marjorie was in the process of delivering babies back to their mothers. When Ray drove up in his red convertible, a Buick, Marjorie was carrying three babies with her, and he thought it was the most beautiful picture. He thought, "How wonderful this is!" That's how he met Marjorie; met her right on the steps of the duplex with her arms full of babies. They started dating after that.

He was so gracious and had never really been to a family dinner I guess. My kids just loved him. I had told my kids to stay in their beds. But my daughter Kay (she's 72 now), when she knew he was coming, she jumped out of her bed and out of her nightie and came running out. She had never seen Ray before, but jumped into his lap. It was the craziest thing, and he was very surprised too. That was 70 years ago.

I don't know for sure [how long they dated] before they got married. Ray said it was the most beautiful thing, he never expected to have a nice wife and children, because he did look a little strange.¹⁴

It took a little time for Marjorie to adjust to the idea of Rap as her future husband. Her daughter Linda Jane said that her mother thought it over before accepting his proposal: "He invited her out and gave her a ring shortly after they started seeing each other. Mom was uncertain as to whether to marry him and carried the ring in her purse for a while. I know they weren't together too long before they got married."¹⁵

Rap, Leroy, Frances, and Marjorie socialized frequently during the courtship. The Yerxa family had adopted Rap as a member of the family. The Yerxa children called him Uncle Ray. Frances continued the story from there:

> When they were just engaged, Ray drove us to Michigan to visit my family and Leroy's mother and father, brothers, and sister. He liked to drive, and the top was down on the convertible and it was fun. Marjorie would go too.
>
> [Ray] loved classical music. In winter in Chicago, people liked to go to the opera, and he'd buy season tickets and often invite Leroy and me and Marjorie to certain operas. It was nice to get dressed up, I'll tell you that. Afterward we usually went to the Shangri-La.¹⁶ The Shangri-La was a very beautiful, exotic restaurant. It was open real late at night, and it was a good place to go for one of those exotic, Hawaiian-type drinks. That was a favorite place where we'd get little tidbits on a stick, that kind of thing.¹⁷

And so it was that the Universe of All Possibilities opened up and gave Ray Palmer what he wanted most. Marjorie Wilson said yes. They were married on Christmas Day 1942. It was a civil ceremony and Marjorie wore a suit. She was Protestant, but Rap was more than willing to ignore his Catholic upbringing. Rap liked to tell a story at family gatherings about the wedding, which Linda Jane Palmer heard repeatedly: "He told everyone that he and Mom got married at 4 P.M. on Christmas Day and that I was born at 4:30 P.M. on Christmas Day. He conveniently left out the fact that they were married in 1942 and I was born a year and a half-hour later in 1943 on the same day. He loved to tease my mom with that story. I believe Mom and Dad went to New York City for their honeymoon. I remember Mom talking about Central Park and an ice skating rink."¹⁸

Ray Palmer and Marjorie Wilson at their engagement, 1942 (courtesy Linda Jane Palmer).

Freddy Funk's Farewell

"Ray was very protective of me after my husband died, and worried about the kids and me."— Frances Ferris Hamling

The years rolled on, the war continued and the friendship between the Yerxas and

Palmers flourished. But Leroy Yerxa had undiagnosed health problems. They came to light when he tried to enlist. The Army doctor's findings resulted in Leroy's 4F, according to Frances.

> Everybody was going to war. My husband was the oldest in the family, but his younger brother joined the Army. And later there was his brother Phillip, who joined the Army as soon as he was finished with high school. Now, my husband was ashamed to be seen on the street because he was a young, able-bodied man, and he wanted to protect the country too, so he went to sign up.
> All the induction centers in Chicago were jammed. He had to take a train to Milwaukee. So he was on this special train that was taking everyone to join up. He was playing poker with the other guys all the way to Milwaukee, having a ball. But when [the Army doctors] got to my husband they took his blood pressure, then took him to a room with a bed and told him to get into bed. He said "Why? I want to be out with the rest of the guys."
> They said, "Well, you could die at any moment, and the Army doesn't want to pay for you." They told him to stay in bed until it was time to get on the train again that night. They told him, "Go to a doctor!"
> So Leroy went to the doctor and the doctor said, "I don't know what your blood pressure is because ... the machine doesn't go beyond 300." In those days, they didn't have systolic and diastolic, it was just one number. The advice from the doctor was ... that Leroy's veins were probably filled with a substance that you find in the veins of very, very old people. Of course now we know that it's cholesterol. They didn't even know the word in those days.

The doctor told Leroy to give up physical activity, like walking up long flights of stairs and bowling. He added that it would be best if Leroy left the stress of big city life entirely. Since the Yerxas lived on the third floor of their apartment building, they decided to move. "Now if you have heart problems they *want* you to exercise," Frances said. "In those days it was the dark ages."

Even in poor health, Leroy was churning out pulp yarns in a white-hot frenzy. Frances began selling science fillers to Rap and even an occasional SF yarn, with a little tutoring from Leroy. Taking his doctor's advice, the Yerxas moved back to rural Michigan.

Leroy Yerxa's writing career ended in 1946, seated at his typewriter. He dropped dead of a massive heart attack while writing "Freddy Funk and the Flippant Fairies." It was a death worthy of any true pulp fiction writer. Frances finished the story, and Rap published it two years later. Rap laid Leroy to rest in "The Observatory" for July 1946:

> As we publish "The Man with Two Minds" by Leroy Yerxa in this issue, it is with a great amount of sadness that we announce the loss of another of our best friends. Leroy has gone to join that other writer he admired so much, David Wright O'Brien, in that land where every story is a best-seller. Perhaps the best tribute we could pay to Leroy Yerxa is to give him the undisputed crown for prolific appearance in *Amazing Stories*.... On one occasion he was the whole contents page of our sister magazine *Fantastic Adventures* and it proved one of our most popular and successful issues....

The aftermath of Leroy's death was difficult for Frances and the Palmers. Frances fell into a deep depression and began to lose weight. This worried the Palmers, who came up with a plan to save her, she said.

> I hadn't been able to eat since I lost my husband and was down to about 70 pounds I'd guess, and the whole family was so worried about me ... and how we were going to divide up four children. [Ray and Marjorie] had me come to their house, and I brought my three year old who was about the age of Linda Jane, their oldest child, and every night they would make hot chocolate. That's how I started to eat again; I started with a cup of hot chocolate at their house.
> [Ray] helped me and my four children an awful lot after my husband died. He and Marjorie

rescued me, as I had nothing. He got together $8000, which was a lot of money in those days. He did it because my husband had written stories and they were accepted but hadn't been paid for because Ziff-Davis paid upon publication.

All of these stories added up to about $8000. He told Marjorie to find a place near them in Evanston, Illinois, where I could move with my four kids, and I could still write filler material to pay for my expenses.... They told me ... that they'd found this little house, a red brick bungalow, and there was room for me and the two girls downstairs and two bedrooms upstairs was made into one big room for my two boys. They wanted $12,000 for it. It had a backyard and everything was wonderful, and I put down the $8000, and had a $4000 mortgage, which was handled by a currency exchange; we didn't use banks in those days. It was like a check cashing place.

I made payments of about $56 per month to pay off the mortgage. I wrote filler articles and was able to take care of the children and pay utilities. I was lonely for Leroy, but we were doing pretty good.[19]

Clash of the Titans

"One thing, you'll never take any buttons off Palmer's shirt, once he's sewed them on."— Ray Palmer

Rewind to the year 1943. The war was still raging. Ray was still cheerleading the war effort while appreciative letters rolled in from soldiers overseas, thanking him for his work on the home front.

His previous seven years at Ziff-Davis had been fruitful ones. He had saved *Amazing Stories* from the brink of ruin and turned it into a bestseller. Through judicious cultivation of contract writers, he emerged as one of the top pulp editors of his day, and he was determined to keep his circulation figures spinning like a set of Chinese circus plates, in the lofty six figures.

Never one to sit on his laurels, Rap was poised to catch the next big wave in science fiction, just as he had done as an editor at *Fantasy Magazine*. After months of wondering what his next breakthrough would be, Rap hooked a live one in October 1943. There was no way he could have known it was about to change the course of his career, create a controversy that would split fandom into warring camps, and bring down a curse upon his name that would endure for the rest of his life, even beyond his death.

The day began routinely. Howard Browne was on fan mail duty, vapidly tearing open envelopes as he sat at his desk high above the unrelenting clatter and fumes of the Loop. Browne figures prominently in this piece of legendary SF romance, and the story has been told a number of ways.

Rap and Browne had vastly different personalities and wrote two different types of fiction. Browne, a bearish, matter-of-fact repo man, was a hardboiled detective fan. Rap, always the impish, ethereal mystic, yearned for worlds unknown. There was an unspoken love-hate relationship between them, which in later years leaked out. Said Browne, "There were times I loved the little bastard; there were times I could've cheerfully strangled him."[20] Browne is forever remembered as the guy who discarded The Letter.

The letter came from a Pennsylvania defense plant worker named Richard Shaver, who was trying to break into the pulps. But there was more to it than that. Shaver was also on a mission. He had secret information, important information of a threat to Humanity far more devastating than Hitler or Tojo. In later years, Browne was often asked about this incident which he retold on several occasions. The following version came in 1984:

6. The Inner Circle

I was at my desk sorting casually through letters from our readers. One specimen caught my attention: a six-page spewing of such egregious nonsense as I've ever run across. The article, written by Richard Shaver, mentioned, among other things, that he had positive proof that a crazed race of sub-humans numbering in the thousands were living in underground caverns throughout the world.... These creatures called themselves "deros" and, unless eliminated, would eventually destroy humanity.... I read portions of the article aloud for the amusement of Palmer and a couple of writers who were in the office at the time, then pitched it into the wastebasket.[21]

Rap went to the wastebasket, retrieved the letter, and told Browne to run it in the next issue. Not only that, he chided Browne for his lack of editorial acumen. It rubbed Browne the wrong way, as many of Rap's comments did. Browne was forced to play second fiddle to Rap throughout his years at Ziff-Davis, but felt he deserved better. Still, Browne and Rap remained friends, at least on the surface. Bill Hamling felt the friendship was prone to conditions, which he explained in 2009: "[Howard is] superior to you, you understand. The fact is, Howard resented that Ray was his boss, see? *Howard* was the genius. Bullshit! He wasn't the genius."

A strange alphabet accompanied Shaver's letter. It had been salvaged, he said, from an ancient civilization. He called it Mantong, the "mother tongue" of the universe. Shaver's letter ran in the January 1944 issue. Reader response was overwhelming. It surprised everyone at the office, including Rap. All at once he knew: This was the next big wave in science fiction.

Shaver's 1943 letter, as it came from Howard Browne's wastebasket:

Sirs,

Am sending you this in hopes you will insert in an issue to keep it from dying with me. It would arouse a lot of discussion.

Am sending you the language so that some time you can have it looked at by some one in the college or a friend who is a student of antique time. This language seems to me to be definite proof of the Atlantean legend.

A — Animal (used "an" for short)
B — be — exist (often command as Ban meant "stay away to exist." Same as quarantine)
C — con — to see
D — de — detrimental or rather disintegrant energy (the second most important symbol in language)
E — energy — an "all" concept including idea of motion
F — fecund (used "fe" as in female) — fecund man
G — generate (used "gen")
H — human (some doubt on this one)
I — self — ego (same as our I)
J — same as generate
K — kinetic (force of motion)
L — Life
M — man
N — child or spore of seed (as ninny)
O — orifice (a source concept)
P — power
Q — quest (as question)
R — ar as horror (a symbol of a dangerous quantity of dis [disintegrating] force in the object)
S — an important symbol meaning sun (sis)
T — te (the most important symbol used; the real origin of cross symbol — it meant integration force of growth [all matter is growing] — the intake is gravity cause — the force is T ["tic" meant science of growth] — remains as credit word)

U — you
V — vital (used as vi) — the stuff Mesmer calls animal magnetism
W — will
X — conflict symbol — crossed force lines
Y — why
Z — zero symbol — a quantity of energy of T neutralized by an equal quantity of D

  A great number of our English words have come down intact as romantic — ro man tick — "science of man life patterning by control." Trocadero — troc see a dero — good one see a bad one — applied now to theatre. This is perhaps the only copy of this language in existence and it represents my work over a long period of years. It is an immensely important find, suggesting the god legends have a base in some wiser race than modern man; but to understand it takes a good head as it contains multi-thoughts like many puns on the same subject. It is too deep for ordinary man — who thinks it is a mistake. A little study reveals ancient words in English occurring many times. It should be saved and placed in wise hands. I can't will you? It really has an immense significance and will perhaps put me right in your thoughts again if you will really understand this. I need a little encouragement.

"S. Shaver, Barto, Pennas."

Part II

Richard Sharpe Shaver

7

Shavertown

"Here I Lie My Weary Feet"—Philip Shaver, 1826

If Richard Shaver had never known a home or boyhood, it might explain why things turned out the way they did. But this was not the case. His lineage stretched as far back as the founding fathers of the Union, and beyond. In fact, the long arm of Pennsylvania Shaver ancestry reaches back to 18th century Vienna, and the birth in 1762 of family patriarch Philip Shaeffer.

As an adventurous young man of 18, Shaeffer threw in his lot with other European immigrants bound for American shores, probably around 1780. How he came to this decision is lost in the mists of time, though it is said that an abundance of push and drive possessed his character. He was not unlike other Germanic Lutherans who sought fame, fortune, and redemption in the New World.

After arriving in his new homeland of New Jersey, Shaeffer jumped on the American bandwagon by changing his foreign-sounding surname. Shaeffer became Shaver. From that moment on, the Shaver surname continued unchanged. Philip became a naturalized citizen at the point of his 1786 marriage to Mary Wickhauser, a New Jersey native of German descent. Before long the two started a new branch of Shaver lineage: a son, John Philip, was born in 1789, Peter in 1790, William G. in 1794, and Elizabeth in 1798.

And yet New Jersey could not quench Philip Shaver's wanderlust. He heard stories of a place called Luzerne County in Pennsylvania, a land of great beauty and natural resources, ripe for enterprising men like himself. Hostile Indians had recently been subdued at the Battle of Wyoming, and that meant Luzerne was wide open for settlement. In 1800, with hope of a better life for his growing family, Philip packed up Mary and the four children and began a second Shaver migration, settling in Dallas Township, Luzerne County, Pennsylvania.

Luzerne County had been founded four years prior to the Shavers' arrival, its outline formed by several creeks and the Susquehanna River. The county name was taken from a popular minister of the French court during the Revolution: the Chevalier de la Luzerne. A new courthouse was under construction in the township of Wilkes-Barre about 12 miles south of Dallas Township. The courthouse would mete out justice to county criminals, ne'er-do-wells, and witches. Witches were a big problem in 18th century Pennsylvania. Unlike the New England states, Pennsylvanians chose to fine their witches rather than kill them. This was only somewhat effective. Local farmers were known to hire African and German witch doctors who filled shotguns with rock salt and fired them into the offending witches. Salt was said to neutralize any witch's spell.

Three more Shaver children were added to the family in Dallas Township: James,

George, and Asa. Philip Shaver's push and drive then set him about doing great things. He became a successful lumberman, said to have built the first sawmill in the township. Shaver men would claim the lumber trade for generations to come.

Philip's success knew no bounds in Luzerne County, and he acquired large tracts of land. He moved from Dallas Township to one of his nearby properties and tried his hand at farming. That, too paid off. By this time he was so well respected that a tiny hamlet sprang up near his farm. The villagers called it Shavertown.

All would have continued in this rosy, upbeat fashion had it not been for Philip's taste for hard cider. Whether the interest was commercial or personal, it led to his undoing nonetheless. That came at harvest time in September 1826, when, at age 64, Philip was crushing apples at his cider mill. Then came the unfortunate accident: The apple crusher crushed his arm. Death followed from complications, likely an infection. He died November 7, 1826.

Prior to his death, Philip Shaver donated the acreage on which the Shavertown Cemetery now stands. A burial plot of illustrious Shavers dominates the cemetery, including Philip's modest grave. His last words, carved on his tombstone, suggest that his push and drive had waned considerably. "Here I Lie My Weary Feet," it read.

Shavertown remains an unincorporated township to this day. Its most significant historical event occurred in October 2005, when Vice-President Dick Cheney stepped out of his steel-plated limousine to speak at a Shavertown fundraiser for Republican Rick Santorum. Santorum lost the election, and Shavertown drifted back into slumber.[1]

Ziba Rice Shaver

> *"The unseen world beneath our feet, malignant and horrible, is complete in its mastery of Earth."— Richard Shaver*

It would take four generations and more than 100 years before a Shaver of Philip's caliber would measure up to the Shavertown legacy. The trail of DNA that went from Vienna to Pennsylvania led next to Philip's son William G. Shaver, who enhanced the Shaver name considerably.

William's marriage to Rachel Ann Robbins in 1816 produced 14 children: Mary Ann, Charles, Lusinda, Elsie, Philip, Philinda, Asa, Betsy Ann, Andrew Jackson, Ira, Jerusha, Olive Ann, Oliver, and William Perry. Our specific interest falls on the 14th and final progeny of William and Rachel: William Perry Shaver, a Union Civil War soldier in the Pennsylvania Infantry, Company A, 28th Regiment. After the war, he suffered infirmities as a result of his experiences and was unable to support himself by his manual labors. He lived with his son or other friends and family, getting by as best he could for the rest of his life. In 1868, three years after his return from the war, he married Rhoda Margaret Anderson.

By 1870, William and Rhoda were living with William's uncle John Philip Shaver, 82, a retired farmer, in Kingston Township. It was not unusual for several Shavers to live under one roof—a tradition going back generations, and continuing well into the 20th century. William was working as a sawyer at Ryman's lumber mill in Wilkes-Barre, as an operator of the huge spinning blade. Also living in the Shaver household was William and Rhoda's one-year-old son William Henry and ten-year-old Clara Shaver, a niece.

Next door lived Ziba Bennet Rice and his wife Elizabeth. Young Ziba was William's best friend and worked in the same lumber mill. William and Rhoda's second son, born in 1875, was named after William's best friend. Thus Ziba Rice Shaver came to be.

Lumberman Ziba B. Rice was a Freemason and attended meetings at George M. Dallas Lodge No. 531. He wore the Masonic apron all the way to his initiation as Grand Master. This was the same lodge where Asa, Ira, Elmer, Lewis, and Joseph Shaver also became Grand Masters.[2]

After the birth of Ziba Rice Shaver, tragedy struck, and life changed drastically within the Shaver household.

Danville Hospital for the Insane

> *"Just soaking your head in a bowl of cold water helps."*—Richard Shaver (talking about brain fever)

Exactly where the illness that swallowed up Rhoda Shaver came from is unknown, but it happened some time after the birth of her second son. In the parlance of the day, Rhoda went mad. Her husband committed her to Danville Hospital for the Insane, 70 miles from Dallas Township, where she spent the rest of her life as a mental patient. Danville asylum was a sprawling 250-acre Victorian estate on the banks of the Susquehanna River. It was on the cutting edge of 19th century Pennsylvania mental health institutions.

Times being what they were, mental health issues were viewed differently than they are now, especially when it came to women. Women were declared insane for reasons considered laughable today, not the least of which was "insanity due to religious belief." That is not to say that every woman committed during the 19th century was of sound mind. The fact that Rhoda Shaver's insanity appeared after Ziba's birth may have resulted from what is now called post-partum depression. It has been known to trigger severe depression, or worse, in some women.

Mania, melancholia, monomania, paresis, dementia, dipsomania, and epilepsy were standard categories of insanity in 1880. But in the case of women, physical issues were also given, such as childbirth, heredity, over-exertion, epileptic fits, domestic troubles, and the frequently used "unknown reasons."[3]

Whatever the diagnosis, Rhoda remained in Danville until her death. This unfortunate turn changed everything. William placed baby Ziba Rice in the care of the widow Catherine Starner, a local German-American. She had the misfortune of marrying a Bavarian man who died before he could raise his five daughters. The widow Starner, always in need of extra income, took in little Ziba as a boarder at the tender age of three.

Meanwhile, Ziba's father moved in with his eldest sister Mary Shaver Frantz, 63. There were other Shavers living nearby. Ira, Phoebe, and Cora Shaver lived in the same neighborhood. Ziba's older brother William Henry vanished from the public record, but resurfaced years later as a married lumberman, in the Shaver tradition.

William Perry Shaver eventually moved to Wilkes-Barre, after the death of his sister Mary. He was living with brother-in-law Bentley Frantz in 1910, and died in 1915.

Ziba and Grace

"Campbell stories don't contain enough sex...."— Richard Shaver

Ziba Rice Shaver met Grace Taylor in her hometown of Fairmount, Pennsylvania. They were married there in 1898. Grace was the only child of Thomas Taylor, a paperhanger at that time, and his wife Kate. Thomas educated his daughter well, and she became a schoolteacher in the small nearby town of Harvey Lake. Grace was a writer, too, and spent much of her time writing poetry and prose.

In 1899, newly married Ziba Shaver found work at the American Car and Foundry Company in Berwick, Pennsylvania, temporarily leaving Grace and their newborn son Donald in the care of the elder Taylors. The plan was to find a home in Berwick when finances allowed. Within a year, Ziba had saved enough from his company paychecks to move his family to Berwick. This was 1901. Berwick became the birthplace of the rest of the Ziba Shaver clan: Catherine Claire in 1902; Taylor Victor in 1904; Richard in 1907; and Isabelle in 1915.

As small as it was, Berwick was a town of big industry. The population hovered around 5000 people, and a third of them worked for the American Car and Foundry Company. The "rolling mill," as locals called it, produced rolling stock for the railroads — railcars of all types. The factory sat on the banks of the Susquehanna River and dominated the town.

Berwick turned out to be a fine place to raise a family. Ziba gained favor at the company and became a supervisor. The pay was mediocre and the work hard and fast. It made a man old before his time. Noise and fumes were mind-numbing. A union strike hit the factory in 1908, shutting it down long enough to make things tough for local families. The company had riled union leaders when administrators began firing employees who dared to become

American Car and Foundry Company, Berwick, Pennsylvania. This was where Ziba Shaver had his most stable job, and his son's first encounter with factory life. As family history has it, Ziba was fired during a union strike.

Formal portrait taken circa 1906. Ziba, Catherine, Donald, Taylor, Grace Shaver. Richard and Isabelle had yet to be born (Dottie Shaver collection).

union officers. Blacksmith's union vice-president W.J. Dougherty said they were forced into the strike: "This is going to be a hard fight and as most of the men had been dealing at the Berwick Company Store, as soon as the strike was on that store would not give any more credit, so it was up to the local to take care of its members...."[4]

The Shaver family weathered the strike, but the lack of Ziba's paycheck during his involuntary layoff forced them open a boarding house. This would explain why the 1910 census found the Shavers living with five roomers: a married couple and three workingmen. A 15-year-old servant girl named Susan Beaver also lived in the house. All but one of the men worked at the rolling mill.

Young Dick Shaver sometimes went to the factory to deliver his father's lunch bucket. He later described the scene in his semi-autobiographical story "The Dream Makers." "The tumult of the snorting metal monsters, the awful smells. Barney Freedman's saloon across from the gate gave off a smell of beer for several blocks. I waited there to give Dad his lunch bucket."[5]

Shaver oral history has it that Ziba lost his job at the American Car and Foundry Company as retribution during another strike, more than likely the strike of 1919. Ziba, it was said, spoke up for the working men of the union. As a company supervisor he was expected to toe the company line, and was fired.

Ziba was obligated to fill out a draft card in 1917, at the age of 42. But it was his oldest son Donald who joined the Army and fought in the First World War. "Ma" Shaver, always the schoolteacher, tutored the children in literature and poetry. Occasionally she sold poetry to popular magazines. Her encouragement rubbed off on Taylor who, on graduating high school in 1921, tried his hand at writing adventure yarns for boys. He sold stories to *Boys Life*, *The Youth's Companion*, and *The American Boy*.

Donald and Taylor, with responsible and worldly acumen, overshadowed younger brother Dick, known more for his mischievous pranks and lack of direction. Dick idolized Taylor and was proud of his brother's ambition. He often recalled how "Tate" joined "the flying cadets. He was in the same bunch of youths as cadet Lindbergh, and went to ground school with Lindbergh,"[6] he said.

Berwick instilled young Dick Shaver with fond memories he retold throughout his life. There were his visits to the Berwick Company Store, and his father's occasional "bouts of reform, when all the liquor in the house was poured down the sink and the kids forbidden to play cards."[7]

He remembered Berwick as an idealized world of grace and charm, lamenting its passing as time went on. Berwick became a mental retreat for his weary mind as his life became difficult. Though he never wrote an autobiography, he did write a kind of memoir in his correspondence and unpublished essays that have survived. What follows are some of those memories in Shaver's own words.

8

The Early Years

"If the man doesn't believe as we do, we say he is a crank, and that settles it. I mean, it does nowadays, because now we can't burn him."—Mark Twain

Dick Shaver longed for someone to help him write his autobiography. Though there were occasional offers, they never panned out, and only six months after this author suggested doing so, Shaver was dead. That left the historical record blank, other than the tidbits of his life that could be mined from *Amazing Stories*. But Shaver was a prolific correspondent, especially during the last five years of his life. Buried within his monologues of pre-Deluge history were tiny vignettes of his early life. Enough of Shaver's letters survived to piece together an image of the real Richard Shaver.

What follows are events from his life that he recalled as his mind wandered back to Berwick, Pennsylvania. As he sat in his wooden shack behind his home in Summit, Arkansas, he typed letters to correspondents like W. G. Bliss and reached far back in time. Thus, what follows is the closest thing to an autobiography Shaver ever wrote, pieced together from those many letters.

The Kissing Ice Man
by Richard S. Shaver

"Dad had to have some con man in him."— Richard Shaver

Time is a thing that stretches out forever when you are small and young and wondering very much about the phantasmagoria of life around you. As you get older this immense time span that is just one afternoon shrinks and shrinks and shrinks into such a little while, that it's hardly worth mentioning. When I was pre-school age, a day was an enormous long time indeed. Now, it's just between meals.

At the age of four, sitting on the doorstep, there was peace. When I was eight, all Europe was killing each other for the Kaiser, that goofy old guy with the handlebar mustache. When I was ten, my brother got on the train to go away to the war. I weighed sixty pounds on the train station scales.

In Berwick, we kids rolled hoops for as long as we could still see them in the twilight. Then we played hide and seek till the bats got too numerous around the streetlights, chasing bugs. That was about the time we slowly meandered homeward in the dark to get our scolding for missing supper.

Looking back as far as I can, my first memories were of the old shoemaker next door.

I remember going in his door, and his grunted greeting as he hammered away at his bench. It was the sort of bench I have seen in late years made into antique tables. You sat at one end, and there were trays for nails, knives and what not. He hammered and I gazed as he carved the leather off the shoes. Knives always interested me, and nobody had knives like he did.

The old shoemaker was about as old then as I am now, I suppose. He had the same sort of gray mustache and the same sort of scorn for the rest of the world. Maybe mine was picked up from him.

On the other side of our house was Mitt's Store. Their name wasn't really Mitt. My mother used to tell me it was Lockwood, and Lockwood wasn't it either. It was an Italian name that had got that way by being misspelled. I never did get the straight of all that. Why Belva Lockwood was called Mr. Mitt was a puzzle that never really bothered me until right now. I bought my false faces at that store, and my firecrackers and my candy and even my valentines on Valentine's Day. In those days they had better valentines, and more of them than they do now by far.

When I went to Sunday school my dad would give me a nickel and say, "Don't stop for a beer on the way," which was his idea of a joke. I would drop the nickel in the plate and take out four pennies. My Sunday school teacher got apoplexy from choking on her tonsils, but couldn't figure out what to say about it, so that established the precedent. From there I progressed to dimes, removing nine cents from the plate, and later it occurred to me it would be just as effective to put my hand in and make a "clink" like I dropped it and keep the dime for myself.

So coming back from Sunday school I stopped at the candy store and bought one yard of licorice for one penny; ten imitation candy corns that looked like big peanuts for one penny; whatever looked good.

When we went to see Granpa and Granma we went in a surrey with a fringe, just like in the movies; five kids and Pa and Ma and a horse all hooked up with harness and fringe, and it was damn near a day's ride, four to six hours, depending on who we stopped to gab with. I stayed with Granpa and Granma some summers, when I was no bigger than a hop toad.

I learned about hard cider from my grandpa, who had a beard down to his knees, believe it or not. He had to tuck it into his shirt and wrap it round his waist. There was a picture of him in his Civil War uniform that shows it round his waist, under his uniform like a spare tire. He didn't tell me about the hard cider, but Granma did in the process of scolding him for taking his friends back to the hard cider keg and getting them all lit.

One of the big tragedies of my life was the chestnut tree blight that killed all the chestnuts. Few people know about the size and beauty of the American chestnut. It was a very big and beautiful tree with shaggy bark and gold yellow leaves in the fall, nearly a foot long. Shaped like a cypress, without the knees. Our landlord inherited a large grove of these fine trees. He hanged himself on one. I was eight or nine. They tried to keep it from me. He was my friend.

In the wooded hollow where I went for peace as a boy, the old world of flowered grass and brooks and streams and endless banks of violets met the new world of banks of slag from the mill that was filling in the place. Those black banks of death marched into my personal hollow of wonder, and kept marching until one day the hollow was gone, and the ground was level with ugly fill.

Somehow I knew there would never be another one like it. Gone were the apple trees

The Shaver family in 1922, minus Donald: (back row) Taylor Victor, Catherine Claire, Richard, Ziba; (front row) Grace, Isabelle (Dottie Shaver collection).

and violets, and the brooks with a dam and a "lake," and its boat and raft, and the long afternoons. And the hollow log where I hid my shoes on the first warm day in spring, and went on to school, barefoot. All black mill dust and cinders. The distant bank of forest now became another field with a fence.

How do you tell about chasing the laughing girls on the way home from school? The time I caught the first one and kissed her. I can't quite accept that that world, a world of lawns and gardens and white houses with smiling oldsters and hawthorn trees and lilacs and beeches and long slow walks muffled in many colored falling leaves, is dead.

And the porches! Once, not too long ago, a porch was an island of beauty and coolness in a street of parched heat. I used to peddle bills, distribute literature, in the modern parlance, but back then we called it peddling bills. Boys would load up with armloads of printed matter and go down each street, dropping one printed sheet on each porch.

Those porches were often the ultimate in luxury, that is, the luxury of the time. That meant gliders, long reclining swings one could lie down on and swing back and forth, causing cooling movements of air. Gliders were expensive, so most people settled for a simple seat on chains. But even so, with porches and swings and awnings and lemonade tables with ice in big pitchers, there was for a time, an island of cool in the hot streets of summer. They usually had plants or ferns, luxuriating in the shade and providing a minimal privacy.

Porches could be particularly wonderful places to a boy who had grown big enough to appreciate the female form. When loaded with teenage girls and chatter and lemonade and elephant-eared plants and soft carpet, and even music from a gramophone, a porch could seem to a boy with an armload of bills, like paradise stretching out in parcels, on and on and up and down each street.

I went around school thinking I was particularly stupid in everything that counted, like social stuff and sports and getting "A's." Then my sister went to Normal School and went through the files and discovered that I, and one girl, had the highest IQs in the whole school. This I could not believe. There had to be some mistake.

Not that it ever did me much good to have an IQ. It only served to show me that I was making all the mistakes, not how to avoid making them. It is seeing your mistake that gives the bright ones that low morale.

A sense of aloneness descended upon me with a crash in the seventh grade, when my teacher, a man named Ryder, Enoch Ryder, lifted me out of my seat and dragged me into the library and beat me with a cane. For what? I was only designing a new kind of bathing suit, with openings at the sides, the kind they wear now, which was so shocking to Enoch he had to beat the tar out of me.

The gulf between myself and Enoch never decreased. It widened and widened between myself and most other people of that time. There was not much chance of communication, and the whole incident of the beating was repeated when he sneaked up behind me as I was making a flip movie with stick people riding horses and rescuing maidens.

When I went to scout camp, I didn't have a uniform. So when a bunch of us set out to walk to town with the scoutmaster, I hung back. I was embarrassed, yet I had started out with them, not yet thinking about my lack of a uniform. The scoutmaster understood what ailed me, asked me if I wanted to return to camp, and I said I did. When I got back to camp the cook asked me "What's up?" I didn't say anything, just grinned. He was a special friend to me for some reason.

Well, cookie assumed the scoutmaster had sent me back because I didn't have a uniform. Now, I knew he was thinking this, yet I could not get the words out to explain the truth — that the scoutmaster was only trying to be kind to me in my embarrassment. So when the bunch returned, the cookie bawled out the scoutmaster, quit his job, and walked back over the mountain, home. So we lost our cook, split up the whole camp in puzzled sides over something that wasn't there at all.

This particular incident followed me all my life in Berwick. The family of the scoutmaster was the most numerous in town, and whenever he explained it, it looked as if I had lied to the cook about why I came back. The scoutmaster's brother was coach of the football team, so as a liar and troublemaker I didn't make the team. It bollixed up my high school days until I left town.

I robbed a graveyard of a skull once when I was a teenager, and let me tell you, no one ever felt the wet earth or clutched a moldy old skull out of a grave and ran like a rabbit through the back streets at midnight like I did to get that thing out of sight before the town night police caught up with me. The aftermath was that Ma found the thing in my bottom dresser drawer and made me bury it in the garden, three feet deep just to keep its relatives off my back in case they heard. They wouldn't have heard about it from me. Half the town was that skull's relatives.

Cats have been a big part of my life back into toddler memories. There is hardly a childhood memory not bound up with some cat or other. When I was three or four, we had a big black tomcat that more or less ruled our house and the neighborhood. He would stand up on his hind feet, turn the doorknob with his paws and walk into the house, and his whole performance with his utter nonchalant capability, was to me nothing short of marvelous.

One time when I was working in a steel mill there was a big black tom, which used to come to me for a nightly half sandwich. I got to know him fairly well and decided such a nice black tom ought to have a better home than his prowl areas under the steel in the mill. So I kidnapped him.

I popped a burlap bag over him, put him into my car, and drove 12 miles home to the little four-acre place where I lived. It was like kidnapping a leopard. He took that burlap sack apart and was all over the car. When I pulled into my drive and stopped, there was no way to hold him. Away he went into the night.

Two days later as I sat eating my "lunch" in the middle of the night, I saw him, back on his prowl of the area he called his own in the steel mill, but he wasn't having any half sandwich from me. I had violated his confidence. He never spoke to me again, though I saw him frequently.

I have had all sorts of jobs and worked in all sorts of situations, and about all I ever learned is that most people are semi-conscious and only looking for a place to lay down and be let alone, like zombies. When I was in my teens I thought they were doing me a favor to let me dig their ditches and crack up their rocks in a quarry, and it wasn't till late years I realized they don't know what they are doing, and working for them is to waste your time literally and you get no where is a fact.

I remember when the Depression was beginning. My brother gave my dad $75 to pay on the house ... a contract-bought house, and instead of walking across the street to the seller to hand it to him, Dad deposited the cash in his bank account so he could give the man a check and so have a receipt without asking for one. Before he could get the check to the man across the street, the bank closed and never did reopen. Eventually he got about $7.50 out of the $75. We nearly lost the house.

That's the sort of memories I have by the dozen, like the time we had a successful restaurant — and it was — a really wonderful business. So what happened? The owner of the building wouldn't let Dad catch him to get the lease signed for next year because he had a buyer, and the buyer bought the building and made a furniture store out of our wonderful restaurant, and we were on the town again.

I could go on like that all night about Dad and his pursuit of the great wherewithal. I can remember his first Ford car, $400 second hand, and it was a beautiful touring car, and he went out in it, selling ... hog tone, cow tone, and hair tonic to the farmers. Anybody that could make a living selling patent medicine to farm animals has to be good, and he did.

I can remember he piled up a stake, a few thousand ahead and went to another town and bought another restaurant that *looked* good. It looked good all right, because it was court week and he never got around to finding out why it was so busy. So what happened, there was no business the rest of the time, only during court week every three months or so. So we were broke again.

I used to crack oysters for my dad's restaurant. They were as big as a big fist; bigger than fried eggs. We used to get them in hundred-pound bags. I was so little I had to have dad set the bags up straight for me to get the oysters out easy ... *now* ... today, try and buy an oyster that size ... they ain't none nowhere.

You never ate anything if you never ate Shaver's fried oysters ... three were a meal. A half-dozen served two. We padded them up in cracker meal and raw eggs ... like great big fat cigars. They were about seven inches long and about three inches through, and fried in good hot lard. Man, what a meal.

My dad walked six miles to school, he used to tell me, whenever I asked for trolley fare. We had a real Toonerville trolley just like in the comic strip. Ma told me Dad walked 20 miles to see her every weekend ... when he was going to college.

Some new cataclysm hit our family as regular as a monsoon every year, or every month, in hard times. Ma always figured a dollar a day to set the table for all of us. Can you imagine setting a table for seven people today on one dollar? And she set it, too, like the Dutch, with everything on it.

We were always broke till payday when I was real small. I was about seven when Dad went out on strike with his pressmen. He was the man who pressed the parts for the *first* steel railroad coach ever made, he used to tell me. They used to be made of wood, you know.

Anyway, he got fired "for siding with the men." Pressmen were supposed to side with management in all labor disputes as they were the high-paid upper class workers, and the labor wasn't supposed to do anything but what they were told in those days. That's when he bought the restaurant. Looking back, I can see it was inevitable. But back then, it was all come by chance to me.

My memories about money go back to the story of the "last nickel in the house." You bought at the company store or you didn't work there any more and if you bought at the company store you never caught up. So I can remember Dad and me walking to the store and Dad buying a lot of groceries at a little store *after* he was fired from the steel mill. Just before we left the house, Ma asked him, "How can you go for groceries when that is the last nickel in the house?"

So all the time he was ordering groceries I keep tugging his coat (I was about knee-

The Shaver children, minus Donald: Taylor Victor, Catherine Claire, Richard, and Isabelle (front). This was taken at about the time Taylor graduated from Bloomsburg High School in 1922 (Dottie Shaver collection).

high) and loud whispering "Dad, that's the last nickel in the house!" at him, and him trying to shush me. We all laughed about it afterward with Ma. I have always wondered how in heck he paid that grocery store.

Then he opened a butcher shop. He didn't know a cow from a mule when it was butchered, I don't believe, and we peddled ice cream from a horse and wagon after dark till midnight, him and me making ice cream cones and putting them on the window of the wagon. So it was fun. He always wiggled out of every tight spot Fate had for him. I don't worry too much, as some of that wiggle is in me, too.

The most fun I ever had was peddling ice in high school. I started peddling ice in the summer, and I was a nice enough looking young fellow so I got in the habit of kissing all the girls on the route who stood still for it, which was more fun than any kid had a right to. The kissing ice man went along all right till the one girl I really had a yen for as the future missus slammed the door in my face and took her ice card down. She had heard about me from the other girls. So it don't pay to have any fun, you pay the worst kind of price for it.

The most embarrassing moment in my life was the time the high school crowd held a swim meet at a big, paid-for swimming pool where it cost a quarter to get in, and I didn't have a quarter. I managed to get in by pointing over my shoulder at the guy behind me in line. I put on my trunks and joined the crowd. The ticket taker got another guy to relieve him at the gate and come after me. He pointed me out and I was forcibly removed from the party for not having a quarter. It was embarrassing because in those days it was embarrassing to be broke. Today I suppose it could be funny.

Nostalgia gets me sometimes.

"The Dream Makers"

"Being broke isn't new with me ... it's the rule of the game. If you've got some money you got troubles and somebody after it."— Richard Shaver

Dick Shaver came closest to writing an autobiography in "The Dream Makers," a fictional story he wrote in 1948 for *The Elder World*. It appeared years later in the Ziff-Davis pulp *Fantastic* for July 1958. Story elements came from his life in Berwick, Bloomsburg, Philadelphia, and Detroit. But more than a chronology of his career, "The Dream Makers" was a history of the intrusive voices that plagued his life. These were the voices from an underworld of ancient machines, manned by creatures both good and evil.

Shaver told of youthful indiscretions and an education fraught with humiliation. The teacher he described in "The Dream Makers" was based on Enoch Ryder, his nemesis schoolmaster. Shaver admitted he was a poor student, but depicted his teachers as authoritarian bullies, if not evil taskmasters, in his story: "Whack! Up went the ruler again.... Whack whack, it went on and on.... The ruler gleamed like tears in my eyes. Whack whack whack.... My face felt like mud was dried on it...."[1]

His academic skills were rewarded with dismal report cards, while older brother Tate was a source of unbounded admiration. "[I looked] in awe at my brother's report card, when he had been late every day for one month."[2]

The American Car & Foundry Company — the steel plant, Shaver called it — was a sprawling labyrinth of smoke, fire, blood, poor pay, and strikes. It remained a glowing ember in the ash of Dick Shaver's memory:

The sun, hot rails burning my bare feet, the stacks belching flame and smoke, and the men with leather pieces on their legs and hob-nailed shoes. The long steel bars and pinchers and paddles, the continuous thunder as of subterranean forces, men with fire playing around their sweat-gleaming upper bodies and their red underwear. The golden showers of sparks from the molten metal at the ends of the tongs.[3]

Young Shaver lusted after everything the Berwick Company Store had to offer. It was a four-story brick building in the heart of town, and he took every opportunity to go there shopping with his father. He recalled it in a series of memory bursts:

The book counter at the company store. Me stealing a book from the tables and crawling under the long tables to read it where no one would see and grab it away. Reaching up and putting it back, grabbing another one.

And the meat counter, a mile long it looked, the thick green glass and the pleasant chill in the hot summer, the red meat making you hungry, and the strange faces of the many clerks. And the fascinating number of dogs that ducked through the swinging doors and hunted carefully the whole length of the sawdust floor, sniffing — all dogs bigger than me, it seemed. Jangling collars and rolling muscles and olfactory organs sniffing up the luscious scent, they swung past me oblivious of all but that ecstatic mixture of odors.[4]

After his termination from the steel plant, Ziba launched his new plan. He had saved every extra nickel he made from the boarding house and a part-time job as a furniture salesman to go into business for himself. Finally giving up on Berwick completely, he moved the family to Bloomsburg, Pennsylvania, where he purchased the Bee Hive Café. Dick Shaver described it from memory in 1948: "It was an immense hotel building. On the third floor was an abandoned ballroom. One end opened on the flat roof. Below was Main Street. I found an air gun in the ballroom. I sat on the roof and shot sparrows. I didn't know anybody in town...."[5]

Two doors down was the Victoria Theater, a silent movie house. The Bee Hive Café, "What you want. When you want it. Music while you dine," got its name from the previous owner, Ralph H. Smoyer. Taylor enrolled at Bloomsburg High School. Dick enrolled in school too, continuing his role as a latter-day Huck Finn. He often helped his father at the café, and enjoyed the work.

Life in Bloomsburg was no different than in Berwick. It was young Dick Shaver against the world. He spent idle hours figuring out how to beat the system, always the rebel. His careless lifestyle made him prone to accidents. He broke his leg in high school, and burned his foot so badly while in the third grade it kept him home for several weeks. He was well-known to other business owners near the family café.

"Next door was the movie house," Shaver recalled. "There was an opening between the two big buildings. I got a long ladder, let it down in the opening. I went up the ladder, opened the long ventilator, and had free movie shows for a month. Then I let the ventilator open too far and they caught me.... [S]tolen pictures are better than paid-for pictures."[6]

Dick watched the ever-changing tableau in Ziba's restaurant — students, troopers, farmers, traveling salesmen, moviegoers, and movie projectionists came and went. Ziba took to the hectic life of the kitchen and became its chef. Dick's job was to take care of whatever his dad said needed taking care of:

I washed dishes, cracked oysters, and kept growing up. Upstairs I had plenty of books, when I wasn't working. I killed the chickens, burned the rubbish.... [M]y brother played football in high school. So did I after awhile. Grandma looked dignified and took Belle to the movies. Belle was four years younger than me. She ate everything, chased the cats into the dining room, let the big turtles out among the startled customers, got a tapeworm from eating raw hamburg.[7]

Apparently the restaurant lasted only a short while, possibly just as Shaver described it, due to a lack of business after "court week" came and went. Grace later opened a tearoom she called The Blue Bowl. This was during Dick's senior year of high school. When she heard that locals nicknamed it The Blue Bowel, she changed the name.

The Bloomsburg city directory said they were living at 526 East Third Street. In spite of his occasional antisocial behavior, Dick seemed to have a good time in high school. In his 1925 Bloomsburg High School yearbook, classmates described him as a fun-loving guy. In writing about him, the yearbook staff highlighted his personal attributes rather than his academic achievements, joking about truancy and tardiness to class. He was credited with a part in the Junior-Senior Vaudeville production "Hearts at Court." He tried out for football, and was listed as a member of the team for each of his three years at Bloomsburg High. They called him "Softy." The rest was laid out for all to see in the yearbook:

Dick is a jolly good fellow, full of fun and always interested in having a good time. He is absent from class quite frequently, but not because of illness — but — guess? Dick is also a little late to classes, occasionally, because of his friendliness to the opposite sex. Shaver is also interested in athletics. He has "starred" in our football team, and is progressing along the line of tennis. Last of all we say he is a good "sport," and his smile is envied by everybody. We all like "Dick" (he is so loving and meek?) and we all like him because he is the Blue Bowl Sheik.[8]

Quotation marks around certain words were code that hinted all was not as it seemed. One of Shaver's classmates — in married life a Mrs. E. Keller — was mystified by the yearbook staff's glowing account of Dick Shaver:

The bio information alongside the photo was mostly the figment of someone's imagination, in my opinion. Dick was *not* athletic. I think he might have suited up for football (he was built for it) but spent most of his time on the bench. At least this is my recollection, and I attended the games — I dated the quarterback! Harry Logan remembered the family as having a little store, but thinks they left Bloomsburg shortly after 1925.[9]

Dick's brother Taylor worked as an electrician after high school graduation. He thought for a time it would be his career, so in 1923 he enrolled at Valparaiso University, majoring in electrical engineering. He completed one semester before joining the Army Air Force. Uncle Sam shipped him to Texas for Flying Cadet training at Brooks and Kelly Fields.

As Dick pointed out, Taylor was in the same class as Charles Lindbergh, and it was a grueling course. Cadets were expected to attend ground school and study hard. Failure on any test meant you were "washed out." Of the 104 original signups, including Taylor, only 18 made the grade. Lindbergh claimed the top position in his March 1925 graduating class, but it appears that Taylor washed out. He went to Philadelphia and took a job as an electrician some time after 1925.

On graduating from Bloomsburg High, Dick soon followed his brother to Philadelphia. In his fictional account based on this period of his life, Shaver began his story in 1926, one year after his high school graduation.

Philadelphia

"Merritt has a perfect technique, and I study it."— Richard Shaver

Dick Shaver packed a few personal items and walked to the highway that led out of Bloomsburg. He stuck out his thumb and was gone. He and his thumb made their way to Philadelphia, which was bigger than any city Dick had ever seen. He moved into Taylor's two-room apartment that faced a newspaper building and a bakery across the street. Each day, the newspaper produced stacks of morning papers and the bakery fried stacks of donuts; of the two, the bakery smelled better. Tate worked as an electrician at the William Penn Hotel, and Dick pounded the pavement until he landed a job.

The brothers were close, more so than most, and Dick's admiration for Taylor was a glory to behold. Long after his brother's death, Dick sang Tate's praises. Not only did he respect Taylor for his accomplishments, but he also felt he could count on him in a pinch, and Tate was always there to help. That he was willing to share his small living quarters was proof of that.

Dick also counted on other family members, most notably his parents and, later in life, his sister Catherine Claire, a teacher like their mother. Catherine eventually married into the New England Haughton family. In the early years, the Shavers were a close-knit family, and like generations of Shavers before them, they cohabited at various times in communal living situations.

Tate was persistent as well as ambitious, and Dick tried to follow suit. He landed a job at Swift and Company, not something he enjoyed, he said, but it supported him. "I finally secured a somewhat better paying job with a packing company selling and cutting meat. The bodies of calves and lambs and sheep hung in long rows before me, chilled flesh, gray and pink and white ... black steel hooks through their Achilles tendons, all those little lives — I thought, hanging for me to hack apart."[10]

He hacked and sawed his way through thousands of those carcasses as one of the "bloody-coated crew." He hung out with his fellow butchers at a nearby diner, smoking cigarettes and listening to their idle conversation. But after-work camaraderie offered no respite from the solitude that haunted him. "My self withdrew slowly from me, and I became just another plodding member of that endless stream of beings who are going nowhere in a hurry but care not greatly if they reach there, for they know it is all nothing and futile."[11]

Big city life, with its liberated women, burlesque theaters and illegal booze, brought new challenges. Dick could not stay out of trouble in Philadelphia, either. He claimed in "The Dream Makers" that while on a date with a waitress, he got drunk and knocked a man unconscious during a barroom brawl. Later, when he asked the waitress for a second date she said, "I don't know if there'll be a next time." This is how it went for Shaver in Philadelphia.

Taylor's life appeared as futile as his younger brother's. At one point he left his electrician job to become a Pennsylvania state trooper. Dick continued cutting meat for Swift and Company. Together they discussed their dilemma, trying to think of a way out. "Our life was one of many hungers and few repletions...." Dick wrote. "We were lonely and cursed with these vaulting ambitions which [would] not take form.... We were intelligent enough to see they were impossible of fulfillment."[12] Tate's vaulting desire was to become an author, an ambition Dick shared, though Taylor was actually making sales.

Grace and Ziba Move In

"My own mother did not know there was any ray, when I talked to hundreds, seemingly, a day."— Richard Shaver

Their loneliness and concern prompted them to send for their parents. A recent letter from Grace said there had been an accident involving their father, who was then working for the railroad. It was a close call, Grace said, and Ziba confessed that he was getting too old for strenuous work. Tate and Dick made their decision after reading the letter:

> My brother looked at me. "I've been checking ads for apartments. There are plenty of vacancies right now. We've got to send for the folks sometime; it might as well be now. Let's go and rent a place and write Ma tonight. Dad's job on the railroad's about over.... We'll write to both of 'em tonight. You write Ma and I'll write the skipper."[13]

They rented a five-room flat fronted by catalpas trees heavy with clusters of trumpet-shaped flowers at the corner of 52nd and Walnut streets. From the fire escape, they had views of their neighbors' tiny gardens in an area of fenced plots overshadowed at times by other apartment buildings.

It was an easy move. Taylor's two rooms did not allow for the accumulation of many personal effects. A taxicab transported their possessions in one trip. "We carried all our collected clothes, bags, books, and many piled magazines down onto the three white worn steps and hailed a taxi.... We started tossing bags and stacks of books into the back."[14]

Ma Shaver arrived in good order. She put a $20 down payment on $100 worth of furniture. That, and what Ziba shipped from their former home, furnished the new flat. Soon Ziba would follow. The Shavers were reunited, and again things felt good for Dick. He enjoyed his mother's cooking and not having to worry about the price of each meal. His young sister Isabelle brought spontaneity and fun back into their new home. "Home was a good thing," Dick said.

The Davey Tree Expert Company

"There are perhaps a million people in the U.S. who know and talk to something— in a confused state, mentally."— Richard Shaver

Dick spent his idle hours at home reading, writing verse, drawing, but still "feeling like a ghoul at work for a race of half-alive carnivores."[15] His job was relentless and exhausting. His mind was usually on other things, and the meat-cutting line began to suffocate his sense of freedom. This lack of attention may have caused the accident that sent a meat hook through his hand. After that, he quit. Ziba was now working as a chef at a local college, but Dick knew the family would not appreciate his lack of employment. "My brother looked questioningly at me, but said nothing—understanding was between us; a year was a long time at an unpleasant job."[16]

Dick answered several want ads. His job search paid off when a reply came from a landscaping outfit owned by the Davey Tree Expert Company. It was springtime, and the landscaping season was about to shift into high gear. The foreman looked him over and asked, "Ever do any hard work?" Shaver replied that he had. His physique confirmed it, and the next day he became a member of the crew. Gardening, it turned out, suited Shaver's

The Davey Tree Expert Company crew, circa 1928. It was exhausting work, but Shaver enjoyed landscaping more than any of his other jobs. He is seen standing with both hands resting on his fellow workers' shoulders (Dottie Shaver collection).

disposition. "These things were alive and good to look at," he wrote. "This was the sun, the open earth, and living things. No cold box full of corpses, but the earth and its beauty."[17]

The next day at 7 A.M. Dick Shaver reported for work dressed as he had when he peddled ice in Bloomsburg, wearing a pair of corduroy pants and a blue woolen shirt. He climbed aboard a Ford truck loaded with crowbars, block and tackle, rope, sledges, a bale of burlap, six-foot anchor bars four inches thick, shovels, and picks. For the next four years he worked as a big tree mover, digging up trees from their original locations and replanting them on rich people's estates.

The fun-loving garden crew whooped and cheered whenever the Ford lurched or backfired on its way to the job site. As Shaver saw it, these men knew how to live life; they appreciated what the world had to offer. "I hadn't enjoyed myself so much for a year. No, not since high school had I had any fun. This carefree rolling was going to agree with me, I decided."[18]

Days moved swiftly, folding one into the next, full of green lawns, graceful trees, and flowering shrubs. Shaver's supervisor noticed his intelligent enthusiasm. His salary increased when he was promoted to second in charge of the work gang. By the time he celebrated his first year with Davey Tree, he was a foreman with a crew of his own.

1929–1930

"The ray killed my brother!"— Richard Shaver

As Dick was ascending the ladder of the Davey Tree Expert Company, Taylor sought a government job with the Federal Immigration Service as an immigration inspector. Passing the civil service exams with flying colors, he was sent to the Detroit Office of Immigration. Once in Detroit, he rented a room in a boarding house at 638 Pingree Avenue.

Dick's job as landscape foreman took him away from the family—out of town and even out of state sometimes, writing up job estimates and hiring local laborers to complete the projects. He liked the change of scenery and he was working on his own, making his own decisions.

With one boy gone and another rarely home, Grace, Ziba, and Isabelle threw in their lot with Taylor. They moved to Detroit in the latter half of 1930, and Taylor again embraced his family. Taylor, Ziba, Grace, and Isabelle moved into larger quarters at 6734 Taft. Again Ziba and Grace started a restaurant with Ziba as chef.

That left Dick without the safe haven of his family, and it began to gnaw at him, made him edgy. One day a problem arose with a client. His supervisor blamed him for the problem. As Shaver explained it, "Then came a slip, a job that took too long, a lost customer, my refusal to shoulder the blame, the argument, and my freedom."[19]

The Great Depression was well underway in 1931. With the loss of his job, Dick followed his family to Detroit. He probably helped out at Ziba's restaurant, as he had in Bloomsburg. For the next few years, Shaver continued to list himself as a landscape engineer in the Detroit City Directory.

In truth, he had slipped from his mooring. He began to reassess his life. Whenever that happened, he usually kicked around until a situation opened up that suited him. At first, he lived off his savings.

"I lazed about, sleeping long hours in the day, reading most of each night, and prowling around the city between times, trying to understand myself. Jobs were not, the Depression was beginning; besides, I did not want to work, I was sick of it. I needed something for my mind to grow on."[20]

9

The Wicker School of Fine Art

"There are friends in the caves who know me, and have watched over me for years."—Richard Shaver

Jim Pobst's *Shaver: The Early Years* (1989) was the first Shaver biography to stress the importance of Detroit on Richard Shaver's art career. A Canadian with a keen interest in Shaver's Motor City hangouts, Pobst traced the streets and buildings Shaver frequented:

> For him, [Detroit] meant Woodward Avenue, especially down toward the river, where there were chili joints, coffee rooms, and all-night theaters that let patrons sleep in them for a dime. The Avenue Theater on Woodward, just around the corner from Jefferson, had a chorus line, and he spent a lot of time there, in the cheap seats.... A few miles north, at 5201 Woodward, was the public library. Across the street, at 5200, was the Detroit Institute of Art. He liked Woodward; it held everything, or so he thought....[1]

"The Dream Makers" placed the beginning of Shaver's art career in Detroit's city center, when an uncontrollable urge to draw came over him. Idly watching the waves of humanity on the city streets, he found himself "mentally sketching the figures of the people, their hats, walk, postures, gestures, and noting the color and the masses of them."[2]

Whether this was a fictional device or a true event, Shaver did find his way to the 15th floor of the Maccabee Building at 5057 Woodward Avenue, where he handed over what little money he had left to pay tuition at the Wicker School of Fine Art. The school's president, John F. Wicker, was a bearded, stocky man, "grizzled and bent, but with an energetically glittering eye" that fixed on Dick Shaver.

"I suppose you want to be a great artist, eh?"[3]

Sophie Gurvitch

"These people have always been there—the hidden people."—Richard Shaver

The course of Shaver's life changed forever when he walked through the doors of the Wicker School of Fine Art. Like the tipping of the first domino, it began an inescapable chain of events. Within two years he would lose his freedom and fall under the control of an evil gang of thugs inside Earth. But in the beginning, the life of an art student seemed to agree with him.

Again his physique came to the rescue. He found that he could earn pocket money as a nude model for figure-drawing classes. It may well have been during one of these modeling sessions that he caught the eye of Sophie Gurvitch, a part-time teacher at the school. Sophie and Dick hit it off, and for better or worse, they became an item.

Sophie was of Russian-Jewish descent, born a subject of the czar in Mirgorod, a town in the Russian Ukraine, on May 2, 1903. Her father was Benjamin Gurvitch, a coppersmith. The Gurvitches fled Russia when the czar's reign of terror against the Jews became deadly pogroms. Ben Gurvitch knew enough to get out while the getting was good, and immigrated to the United States in 1904.

Once established in America, he sent for his wife Anna Mintz and their daughter Sophie. Anna purchased two steerage tickets on a steamship bound for America in 1905. They settled in Detroit, where Ben opened a hardware store, Star Hardware and Paints. They became naturalized citizens in 1911, and cheered the Communist takeover that brought a bloody end to Czarist Russia. Though they were now American citizens, Gurvitch family politics were rooted in the Russian revolution.

Ben and Anna became first generation Communist Party members, and when Sophie was old enough, she joined the Young Communist League. This was not unusual in the teens and twenties, long before World War II and the Cold War. Many young American artists identified with worker rights and socialist ideals, and as the Depression deepened, it nourished the Communist credo.

Working Americans generally loathed the back room deals of Wall Street and the banks. The Gurvitches were proud of their Red heritage, according to Shaver's daughter Evelyn Ann:

> Mother belonged to the John Reed Club.... Right up until, and during, the Second World War my Aunt Evelyn had people staying over that the U.S. government was interested in. I think they were Communists. Aunt Evelyn complained bitterly that she had newly carpeted the apartment, and [the Communists] put out their cigarettes on the floor. At that point, she dropped them. My grandmother was a Communist until Russia invaded, at which point she dropped them too. I understand that in the 1920s they had guests from Russia that were studying here.[4]

Between 1931 and 1932, Sophie was living with her family above Star Hardware and Paints at 8715 East Forest Avenue. The entire block where the hardware store stood is gone now, according to Evelyn Ann. It fell victim to Detroit urban renewal, she said.

Ben saw to it that his children were well educated. He sent them to the best schools he could afford. Sophie attended art school for a career as a commercial artist. Her younger sister Evelyn became a concert pianist and earned a living as a piano instructor. Sophie grew up as a free thinker, a feminist, and suffragette, and for a time lived in a commune called The Carriage House, with like-minded socialists and Bohemian artists. Her parents occasionally took the streetcar to visit her there, said Evelyn Ann. "It was a very different life than what they were accustomed,"[5] she said.

Komrade Shaver

> *"... in my day if you could say 'dialectic' you were a top-notch Communist. Nobody else knew what the word meant."*— Richard Shaver

American Communists were handed a victory in 1930 when Detroit elected a mayor openly supported by the Ku Klux Klan. This marginalized the city's black population more than usual, and played into Bolshevik hands. Detroit was full of Reds and people with Red sympathies. This was due to the abundance of assembly-line workers — thousands of them — many of whom were out of work and angry, thanks to the Depression. Capitalist overlords of the era often hired goons as enforcers to spy on factory workers and keep them in line. There were threats of dismissal or worse, for siding with labor unions.

The greatest corporate master of them all, Henry Ford, was the undisputed richest man in the world. American Communists viewed him as the Darth Vader of his empire, the scourge of the plucky American factory worker. Massive layoffs at the Ford plant were rampant in the early 1930s, as were dangerous assembly-line speedups to make up for the lost labor. Workers were at the mercy of their employers. There was no unemployment insurance, no medical benefits, no sick leave, and no rest breaks. If the line stopped for any reason, workers got no pay. Graft was endemic throughout the hiring process, and blacks were barred from working at any Ford plant.

These grievances and more became the driving force behind a protest march at the Dearborn, Michigan, Ford plant on March 7, 1932. Not all of the thousands of protesters who showed up were card-carrying Communists. Many were former Ford workers hoping to reclaim their jobs. That morning, they marched toward the plant, singing songs and carrying signs. As it happened, Clyde Ford was Dearborn's mayor. It was no coincidence that he shared his last name with auto mogul Henry Ford. They were cousins. Mayor Ford confronted the protesters with city police and tear gas at the Baby Creek Bridge on Miller Road.

The thousands of workers, now angry, beat back the 30 police officers. They showered them with rocks and frozen mud, and for a time had the upper hand. They even reached the plant gates. There the Ford Hunger March, as they called it, became the Ford Massacre. Dearborn police were reinforced with Detroit cops, firefighters, state troopers, and the Ford plant's own goon squad, innocuously named "The Service Department."

Services rendered that day began with a water barrage from fire hoses, accompanied by live rounds of ammunition from police. When the unarmed workers panicked in retreat, Ford's Service Department opened fire with machine-guns. It was a miracle only four men were killed outright. Fifty more were wounded, 29 of them seriously. Some would later die of their wounds. To add insult to injury, police tracked down 48 wounded protesters and arrested them in their hospital beds.[6]

Police claimed the riot began when a Communist hiding behind a parked car fired six shots. Reporters quoted a Ford spokesman who was "mystified" by the riot. He said Ford Motors was generous to its workers, more so than most auto companies.[7] The papers had a field day with it. They reported 2,500 marchers were beaten and dispersed. To protect the Ford plant from further disruption, the Michigan National Guard First Battalion, 125th Infantry, circled it for the night.

This was life in Detroit at the time Dick Shaver and Sophie Gurvitch met at the Wicker School of Fine Art. The school had its cliques, one of them being a group of young artists with proletariat leanings. They called it the John Reed Society. John Reed was a well-to-do Bohemian artist and journalist from Portland, Oregon. The Communists claimed he was the first native-born American to join the Party. Reed's membership resulted from a trip to Czarist Russia, where he found himself swept up in the fervor of the Bolshevik revolution.

Young Communist League members with a yen to create art for the masses founded the John Reed Society in October 1929, and the club was gaining steam in the early 1930s when Sophie joined in Detroit. She educated Dick on the Communist movement as they whiled away their time together. Eventually he became a member too, though he waffled as time went on.

Better Well Read Than Red

"They used to say I was a Communist, which was reason enough for torturing me."—Richard Shaver

Shaver's Communist Party membership happened more by accident than by love of ideology. Memories of his Party affiliation were not proud or defiant as he recalled them years later. Instead, he blamed his Red ties for sinister events that plagued him throughout the years following art school. He explained it vaguely, but entertainingly, in a letter dated July 21, 1973:

> I spent twelve years in various incarcerations because of getting on a list while in art school.... [E]verybody who [went] to an art school [got] listed as a radical because in those days radicals did permeate art schools with a thing called the YCL, the Young Communist League. Members of the YCL professed to be followers of one famous radical who happened to be an artist in Russia at the time of the revolution. I don't remember his name.
>
> I knew some of these people and was listed as a YCL member because they passed around a charter paper for a chapter in the city, and I signed it just to be friendly. That signing thing cost me twelve years of freedom, and my brother was murdered outright by "counter-revolutionaries," actually members of criminal syndicates who used "counter-revolutionary" labels as a cover for criminal activities, because it kept them good with police....

What Shaver was doing at a YCL meeting in the first place is a curiosity, since he had so little interest in ideologies. But his girlfriend Sophie was a card-carrying member. Her entire family had joined the Party, even fun-loving Uncle Harry. Everybody liked Uncle Harry, so Dick became a member too. His belief that counter-revolutionaries murdered his brother is strange indeed. But since our story has not yet reached the year 1934, Taylor will remain alive a while longer for the sake of chronology. Taylor's was not the only untimely death in Shaver's future. More would follow.

The Day the Dollar Died

"Do you hear voices? What would you say if someone asked you that question?"— G.H. Irwin, "20 Million Maniacs"

Young Communists Dick and Sophie followed newspaper accounts of the Ford riot in all its bloody detail. The Young Communist League felt that a counter-punch was in order. The heavy-handed tactics of the cops and Henry Ford's Service Department would not be tolerated. They planned counter-demonstrations — consciousness-raising for the masses.

Shaver said he took part in one of these rallies. Some of the details were fuzzy by the time he wrote about it in 1973. Names and dates had been reduced to shadows flickering on the cavern wall of his memory. Nevertheless, he seemed to have an insider's knowledge of an event that sounded much like those in 1932. He was involved, he said, in a big way, and his high profile brought him to the attention of Big Brother.

> It was a big demonstration arranged by the YCL. We had about a thousand youngsters ... and we rehearsed a big program and hired the biggest skating rink and coliseum in town. We had a big sort of pyramid in the middle of the rink, with spiral ramps going round and round ... and on the top of the pyramid was a big gilded dollar sign rampant above all ... about six foot high....

Our program was flower girls singing ... going up the ramp, to be broken up by a bunch of club-swinging cops. I cut the clubs out of broomsticks and put them in the dressing rooms. I had been saving old broomsticks in my basement. I lived about two blocks from the big rink.

Anyway, somebody got cold feet and cancelled the club-swinging-cop-brigade-breaking-up-the-flower-girls scene, because it was too much like inciting a riot ... and we didn't have much of a program left. So we sat around the dressing rooms while the rink filled up ... and it filled with thousands and thousands of people. We were wondering how to have a program for all those people when most of our original plan was canceled by the cold-water brigade.

So an old Italian whispered in my ear how to put a cap on it ... he was what you'd call an old-time bomb-throwing type from Europe, and had some experience with the whole scene. So when we got to parading up the spiral ramp, I got into the first bunch of girls and flowers and singing, and when I got near the dollar I jumped up ... pulled it up out of its roots and stood on it and held up the workers' fist.

To me it was all fun, just to fret the stodgy oldsters, but what happened was it got me in a news picture, stepping on the dollar and holding up a fist, and it never occurred to me that I'd be labeled a radical ... it was all just fun to me.[8]

A merry prank, or so he thought at the time. Afterward, his name found its way onto a *lot* of lists, he said. And that meant trouble. It was as if the ghost of Enoch Rider, his old schoolmaster, was haunting him, still calling him onto the carpet. In researching this dollar sign incident, the Detroit Public Library's Burton Archive revealed no photo of Shaver holding up the workers' fist, and nothing resembling Shaver's rally. But there was a short piece in the *New York Times* on March 11, 1932, about an incident that sounds like a possibility:

COMMUNISTS MEETING IN DETROIT, DEMAND TRIAL FOR HENRY FORD.... Five thousand persons packed the Arena Gardens tonight for a meeting avowedly sponsored by Communists, and heard speakers demand the "trial and conviction of Henry Ford for countenancing the murder of our comrades."

The meeting was called because of Monday's riot in front of the Ford Motor Company's plant in Dearborn, in which four unemployed marchers were killed. Most of the five thousand spectators within the hall and the one thousand who gathered outside, unable to gain admittance, apparently were curiosity seekers, hundreds of them boys and girls.

The Arena Gardens was Detroit's most famous skating rink and coliseum. Could this have been the scene of Shaver's dollar sign incident? We may never know for sure.

Hard Times

> *"Although I have never experienced memories of Lemuria or Atlantis, I believe they may have existed, and I want to know more of them."—1945 Fan letter, Maxin 92*

In the beginning, Shaver's modeling job at the Wicker School of Fine Arts paid 35 cents an hour. As the Depression deepened, it dropped to 25 cents. Shaver had to scramble for extra income. Biographer Jim Pobst discovered how he did it: "The modeling gave him an idea. He rented a loft, a cheap place nearby and hired a model for $10 a day. He sold tickets for $1 a head through the school, and on good days, sold thirty or forty tickets.... On warm sunny days he would go to one of the city parks, and do quick sketches of passersby and tourists for 25 cents. One week he took the money he had earned and bought a ready-made suit for $22.50."[9]

But this was pennyante stuff. Sophie was the one making good with an art career; she was on the way up. Her Wicker School teaching job was just a stepping stone. She had studied at the Chicago Art Institute and at the Art Student's League in New York City. The Art Student's League was a prestigious feather in Sophie's cap. Jackson Pollack and Man Ray were said to have attended the ASL at one time or another. Sophie became proficient in oils, watercolors, and pen and ink. She painted in a realistic style, according to her daughter Evelyn Ann, who later began her own career in art and teaching.

The Depression continued its downward spiral. The Wicker School's enrollment fell until it hit bottom. After 22 years of art education, Mr. Wicker closed the school in 1932. It was an untimely development for fair-weather Communist and now former art student Dick Shaver. It was even worse for Sophie. She lost her teaching income. Hard times often bring people closer together, and in this case, it happened to Dick and Sophie.

Against the wishes of both the Gurvitch and Shaver families, they were married on July 5, 1932, by a Detroit justice of the peace. Witnesses that day were Sophie's sister Evelyn and friend Goldie King. The newlyweds moved into the Shaver family household on Taft Avenue, which was nearing overflow capacity. This may have put some strain on Taylor, who knew of Sophie's Communist sympathies. He was, after all, an employee of the U.S. government. Further stress came from Sophie's parents, who were unhappy she had married a gentile. The clash of cultures sparked an inability of both families to accept the marriage.

Sophie made plans to scout for work as a commercial artist in New York. Shaver also began to job-hunt. He lucked out and was hired by the Briggs auto body plant in Highland Park as an assembly line worker. This was Henry Ford's original auto plant. Now it produced Briggs bodies for the new V-8s. Like everywhere else in Detroit, working conditions were rough:

> Rules then in force allowed pay only for time the production line was in operation. It was common to spend ten hours on the line, only to be paid for four or five. The starting rates were 10 cents an hour for men, four cents an hour for women.... Briggs had the reputation of being a "butcher shop" with speed-up rules that led to an increased accident rate and fatalities. It was a tough employer.[10]

His supervisor handed Shaver a welding gun and showed him how to use it. The Briggs plant, along with many other factory jobs, became a source of dread and hatred of assembly line work. Gigantic machines stamping out auto bodies from large steel sheets pounded Shaver's ears ten hours a day. Shaver described the scene:

> Overhead conveyers shot diagonally across the spaces which are the light wells, around me were welding jigs, and every few seconds I had to duck a welding gun. Two of them hung on swivels and were used in

Sophie Gurvitch Shaver, age 33, as she appeared prior to her tragic death in 1936. She died of accidental electrocution. (Richard Shaver collection).

succession for two different sizes and shapes of welds. The swinging gun timed our action, and gave a pulsating rhythm to our movements.... I was the man doing the welding. I grabbed the gun as it swung, welded, pushed it away and ducked its mate as it swung into position over me, then straightened and shot the juice to the next weld.[11]

Sophie returned from New York City without the job she hoped to find. She became pregnant the following year.

10

Through the Looking Glass

"The voices came from beings I came to realize were not human."— Richard Shaver

"**Adventure Writer Stricken Suddenly**. Taylor V. Shaver, Author of Boy's Stories, Dies at 30."[1]

Taylor began to suffer chest pain as February was just getting underway. He remained at home in bed, but by February 20 he came down with pneumonia and the pain was so great his doctor sent him to East Side General Hospital. He died there four days later. The doctor's scrawl on Tate's death certificate said it was cardiac hypertrophy complicated by lobar pneumonia. Cardiac hypertrophy is a thickening of the heart muscle associated with untreated high blood pressure. It decreases the capacity of the heart chamber to move blood.

The Shaver family was devastated. Dick went on a drunken bender the day Tate died. Funeral services were held on February 26. After that, things were never the same. Taylor was the rock on which the family anchored itself. With Tate gone, Ziba and Grace decided to move to Barto, Pennsylvania, back to the few acres they owned there. They called it Bittersweet Hollow Farm.

That left Dick and Sophie alone at the Taft Avenue flat. Within six months the baby would arrive, but the flat seemed empty without Ziba, Grace, Isabelle, and most of the furniture. A vague and desperate cloud descended over Dick. He began to suspect Tate's death was murder. His suspicion turned into obsession. Months before Taylor had died, he told Dick of problems he was having along the Canadian border. Organized crime was involved with bootleg booze brought in by runners sneaking across the border.

Things were getting so bad for immigration inspectors that the U.S. Border Patrol took charge. The Border Patrol stationed one of its two directors at Detroit's immigration office in 1932 to cover the Canadian border. Prohibition was being enforced in the United States, but booze was legal in Canada. Organized crime began recruiting illegal immigrants to smuggle alcohol across the border. It was a violent time in Border Patrol history, and immigration inspectors were on the front lines of the war on illegal immigrants and illegal booze.

Whatever Shaver's suspicions, they began to encompass more than the Canadian border. He told Sophie that people were watching him, following him. He began hearing voices, and believing that someone was reading his thoughts.

"There was a constant sly perception and reaction going on that was not my own thinking," said Shaver. "There was a listening, a watching, a weighing of me. Some other mind was getting more and more familiar with mine. The most secret vistas of my youthful dreams were being calmly, ignorantly, and ruthlessly pawed over by a definitely intruding personality—and the intrusion was strangely revolting and resented."[2]

As the voices continued, Sophie worried that something was going terribly wrong. At first, Dick thought the voices came through his welding gun; that somehow the wiring had become a receiving unit, allowing him to overhear conversations of other plant workers. But when the voices began to follow him home, he knew he was in trouble.

"For the next few weeks I spent a lot of time reorienting my thinking, adapting my viewpoints and attitudes toward life to fit this tremendous new fact — that there was *an important part of life which might even rule me and most men, about which I knew nothing at all!*"[3]

The voices, he said, could be loud or soft, and were sometimes masked within other sounds, like "a fly buzzing by your ear," or embedded within the din of a machine. He began to differentiate between his own thoughts and the ones telepathically inserted into his mind by mysterious rays. "Telepathic talking is like phoning," he said.[4] Good rays could make the birds sing to him in the morning. The voices refused to talk to anyone who did not know about them, he said. This made matters worse. No one understood.

Shaver began a new life as his old one collapsed around him. The rigors of the factory, stress between his in-laws and parents, the prospect of becoming a father, the death of his brother Tate; it all became too much. No one knows for certain what makes the voices appear, but once they do, the most common diagnosis is schizophrenia, and Shaver became its poster child.

Acute paranoia, often associated with schizophrenia, overtook him as the voices intensified. They began to answer questions before he asked them. Initially, Shaver reacted like anyone would when they begin to hear voices for the first time. Who are they? Where do they come from? What do they want? Doggedly determined, Shaver set out to find answers.

In the beginning he was fearful. The voices knew his innermost thoughts. They accused him of being a Communist and of being homosexual. Voices at the steel plant whispered that he was a "morphydite," that he had no penis. It all became too much to bear. He may well have told his parents about the voices, and (possibly at his mother's urging) he left Sophie and traveled to Bittersweet Hollow Farm.

"I began to believe in untrue things and realized I must do something. [When] we got a week off the Fourth of July, I went home to Pennsylvania. But they followed me all the way, several of them with whispers and wool of the most revolting kind.... Now all the time, they lied ... about me, friends would come to me with the most astounding stories circulating about me, were they true, they would ask. Of course they weren't...."[5]

Sophie, frightened, alone, and pregnant in the Taft Avenue flat, told her father of the new developments. He became enraged at Dick's irresponsible behavior.

Shaver may have returned to Detroit for the birth of his daughter, Evelyn Ann, born August 31, 1934, but he remained in a paranoid state, too unsettled to return to work. He struggled with the voices and his marriage. "The hindrance I received was a vicious impulse toward leaving undone the most necessary tasks, toward slighting the best of my friends, toward forgetting the most sacred duties. The hindrance was a wicked, slothful, ill-intended lethargy that dragged its feet, pulling on my coattail every time I found a way toward love, friendship, better living, spoiling every little success, soiling every pleasure."[6]

Shaver blamed his condition on a case of sunstroke. It was a common story among the Gurvitch family, and may have had some basis in fact. Men who were overly exposed to the hot, dry desert, Shaver said, became "cafard." Cafard is usually defined as deep melancholia, but Shaver gave it another meaning. He saw it as a kind of brain fever that made men susceptible to mayhem.

If his sunstroke happened at all, it appears to have occurred sometime after Taylor's death. In truth, the voices and his growing paranoia were more than a case of sunstroke.

Terror gradually crept into his life. At first it was a matter of finding out where the voices came from. Next, why were the voices focused on him and not others? And finally, what was their purpose? Gradually the pieces began to fall into place. He deduced that underground rays were putting the thoughts in his head, and that a malevolent purpose was behind them. "Then my growing understanding was amplified by a horrible experience, and brought me into the class of 'the accursed'.... I understood why and how my watchers had to justify their existence to their superiors, and how in their reports they were apt to enlarge upon my efforts to perceive and understand them. For I was suddenly graduated from a nobody to a somebody very dangerous to *them*."[7]

Shaver kept the "horrible experience" to himself, but it involved the law. It was serious enough to make his wife and friends think he had finally gone off the deep end, and it came at the urging of the voices. If the intention was to put him out of circulation, it worked. It led to a decade of incarceration within Michigan's mental health system. Shaver hid this part of his past whenever he talked about his past. He would rather people think he spent time in prison than in the "bug house."

"I shall not ... give you the details of how the axe fell on me; it is all too sordid. I assure you it did not do me credit, and I would much rather forget it.... [My] enforced escapade, which I was blindly urged into by the subtle energy of the telepathy machines ... ended with my arrest...."[8]

Flight into Futility

> *"I know those dero only let me live because my life was a burden to me, and because my torture was a delight to them...."*—Richard Shaver

Ben Gurvitch grew up in the final decades of Czarist Russia. He survived the czar's pogroms because he was smart enough to know trouble when he saw it. Now, in Detroit, the trouble he saw was a son-in-law who deserted his pregnant daughter because of the voices in his head. Gurvitch was a practical man; a man who, above all, knew how to protect his family. And as he saw it, Dick Shaver was a threat to that family. He made up his mind to neutralize the problem for the sake of his daughter and granddaughter.

And so it was that Gurvitch left the hardware store one day to seek advice from a friend, a well-respected lawyer and Detroit newspaper reporter named Louis Tendler. A Russian Jew like himself, Tendler had immigrated to America with his mother in 1906.

Tendler's advice was simple. Shaver was obviously insane, he said, and Sophie, his wife, had the power to commit him to an asylum. Even if Sophie still loved her husband, she had to think of her career and the new baby. Private treatment was out of the question; it was far too expensive. The state must get involved.

With growing pressure from her father and Tendler to move ahead with the plan, Sophie acquiesced. With Tendler's help, she petitioned the court to declare Shaver incompetent due to insanity. Thus the gears of the Michigan state legal system were set in motion. They gnashed their teeth as they ground up Dick Shaver in the process. He was about to embark on a forced pilgrimage—first stop, the Detroit Receiving Hospital Emergency Ward, where he was admitted as case 200014. The Court documents said it all: "White married male aged 27 years. At time of entrance to hospital he refused to cooperate and had to be restrained. Admits of auditory hallucinations but says he is much improved at present. He hears 'echoes' of voices talking about him. Patient disturbed and confused at times. Advise he be committed as insane."[9]

On July 27, 1934, Sophie signed the petition to have Dick committed. She said his paranoia had overtaken his better judgment. He thought people were following him, talking about him, that doctors were trying to poison him. She stated that Dick had no estate and no income, and that his parents, who were now living in Pennsylvania, had no means to support him in his present state. These events came just six months after Taylor's funeral; 1934 was shaping up as a dark year indeed for the Shaver family.

Ziba's memory of his mother Rhoda, and her own mental breakdown, may have made the news about Dick's mental collapse more believable. As Grace put it, Dick's condition was "a long time in coming."[10]

Things began to move swiftly as court dates came and went one after another. On August 2, Sophie filed a petition to become Dick's legal guardian. This time she stated her husband's estate was $100, and that he had a monthly income of $10. Dr. Jack Agins examined Shaver on August 5 and recorded his condition:

> Richard Shaver is a young white male, 27 years old, confined in the psychopathic ward of the Receiving Hospital since July 16, 1934. He gives a definite history of persecution for alleged imaginary communist beliefs and ridicule by his fellow employees for supposed homosexual practices. He thinks he was hypnotized at the time and has a definite consciousness of a "dual mental personality." When he speaks he wonders if his words are uttered by someone else. The last affliction is still present to a definite degree, although in general he is able to rid himself to an extent from the ideas of persecution. As he is not entirely free from his mental affliction, he should be institutionalized.[11]

On August 6, the probate court clerk sent a registered letter to Ziba and Grace notifying them of the petition to commit. Richard, Ziba, Grace, and the superintendent of Shaver's hospital ward were summoned to appear before Judge Murphy in Room 305 of the Wayne County Probate Court on August 17.

It is doubtful that Ziba and Grace could afford the trip to Detroit for the court hearing. On August 17, the superintendent of the Receiving Hospital brought Shaver before Judge Murphy. A clerk at the Detroit Department of Public Welfare telephoned Shaver's parents on August 20, informing them that Judge Murphy had contacted a Dr. Inch at the Ypsilanti State Hospital, and that this same Dr. Inch said he would admit Shaver into his care "at the first vacancy."

Sophie became guardian on August 29. The next day, sheriff's deputies Blume and Ligarness arrived at the Hospital Receiving Ward. They handed their orders to Shaver's ward superintendent: "It is ordered that the Sheriff in and for said County be and he [sic] is hereby authorized and directed to remove the said Richard Shaver to the Ypsilanti State Hospital at Ypsilanti, Michigan, with full power and authority for that purpose."[12] They drove him to Ypsilanti State Hospital where they put him in the care of Dr. G.F. Inch.

Ypsilanti State Hospital

"I, Richard Shaver, was going insane."

At the time Shaver entered Ypsilanti State Hospital, it was a state-of-the-art facility. It opened its doors on July 28, 1931, three years before Shaver moved in. It was a $1.5 million dollar brick behemoth, with an expansive neo-classical entrance comprised of six white, fluted columns.

Shaver's treatment included one or both of the hospital's two specialties: hydrotherapy and physiotherapy. Hydrotherapy used water, and lots of it. Patients were treated to sitz baths in oversized bathtubs, needle showers that included fan douches and jet douches. They received footbaths, cold, wet sheet packs, bubble baths, salt glows, hot fomentations, and colloidal baths. Physiotherapy included all types of massage, electric light cabinets, electric light bakes, ultraviolet radiation, and surgical dressings.[13]

As soothing as this sounds, Ypsilanti State Hospital was no health spa. The massive A building, with its adjoining C-1 and C-2 blocks, was designed to hold 900 patients for the "custodial care of the insane, and was not well-suited for a therapeutic program of care and treatment for the mentally ill."[14] By the end of its first year, the hospital had 922 patients. The daily cost of maintaining one patient at Ypsilanti was 80 cents.

Shaver felt he had been railroaded. He used to say that almost any odd behavior is excuse enough to commit someone to a mental hospital. He cautioned Ray Palmer about loose talk to the wrong people in a 1944 letter:

> Your friends can be very sly and evil if they think you are cracked — they — your own wife, will lie to you and say she met the most wonderful doctor, and she wants you to see him and she insists. You can't refuse your dear wife, particularly because you are at that very time controlled by the dero ray — the mental hospitals are one of their favorite hells where they torment their victims for years without anyone listening to the poor devil's complaints — for the "patient is having delusions." ...[B]e very circumspect how you talk about these things, for it is their favorite stunt to put a guy in the nut house....[15]

Shaver was in and out of Ypsilanti, thanks to a growing

Evelyn Ann Shaver, 20 months, 1936. Within months of this photograph being taken, her mother's tragic electrocution would result in her adoption by her grandparents and a name change to Evelyn Ann Gurvitch (courtesy Evelyn Ann Bryant).

patient population that caused major overcrowding. The crisis gave rise to a liberal off-campus visitation program for its more trustworthy patients. As long as Shaver behaved himself, and his guardian approved, he was free to return home for visits. Sophie frequently brought Dick to their apartment for short stays. He eventually went for an extended stay on his parents' farm in Pennsylvania. At the end of each visit with Sophie, he would simply check back into the hospital.

1935–1936

> *"I do not think that the [marriage] had anything to do with Dick's mental collapse — it was a long time in coming...."* — Grace Shaver

With Dick in Ypsilanti State Hospital, Sophie found the size and expense of the Taft Avenue flat unsuitable. She and the baby moved to a smaller apartment at 8866 David Street. At 35, she was working at a Detroit advertising firm as a commercial artist and was active in Detroit's art scene. She participated regularly in annual art shows and the Detroit Society of Independent Artists. She was featured in an exhibition of Jewish artists from Detroit. She signed up to work as a WPA artist, and in 1935 was an employee of the U.S. government, painting illustrated nursery rhymes on the walls of child care facilities.

For reasons known only to Sophie, she kept Dick's name with hers on the David Street apartment, even though he never lived there. As his guardian, Sophie could bring him home, and she did. This continued the following year, when Sophie moved to 3009 Holcomb Avenue, Apartment 16. Though Dick lived in Ypsilanti, Sophie continued to include his name in the city directory. It was on one of these visits that Sophie sketched Dick's portrait, according to Evelyn Ann. The portrait is the only image of her father she still possesses:

> I know he came back to visit my mother, and that's when she did that portrait. Why he had to go back [to the hospital], I don't know. My family had him committed; we had a friend who was a lawyer. They committed him because they were worried about the fact there was a baby in the house. They really suspected him of treachery, because he left [Mother] when she was pregnant. Some guys can't take responsibility.... Now I wonder whether [my mother] didn't have some kind of agreement with him to have a child. And after that he just left.[16]

Treachery came from both sides. Apparently Grace did not approve of Sophie. Her politics, religion, and family were nothing like the Pennsylvania-bred Shaver and Taylor families. From the moment Dick and Sophie announced their marriage plans, Grace knew there would be trouble, but stifled her objections. Hard feelings surfaced after Dick's breakdown. Sophie accused Grace of hating her, and felt that Dick's mental collapse resulted from stress caused by the Shavers' inability to accept her or their marriage.

Sophie also accused Grace of attempting to split them up after Taylor's death by suggesting Dick come to Barto without her.[17] Grace denied the allegations in a letter to Sophie, saying it was not her custom to meddle in either of her sons' affairs. "I feared to alienate them with nagging — for a long time we looked at your intimacy as temporary — when you were married he talked it over with me and I thought it for the best, but I should have gone to see you first — I might have saved you both a lot of trouble if I had voiced my objections first.... Since he has been ill I have been very careful to speak little and kindly [of you]...."[18]

As a gesture of good will, Sophie arranged to send Dick for an extended stay on the

Shaver farm. Everyone agreed that normal surroundings might help with his recovery. Dick returned to the farm in June 1936 and spent the next several months hoeing weeds, grafting fruit trees, and feeding the chickens and goats. Sophie offered to send art supplies as her finances allowed, so Dick could keep up with his drawing. Ziba's plan to become a successful chicken rancher went bust, and the family was broke, with no money to pay for luxuries like drawing paper and colored pencils.

Shaver was emotionally torn about his marriage. He loved Sophie, but friction from both families from the clash of cultures wore on him. He tried to leave Sophie more than once, but always came back. He told his mother, "I thought I'd leave her, but I couldn't."[19]

Cold Dead Winter

> "Regardless of whether Shaver is right ... the good and the evil forces do exist, *and this investigation is bound to lead us to ... a worldwide cleansing of false beliefs....*"— David D. Dagmar, Maxin-96

Sophie's Holcomb Avenue apartment was part of a working class neighborhood, with Star Hardware and Paints only a few blocks away. With her commercial art career beginning to take off, she moved into a better apartment in the same building. But it was winter, and the rooms were hard to keep warm. Louis Tendler, friend of the family, learned of her dilemma and bought her a housewarming gift—a portable electric heater. Sophie accepted it with gratitude.

Portrait of Richard Shaver painted by his wife Sophie, circa 1934–1935. Sophie drew this while Dick was on leave from Ypsilanti State Hospital (courtesy Evelyn Ann Bryant).

Things were getting back to a normal routine for Sophie, what with Dick living on his parents' farm. On December 29, 1936, she had just completed a job for clients Fred Lister and Horace Cross. They were to meet her that day to pick up the artwork at her apartment. Knocking on her door, they got no reply. Newspapers, including the *Detroit News*, carried the story the following day:

Woman Artist Dies of Shock—Sophie Gurvitch Shaver—Victim of Heater.

An electric heater grasped in one hand, Mrs. Sophie Gurvitch Shaver, one of Detroit's best known young artists, was found dead in a half-filled tub in her apartment at 3009 Holcomb Avenue, Tuesday evening. Detectives Lawrence Sheehy, of the homicide squad, and Albert Kean, acting deputy coroner, said the young woman apparently lifted the electric heater with damp hands while standing in the water to take a bath and was killed by the current passing through her body. The body was found by

Horace Cross, 4837 Wayburn Avenue, and Fred Lister, 2206 Alter Road ... who investigated when they found the lights on but received no response to their calls.

Conflicting versions of the story appeared in other newspapers, with no accounting for accuracy. The *Detroit Free Press* stated, "Her husband is in a sanitarium in Pennsylvania and her two children are in a hospital." *The Detroit Times* added even more detail, with human interest: "**Electrocuted in Bath, Leaves Sick Child....** Little Evelyn Shaver, five [she was two], lies ill with scarlet fever today in Herman Kiefer Hospital, unaware that her mother, Sophie, 35, an artist, accidentally electrocuted herself while bathing in her apartment...."

They buried Sophie on New Year's Day, 1937. In keeping with Gurvitch family tradition, she was laid to rest in Workmen's Circle Cemetery, a favorite resting place for Jewish families involved in Socialist politics, the labor movement, and Eastern European Jewish tradition. One of the cemetery's most famous residents at the time of Sophie's internment was Harry Millman, a member of Detroit's notorious Purple Gang.

Louis Tendler's guilt for giving Sophie the instrument of her death burned into his soul like red-hot coals. More than ever, he felt responsible for Evelyn Ann. The untimely death of her mother presented Ben Gurvitch with a new problem. Evelyn Ann had but one parent, her father Dick Shaver. This could bring further woes to the Gurvitch family if Shaver should decide to claim his daughter.

Complicating matters further was the fact that Shaver now had no guardian, and was living outside the asylum. These were the circumstances leading up to phase two of the plan to control Dick Shaver's life. This time it was a two-pronged attack. First, Shaver must relinquish all rights to his daughter. Ben and Anna Gurvitch would then adopt her. Second, Gurvitch would petition the court to appoint his friend Louis Tendler as Shaver's guardian. This was the knockout punch in a series of legal maneuvers to dispose of Richard Shaver.

Tendler sent a letter to Ziba and Grace presenting the Gurvitch adoption proposal. Tendler reasoned that it was in the best interest of Evelyn Ann to be raised by her mother's family, in a Jewish household. After all, her father's fragile mental state made him incapable of caring for her. He asked Grace to convince Dick to sign the papers. Making matters worse were the voices in Dick's head, which had not subsided. Ziba and Grace decided it best for the child to leave the Shaver family and become a Gurvitch.

Shaver was grief-stricken on learning of Sophie's death, but after reading Tendler's proposal he became outraged, calling it "loathsome." He would have no part of it, he said. His older brother Donald, who happened to be staying over for the Christmas holidays, sided with his brother. A heated debate ensued, with Ziba and Grace for, Dick and Donald against. In the end, the elder Shavers won Donald over, and Donald convinced Dick to give in. Grace explained their decision in a letter to Louis Tendler, dated February 12, 1937: "My Dear Mr. Tendler, Enclosed find the paper which you forwarded me, duly signed. I was not able to go to a notary until today.... Richard thoroughly understands — but is *no better*. Personally I feel that it is right that they should have a legal right to keep their daughter's baby. And I thank you for assisting in the matter."

Years later, Shaver contradicted this version of the adoption, telling his third wife Dorothy that he was still in the hospital when presented with the adoption proposal. He claimed he misunderstood what he was signing. A member of his own family, he said, tricked him into thinking the papers would bring about his release from Ypsilanti State Hospital. This was Shaver revisionism, because in 1944 he informed Rap that Sophie had died while he was on leave in Pennsylvania. His new version of the adoption story may well have salved the guilt he felt for giving in to family pressure.

On January 20, 1937, less than a month after Sophie's funeral, Ben Gurvitch petitioned the court for a hearing to appoint Tendler as Shaver's new guardian. Gurvitch described himself to the court as Shaver's "father-in-law and friend." The judge set a hearing for February 24, but only Gurvitch and Tendler were in attendance. Without any objections, the judge appointed Tendler as guardian.

Gurvitch now held the key to Shaver's freedom or incarceration. That was not all. He had adopted Evelyn Ann Shaver and planned to erase her father's memory completely. Thus ended the emotional roller coaster that began with Shaver's arrival in Detroit. During that time, his life was turned inside out. What happened next was Dick Shaver's answer to the years of pain.

11

Period of Abandonment

"The real truth is that you are pretty continuously tampered into your rather blind view of this whole thing."— Richard Shaver to Ray Palmer

What Louis Tendler planned to *do* about Richard Shaver was the big question. Shaver chose not to wait to find out, and fled the farm for parts unknown. He left his parents holding the bag, for they were responsible for him. From that point on, Shaver was a fugitive from Ypsilanti State Hospital. It was easy for him to melt into the Depression era's vast legions of nameless tramps and hobos. With nothing but a "cheap Indian blanket, a genuine Navy wool blanket, matches, and a pocket knife,"[1] Shaver traveled across the eastern United States and Canada. He rode buses, hitchhiked, and did not stay for very long when he stopped. He rode boxcars and stowed away on tramp steamers. As an old-timer, Shaver recalled his rambling days with a touch of nostalgia, often recounting it in correspondence: "I went clear across Canada with a blanket roll," he said, "staying away from people except to work for a few days to pick up grocery money.... [T]here is great satisfaction in being strictly on your own and able to keep yourself comfortable and free and warm. This can be a problem just keeping warm, you know, if you don't know how."

Shaver exaggerated his account. He did not go clear across Canada, though he did cover a few eastern provinces. He worked at odd jobs: cutting up fish in a fish cannery, and as a crew member on a fishing boat. He worked any job where few questions were asked, and he kept moving.

He was proud of his survivalist lifestyle, describing in detail how he got by with "a little coffee and bacon, that's all. Hang a can for coffee on a stick stuck [in the ground] on a slant. If you don't carry a pan as a mess kit ... you can just heat a rock that is flat for bacon and eggs, and you can find the eggs in birds' nests once you get used to the idea ... even turkey eggs. With a compass you can travel round the world with nothing else. During the Depression a lot of people saw the world with a blanket roll ... they didn't even call us bums, there were so many of us."[2]

A 1945 letter from Shaver to Ray Palmer described his circuitous wandering during this period. His first stop, he said, was his former haunt of Detroit. Having little money and fearing the long arm of the law, he camped in secluded areas on the outskirts of town. From Detroit he traveled to upper Michigan. He migrated to Akron, Ohio, to Pittsburgh and then Philadelphia. From there he went east to New Jersey and New York.

By the time he reached Boston, he realized big cities made him easy prey for the tormenting rays coming from the cavern people, so he turned north to Vermont and open country. He was wary of being caught and taken to the asylum. "I like to stay out of the big cities and away from circulation, because too many things happen which I can't be fore-

warned of. That is, I walk down the street in the city and a half a dozen guys make remarks....
And if I lose my temper and grab one of them, I'm in jail...."3

Max, his dero tail, unrelentingly continued to pursue him. People who met Shaver along the way thought he traveled alone, but they were mistaken. There were always the invisible "others" following his every step. Finally, he left the United States altogether:

> I went on up to Newfoundland trying to shake the tail, invisible but almighty tormenting. Just like the Maupassant Horla, only incredibly stupid and revolting ... there was some mighty good ray in Newfoundland, they treated me fine and a little of the old magic came back into life ... a ray called Sue, brought ... (I got twenty days for stowing away...) every animal and insect into my cell to make mystic love to me. She was immensely talented and had a little blind girl from the caverns with her (I suspect she was surface ray) with whom I fell hopelessly in love....4

Shaver would later name the blind girl "Nydia."

Newfoundland Stowaway

> *"If you want to stow away in the dark through the hatch, always pick small ships with a shallow draft...."— Richard Shaver*

Shaver purchased a bus ticket on his last day in Vermont; destination, Quebec, Canada. It took what little cash he had left, and he was disappointed when Canadian border guards near Montreal refused him entry once they learned he was broke. They put him back on the bus and returned him to his point of origin. Not one to give up easily, Shaver said he walked back to the border and crossed unnoticed.

He liked Montreal well enough to stay a few weeks. When it came time to move on, he stowed away on a ship bound for Halifax, Nova Scotia. In Halifax the captain spotted him as he was leaving the ship "by the stowaway's exit," but he managed to escape.

By this time it was late 1937 and Halifax was cold. Loafing about the docks, Shaver learned that his best bet for transportation was the SS *Nova Scotia*, which was taking on cargo bound for Liverpool, England. Shaver hung around a few more days, waiting. On the night before the ship's scheduled departure, Shaver launched his plan to sneak aboard:

> I stowed away on ship by taking off the hatch cover in the dark, and dropping in to reach the ladder with my feet, and there wasn't any ladder, and my wet overcoat was turning into ice. I was just too lazy to pull back up, so I let go, thinking it was only a twelve-foot drop....
>
> Well, about two minutes later I was still falling. That was about a forty-five- to fifty-foot drop. I landed on the boiler, which was warm anyway. [It] saved my life and I didn't bother moving till they came and got me in the morning. If it hadn't been a warm boiler I'd have frozen. Luck ... I am always lucky. But I still limp from that one...."5

The *Nova Scotia*'s first stop was St. John's, Newfoundland. There the crew was surprised to learn they had damaged cargo by the name of "Leonard Hogan." That was the name that popped into Shaver's head when he was questioned by crew members. On December 6, 1937, the St. John's *Evening Telegram* carried the story "Stowaway Found in S.S. *Nova Scotia*":

> Yesterday when the hatches of the S.S. *Nova Scotia* were removed to load cargo a stowaway was discovered in No. 4 hold. He gave his name as Leonard Hogan, a seaman from Belfast, Ireland.
>
> As far as could be learned he had been stowed away on the ship ever since she left Halifax on November 27th. When discovered yesterday he appeared to be suffering great pain and when examined by the ship's doctor it was found that his ankle was fractured. He was sent to hospital

for treatment.... He evidently was prepared for a trip, as he had a flashlight, magazines, water, and provisions with him.

The main hospital in St. John's, Newfoundland, was St. John's General, but Shaver, a vagrant, was not taken there. Shaver said he was treated at a local charity hospital instead. In looking into 1937 St. John's city records, Shaver biographer Jim Pobst found something that fit Shaver's description: "a home run by a family named Hull. Readers of Shaver's stories will recall the character 'Mother Hull' as an important element in those stories which he wrote about his flight across the U.S."[6]

His convalescence lasted a few months. News about Leonard Hogan turned up again on April 9, 1938, when a Constable Noseworthy filed a complaint in Magistrate's Court charging "Hogan" with vagrancy. Judge H. O'Neill meted out Hogan's sentence. Pobst picked up the thread from there:

> At 8:30 P.M. Case No. 312 was heard and the defendant was described as "Leonard Hogan, 35, Ireland." The sentence was ten days in the St. John's Penitentiary, but there was a note on the court record that read: "Remanded to Probation Officer." On the tenth day following, April 18, 1938, acting Sergeant Mahoney of the Newfoundland constabulary swore a similar complaint, the difference being that Shaver's correct name, if not correct age, first entered the record here. He was listed as "5 feet 10–½ inches, Eyes Blue, Hair Black, complexion Dark."[7]

On April 28 the court decreed that "Richard Shaver, 35, single, Ireland, Under Warrant" was being held over for deportation to the United States. He was escorted aboard the SS *Newfoundland*, bound for Boston, Massachusetts, via Halifax on April 30, 1938.

Where Is Richard Shaver?

"Teros, not deros is what I sell ... what people get is their own fault."— Richard Shaver

Louis Tendler undoubtedly wondered what happened to the man placed in his care. It had been a year since Shaver disappeared, with no word of his whereabouts. Ben Gurvitch was on edge, not knowing if or when Shaver might appear on his doorstep looking for his daughter.

Gurvitch would spend the rest of his life shielding Evelyn Ann (his adopted daughter) from her father Richard Shaver. The easiest way to explain her adoption was to tell her Shaver was dead, which is what Gurvitch did. An unexpected visit from Shaver would expose Gurvitch as a liar. It became a troublesome skeleton in the Gurvitch family closet. It rattled now and then as years went by, just to make sure Evelyn Ann knew it was there. "I couldn't get anything out of my family at all," she said. "My sister Rose, who is also my aunt, told me that she knew very little. She told me that he did come to ... see me, but they wouldn't let him because they told me that he died of sunstroke. So here they were caught in a lie, which wasn't their thing, but they lied about this because they felt they were protecting me. He wasn't Jewish either, so they were suspicious."[8]

The SS *Newfoundland* steamed its way into Boston Harbor on May 4, 1938. Shaver learned on his arrival that Boston had changed since his last visit. "A bunch called the Wasps had taken over the caverns under Boston and were hell — they got me in trouble," he said.[9] The trouble began on the day of his arrival, when Immigration Service Inspector J.W. Daley sequestered Shaver for a Board of Special Inquiry (BSI).

BSIs were standard procedure for passengers whose papers were questioned by the U.S. Immigration Service. Shaver's Canadian deportation was likely what flagged his name on the ship's passenger list. There was also some confusion about his citizenship. He claimed he was Irish in Canada, but reverted to U.S. citizenship on his arrival. Other strangeness may have revealed itself during the inquest, like talk of voices, underground rays, and his dero tail Max, but this is not known for certain.

Shaver gave Ziba's name and address to Inspector Daley, confirming that he had roots in Pennsylvania. The results of Shaver's BSI were duly recorded and placed in Immigration Service files. As years passed, the record went to the Washington, D.C., National Archive. After that, it went missing. This presents a problem. Was Shaver released after the inquiry or was he found out?

He was on the lam from Ypsilanti State Hospital, and his guardian was waiting for news of his whereabouts. If Daley checked out his story by contacting Ziba, he may have learned the truth — that Shaver was away from Ypsilanti without permission. Just how much Shaver told the board of inquiry about Max, Sue, Nydia, and the rays is not known. But individuals who exhibited aberrant behavior in front of Boston Immigration agents usually got a one-way ticket to Grafton State Hospital. Shaver told Ray Palmer that after being held over in Boston he was taken to Grafton, which he said was "about 20 miles outside of Boston."

Grafton — Gateway to Hell

"I hesitate very much to tell you the many things I have learned ... for you would think me insane and my work cannot afford that mischance."— Richard Shaver

Grafton was perhaps the most puzzling of Shaver's destinations. He withheld key elements from his Grafton narrative; information that would have revealed how his rambling ended and his enforced stay at Ionia State Hospital for the Criminally Insane began. Shaver's repeated references to Grafton and the phantasmagorical circumstances surrounding it made Grafton a turning point, eventually figuring into a series of stories with Shaver and the blind girl Nydia in the starring roles.

Shaver believed his Grafton experience was tied to the cavern dwellers, Sue and Nydia. They had been his allies since Canada, following him all the way from Newfoundland to Boston. The malignant dero, Max, also followed him.

Grafton, Massachusetts, was originally a Puritan settlement, purchased from the Nipmuck Indians in the early 1700s. It enjoyed relative quietude during its first 200 years, until Hollywood made it the location for *Ah, Wilderness* in 1935. On Shaver's arrival three years later, it still seemed harmless enough, except for one thing.

Grafton's largest employer was Grafton State Hospital, an insane asylum founded in 1912. The hospital was nestled in the suburb of North Grafton, and it was not uncommon for people exhibiting odd behaviors on the streets of Boston to find themselves taken to Grafton for observation.

It is not known for certain if a stay in Grafton State Hospital was the sole reason for Shaver's mysterious Grafton visit. Perry Mason would have called it circumstantial evidence. Still, one feature that adds allure to this possibility is the extensive tunnel system under the hospital grounds, which often became the refuge of its patients. Those who found their way into this underground labyrinth could hide for hours before being found out. Shaver described his Grafton experience to Ray Palmer in a vague but dramatic fashion in 1944:

> I was deported [to] Boston, see. Sue and her blind girl seemed to be on the ship.... I was held up for a day, but was told Sue was taken captive and taken ... to the town of Grafton....[10] She did a great deal for me in Newfoundland and came home with me on the same ship. As she left the ship, they kidnapped her ... to a stronghold about twenty miles from Boston. There after a time, she was killed. I myself was taken, through means I don't want to talk about, to the same location.[11]

Grafton and the cell where Shaver languished became a cornerstone of the Shaver Mystery legend. He told the story many times in his essays. It became his portal to the underworld, thanks to the blind cavern girl Nydia. His Grafton guard was defenseless against the power of the ancient machine Nydia used to free Shaver from his imprisonment. Thus Nydia earned a leading role in the Shaver Mystery. Shaver said he fell for her in a big way, and according to his stories, Nydia returned his longings.

An avid reader of mythology, history, and literature, Shaver named Nydia after Bulwer-Lytton's blind slave girl from *The Last Days of Pompeii*. Bulwer-Lytton's Nydia loved her Greek master, ultimately saving him from a devastating eruption of Mt. Vesuvius. Shaver's Nydia rescued him from his cell in Grafton. Both Nydias were young and blind, and wore similar clothing.

Nydia's proposal was simple: All Dick Shaver had to do was accompany her through the looking glass. "If you are willing, I can take you to a place where no police have ever shown their face, and where none ever will. You have only to agree to do as I tell you, without argument, for one year. I can free you quickly and in truth I need your services."[12] As the story goes, Shaver agreed. What happened next was something he told throughout his life, and the story never wavered. A guard came to his cell in the dead of night, dazed, as if mesmerized:

> By then I understood something of the powers of my cavern maid, and understood that he was a man under mental control. Behind him I could see reproduced the form of the blind girl, her transparent form bending over a huge old mechanism, her face a mask of concentration. The guard waited until I had emerged, almost cringing in my dread lest this was just another dream from which I might awaken, then he locked the cell door behind me.... We walked to the outer door that led from the corridor. This he opened and stood waiting to lock it again after I had passed through it.[13]

Shaver knew his story would be difficult for others to believe, but emphasized it *was* true, and that Grafton was the key. He told Ray Palmer, "[T]he incident I described in the story where Nydia gets me out took place outside of Boston in Grafton. She really controlled the guard and got me out. He unlocked the door in a trance in the middle of the night. I went to her ... the caves there were not deep, only a mile or so and water under that. The lower caves are sometimes filled with water."[14]

12

Ionia, 1938–1943

"[H]alf the guys in here hadn't ought to be here if there was any justice."—Butch Taylor, "The Mind Rovers"

Richard Shaver sat in the back seat of the Wayne County sheriff's black Ford sedan as a deputy navigated the winding driveway to Ionia State Hospital for the Criminally Insane. Through the car window, he glimpsed Ionia for the first time.

It was a pastoral setting except for the castle-like structures that were its centerpiece. Shadows from gothic stone towers crept over sloping green lawns and a murmuring creek with an ornamental water wheel. The wheel seemed out of place. It turned but had no mill house to go with it.

The meticulous grounds were a testament to the vigilance of Ionia's male patients who tended them daily. Shaver saw them pushing their wooden carts with tall steel wheels, as they scoured and trimmed and clipped every square foot of the hospital's 529 acres.

The hospital's admissions officer ushered Shaver into an examination room where a staff doctor asked him questions. The doctors asked the same questions of every new Ionia patient: "Can you tell me, please, your full name? Can you tell me the date, month and year? Say the alphabet. Count from one to fifty. Name the months. Repeat the Lord's Prayer. What is the largest river in America? What is the largest city in the world? What was the War of the Revolution? What was the Civil War?"[1] The doctor wrote down Shaver's replies and placed them in his new file. He was given a number: patient 3234.

This was definitely not Ypsilanti, where Shaver used to check in and out for visits with Sophie in Detroit and his family in Pennsylvania. The more he talked with other patients, the more he feared he would leave Ionia. The asylum averaged 1,500 patients, and each year about 15 of them were released.

Dr. Jonathan Metzl spent five years studying the charts of 1930s Ionia patients as research for his book *The Protest Psychosis*. He found that short sentences at Ionia often turned into lifetime incarcerations for no apparent reason:

> A number of charts contained yearly notes from patients to their doctors voicing such sentiments as "Doc, I really think I am cured," or "You have no right to keep me here after my sentence is over." These letters, stacked thirty deep in some files, signifying years of pleading and longing and anger, with thirty years of responses from clinicians urging "You are almost there," or "Perhaps next year." Invariably, the last note in each stack was a death certificate from the Ionia coroner.[2]

Shaver's visitors were few and far between. As his fictional protagonist Butch Taylor in his story "The Mind Rovers" said, "My people dropped me like a hot potato when I got framed into jail." This was as true of Dick Shaver as it was Butch Taylor. After he escaped Ypsilanti State Hospital, the state would see to it that he never did it again. But why the judge chose Ionia, a facility for the criminally insane, no one seems to know, including Shaver's daughter Evelyn Ann. She discussed it with Ray Palmer's widow Marjorie at the Palmers' Wisconsin farm in the early 1980s: "Marjorie Palmer thought he'd escaped. She said there was nothing wrong with him. Why they had him put in Ionia, I don't know. It was for people who were criminally insane. My sister could not tell me why he was there.... After my mother died, no one went to see him, but my sister Rose felt sorry for him. She visited him there and took him some flowers."[3]

Shaver's sister-in-law Rose Gurvitch was 18 at the time of her visit. Rose was born in 1920, which would have placed Shaver's admission to Ionia in 1938 or early 1939. But a dark chasm of unknowing exists prior to Ionia. Did the Immigration Service turn him over to Grafton State Hospital, which in turn notified his guardian Louis Tendler? Did Immigration release him, allowing him to continue his rambling from job to job until he came to the attention of law enforcement?

Shaver told Ray Palmer that he traveled to Reedville, Virginia, getting a job on a fishing boat after Grafton. No one knows for sure, and records are either buried in red tape or missing. Once he was in Ionia, his family seems to have dropped him, keeping his whereabouts a secret from friends and relatives.

With so little outside contact, Shaver began to despair. Instead of freeing him from the tormenting rays, Ionia made them stronger. His dreams and imaginings, guided by the voices, gave him access to a world Ionia could not take away from him. He learned more details of their science, of cataclysms that befell Earth 12,000 years ago.

In his spare time, which was plentiful, he learned the nuance of ray technology and eventually classified scores of rays, having experienced them firsthand. Most frequently used were stim ray, ben ray, aug ray, pain ray, crueling ray, police ray, medical ray, and penetray, but there were many others. Shaver came to believe that he alone held the key to a vast secret few others knew.

"It has taken me years of meditation and contact to connect my own ideas of what and where secret ray is, and I suspect ... I am almost the only man who really understands ray who has not joined them in the caves permanently."[4]

Shaver may well have been subjected to Metrozal shock therapy, which was routine treatment for Ionia patients diagnosed with schizophrenia. He once told Rap that Metrozal, the drug used to induce shock, was an ancient cure for a "sun robot." Since he often claimed he was the victim of sunstroke, this may have been his reasoning for the treatment.

In "A Witch in the Night," Shaver wrote that Nydia used a device that allowed him access to thought records of the vanished civilization of Lemuria. These records were the actual experiences of ancient people recorded onto reels. They gave Shaver a glimpse into a long-forgotten world. This is how he learned of Lemuria's science, history, and customs. His description of the device is worth noting:

> Into yet another chamber Nydia led me and guided me to a huge chair, like a giant's dentist chair, although the upholstery was missing.... There were several flexible metal straps, which she fastened about my wrists, waist, and neck. Then she took a strange helmet, fastened to a heavy cable, and placed it on my head.
> Lie back and relax. You will soon be another person entirely in another period of time. Do not let the double sensation of being two people at once worry you; it does not last long. This is the greatest experience the ancient wisdom of the caverns can offer you....
> I saw her throw a Titan-size switch on the wall and in a flash — I was not Dick Shaver, but another man entirely![5]

Nydia's similarity to a nurse administering a shock treatment is hard to ignore. Nydia spoke of his two personalities as if she were referring to his diagnosis. But the real question was and still is: Where *was* Richard Shaver and who was Nydia?

Patient 3234

> "You've got ten years of my life, and you can't give it back."— Butch Taylor, "The Mind Rovers"

Shaver recorded his notes about Lemurian science on the back of hospital breakage report forms. The machines within the caves were varied and numerous, he said, but most of his experiences could be attributed to three of them: the Telaug (a thought inducer), the "superior X-ray," and the "projector." These, he said, were not a figment of some science fiction writer's imagination but down-to-earth technology anyone could understand.

"[T]he simple answer to produce such phenomena is *not* fantastic and incredible," he wrote in a letter to Ray Palmer. "They are simple things that could be produced today.... Is a projector fantastic? Is an X-ray fantastic and antique? Is a movie machine coupled with X-ray to project pictures through a wall fantastic? That is all you have to admit to explain every one of these phenomena."[6]

The underground rooms that housed these machines were a wonder to behold: During his time spent with Nydia, Shaver saw many of them, "pillared by mighty simulations of trees, hung with crystalline, glittering fruits. In every one of these great rooms stood several of the enigmatic ancient mechanisms, themselves beautiful of form and shimmering with prismatic color." Some machines spoke to him incomprehensibly, with strange but beautiful-sounding words. "I suspect that they were equipped to announce their need of oil or other minor adjustments, as we would equip mechanisms with red lights," he said.[7] He walked on cavern floors "super polished and super hard ... inlaid with beautiful designs and symbols which I deduced were writings in the ancients' lost language."[8]

Shaver's information about the cavern world came from an inner knowing that was as real as the Empire State Building. He deduced answers by simple reasoning. For instance, during his rambling period he discovered that the rays followed him wherever he went. How did that happen? Like a good auto mechanic, Shaver went for the simplest diagnosis: He concluded the cave people used trucks to transport ray instruments through their vast cavern system. He put two and two together and it always came out as it should, and no one could convince him otherwise.

He also learned he was not the only Ionia patient to be railroaded into the state asylum system. As he saw it, fat cats made huge profits from the state, as long as they kept a steady stream of "crazies" locked up in the nut house. Shaver's fictional alter ego Butch Taylor learned to hate the backroom racketeers who kept him confined long after he should have been released. Butch revealed their M.O. in "The Mind Rovers": "All the docs have to do is say a man's crazy and he's sunk — and they ain't gonna say nothing else when their outfit gets six bucks a day for their keep."[9]

In "The Mind Rovers," the racketeer boss behind the scam was a former Nazi agent who ran a shadow company called the Ajax Film Exchange. Shaver said that once the police caught a potential victim, the doctors made sure he stayed crazy through various treatments. "I don't want any of them docs putting me under observation," Butch said. "You know what that means."[10]

And Shaver was right. Dr. Metzl learned years later that during the 1930s, 1940s, and 1950s, "prisoners often felt, rightly, that a trip to Ionia meant detention without end."[11]

Rap said that he learned of Shaver's stay in the asylum not from Shaver, but from a mysterious nurse who presented him with Shaver's medical records. The file allegedly revealed a "catatonic" Shaver, unable to take care of himself. Rap's claim is doubtful considering Shaver's outpatient visits with Sophie in Detroit, with his parents in Barto, and his escape as a tramp on the road. A nurse caught stealing patient records in order to turn them over to the editor of a science fiction magazine would jeopardize her job if not her career.

Rap later changed his story in a videotaped interview. Stan Deyo's 1977 production *UFOs Are Here!* reveals a 67-year-old Rap who, with camera rolling, said Shaver "originally claimed that he spent eight years in these caves.... I discovered later, much to my embarrassment, that he had spent these eight years in the Ypsilanti state hospital for the insane in Michigan. I contacted the doctors, and they said he was catatonic; they even had to feed him, in this imaginary world of his...."

The mystery nurse and Shaver's medical file were not mentioned. But Rap was no dummy. He must have known as early as 1945 of Shaver's stay in the asylum. Shaver's letters to him were full of talk about mental hospitals, incarcerations, voices in his head, fear of being arrested, and distrust of doctors. Rap's yarn about the mystery nurse and a catatonic Shaver lent credence to his personal theory that Shaver was, in fact, wandering the astral plane, not the underworld, during his incarceration.

The Telaug

> "For anyone who has since had messages beamed at them through their fillings or their TV sets, or via high-tech surveillance, MI5, Masonic lodges or UFOs, James Tilly Matthews is Patient Zero."—Mike Jay, The Air Loom Gang

Richard Shaver's telaug, with its ability to implant thoughts in his head (and generally confound those around him), has a precedent in the historical record. Englishman James Tilly Matthews described a similar machine in the 1790s. Matthews is credited with the first historical account of an "influencing machine." Like Shaver, he was taken on a short trip for a long stay in the asylum. In Matthews' case, it was London's infamous Bethlem Hospital, also known as Bedlam.

Matthews claimed that a machine called the Air Loom controlled him and members of the House of Commons, among others, by pneumatic power. The Air Loom, a huge machine with tubes, dials, and sails, projected invisible rays that influenced his behavior. A gang of miscreants operated the Air Loom in subterranean secrecy from a cellar near London Wall. Matthews eventually died in Bedlam, but not before contributing a vast and valuable library documenting his tormentors and their incredible power.

Matthews had the distinction of being diagnosed posthumously as the first case of paranoid schizophrenia. His affliction was simply called madness in 1797. It took the hindsight of 100 years of psychiatric progress to determine a new diagnosis, and to identify the source of his Air Loom. So-called influencing machines, defined at the turn of the 20th century, had roots in the industrial revolution and the quasi-scientific experiments of Franz Anton Mesmer, who demonstrated that people could be affected by invisible magnetic waves.

Like Shaver's cave people, Matthews' Air Loom gang had names and distinct personalities. Bill the King, Jack the Schoolmaster, Sir Archy, the Middle Man, and Augusta were Matthews' main characters. Shaver's revolved around Max, his dero tormentor, Nydia, his blind lover, and Sue.[12]

Matthews spent much of his time in Bedlam writing about the types and uses of the invisible rays that afflicted him. "Kiting," he said, was a ray that could put an idea into his head that "floats and undulates in the intellect for hours."[13] "Lengthening the Brain" gave his thoughts a funhouse mirror effect, causing "good sense to appear as insanity."[14] A "Bomb Bursting" ray can fill the stomach with gas and detonate it from afar, with "a horrid crash ... heard in the head."[15] Gaz-plucking, dream-workings, laugh-making, brain-sayings, foot-curving, vital-tearing, and lobster-cracking were also on Matthews' ray list.

The Air Loom Gang by Mike Jay is a thorough and thought-provoking study of the Matthews case, which has so many similarities to Shaver's experiences that Jay mentions him in passing. One of the most striking similarities is the importance the two men placed on their dreams, which were not dreams at all, but schemes placed by their tormentors. "It's significant that the part of Matthews' world where the gang have the most powerful and regular control over Matthews is in his dreams," Jay writes. "It's when he sleeps that they assemble their new projections, 'forcing their phantoms and grotesque images on his languid intellect.' They begin to manipulate 'puppets of uncouth shape, and of various descriptions' into obscene travesties of the waking world.... When he wakes, they have all the information they need to plot his assailment for the following day."[16]

Shaver, too, confirmed the hidden source of his dreams: "That night I slept, knowing *they* would come in my sleep to see who this was who *knew*, and what I was doing in their city. In my sleep they came, and that is always like a dream."[17]

Shaver's Science

"The truth is you can't ever listen to ray about anything because of tamper, and a surface man can never be sure a certain message is not tamper because they are so expert at imitation...."— Richard Shaver

At what point Shaver began to expound scientific theories based on Lemurian physics is a mystery like many others nested within the many-layered Shaver Mystery. It began, more than likely, when Shaver sought the source of the rays that bombarded him. He knew they were real, but wanted scientific proof. In search of an answer, he mined a vein of fringe physics that was championed by a handful of early 20th century scientists. Their research confirmed he was on the right track. He told Ray Palmer of his interest in these scientists, which probably began in Ionia, when he had plenty of time for rumination and study.

For a time in the early 1940s, he corresponded with Professor Albert Cushing Crehore (1868–1958), a scientist whose theories about molecules led him to postulate the nature of gravity. According to Crehore, the speed and movement of molecules within a charged electric field was its source. His book *Analysis of the Cause of Gravitation* inspired other researchers to experiment with anti-gravity drives for spaceships. This, and Crehore's thoughts on the prevention of aging, inspired Shaver. He suggested that Ray Palmer consult with Crehore on some of the finer points of Shaver Mystery science.

"Am enclosing some research I have had done by Crehore on age — I have had in mind a pamphlet including quotes from authorities and have had some work done by Crehore before — he found George Crile's book on *The Bipolar Theory* for me when I could not buy it. I have corresponded with him for some time and recommend him to you if you do not already have anyone working on research along this line.... He is honest, reliable, and enthusiastic."[18]

It was about this time, 1945, that Shaver wrote a letter to Albert Einstein detailing his age theory. This turned out to be a bad idea, when Einstein sent Shaver a reply. He gave two thumbs down on Shaver's theory that humans could live forever in hermetically sealed chambers with purified food, water and air. Einstein's off-the-cuff dismissal angered Shaver mightily. Nevertheless, he continued his research.

Shaver eventually came up with his own theory of gravity, explaining it within the context of the ancient science of Earth. It became one of Ray Palmer's scientific proofs of the Shaver Mystery. Gravity is a push, not a pull in Shaver's theory, caused by the friction of a universal element permeating all space called exd.

Exd, Shaver explained, is an invisible ash — the disintegrated matter of super-novas. It permeates the entire universe. The ash is so fine it can become energy, and is attracted to larger accumulations of matter like planets and suns. The friction that exd creates in the process of being absorbed into planetary bodies is what we experience as gravity. In other words, the apple that dropped on Newton's head was pushed off the tree by exd particles. This constant accumulation of exd in a celestial body increases its size over a vast period of time. Hence, exd is an integrant process in the universe, as opposed to disintegrant processes, which destroy.

The foundation for Shaver's new science was a delicate balance of two universal forces: *de* disintegrant, and *te* integrant. Even his cave people reflect these concepts: The dero represent disintegrant force and the tero the integrant. It was easy to tell who is good or evil by their allegiance to *te* or *de* universal energies. Shaver expounded at length on the theory of *de* and *te*, penciling notes on sheets of pulp paper during the development of the Shaver Mystery between 1943 and 1944.

He determined that Atlans had learned how to neutralize the exd flow with a kind of anti-gravitational device on their spaceships, explained in a footnote of his debut story "I Remember Lemuria!" in *Amazing Stories*:

> Light speed is due to "escape velocity" on the sun, which is not large. This speed is a constant to our measurement because the friction of exd, which fills all space, holds down any increase unless there is more impetus. The escape velocity of light from a vaster sun than ours is higher, but once again exd slows the light speed down to its constant by friction, so that when it reaches the vicinity of our sun, no appreciable difference is to be noted. A body can travel at many times the exd constant, under additional impetus, such as rocket explosions. A ship whose weight is reduced to a very little by a reverse gravity beam can attain a great speed with a very small rocket. Once beyond the limits of matter, gravity ceases and the ship becomes weightless.[19]

Shaver theorized there are ways to stop the aging process, which he believed was caused by harmful solar emissions. The ebb and flow of the sun's magnetic fields produce both integrant and disintegrant energies. He believed there was a way to filter out the destructive, disintegrant rays that were harmful to life on Earth. He cited the Zeeman Effect as proof.

The Zeeman Effect demonstrates that a beam of light can split into several atomic-energy levels simply by introducing a magnetic field at the light source. Shaver surmised the disintegrant energy could be filtered out, resulting in the sun's beneficial rays falling to Earth, thus slowing if not halting the aging process. Shaver said, "By varying the proportionate strength of the unit rays making up the multi-beam [we might] control the nature and form, even the character of animals grown under the beam's beneficial force."[20] This would include altering the nature of human beings.

Shaver told Rap that much of his information on life extension came from his cave

One page of Shaver's notes on the concept of *de* and *te*, probably written around 1944. Richard Horton saved these notes from oblivion in the early 1950s, while he was working on the Shavers' farm.

contacts, who "had the problem of age whipped." The revelation came to him during his convalescence in Newfoundland. How much of it came from the caves and how much from George Crile or Raymond Pearl (who published *Biology of Death* in 1922) is not known, but Shaver enthusiastically endorsed both men's work.

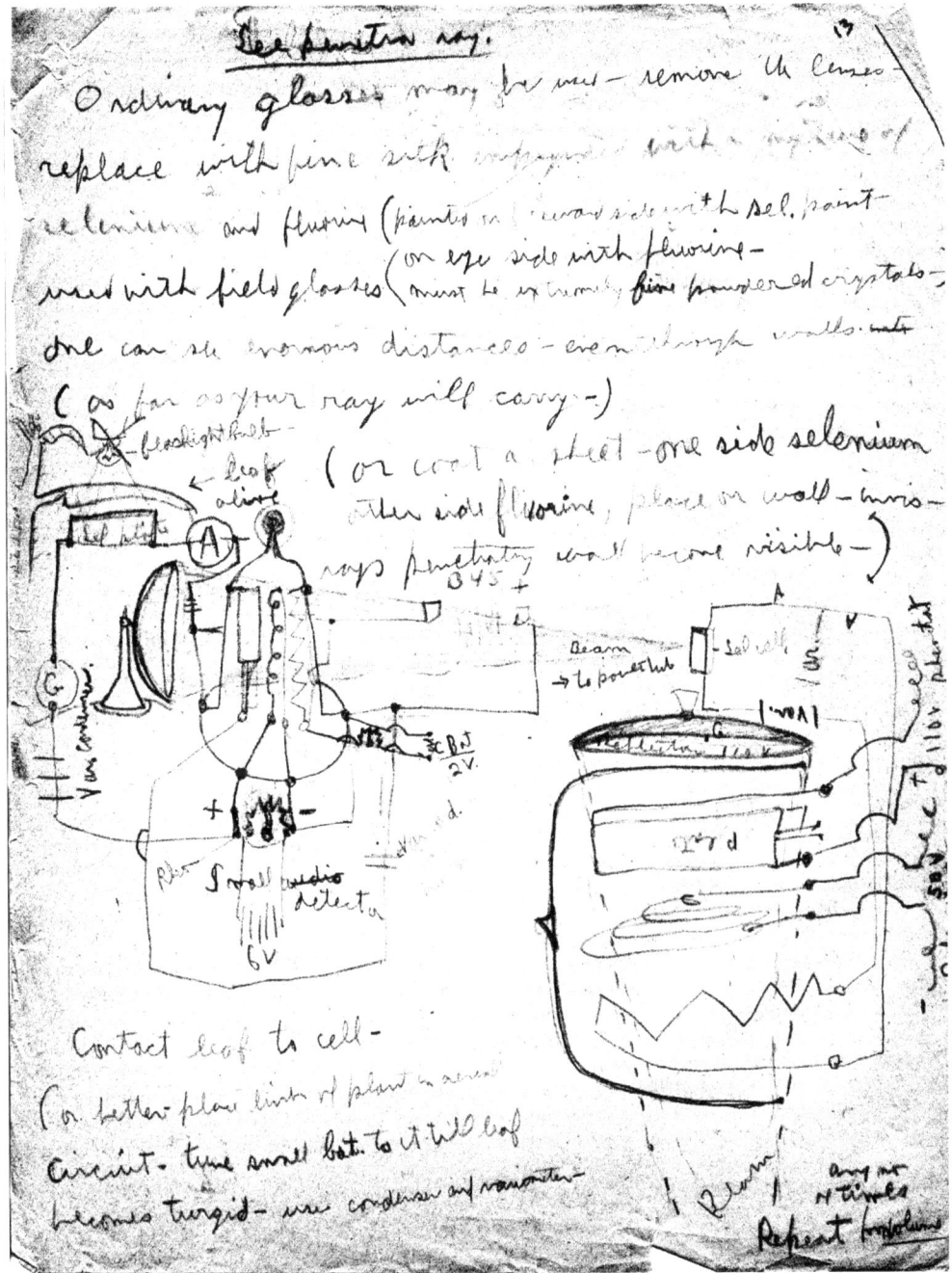

One page of Shaver's notes and diagrams of the science he learned from the thought records of the cave people. This was probably written after he got out of Ionia State Hospital in 1943.

One theory built upon another. In time, Shaver realized that his beneficial rays might be put to practical use. He tried to convince Rap to assemble a team of scientists to build a "Life Chamber." The chamber would prove his theory that by filtering the harmful rays of the sun, life could be extended far beyond man's meager lifespan.

The description of his Life Chamber calls to mind another unconventional life extension researcher, Wilhelm Reich, who developed an Orgone (life force) accumulator resembling an electrical condenser that used layers of organic materials. In a fictional short story that Shaver sent to Rap in a letter, the Atlan "Wizard of Growth Cultures" explained the life chamber's construction:

> I prepared insulated chambers, with both vacuum walls and condenser walls. That is, I used layers of dielectric and layers of metal foil alternately, some of them hundreds of layers thick. Upon each of these sheets of foil I placed electric charges of varying attunement, running progressively through the whole range of wavelengths.... Within these tiny sealed worlds I found I could control all the factors of environment completely.... I have discovered that creatures in many types of these sealed little worlds do not die, they do not even become adult. They just keep growing in strength and size and speed of activity.[21]

This echoed the research of Raymond Pearl, who wrote "That the individual cells and tissues of the body, in and by themselves are potentially immortal...."[22] Shaver also drew upon another of his scientific mentors, George Crile, Sr. (1864–1943). Crile's book *The Phenomenon of Life, a Radio Electric Interpretation* (1936) spelled out his crusade to determine the cause of death at the cellular level.

Crile said that a cell's nucleus holds a positive charge, while its cytoplasm holds a negative charge. He believed the acid-alkali balance between nucleus and cytoplasm created tension that furnished an electrical charge to the cell. This spark of electricity is what we call life, he said. Absence of this delicate balance — stasis — means death. The key here was to keep the tension between nucleus and cytoplasm going. Crile's work enshrined him in Shaver's eyes.

Shaver also followed the work of Alexis Carrel, especially his "immortal chicken heart" experiment. Carrel's chicken heart tissue began life in 1912 and was still alive 20 years later. It was a piece of embryonic heart tissue that lived in a super-purified solution in Carrel's lab, where it appeared to be immune to the aging process. Carrel's nutrient solution was processed in a centrifuge to remove all impurities. Shaver brought up the immortal chicken heart whenever he spoke about his theory on life extension.

The chicken heart experiment was never replicated by anyone but Carrel, and because of that Carrel has been discredited, though it seemed valid at the time. Scientists now believe Carrel may have inadvertently added new cells to his chicken heart through the nutrient solution. But during Shaver's day, Carrel was lauded as a pioneer in the crusade against age.

Prodigal Son

"I have been out of circulation — in the wilds — for some ten years." — Richard Shaver

Just as mysteriously as he was committed to Ionia, Shaver was discharged in May 1943. This may have been due to his father's ill health, and the fact that his mother Grace was about to lose her only support. Grace was on good terms with Louis Tendler, having assisted him with the Gurvitch adoption. She could have asked Tendler to put in a good word with

Richard's doctor to consider him for release under special circumstances. The doctors, of course, would have to concur that he was capable of living and working on the outside, and apparently they believed he could. After nearly five years a prisoner in Ionia, Shaver was at last a free man.

The welcome mat was conspicuously absent on his return to the family fold. Though Grace and Ziba were willing to take him in for practical reasons, his sisters and brother were less magnanimous. Shaver's third wife Dottie described his homecoming in an August 24, 1980, interview: "They were so scared their reputations would be marred that they kept it a secret. When he got out, he went to visit his older brother Donald in Pennsylvania; he drove there in his Dodge. When he got there, his sister-in-law wouldn't let him in the house."

On returning to Bittersweet Hollow Farm, Dick found his father clinging to life. Grace was caring for him. She was a retired schoolteacher now, after 30 years of service. Ziba knew he was dying, and because the other children had moved away to demanding jobs or marriages, he knew Grace and Dick could help each other. She needed someone to tend to the farm and watch after her. He needed someone to help him integrate back into a normal life.

Dick would take care of Grace off and on for the rest of her life, which is why his sister Catherine Claire begrudgingly helped him with living expenses whenever he fell on hard times, which he often did.

Ziba died on August 10, 1943, three months after his son's release. The family buried him in the Fairmount Springs Cemetery, along Old Country Road in Grace's hometown of Fairmount. With the funeral behind him and his siblings gone, Dick was head of the household. He got a job at the Bethlehem Steel plant in nearby Allentown. It had shifted production to the war effort.

But Dick never forgot his conversations with Tate and their shared dream to become accomplished writers. He dug into an old trunk Grace had stored in the farmhouse and found his early manuscripts were still there, as were Tate's unpublished works. He began to revive his stalled career, reworking stories and writing new ones. He bought *Writers' Digest* and sent stories to pulp magazines.

There was a marked change of direction since his first attempt at writing. The voices had taught him there was something far more important to write than mere fictional stories. He read books on physics, biology, and mythology, and studied the elements of radio hoping to learn how to build a telaug, the telepathic machine that put thoughts in his head. He was also working on his Mantong alphabet—and getting plenty of rejection slips in the bargain.

Shaver worked his way up to crane operator on the graveyard shift at Bethlehem Steel. Sometimes work was slow, so he jotted notes for stories as he lounged in the cab of his crane. How he managed to keep his stays at two state asylums a secret from the hiring boss is a mystery, but the shortage of male workers on the home front got him the job without a hitch. He rented a room in a cheap Allentown hotel and came home to check on Grace most weekends.

Grace wanted Dick to avoid further mishaps with the law and was anxious for him to "straighten himself out." Now that he had a steady job, she felt he should settle down and marry. He found a fiancée through a *Lonely Hearts* magazine ad: secretary Virginia Fenwick, 29, formerly of St. Louis, Missouri. Shaver had a good job, needed female companionship, and she was willing.

They married on January 29, 1944. Unwilling to reveal his past, he failed to mention Ionia. As Shaver filled out his marriage certificate, he answered "No" to the question, "Has applicant within five years been an inmate of any county asylum or house for indigent persons?" This came back to haunt him within a few short weeks, when Fenwick saw documents, carelessly left out, that revealed her husband's history in the asylum. She packed her bags and took the next train to Philadelphia. The divorce papers arrived by mail four weeks later.[23]

Regardless of the setback, Shaver was enjoying life as a free man. During his short-lived marriage, he met a feisty defense worker named Dorothy Erb at a local juke joint. Everyone called her Dottie, and she worked the 11 A.M. to 7 P.M. shift at a nearby manufacturing plant. She was getting a divorce too, she said.

"He was very dignified," Dottie recalled. "He always was and always has been. He was different, not like everybody else. He said 'Hello,' and we got into a conversation every day for the next three weeks. He said that he wrote, but I didn't know what until about a year later."[24]

When his divorce to Fenwick became final, Dick and Dottie began to get serious. Though Dottie never did warm to Dick's talk of rays and cave people, she had her own set of supernatural beliefs and experiences. At the age of 12, she began to see strange people who looked like witches and ogres lurking about the house. Her family concluded that a jealous aunt had put a hex on her, and they took her to a German hex doctor to have it removed. From then on she was a firm believer in witchcraft. She hung a Pennsylvania Dutch hex sign in her house to ward off witches, until she finally became a devoted Baptist in the 1960s.

Dick eventually moved Dottie onto the Shaver farm to "take care of the house." That was when she realized the modest farmhouse had its share of Pennsylvania supernatural phenomena. "That was a funny section of the country," she explained. "You'd hear the gate open and nobody'd be there, and hear car accidents when there were no cars on the highway in front of the house. That was a screwy place."[25]

Grace thought Dottie was far too vulgar; not what her son needed to dispel the voices. Dottie proved otherwise. "Well, he took me home to meet his mama. Mother hated me. She said I wasn't educated enough to do what he needed. But then later on he took me in, and what a help I was. I pulled him out of it, you know, the voices and things like that, in his head...."[26] Dottie was optimistic. She always was when it came to Dick. Their marriage came a year later.

1944

"My own daughter by my first wife is eight or nine. I never see her. Her mother's people ... are angry at me over a long absence which was unavoidable."— Richard Shaver

Dick Shaver kept writing and mailing manuscripts. He was on a crusade to expose corruption in the U.S. mental hospital system, "Where all treatment is torture, and all medicine is poison...."[27] It was almost as important as spreading the word about his discovery of the Mantong alphabet. In both cases he had a message and a burning desire to tell his story, up to a point. Either through self-preservation or on advice from Grace, he kept his mouth shut about Ionia, rays, and the cave people during polite conversation. Revealing too much information to the wrong people, as he had learned the hard way, had serious consequences. But in his writing, he was willing to reveal all.

In the summer of 1943 he sent a letter, along with the latest version of his Mantong alphabet, to the editor of *Amazing Stories*. According to *Writers' Digest*, the editor was Raymond A. Palmer. The letter fell on fertile ground. He got a reply from the editor, asking for more material. Not only that, he wanted to know more about Shaver's ray people. Thus began Shaver's voluminous correspondence with Ray Palmer. Things were indeed looking up.

Shaver had not forgotten his daughter Evelyn Ann, and often wondered what she had become in the years of his absence. He sent copies of his published stories in *Amazing* to her sister Rose, the only Gurvitch other than Sophie who showed him kindness. He hoped Rose would give them to Evelyn Ann. Once he tried to see his daughter at school, away from Star Hardware and Paints, where she lived upstairs. The family got wind of Shaver's plan from the school principal. Evelyn Ann remembers,

> What happened in school was the principal called me into the office and asked me what my dad's name was. It seemed odd to me. My grandfather was my legal, adopted father.... So I said, "Richard Shaver" and went home for lunch. I told my grandmother and she hit the ceiling. "Don't you ever tell anyone that, your father is Benjamin Gurvitch!" I was confused.
>
> That day they whisked me out a side door at school at the end of the day. I was picked up by a family friend who had a car. She took me to her house, which was in the cultural center of Detroit. From there my brother-in-law picked me up and I went to my sister Rose's house. She was just married and living in a flat on the west side.
>
> I guess they had some plans to go to a party, and left me in bed and I was lying in bed looking up in the closet, and I saw some magazines. With nothing else to do, I dragged them down, and looking through them, I found a little note that said "Give these mags to little Ann. Signed, Dick." I didn't know Richard was "Dick." But somehow I knew these were my father's.[28]

She fell asleep, she said, and on waking the next morning the magazines were gone. They went back with the skeleton in the Gurvitch family closet. If it could talk, the skeleton could explain why Evelyn Ann never knew her father, and why he was sentenced to ten years in the Michigan state hospital system.

PART III

The Rise and Fall of the Shaver Mystery, 1945–1948

13

Howard Browne

"If fans have cosmic minds, as some have claimed, the cosmos is in big trouble."—G.W. Page

Ray Palmer and Howard Browne took to each other like oil and water. Scientifically they behaved as nature intended: When put together, they produced an appealing rainbow sheen. But as any scientist will tell you, only one comes out on top.

Rap was already a seasoned editor with a snappy office, a gorgeous secretary and thousands of adoring fans by the time Browne arrived on the scene in 1942. Fate had plucked him from the oblivion of a Chicago "No Money Down — Three Full Years to Pay" furniture store credit office where he endured five dreary years "repossessing beds from under sick women."[1] An unhappy marriage added to his despair, and he spent a sizable chunk of time dreaming of a world without furniture payment plans and wives. A diehard Raymond Chandler fan, Browne decided the glamorous life of a writer was the way to go and he set out to change his career.

Like most of Rap's writers, including Rap himself, Browne was self-taught. This was not enough to keep him from launching his new career to "Enjoy the good life, buy an A-frame chalet in Switzerland, [and] make time with the pretty girls."[2] He enrolled in a typing course and polished his grammar and punctuation. With his new typing skills, he went to work pounding out two detective yarns that — with help from the U.S. Postal Service — found their way to the desk of Bernard G. Davis, managing editor of the Ziff-Davis Publishing Company.

This is where the miracle of Browne's story comes in, because at that very moment, Davis was in need of an editor for his newest magazine, *Mammoth Detective*. It may seem odd in the world of today, but Davis hired Browne entirely on the weight of his first two submissions. As a writer, Browne was an unknown. His editorial experience was as thin as a smoke ring. But Davis saw his potential as a writer, a damn good one who would know a good story when he saw it, and for that he was just what he needed. He hired Howard Browne on the spot.

Then the other shoe dropped. Davis flipped the switch of his intercom: "Would you ask Mr. Palmer to come in?" Rap entered. After formal introductions, Davis turned to Browne, "Since *Mammoth Detective* is still a quarterly, you'll be free to give Ray a hand with *Amazing* and *Fantastic*," he said.[3] On his way out, Rap handed Browne a manual on proofreading symbols. He and Rap would share the same office and the same secretary.

That was A-OK with Browne: "Every secretary was well under thirty and a beauty pageant finalist, while the receptionist had to have been a former Miss America."[4] Browne's enthusiasm grew, but not for science fiction. Everyone in the office knew that he was a detective fiction fan. He had no use for SF. And so for the next five years he helped Rap with *Amazing* and *Fantastic* as he edited *Mammoth Detective*.

It was during this time that Browne began work on a new series of detective novels — his Paul Pine series. Writing under the name John Evans, he kept his detective novels on the QT at work. That is, until he ran into Bill Hamling and Chester Geier at the office one day. Both Hamling and Geier had read the first John Evans novel, *Halo in Blood* (1946), and thought it a "top flight job" according to Geier, who remembered the encounter that day with Browne:

> Bill Hamling and I read the story when it appeared.... I think Browne recommended it to Bill, but without revealing that he was the author. Not long afterward, Browne showed Hamling and me the start of a story he was working on, with the name "John Evans" on the title page. Hamling was amazed, and exclaimed, "Why, you son of a bitch!" Browne sort of shrugged it off and said, "What's the matter?" Hamling said, "You never told me you were John Evans."[5]

Some 60 years after that incident, Hamling still considered Browne a member of Rap's inner circle. But even card-carrying members were not obligated to like one another. "[Howard] was a member of the Ziff-Davis editorial department, and that's the only reason he ever got connected with Ray Palmer, or me, for that matter. Howard never gave a shit about Ray. And Ray simply didn't like the detective magazines.... Howard Browne strictly was ... with guys like Paul Fairman and did only the detective magazines. He didn't give a shit about science fiction —*at all*!"[6]

Wastebasket of Discontent

"I am the most curious person I know."— Ray Palmer

After reading excerpts of Richard Shaver's letter aloud for the amusement of his fellow editors, Browne crumpled it into a ball and tossed it in the circular file. Then Rap did something strange. He got up from his desk, walked over to the wastebasket and retrieved the letter. With that, he put a shiner on Browne's vulnerable ego.

He smoothed out Shaver's letter and handed it back to Browne with the admonition, "And you call yourself an editor? Run the entire thing in next issue's letter column."[7] Browne was dumbfounded, recounting the incident in his memoir. "I said, 'As a fledgling editor anxious to learn the trade, I'd love to know why you want it run.' He gave me his cherub-type smile. 'One of these days,' he said, 'I'll tell you why.'"[8]

This is the question that seems to have outlived them both. Why did Rap run a letter that Browne so roundly ridiculed? Several theories have been advanced, though none in themselves have satisfied historians. Taken as a group, they may hold the answer.

1. Rap ran the letter because he sensed significant truths in what Shaver had to say. (This is what Shaver thought.)

2. He ran it because he was P.T. Barnum incarnate and knew controversy would sell his magazines. (This is what Browne thought.)

3. He ran it to prove a point to Browne, his assistant editor. (This was what Rap claimed.)

4. He ran it because Browne called Shaver a nut and a crackpot, which automatically conferred underdog status to Shaver. (Due to his own life experience, Rap favored the underdog.)

5. All of the above.

Reader response to Shaver's letter hit the Ziff-Davis mailroom with gale force. In retrospect, Rap would remember the incident much like the courtroom scene in *Miracle on 34th Street*, when mail sacks full of letters addressed to "Santa Claus, North Pole" were wheeled into the courtroom; the letters were proof of the existence of Santa Claus. Rap told the story of those letters to his dying day. There were thousands of them, he said, about 50,000 by his reckoning. It became a high-water mark of his career, and yet it turned hardcore fandom against him in a big way. As the letters rolled in, Browne was finally given his long-awaited answer: "Now you know why I wanted that first article of Shaver's run," Rap said (as told by Browne).

"Tell me anyway," Browne replied.

"Any editor worth his salt has one goal: to increase circulation figures. When an opportunity to do that comes along, he has to know how to recognize it, make it work for profit."[9]

Chester S. Geier and William L. Hamling

"Everybody in those days tied in to somebody in the inner circle."—Bill Hamling, 2009

Army Lieutenant William L. Hamling, former *Stardust* executive editor, dropped by Rap's office in February 1944. He told Rap of a run-in with a landmine that had taken him out of the war. *Amazing*'s all-serviceman–written issue was coming up, and Hamling handed his contribution to Rap in person; he also explained that he was back in Chicago for the duration, determined to make his mark as a writer, preferably working side by side with his old mentor, Rap.

Hamling and Lane Tech High School buddy Chester S. Geier picked up where they had left off. Geier's hearing, or lack of it, exempted him from military service, and they began cranking out pulp stories from a shared office on Lawrence Avenue in Chicago. Most of their stories were produced for Ziff-Davis publications, written to Rap's specifications. Hamling edged ever closer to Rap's inner circle and a desk of his own at Ziff-Davis. Over time he became one of Rap's closest friends and confidants. Hamling said:

> I used to baby-sit Ray Palmer's children. Ray Palmer was my closest friend. As far as Dick Shaver ... was concerned, Ray discovered the guy because he had submitted a manuscript.... That brought Shaver into Ray's and my life. I said, "You know, Ray, this guy's a nut." And Ray said, "But he has a subject that will sell copies of *Amazing Stories* and we work for the Ziff-Davis people." Dick Shaver became a good friend of both of us, in addition to his professional status as a writer. He didn't know how to write properly, and Ray spent half of his goddamn time editing Shaver's manuscripts so they could be published.[10]

Hamling was an agnostic as far as Shaver's voices were concerned. Unlike Browne, Hamling never criticized Rap's handling of the Shaver Mystery. Rap had given Hamling his first and second biggest breaks of his career—something he would never forget. Loyal to a fault, Hamling sided with Rap and the Shaver Mystery even when fandom turned savagely against it. In 2009 Hamling said:

> [The Shaver Mystery] was not done maliciously. Palmer was a believer, and he wasn't a phony. I'll verify that. He was a top-drawer editor, and he had the record to prove it. Ray had strong convictions. He really and factually believed Shaver, but he didn't promulgate fantasy ideas out of it. He *molded* the Shaver Mystery as a record of an era of hidden truth. I always used to laugh

at that kind of thing, but you know, who the hell am I? I don't know whether that's truth or fiction. I was there, but I don't know if it's true or not.[11]

As Rap expanded the Mystery and *Amazing*'s circulation rose, Browne faded into the shadows. Rap had become the alpha dog of pulp editors. He christened his new promotion The Shaver Mystery, using the name of the man whose revelations altered the course of *Amazing Stories*. It was all about circulation and it was all about hidden truths, as Hamling said. Rap, a mystic by nature, was drawn to Shaver's worldview. He took the parts that fascinated him and worked them into a personal vision of the universe.

Sixty years removed from the Chicago Loop and Ziff-Davis Publishing, Bill Hamling relaxed behind the small, tidy desk in his Arthur Elrod–designed Palm Springs mansion. Behind him, floor-to-ceiling windows faced a lush, palm tree–shaded swimming pool. He was dressed as a Southern Californian — Bermuda shorts and polo shirt, his hand-carved cane propped against the desk. In time and place, he was as far removed from his Chicago roots as an Eskimo kayaking down North Palm Canyon Drive. He said he would never forget his years with Rap, which he fondly recalled in his office that day.

"Ray was actually the father of the Shaver Mystery, not Shaver," he explained. "You have to find out who Ray Palmer was. Ray took the essence of what Shaver gave him and he molded it. That's what he did. Dick Shaver didn't like some of the embellishments of the Shaver Mystery."[12]

The "mystery" did in fact come from Rap, a man whose life was a mystery long before Shaver appeared on the scene. It was Rap who chose the name Shaver *Mystery*. Why not the Shaver *Terror*, or the Shaver *Enigma*, or any number of other titles? Rap explained his reasoning years later. A mystery, he said, is something that should never be solved because it encourages thoughtful curiosity. A mystery makes one *think*, he said. Speaking at a 1977 conference on flying saucers a few months before his death, Rap discussed the flying saucer enigma as if he were talking about Shaver's mystery: "If we knew exactly what the flying saucers were ... we would have solved the mystery, returned to boredom, and stopped thinking again. I hope we never really solve the mystery of the saucers...."[13]

Rap's desire to promote mystery as an exercise in thinking came from his conviction that 99 percent of the population is brainwashed by educators and religion. Through his judicious use of entertaining SF and a confrontational editorial style, he hoped to change the world. He felt that science fiction and provocative ideas inspire people to think for themselves and become useful citizens, and this was far better than a classroom education.

Some call it education; I call it mental enchainment. We *believe* too much. We *believe* Einstein, we don't *understand* him! We *believe* the textbooks, when we should *constantly question* them. If they are *right*, our questions won't destroy them. If they are wrong, their wrongness *will* destroy us![14]

...I see so many of you asleep, hypnotized by "facts" and by "knowledge." There is only the mysterious horizon beyond which lay unborn facts, and unresearched and unproved knowledge. If you don't see that, you are hopeless.[15]

The Care and Feeding of a Mystery

"Why do we die? What is gravity? How did life come to Earth? Are there beings on other worlds? Did ancient Mu exist? If you have any of the answers to these questions, they are either wrong or inadequate! The true answers are contained in the True Story

of Lemuria! *And when we have completed the assembling of a mass of sensational theory and fact and a thrilling story of adventure, we intend to present it to you, take it or leave it. But we believe it to be true!"*— Ray Palmer

Rap's frantic behind-the-scenes buildup to the Shaver Mystery shifted into high gear in May 1944. He had an open line to Shaver and was burning the midnight oil preparing the first installment of what would become a series of stories based on information from Shaver's voices, that is, the cave people. He began with a major rewrite on a rambling 10,000-word manuscript Shaver called "A Warning to Future Man." Soon it would become a 31,000-word science fiction adventure epic worthy of Rap's legendary plotting skills. Rap kept Shaver apprised of his progress: "I am now ready to begin the writing of the fiction story which must be published first. I feel that with this to go on, many people will write me, and add to what we already have. Once we have several hundred interested, we can proceed to more earnest work. I propose a book outlining this new 'or old' science in complete detail. It would probably have to be privately published."[16]

Instead of coaching Shaver to rewrite his own manuscript as he did with other new writers, Rap rewrote it himself. This would not only get it into print sooner, but also allowed him to mold Shaver's material to his liking. Rap was in the process of constructing his vision of what the Shaver Mystery should be, while retaining Shaver's basic story elements and characters. A rapid-fire correspondence ensued. Rap told Shaver to send all the fiction he had on hand.

But Rap's plan to debut Shaver's first story hit a snag. Hitler's war was drying up the paper supply. Ziff-Davis published only five issues of *Amazing Stories* in 1944, and the paper shortage was about to slow the publishing schedule even further, making it a quarterly beginning with the March 1945 issue. With only four issues allotted for *Amazing Stories* in 1945, Rap planned every cover would feature his new Shaver Mystery — a "new wave" in science fiction.

While Rap saw in Shaver a potential sensation, Shaver saw Rap as a means to spread the word of imminent danger; hence the title of his original manuscript, "A Warning to Future Man." He immersed Rap in the strange world of his everyday life — the voices in his head that were not his own, the threat posed by the deros, rays (both good and bad), the cause of human aging, the science of *de* and *te*, Earth's pre-history, the Mantong alphabet, and the subterranean machines that plagued him. The amount of information was overwhelming, but Rap was a good student and did his homework.

He confessed to Shaver that he, too, was not immune to the strange influences he spoke about; "tamper," Shaver called it. Their mutual understanding established a kinship, creating an inner circle within Rap's inner circle. They were a team.

"I am not troubled with dero, although they have not neglected me," Rap told Shaver. "I perhaps am fortunate in being able to see through their tricks easily. Only once was I duped, and it gave me an advantage, because ever after I was able to see through their attempts.... I have gotten where I am by direct intent and constant direction by these same sources. And I haven't been tripped up because I saw the pitfalls first."[17]

Shaver later began to have doubts about that. Nevertheless, his letters arrived nearly every day at Rap's Chicago office. Rap eventually bound Shaver's huge letter file into a single volume for future use. These letters, some of them reprinted in Rap's *Hidden World* magazine series, provide ample proof that although Rap was the brainchild of the Shaver Mystery, they developed it as a team, at least until disagreements arose.

Shaver changed the name of "A Warning to Future Man" to "Ware On," but Rap ignored both titles. He called it "I Remember Lemuria!" Visions of sequels danced in Rap's head, and Shaver was only too happy to oblige by sending more material. He was on a roll and, with Rap's encouragement, writing new yarns and refurbishing old ones based on information the mysterious voices had been giving him for more than ten years.

14

Lemuria, My Lemuria

"Now, on the threshold of 1945, we have finally realized that the future has caught up with us."— Ray Palmer

December 1944. Snow settled over the Loop like a goose down comforter. On the 22nd floor at 608 South Dearborn Street, Rap was at his typewriter, fingers flying so fast they were barely visible to the human eye. His typing prowess was another of his acknowledged super-abilities; even Howard Browne gave him that. Sometimes he topped speeds of 90 to 100 words per minute, a tidal wave of words flooding the page. Rap was writing his editorial for the March 1945 issue, making his case for "the next big thing" in science fiction — "I Remember Lemuria!":

> Primarily, the concept of *Amazing Stories* was that of a stimulus to imagination.... For several years we have been wondering as much as you what that new evolution in science fiction would be. Now, with this issue, we believe we have the answer.
>
> Beginning with this issue, we are introducing something new in stories of the past. We are taking the strange things that have always made Man wonder ... and are projecting them into a field of logic in an effort to arrive at truth by beginning with what is accepted as fantasy.[1]

Rap was holding back a punch. He was still not ready to admit, as Shaver had, that these revelations were based on fact. So Rap came up with his first interpretation of Shaver's claims — one of many that would ruffle Shaver's feathers. He said the story sprang from Shaver's racial memory: "We have begun to tap one of the most mysterious corners of Man's mind, and with truly amazing results, as you will discover when you read this first story. Something new in science fiction is here!"[2] Rap announced his plan to document his readers' racial memories too, with the hope that his work "may lead to the answer to many mysteries of the past that have been hidden from the eye of research up to now."[3]

Instead of conquering distant planets in Man's future, Rap returned to the distant past. He began to ponder the life of Cro-Magnon man, and marveled at the mysteries of Angkor Wat. He challenged his readers in editorials. How were the pyramids built? What about the Chinese legends of visitors who came to Earth from the moon? More importantly, what was "orichalcum," the Lemurian metal Shaver described in "I Remember Lemuria!"? It was science fiction come to life. It was more than a pulp story; it was alive and all around us, waiting to be discovered if we just opened our eyes.

The die was cast.

Amazing Colossal Mystery

"I feel that the first thing to do is to marshal together all we know, and get it published."— Ray Palmer, 1944

Shaver's subterranean worldview had become quite complex, so Rap had a lot to learn. It had grown to mammoth proportions during his stay in Ionia, and was now replete with hidden influencing machines, sinister underground mutants, corruption within the U.S. penal and mental health systems, aging and gravity, the discovery of Earth's oldest language and the science of *de* and *te*, the cornerstones of Shaver's ancient physics. Shaver brought Rap up to speed through his extensive correspondence.

As Shaver was resurrecting his lost writing career, he got a middle name: Sharpe. This middle name was conspicuously absent from his birth certificate and first two marriage certificates. He debuted as Richard S. Shaver when his first SF stories appeared during the early 1940s. He told a correspondent that an editor gave him the middle name, and he decided to keep it.

While preparing to debut Shaver's first story, Rap hit another snag and had to postpone its 1944 publication date. He was awaiting the results of radiation levels in meat samples at Armour Laboratories. The tests were meant to confirm Shaver's age science — that sun radioactivity accumulating in the flesh causes age.

Richard Shaver, Lily Lake, McHenry, Illinois, 1945. His first Shaver Mystery stories were then hitting the newsstands (Dottie Shaver collection).

But the lab tests were not in the best interests of the Armour meat company, and their PR people hedged on releasing them. Shaver feared Rap's hesitation to release his story would cost them their edge, allowing another magazine to scoop them on his groundbreaking discovery.

Their schedule was back on track when Rap sent Shaver the proofs for "I Remember Lemuria!" now rescheduled for the March 1945 edition. Shaver was pleased.

"I have no kicks or major corrections on the proofs you sent," he told Rap. "I am intensely delighted at your grasp of the theory and science in the story. To be really understood ... is a relief beyond words."[4]

The publication of "I Remember Lemuria!" secured Shaver's devotion to Ray Palmer as an editor and friend. He knew he had found the right man to spread his message to the masses. Not only that, Shaver was pleasantly surprised to find himself featured as the magazine's cover author. It so encouraged him that he "sent for a couple of books on plotting."[5] Plotting was his biggest challenge then, and throughout his writing career.

When Rap grumbled that it took him several days of hard work to bring the manuscript up to *Amazing*'s editorial standards, Shaver's mood changed. "I was ashamed at first that you had to do so much rewrite work on my first story...." he told Rap. "But now I realize that you put this work on my story because of the importance of the material and your own interest...."[6]

Shaver, new to the writing scene, was insecure. To ease his anxiety, he collaborated with a radio announcer named Bob McKenna. McKenna, who worked at station KDKA in Philadelphia, did ghostwriting on the side. Shaver sent McKenna his rough drafts for polishing. McKenna also assisted Shaver with his Mantong alphabet, placing a "help wanted" ad in *Writers Digest*, seeking scholarly input. McKenna received 100 replies, but when Shaver revealed the source of his alphabet, the offers vanished.

The Shaver-McKenna team eventually shared credit in *Amazing Stories* for the novels *Cult of the Witch Queen* (July 1946) and *The Return of Sathanas* (November 1946). Shaver paid McKenna by the word out of his paycheck from Ziff-Davis. His overhead increased further when he hired a typist. She got 50 cents for every 1,000 words. Shaver's typing skills, or the lack of them, were legendary.

He also worked with a female author named Greye LaSpina, a baroness by marriage to the Italian aristocrat Baron Robert LaSpina. Her first supernatural fiction appeared in *Thrill Book* in 1919. Shaver, who found her through an ad, hired her to work on "Thought Records of Lemuria," which appeared in *Amazing*'s June 1945 issue. He was not pleased with her style. "She is a bit old-fashioned in her wordings and I think I will not have any more done by her,"[7] he told Rap.

Shaver's first solo attempt at a major story came with "Invasion of the Micro Men" (*Amazing Stories*, February 1946), which was entirely Shaver-written. Rap tried to soothe his insecurity: "In the future do not employ help on important stories. You can write very well," he said.[8]

Nevertheless, Shaver pressed Chester S. Geier into service, and they shared credits on "Ice City of the Gorgon" (*Amazing Stories*, June 1948), "Fountain of Change" (*Fantastic Adventures*, December 1948), "Battle in Eternity" (*Amazing Stories*, November 1949) and "Lightning Over Saturn" (*Other Worlds Science Stories*, October 1951).

Rap bought all rights to Shaver's stories. At first this presented no problem. Shaver was ecstatic that an editor actually saw value in his work. But when the Shaver Mystery quickly turned into a national sensation, he began to have second thoughts. He told Rap he was unsettled about selling all rights, but since they were so heavily rewritten he wasn't sure how to approach the issue. In the end, he put doubts aside and placed himself in Rap's hands. "I trust you implicitly, Rap, and I do wish to help you make the most out of this thing and you are the one man I know who understands ... the immense possibilities of this work."[9] As time went on, his attitude would change about that.

He began to feel the pinch of his penny-per-word pay scale as sales of *Amazing Stories* continued to skyrocket due to his stories. He knew that Rap was paying more to other writers that did far less for circulation. So Rap gave him a raise in June 1945.

"Right now I guarantee you a living," Rap said. "Later on, you'll get better than a living. To do that, your rates are now two cents a word.... I attach highest importance to the truth of your writings, and am anxious for you to get them on paper...."[10]

Shaver Mystery yarns that followed "I Remember Lemuria!" and "Thought Records of Lemuria" in 1945 were "Cave City of Hel" and "Quest of Brail." Reader letters flooded the Ziff-Davis mailroom. The Shaver Mystery was by all reckonings a hit. Nevertheless, William B. Ziff was uneasy. He wondered if Rap's sensationalistic approach to SF was creating *too* much controversy, or worse, making Ziff out as the laughingstock of the publishing industry. Shaver on the other hand, was totally on board with Rap.

"I think you are wholly right in making it as sensational as possible," he told Rap. "The conservative attitude can throttle all new things...."[11]

Suddenly, Bernard Davis cut Rap's budget and nixed his plan for a Ziff-Davis book based on Shaver's scientific revelations. Rap wondered if they doubted his savvy as editor. He told Shaver about the new development. Shaver clued him in on the source. It was dero tamper coming from the caves, he said.

"The cut in your budget tells me ... that [the dero] have aroused an animosity in Davis against you.... It is very possible that both Ziff and Davis think you are too wrapped up in the mystery of ray secrets and have gone off the track of fact...."[12] Shaver advised him to counter the negative thoughts rayed into Ziff and Davis' heads. Rap had to convince them he was the right man for the job. Said Shaver, "[D]on't be modest — blow your horn fully and crow a little over those who deplored your interest in our subject.... If you know that they think the subject an irrational one ... laugh that the interest in ... race memory and Lemuria is so general that we must go ahead anyway."[13]

Dick and Dottie Shaver, 1946, Lily Lake, McHenry, Illinois (Dottie Shaver collection).

A Meeting of Minds

"Neither Dot nor I are as ignorant or uneducated as I fear we sound to one who doesn't know us well."— Richard Shaver

Shaver was essentially an idea man, always on the lookout for a scheme that would strike gold. Most of his ideas never bore fruit, but he never stopped planting seeds. One of his ideas was a comic book based on the Shaver Mystery. He was a comic book fan from way back (Wonder Woman being his favorite superhero) and felt that comics had potential as a vehicle for his stories — something like Flash Gordon, only better.

Shaver asked Rap to pitch his idea to Mr. Davis, "simultaneous with the publicity that is bound to come ... when the full impact of our work is realized."[14] He made a rough draft of the first issue, hoping Rap's artists would add polish. "You remember when Buck Rogers came out in the first issues of *Amazing Stories*? Well, look at the way it was developed through the years.... I think we could do better than Buck Rogers or Flash Gordon and certainly far better than Superman with our data as a base...."[15] He called it *Space Ace*, similar to Smith & Street's *Air Ace*. In the end, his Space Ace never escaped Earth's atmosphere, much to Shaver's dismay.

Rap and Shaver quickly pieced together the Shaver Mystery in 1944. After publication of "I Remember Lemuria!" their names were forever linked within the science fiction genre. In January 1945 Rap decided it was high time to meet his new discovery in person. Shaver was thrilled at the news. He gave Rap instructions on train schedules to his rural part of Pennsylvania. "Get off at Pottstown and phone me and I will pick you up," Shaver wrote.[16] If Rap arrived while Shaver was still at work, he was to call the Bethlehem Steel plant. "Ask for crane operator Shaver," he said.

Shaver lived about 12 miles outside Pottstown, a 20-minute drive on a good day. Dorothy Erb, Shaver's new love interest, was now living on the farm. She was unsure what to think of their impending visitor from Chicago. She told Dick that she "don't know whether to act like a lady or act normal."[17]

After several postponements blamed on his busy schedule, Rap arrived at Pottstown station in March 1945, suitcase in hand. Shaver was impressed with his new editor and friend, but unsure of what he would think of his country image. "You were the first visitor I and Dot have had," Shaver said, "that is, a visitor whose critical eye we had respect for. So put our deficiencies down to our lack of social life...."[18]

On returning to Chicago, Rap wrote in *Amazing Stories* about his sleepover at the Shaver farm, describing it in broad strokes as it fit the Shaver Mystery mythos. Yes, he had heard the voices, he said, after Shaver had gone to bed. But he failed to tell his readers that he knew the voices had come from Dick Shaver in a trance-like state. Thus began Rap's search for an explanation, which he confessed to Shaver a year later, in 1946:

> Maybe there was something to this "trance" business. How could I say definitely it was not you who spoke, even if you didn't realize it while in some sort of a "trance" (for lack of a better word).... I turned my attention to mediums, to spiritualists, to Oahspe, to the Book of Mormon, to Indian legends, to voodooism, to anything occult.... I learned that when you talked of caves, others talked of "planes" or "astral spheres" or just of heaven and hell.[19]

This was the last thing Shaver wanted to hear. He considered himself a strict materialist, drenched in the atoms of the physical plane. It was not spirits of the dead that tormented him, but actual people, strange as they were, sitting at the controls of machines in real caves. Unknown to fans, the divide between Rap and Shaver widened as the Shaver Mystery continued its run in *Amazing*.

Rap was not the only Palmer to hear Shaver's voices. It happened to Linda Jane and Jennifer Palmer on a Christmas holiday some time in the early 1950s. One afternoon the sisters were at home and happened across Shaver lying on the sofa, asleep. Linda Jane mentioned it in an email to the author on April 26, 2012:

> They were at our house for Christmas and he appeared to be taking a nap, and I heard voices that weren't his. [The Shavers] were always at our house for the holidays. He and Dad played chess a lot. It was eerie and I remember staying away from him that day. I guess I saw too many strange visitors with stranger stories when I was growing up and just felt it was something to ignore because I wanted a normal life like everyone else. I still have mixed feelings about Shaver because the guy I knew was a gentle man who was a little different.... But he didn't scare me except that one Christmas day when my sister and I made sure we avoided him after hearing the voices.

Mutan Mion and Oahspe

> *"I myself cannot explain it. I know only that I remember Lemuria!"*— Richard Shaver, 1945

Oahspe was a kind of alternative bible dictated through automatic writing to an American dentist named John Ballou Newbrough in 1881. Rap became a big fan of Oahspe, though Howard Browne doubted he really believed in it. Oahspe is where Rap learned of Atmospherea, a place inhabited by so-called spirits of the dead above the Earth. Said Rap, "The Earth is inhabited by more than Man. It is inhabited in an area we call the atmosphere. A hundred miles above our heads there is intelligent life. A thousand miles up there is more intelligent life — a life form much more intelligent."[20]

He gave a copy of Oahspe to Shaver, but the book fell with a dull thud against Shaver's belief system. Oahspe teaches that these so-called spirits are as real as human beings. That riled Shaver, for instead of deros and teros living in a cavern system, Rap said we shared the planet with countless invisible "others."

"These others exist in varying degrees of civilization, some highly advanced, others quite degenerate and vicious," Rap said. He identified one of their strongholds: "The major and best of these empires ... is located approximately 1,000 miles from Duluth, Minnesota. Straight up."[21] Rap was becoming a dyed-in-the-wool spiritualist right before Shaver's eyes.

Rap of course disagreed. "The word spirit is a fooler," he told Shaver. "It is *all* people. When you speak of Gods and Dark Goddesses, I don't believe you any more than I believe in the Catholic god. I know they are all only people.... I know they once existed here on Earth, on the surface, because I know the ruins of their buildings still exist. In the caves? I don't know. I have no proof. When you speak of a woman at a ray machine, I do not know that."[22]

In spite of these setbacks, *Amazing*'s circulation flew higher as the Shaver Mystery continued its run. Harry Strong, Ziff-Davis circulation manager, confirmed the heady rise in sales and routinely sent them to William B. Ziff. Bill Hamling followed circulation figures religiously.

"Hell, I'd go into Strong's office and ask his girl, 'What'd we sell last month?' And she'd open up the notebook and would tell me. It always amazed them, particularly Bill Ziff, the owner of the company, that a goddamn pulp magazine could be selling hundreds of thousands of copies with a lunatic writer."[23]

Rap may have sensed the doubt coming from William B. Ziff, but Mr. Davis gave him a raise — his reward for the magazine's soaring circulation.

15

Conflict

"[N]o one knows better than I that it is not I that is mad in this world—but the great mass of men who are illogical to the point of madness for all."—Richard Shaver

What riled fandom's intelligentsia even more than the Lemurian Hoax, as they began to call it, was the fact that Rap had written himself into it. He was as much the crusading hero as any of Shaver's fictional characters. Next to Shaver (maybe more so), Rap became the face of the Shaver Mystery. Shaver, meanwhile, bent over backward to show appreciation to his new mentor: "And to editor Ray Palmer I express my unbounded gratitude. I know that if even a few of you go to the lengths he has gone to check many of the things I remember, a beginning will have been made to something, the ending of which awes me beyond my poor power to express my feelings."[1]

To explain the scientific component of "I Remember Lemuria!" Rap wrote extensive footnotes. They added a sense of realism, as if groundbreaking research was taking place, not just at Ziff-Davis, but also within the scientific community. The story opened with its hero Mutan Mion—actually Richard Shaver in a Lemurian incarnation—hard at work on a painting. This seemed to fit, since Shaver considered himself an artist too.

Woven like fine thread throughout "I Remember Lemuria!" was Shaver's cosmology—a dying sun spewing "dis" (deadly radioactivity); an elder race of highly evolved, ageless beings who prospered on Lemuria (their name for Earth) until the sun began to poison them. The various races (Atlans, Titans, and Nortans) prepared to abandon Earth for a migration into deep space. The evacuation was sabotaged by an evil Rodite named Zeit. These Rodites were also referred to as Derodites, or simply *deros*. Whatever their name, they were bad news.

Reader response to "I Remember Lemuria!" was an eclectic outpouring of enthusiasm, disbelief, and curiosity. Rap carved out a special section in the magazine to handle the overflow of letters. He called it "Report from the Forgotten Past." He made his first Shaver Mystery confession, too, but this time he said it was the straight dope:

> When Richard S. Shaver sent in his first story, we didn't believe Mr. Shaver's explanation of where he got it, and because we didn't want to look silly we figured out a "very good" source. We called his story "racial memory." "I Remember Lemuria!" was not a racial memory, but a thought record! In order to understand what that is, you'll have to read the story that begins on page 16.[2]

Amazing's second Shaver Mystery cover story, "Thought Records of Lemuria," proved the Shaver Mystery had legs.

Robert Gibson Jones painted this cover for *Amazing Stories*, June 1945. It illustrated Richard Shaver's story, "Thought Records of Lemuria."

Shaver Mystery Juggernaut

> *"The Elizabethans said ain't and so do I. I can't help it. Probably the Lemurians said ain't too."— Richard Shaver*

Readers' letters about the Mystery were getting longer, *a lot* longer. Nine to 40 pages were not unusual. Not only that, these new letters were some of the most entertaining to date, transforming Rap's "Discussions" letter column into a rollicking good read. The 40-page missive came from Bruce and Wesley Herschensohn, aged 12 and 16, of West Los Angeles. They told of their pet turtle. As their story goes, the turtle died. Then a miracle happened. A voice they believed to be that of the turtle intruded on their minds. The turtle made telepathic contact with its former owners, giving them curious information. "[I]t has told us many things," they said, "among them the alphabet of the language of Lemuria of Mr. Shaver."

Why the turtle kept silent during the time it lived with the boys was never explained. Once dead, however, the turtle pulled out all the stops, corroborating everything Shaver was saying. Rap thanked the boys for "all the things they have told us in support of Mr. Shaver's story and the science it contains, especially concerning racial memory, the alphabet and the mechanisms of the Titans and Atlans." Shaver explained the turtle's purpose in a letter to Rap: "The kids are controls for the turtle.... They will be super kids having the turtle behind them."[3]

Rap had all his oars in the water and was rowing full speed ahead. A topic of great debate among readers was the Mantong alphabet, discussed at length throughout the Shaver Mystery issues. Rap, who considered himself a Mantong scholar, faced many challengers in "Discussions." One dissenter was a professed linguist who scoffed at Shaver's rules for Lemurian root words:

"Mr. Shaver's contempt for the basic history of his vocabulary is startling. He neglects completely the fact that every word in the English language has changed tremendously both in spelling and in pronunciation and often in meaning." Said another, "Please put me down with those who regard Richard S. Shaver's various theories as completely unscientific and unfounded on any known fact." Rap even gave readers the Mantong meaning of Shaver's name. Roughly translated it meant "I see horrible human animal with detrimental power."

A few readers mailed clues to help Rap locate the hidden telonium thought records from which Shaver got his original information. One mentioned Italy; another said that Moses got most of Genesis from them; another named a site in the United States. Rap claimed that he was organizing an investigation to track down the missing thought record. The investigation ended in failure.

Regardless of this continuing lack of tangible proof, reader interest in the Shaver series managed to feed Rap's hunger for controversial new ideas, which he offered up in heaping spoonfuls to cure his readers' war-weary gloom. Everyone in the known SF universe was talking about *Amazing Stories* and what was now termed "Shaverism." Challenging his readers with ideas, no matter how contentious, was Rap's *raison d'être*. He was living in the eye of a hurricane of his own design, and it was exhilarating.

Chester Geier Remembers

> *"All I am is a witness to human events."—William L. Hamling, 2009*

William Hamling and Chester Geier became regulars at the newly relocated Ziff-Davis offices at 185 North Wabash Avenue, where they, too, were caught up in Ray's latest science fiction blockbuster. Three decades later, Geier recalled his time at Ziff-Davis in a memoir that appeared in *Shavertron*. Due to its tell-all nature, Geier added one proviso: He wanted to embargo it until after his death. That came on September 10, 1990.

The title of his memoir was as unpretentious as Geier was himself—*Re: Richard S. Shaver*. It was a blend of first person narrative and analysis. Like Howard Browne, Geier was suspicious of Rap's handling of the Shaver Mystery. At the time he wrote it in 1980, he believed a new generation of fanzines like *Shavertron* would glamorize an historical event in which key players—Shaver, Rap, Hamling, Browne, and himself—were working stiffs simply trying to eke out a living. Nothing extraordinary about it, he said. Hamling echoes this view, purporting to be as mystified as his former office mate by any interest in his part of the story.

Like most pulp writers, Geier had a family to support. When public interest in science fiction magazines was fading in 1952, he got a job as an associate editor at *Today's Science*, a new pocket-sized slick. That folded in record time, so he made a hasty call on one of his former Ziff-Davis contacts and snagged a job as managing editor at Rap's *FATE* magazine. He would never become the acclaimed author of his high school dreams, but instead of the feast-or-famine lifestyle of freelancing he had a steady paycheck. He remained with *FATE* until his retirement in the mid–1980s.

And so it was that in 1980, Chester Geier took time out from his job at *FATE* to walk the dimly lit alleyways of his past. As it turns out, he played a significant role in the Shaver Mystery saga, far more than historians have given him credit.

Regarding Richard S. Shaver
By Chester S. Geier

> *"Berkeley Livingston was a Howard Browne protégé, a natty and I thought rather ratty fellow...."*— Chester S. Geier

At this time Bill Hamling and I used to visit Ray Palmer and Howard Browne at the *Amazing Stories* offices about once a week. An air of excitement, of things happening hung around Rap. He mostly talked about DS [Dick Shaver] and of the subjects and incidents that arose in connection with DS. Bill and I were told (or Bill told me, acting as my interpreter) how DS heard strange, ghostly voices, how DS was tormented by mysterious rays employed by demons, or deranged robots, in underground caverns, and how DS claimed his brains had been scrambled by these rays.

Browne was skeptical and razzed Rap or made sarcastic comments. Bill gleefully told me Browne once remarked that "Claiming to have scrambled brains was just an excuse for not having any to start with." Bill and I did not know exactly what to make of the hullabaloo about DS. What kept us off balance is that Rap seemed convinced that what came to be called the Shaver Mystery had a deep significance, that the claims had a basis in truth, if not absolutely true. It was an attitude, or a pose, that Rap was to maintain with quite some consistency throughout his exploitation of the Shaver Mystery.

After publication of the first Shaver Mystery stories in *Amazing*, DS moved to McHenry, Illinois, apparently to have direct and personal benefit of Rap's mentorship. One Sunday afternoon Rap drove with Bill Hamling and Howard Browne on a visit to DS.

While at the small summer home DS was renting in McHenry, which then was largely a summer resort area Bill told me later, they were all seated around a table, chatting, when suddenly DS leaned over and peered under his chair. In the momentary pause in conversation, while the others eyed him curiously, DS said, "That was Max." DS explained that

"Max" was a dero.... Bill said DS seemed perfectly serious and solemn and the incident gave him a cold chill....

Time passed and Rap huckstered the Shaver Mystery with consummate skill, like a maestro leading a symphony orchestra, wielding his typewriter like a baton. He continued to appear perfectly serious.... He continued to make claims and drop hints like bombs. *Amazing* now had a huge readership — which Rap believed was due to the popularity of the Shaver Mystery — and from this readership, which included many educated skeptics, came strong challenges.

Many criticisms and rebuttals of details of the SM were made in letters Rap published in *Amazing*. He argued, ranted, wheedled, zigged, and zagged. When the pursuit got too hot, Rap claimed that DS had been misunderstood and that remarks Shaver had made in editorials or in answer to letters had been misinterpreted. In setting the record straight, he added to the confusion. *Amazing* became a strange cacophony of conflicting voices.

The Shaver Mystery, and *Amazing Stories* itself, got to seem chaotic and I'm sorry to say I no longer paid much attention to what was going on. I was working hard to develop as a writer. I had a wife and a child and another child on the way. I found myself facing much competition for story checks. Rap had acquired too large a stable of writers who depended on him for a living, and he was practically forced to ration them.

After publication of the first Shaver Mystery stories, all sorts of odd characters came crawling out of the woodwork. A few of these became writers for Ray Palmer. One in particular became a featured writer in Rap's own magazines by claiming at the outset that he was a Titan, a member of one of the ancient races mentioned in the Shaver Mystery stories. I don't know if he convinced Rap, who knew what was fact and what was fiction about the Shaver Mystery, but this man was solemn and reflective and sat at Rap's feet with a dog-like patience and reverence.

Ray Palmer ... liked to be admired and have devoted followers. Some of these were sharp enough to realize that becoming a disciple was their ticket to board the gravy train. Although the self-styled Titan was not a writer, Rap encouraged him to write, explained how in great detail, and published the Titan's first efforts, which discerning readers roundly booed, a strange way for an otherwise astute editor to perform. Mention of these side issues may help to get the Shaver Mystery into perspective because it had a foundation in Rap's own unusual and complex personality.

16

Line in the Sand

"[Ray Palmer] and Shaver met on a plane that was a little bit different than the rest of us."—William L. Hamling

If *Amazing*'s first two Shaver Mystery issues were not enough to convince readers of Rap's intentions, the September issue with its cover story "Cave City of Hel" would. That was when he drew his line in the sand. That was when he stated that the Shaver Mystery was fact, not just swell science fiction.

Fan clubs across America were buzzing over Rap's new revelation, though most fans already knew where they stood on Shaverism. Some SF clubs tried to take a stand by voting on resolutions to boycott the Shaver mystery, but internal bickering usually shelved the effort. Members of the Eastern Science Fiction Association voted 21–4 stating that Shaverism was *not* fact but fiction. Even worse, "Members booed Shaver loudly when he showed up at a fan meeting."[1]

While Shaver became the whipping boy of Shaverism, it was a win-win situation for Ray Palmer. He was promoting a subject that fascinated him, which in turn created controversy that stirred up the fan base and sent *Amazing*'s circulation through the roof. Emboldened by the overwhelming response to Shaver's stories, Rap upped the ante by declaring that he, too, had memories of a strange and distant past, and implored fellow Lemurians to rally 'round the flag.

> Your editor believes that the time has come for a frank discussion with you.... First of all he wants to point out that Shaver actually believes his own statements to be the truth and that these convictions of his are woven into an entertaining series of stories for a definite purpose. This purpose is (1) to find others who have had experiences of the same sort, get them to write, and compare their experiences with those of Mr. Shaver and of one another, so as to confirm or corroborate his statements by the only means possible at this time.
>
> Thus, we urge every reader who has such convictions within him, who believes there is a mystery connected with his purpose here on Earth, who believes he has a work of some far-reaching scope to perform, who believes he is part of a great plan, and who is convinced that he knows things today unknown to science, to write to your editor, WHO IS ONE OF THOSE PEOPLE! TIME HAS COME FOR ACTION![2]

Those who did not know Ray likely thought this a completely outlandish statement. But truth, as they say, is stranger than fiction, for Ray did believe that a mystery surrounded his life's purpose. More than that, he felt that he had work of a far-reaching nature to perform. Bill Hamling, the one man who says he knew what made Rap tick, contradicts the image historians have given his former boss:

> I knew more about Ray Palmer than any living person. That's a fact, not a fantasy. Ray was always considered a little bit wacky, but they were wrong. That's why he took up with the Shaver Mystery,

because he was akin to that kind of thing. He and Shaver met on a plane that was a little bit different than the rest of us. I don't believe that Dick Shaver was a nut. I think whatever voices he heard *were* voices. That didn't make him a nut in my book. I don't think he was hallucinating, really. But I'm no authority, all I am is a witness to human events....[3]

The Fen of Fandom

> "The ball sped down the alley with a skidding hook. It caught the headpin and the number two on the Brooklyn pocket. The pins scattered."—from "The Animated Tenpin" by William L. Hamling

Critics were nothing new to Ray Palmer. He had them as far back as *Fantasy Magazine*. But fans of third and fourth fandom were far different from their first and second fandom counterparts. They saw themselves as insurgents, Communists, atheists, and just plain rebels. *Amazing Stories* for September 1945 contained the first hint of an opposition to the Shaver Mystery, though Rap brushed it off like lint on his collar in his editorial column, "The Observatory":

> There have been some odd reactions, one of them being a promise by a fan group to "expose" our "hoax" (which was a compliment, by the way, because it was termed the "biggest ever attempted in modern science fiction history").... We realize that a lot of our readers find it difficult to believe that we ourselves believe one single word of what Mr. Shaver tells us in his stories, but we'll keep on presenting the evidence as it comes in, and you can judge for yourself.

The chasm between Rap and fandom widened. Fandom, dogmatic in its own right, picked up the gauntlet to confront Rap head on. The insurgents began to refer to Shaver Mystery fans as lunatics. During the Shaver Mystery's first year, Rap overwhelmingly published letters of corroboration and praise for the Mystery. The opposition changed all that when it came up with a plan to subvert Rap's fan letter gatekeeper, Howard Browne. Hoax letters began to slip through undetected (or maybe with help from Browne) that chipped away at Rap's credibility.

Said one hoaxer, "I am a graduate in occult sciences of Miskatonic University and have been engaged in conflict with Mr. Shaver's 'underground deros' since my graduation there in 1935.... Translation of the seventh chapter of the 'Necrominicon' [sic] using the 'Lemurian alphabet' should aid greatly in discovering the missing plates. John Poldea (address deleted)."

Rap failed to notice the misspelling of H.P. Lovecraft's *Necronomicon*, as well as the phony Miskatonic University. Said Rap, "Your use of quotation marks around 'underground deros' interests us greatly, because it is exactly what we would have done, knowing what we know now!"

Rap learned he had been punked when a subsequent confession arrived in the mail. It was one of many fan hoaxes foisted upon the champion of Shaverism. True, there were far more readers with a keen to casual interest in the Shaver Mystery than those who reviled it. But the disgruntled fans were the ones who produced fanzines, attended SF conventions and joined active fan clubs. They were the voice of the SF movement, and would go on to write its history. Like Rap, many became prozine editors. These were the fans that did not take kindly to Shaverism.

Meanwhile, Richard S. Shaver, self-proclaimed SF fan, found himself banging his head against the brick wall of fandom. These fans wanted nothing to do with him, and Shaver, being low-key and somewhat sensitive, took it to heart. His name was being slandered in fanzines across the country.

One of those fanzines was Joe Kennedy's *Vampire*, the most popular fanzine of the Shaver Mystery era. Kennedy enjoyed writing about the Mystery, both pro and con. One *Vampire* piece, embraced by fans as a hilarious satire aimed at Rap's Lemurian stories, was "You Must Believe!" by Al Weinstein. Its main character, a Lemurian, was compelled to inform his fellow Lemurians: "I hear voices ... I REMEMBER EARTH!" This cracked a few ribs at local club meetings.

What finally dragged Dick Shaver into the public arena was something else entirely.

Vampire had recently printed a scathing review of *Maxin 96*, a Shaver Mystery–occult fanzine published by David D. Dagmar of Hollywood, California. Adding insult to injury: *Startling Stories*, Ray Palmer's competition, picked up on the *Vampire* review and republished it. Shaver was mortified and anxious to set the record straight. He mailed Kennedy a rebuttal, which never saw print, according to fan historian Harry Warner, Jr.:

> Kennedy rejected a four-page "prose poem" submitted to *Vampire* by Richard Shaver. Kennedy described it as beginning with a blank verse discussion of Palmer and deros, then shifting into straight prose as more appropriate to its consideration of the dero-controlled fans, finally assuming the guise of an ordinary letter, and ending without the least warning.[4]

Kennedy and Shaver struck a compromise and, in *Vampire*'s June 1946 issue, Kennedy ran Shaver's rewrite. Kennedy titled it "Lovecraft and the Deros" and made it clear to readers that he was "completely convinced of the author's sincerity," but that Shaver's views did not reflect those of *Vampire*'s staff. Shaver began by stating that up until twelve years earlier, he had been an SF fan like many of those who read *Vampire*:

> I thought I knew exactly what was true in science and what could happen and that I could draw a precise line in my reading between fact and fancy. Then it happened, almost exactly as I tell it in the stories I write. Things that couldn't happen except through a wonder-science never produced by modern men of science at all.
>
> There were three conclusions. The first, that these machines and rays came from space (visitors). The second was that they were *modern secret science*— things that science had developed and kept to itself as a monopoly, for the power and wealth the advantages of using these apparatuses would give them. This second conclusion was my conclusion until I knew more about it, which took many years. It is the usual deduction of the person first contacting secret ray.

After expounding on the hidden truths of Earth's ancient past, Shaver noted how *Vampire* reported that fans booed him at the convention in Newark. "All this active fan opposition hurts like hell — but the truth of it is — they lose so darn much I could give them —*if* THEY UNDERSTOOD! But they are not my worst worry. My worry is the mad dero of the caverns — and they do our country even more harm...."

In the end, Kennedy invited readers to comment, adding, "Please, though, no descriptions of weird dreams or talking turtles."

Shaver's emotional op ed did nothing to quell the insurgency against *Amazing Stories*. He and Rap began circling the wagons to fend off 175 (give or take a few) enraged fans who appeared to be permanently on the warpath.

The continuing barrage of rocks thrown against his good name may have given Shaver the idea to disappear. This happened around the time his story "Masked World" appeared in *Amazing*'s May 1946 issue. In a letter to Rap (reprinted in *The Hidden World*, Winter 1964, page 2864), Shaver proposed that it might "be a good publicity angle for Dick

Shaver to be reported disappeared — and for 'Vic Valentine' to carry on.... [I]t should be considered if interest drops off ... and did or did not the deros run away with [me?] ... and an issue or so later I came back with a story about it...." His plan with the fictitious Vic Valentine never came to pass, and Shaver was forced to remain in the crosshairs of an angry fandom.

17

Science of the Damned

"Fandom didn't like Ray Palmer. They simply didn't like his appearance. He was a hunchback."—William L. Hamling, 2009

December 1945 saw a more confrontational Ray Palmer, who pointed out that scientific arguments against the Shaver Mystery were invalid. Why? Because the Shaver Mystery was not amenable to scientific observation; therefore scientists could not comment on it. Besides, scientists were known to change their minds frequently. The scientific facts of today will be refuted in days to come, Rap said.

"[The scientist] COULD be wrong in his conclusions. And he is LOGICALLY wrong in supposing that only that exists which he has SEEN and MEASURED and PROVED by EXPERIENCE."[1] He reminded readers that proponents of a flat Earth were thoroughly validated and later thoroughly disproved. Meanwhile, the Shaver Mystery was becoming so important to *Amazing* (and its soaring circulation) that Rap even dropped stories by Henry Hasse and Ray Bradbury to make room for more Shaver, who was now being touted (by Rap) as a writer whose work was "almost lyrical."

Again, Rap encouraged readers who heard voices to share their experiences. "We have conclusively established that there are voices, and we are prepared to prove it to anybody who wants to find out without presuming to ask us to do all the doing while he sits on his fat and drools, 'put up or shut up'.... [W]e aren't interested in satisfying curiosity seekers and those mentally blind ones who never thought an actual thought of their own...."[2]

Rap was asking for trouble, and he got it in spades. The insurgents increased their prank letters. Sometimes Rap caught them, but his enthusiasm often clouded judgment. It was hard for an old-time fan and prankster like Rap to find himself on the receiving end of a fan hoax. He denounced it as dirty pool, "unsportsmanlike planting of fake bones" in the bone yard. "They are not a credit to the great traditions of science fiction, the living illustration of the maxim 'What man would create, he must first imagine.'"

Somehow Rap had forgotten his own pranks, even ones he pulled as editor of *Amazing Stories*. He wrote fake "Meet the Authors" profiles for A.R. Steber and Frank Patton, two of his pen names. Steber had three such profiles, all of them different. In one he was a secret agent fleeing Nazi Germany in a submarine. In another he was forging across Canada by dog sled on his way to the Yukon gold fields.

One of the phony profiles featured a photo of Rap dressed as the fictitious Steber, wearing a monocle, gold braids, and antique military uniform. He featured Frank Patton, with a bogus bio and a grainy photo of a man (not Rap) sporting a smarmy pencil mustache.

Howard Browne, on the other hand, believed that nearly *everything* Rap did was a hoax. In a 1988 letter to Chester Geier, Browne claimed Rap used self-induced trance to appear sincere to his readers. "Ray was interested in the 'occult and paranormal,' yes. But only as a means to an end: the profit in publishing and promoting it. He had that ability to induce a kind of self-hypnotism to make himself 'believe' what he preached, for the sake of enforcing reader believability, knowing all along that the material was nonsense, such as the Oahspe 'bible,' for example. He would go on and on about it to me, about how valid it was. And always there was that almost undetectable look about him that said something far different."

Regardless of Browne's assessment, there is no doubt there were times when Rap pulled a fast one. It was part of his DNA as an old-school science fiction fan. When fandom's criticism got serious in 1946, he and Bill Hamling started a rumor with a phony letter that Hamling allegedly mailed to a "gullible" fan. The news it contained went something like this. One warm summer evening, Rap suddenly went missing. He was later found hiding in his basement, clutching a lump of coal in one hand, a magnet in the other, and babbling incoherently. Diagnosis: nervous breakdown. The letter said he was rushed to a sanitarium. This was easy for Rap's critics to believe, and sure enough, word of his insanity tore through fandom like bedbugs in a Tenderloin flophouse.

Rap later confessed to the prank, or Hamling did, but not before the letter circulated among Big Name Fans. Forrest J Ackerman "generated much excitement" when he read a copy to members of the Los Angeles Science Fiction Society at its June 20, 1946, meeting. The letter also revealed a defiant Bill Hamling, who blamed fandom for causing Rap's mental breakdown: "The greatest mistake the fans ever made with their dealings with a professional house, they made with Ray Palmer and *Amazing Stories*. *Amazing Stories* and its companion, *Fantastic Adventures*, are the leaders in the field today. The Shaver Mystery, true or untrue—and what difference it makes I fail to see—will continue.... As usual, the fans and the minority they represent have missed the boat.'"[3]

In a reply to a reader in the April 1962 *Forum*, Rap gave his version of the story "As for the 'basement incident' that was a joke played on me by my associate editors, who were at that time scoffing mightily at my experiments with pure carbon, magnets and vitic (whatever it is).... We did earn the belly laughs of our pals at the office, who dropped a card to one of our more gullible science fiction fans informing him that Ray Palmer had been found crouching in his basement...!"

This, too was a fabrication, as Bill Hamling explained in 2010. "Baloney!" he said. There was no letter sent to an unnamed fan. It was Ray Palmer's way of finding out who his friends and foes were. Hamling was merely his accomplice.[4]

No one has ever stepped forward with first-hand information that Ray secretly told them the Shaver Mystery was a hoax. That included his kids. Rap's daughter Linda Jane said she found her dad's mystical beliefs too strange and embarrassing to discuss with her school chums. She still wonders what went on with her dad when it came to the Shaver Mystery. "Personally I don't think my dad believed in the deros.... I don't ever remember him talking as if he believed it."[5]

If Rap's plan was to hide the fact he had perpetrated the greatest hoax ever to hit science fiction, he was a spectacular success.

Bigger and Better Hoaxes: Steve Volto Dero

"The most unusual letter I received so far is one from a person claiming to be a dero."—Norman S. Kossuth, SF fan

Perhaps the most elaborate hoax to appear in *Amazing*'s letter column was the fan-inspired "Steve Volto Dero." It sprang from its lair and sank its fangs into the necks of Shaver Mystery fans across the United States and Canada. It began with a letter to Rap from 18-year-old Norman S. Kossuth, Shaver Mystery fan and member of Detroit's legendary Michigan Science Fiction Society—aka "the Misfits."

Kossuth liked to think of himself as something of a psychic. He radiated a blue aura, according to an occultist who visited their club one evening. Far more damning than Kossuth's metaphysical leanings in the eyes of his Misfit brethren was his interest in the Shaver Mystery. Fellow member Charles Metchette, who documented Kossuth's allegiance, explained, "Norm Kossuth was ... a devotee of Richard S. Shaver. He went to Illinois to visit the guy, and returned convinced that Richard should be listened to...."[6]

It should be noted here that Kossuth was not the hoaxer, but the patsy in the Steve Volto Dero hoax. Kossuth explained he had been picking up strange mental impressions—answers, if you will—to his thoughts about the Shaver Mystery. Some of the answers were "so full of foul language and lies" that Kossuth came to the conclusion they were sent by Shaver's deros.

The teenager went on to say that some of the cryptic messages included locations of cave entrances as well as plans for a radiophone and a "degravitator." Kossuth learned that the data was coming from "a dero named 'Steve' in Detroit, or rather, from under Detroit.... I proceeded to ask him questions and I'll be darned if he didn't seem to give some answers that made sense.... I have been stung by a few rays (from the dero). Not a pleasant experience!"[7]

Ray, mentor to all teen SF fans, counseled Kossuth on his dilemma. Any statements coming from a dero, he said, are "outright lies." Having said that, Rap ignored his own advice and suggested Kossuth ask Steve the dero a few questions, like "What is your full name? Did you ever live on the surface, and what was your address then? What do you eat?" Rap further comforted Kossuth with, "We have no reason to doubt the authenticity of your letter or of your experiences."[8]

Rap's reply seems to have encouraged the boy, but it antagonized Steve the dero, who began sending threatening postcards from Detroit to a select group of fans. The cards had ominous warnings, hinting that the perp knew what the fans were up to. They were signed Steve Volto Dero. Apparently the dero was using his full name now. Teen SF fan Vaughn M. Greene, enrolled at San Francisco's Lick-Wilmerding Vocational School, received one of the dero's postcards. Now in his 80s, Greene remembered that the card arrived at his boarding house in 1946. "It had a photo of a town square—a picture postcard like you can buy at the drug store. It was [from] this guy bragging about himself in a vaguely menacing way, telling me not to 'get into' the Shaver Mystery stuff. It was signed 'Steve Volto Dero.'"[9]

One card that survived, typed and signed by Steve Volto Dero, said: "Keep out of our caves or else. We do not want anyone exploring our caves. This is a warning from us deros. You will get nothing but troubles. Beware deros hate all humans."[10]

Greene learned he was one of a half-dozen *Amazing Stories* readers who received similar warnings. The others, like Greene, were letterhacks whose addresses appeared in "Discussions." Rumors of the perp's identity focused on two people. Heading the list was Norm Kossuth, as he was first to reveal the existence of Steve the dero. Second on that list was a 21-year-old Nova Scotia woman who claimed to be a victim of the very same dero. She collected Hindu idols, read *Amazing Stories*, and corresponded with Richard Shaver. She laid the blame on Kossuth. In handwritten letters sent to other victims, she accused Kossuth of being Steve Volto Dero.

"He has sent me threatening cards and letters — this has been going on since 1946. I will quote some of his threats, and I am not the only one who received them. Quote: 'We are coming to get you. You will die by my hand ... Steve Dero.' Quote: 'I know a girl who was mixed [up] with the black brotherhood. I talked to her on the phone last week, now she is dead.'"[11]

Kossuth denied her accusations, arguing that it could have been *she* who masterminded the hoax. Casting further suspicion on the Nova Scotia woman were rumors that she dabbled in witchcraft. This only increased her anger. She determined to expose Kossuth, Rap, Shaver, and others she now believed were persecuting her. Greene, on the other hand, thought it was all a big joke, as he stated in a 2008 interview:

> I was in contact with John Hart at the time, and we were pretty hot on this Shaver Mystery business back then. He was the one who told me that [the postcards] were from this girl in Nova Scotia. I presume that he learned it from Norm Kossuth in Detroit. John knew Norm quite well, so maybe Norm told him that just to get him off the track.[12]

Exasperated, Kossuth sent a letter to Greene confessing that his communication with the dero named Steve had actually come through automatic writing, not via rays from the caves. Thanks to debilitating harassment over the Steve Volto Dero affair, he had recanted his belief in Shaverism:

> I admit I halfway believed the Shaver stories at the time. The letters I wrote to *Amazing* did describe the true phenomenon of automatic writing.... I have learned since that the operator is moving the pencil himself although he is completely unaware of it. The subconscious mind can make you write anything you wish. The whole thing is sort of scary but I think that's how I got that dero junk.[13]

The enigma that was Steve Volto Dero has never been solved.

Critics' Choice

> *"I believe Richard S. Shaver to be the most unjustly maligned writer of all time."—*
> *Arthur Temby Janes, SF fan*

There was no monopoly on the brickbats pummeling the Shaver Mystery. Fandom got moral support from literati like Thomas S. Gardner, a science fiction fan and commentator with a Ph.D. who wrote two scathing essays denouncing the Mystery. Gardner revealed his gut-wrenching fear that Shaver, with his talk of ancient science and rays from malevolent deros, would transform the weak minds of his readers into Manchurian candidates. (Gardner is also remembered for his crusade to develop a university degree for SF buffs, as well as his two 1949 essays, "An Open Letter to Walt Disney" and "The Works of Edgar Rice Burroughs and the Sands of Time.")

Nipping at the heels of Shaver's "I Remember Lemuria!" Gardner gave the editor of

Fantasy Commentator enough anti–Shaver Mystery ammo to put Ray Palmer on defense for the rest of his Ziff-Davis career. Gardner's "Calling All Crackpots" appeared in the spring 1945 issue of *FC* as a line-by-line repudiation of the science and sanity of Shaverism. Said Gardner,

> The reader group catered to by Palmer consists of the average person with a sixth grade educational level, who wants in his fiction very little plot or characterization, plenty of action, and a love story ending of a clinch.... I would advise our editor and author to spend a year or so in an actual laboratory, where they might learn a few accurate facts.... Of course it is possible to locate the sites of the lost cities Mr. Shaver claims to have discovered. But do not be surprised if the usual fictional earthquake, landslide, or tidal wave has destroyed the entrance — with, in my opinion, the fictional civilization that was supposedly beyond it....

Like other critics, Gardner found it hard to fathom that Rap actually believed the science he propounded, "for if this were true it would be necessary to assume that he knows little or nothing about geology, industrial processes, potential theory, anthropology, and other scientific subjects."

This was the first mainstream effort to eviscerate Rap's "Lemurian Hoax." It was so well received by the anti–Shaver camp that Gardner wrote a sequel titled "Crackpot Heaven." This time he took aim at the *readers* of *Amazing Stories*, whom he denounced as a group of psychopathic, maladjusted, undereducated goofballs living solitary lives in ignorance of real science.

The social implications of such a hoax, Gardner said "are much greater than most fans imagine...." Five percent of the American populace (by Gardner's calculation) belonged to the lunatic fringe. He estimated seven million of these lunatics were "living their daily lives under delusions of grandeur, believing in lost races, 'ancient wisdom,' astrology, pyramidology, and the like." Even worse, this fringe population might conceivably influence the direction of public school education. If Ray were to unify the disparate elements of the lunatic fringe, "he would have created a powerful public opinion backed by people with a crusading spirit...."

Gardner also feared Rosicrucians could gain seats on Hometown USA's school board. In any case, his Shaver Mystery roast ended with the prediction that Rap's "new policy will be an outstanding success, and the Lemurian Hoax will go on for years, possibly becoming a permanent esoteric feature of *Amazing Stories*."

Gardner set the tone of future criticisms of the Mystery, and each year the criticism grew more strident until even William B. Ziff in his ivory tower began to hear it. *Harper's* followed up on Gardner's essays with an article about SF fandom by William S. Baring-Gould. Baring-Gould covered SF pulps in general and *Amazing Stories* in particular, showing no mercy for the Shaver Mystery: "[A] place at the very bottom of the list, in the opinion of most fans, should be reserved for *Amazing Stories*, the one time 'Aristocrat of Science Fiction....'"[14]

Baring-Gould reiterated Gardner's claim that Shaverism was "probably undesirable and even dangerous. ... [T]o many an honest science fiction fan, whose hobby has suffered so much, this will undoubtedly go down as the year's greatest understatement."

Meanwhile

> *"No giant stone monuments will be erected to Roger Graham unless he builds them himself...."— Richard Shaver*

On the flipside of Ray's new Shaver Mystery anthem was an entirely different tune. Behind the façade of his entertaining new controversy was a strictly human drama playing out in a parallel universe called Life. It was as far removed from Lemuria as the moon is from Pasadena. Lead characters in this melodrama were as secretive as they were vocal, and their behind-the-scenes melee was kept hidden from fans and foes alike.

William B. Ziff, not one to pay much attention to the inner workings of his fiction group, obsessed over his own pet projects. He was a flyer during World War I and made his fortune with, among other things, books and magazines devoted to flying, photography, radio, and TV. He had aspirations of legerdemain, too. With coaching from Howard Browne, he authored several books, three of which were published between 1942 and 1944. Word around the water cooler was that Ziff and Browne had formed an exclusive writer's workshop. Bill Hamling frequented that water cooler and knew all the details:

> Ziff used to call Howard to New York for conferences, because Ziff liked to write. Howard was a goddamn good writer, and so he would council Ziff, and that's how they had a good relationship. Bernie Davis was close to Ray Palmer, and after Ray, me. There was this split relationship in that corporation. You had your own bosses, so to speak, and everybody understood everybody else.[15]

Browne's relationship with the president of the company set him apart from other Ziff-Davis editors, especially Ray Palmer. Although the fiction group functioned amiably on the surface, its members had their allegiances. Browne had Ziff's ear, and Browne did not like Rap's style.

Rap's loyal wingman, Bill Hamling, became part of the Davis camp. Nearly 70 years later, Hamling's allegiance to Davis remains intact. "Ziff didn't know shit from Shinola," said Hamling. "Bernie Davis knew it all, and Bernie was the executive in charge of our little club, and he didn't care as long as we made his company *money*! I didn't think too much about Ziff."[16]

Other allegiances came and went within the fiction group. Causing Shaver great personal consternation was a young gun named Rog Phillips (Roger P. Graham), who became part of Rap's inner circle in 1946. He appeared to be a convert to Shaverism on his debut in *Amazing Stories*, but reversed course after Rap drove him to McHenry to meet the Shavers.

Always mindful they might appear unsophisticated to big city folk, Dick and Dottie Shaver were not impressed with Graham's acerbic remarks and high opinion of himself. Things went downhill from there.

Graham moved to Chicago and hobnobbed with Rap and his closest friends. He put his proximity to good use by filling Rap's ear with doubts about Dick Shaver. For a time, Graham corresponded with Rap. (His job as night watchman at a casket factory offered him plenty of time to knock out letters on the office typewriter.) Graham argued that Shaver was completely off course—about the caves, about the voices, and about his ancient science. He told Rap the telaug Shaver hoped to build was nothing but a pipe dream.

About a year after Rap had taken Graham under his wing as an aspiring writer, he did something strange: He sent his entire file of Graham's letters to Dick Shaver. This was in the summer of 1946. On reading them it became crystal clear to Shaver that Graham had been sucking up to Rap to gain favor, and he thought Rap was falling for it. Horrified, Shaver fired off a reply to Rap saying he was dumbfounded and discouraged by Graham's attacks and Rap's acceptance of them:

> [I] have finished the file of Rog vs. Shaver ... and can't say I admire the deal I seem to have been getting all around. Was the most discouraging reading I have ever ever ever indulged in. It seems

to me that neither Rog nor you, Ray, have ever bothered to really understand me.... Do you realize that ever since Roger stepped into the picture you have been mentally doubling on me? ... [I]t is evident that Roger has been working against me steadily."[17]

Shaver wrote several pages of heated response to Rap's apparent callousness and Rog's personal attacks. He was obviously hurt, and felt that Graham was using flattery to enhance his standing with Rap. Worse, he was out to destroy the Shaver-Rap friendship and discredit the Shaver Mystery. Rap had to use some fancy footwork to calm Shaver down.

"You see, I am not taken in by Roger," said Rap. "You ask Margy. She will tell you that I often talk with her about Roger. We know he is bombastic, we know he likes to be a big shot, we know he lies, we know he is uncharitable in his choice of words, we know that up to now, he hasn't really proved anything. But we always hope somebody will eventually. Meanwhile we take nobody's word, but always act only as our best judgment tells us based on what people do tell us."[18]

It was a struggle, but Shaver let it go. His friendship with Rap again took hold, with a few scrapes and bruises in the process. Shaver was well aware of the fact he was not a member of Rap's Chicago inner circle, and that added to his insecurity. "I want to play poker with the boys and to bowl and all, but I can't make it out there, and that is that," he said.[19]

Even at the height of his career at Ziff-Davis, Shaver's lack of personal contact with Rap made him nervous. "I trust you, but I am pragmatic," he told Rap. "I know I can trust you only so long as I am of real value to you.... But if I never read another Roger Graham missive I will survive."[20]

Rap suspected the real reason Shaver remained aloof was Dottie. She sized up Shaver's friends the minute she met them. Party boy Bill Hamling made a bad impression on her, as did Graham and others. That meant poker night with the boys was o-u-t. Rap admitted to Shaver, "I find Hamling's youthfulness and his ideas of what is 'fun' rather childish too. He does bowl and play cards and I like both."[21]

But everyone agreed with Dottie's assessment, that Chester Geier was "a wonderful man."

18

Fanfeud from Hell

"Palmer hates our guts and regards us as a bunch of stinking rats."— Don Wilson, SF fan

Rap could take criticism (sometimes) and he could dish it out, too. After months of repeated personal attacks, a fan letter sent by Don Wilson of Banning, California, sent him over the edge. Wilson, a frequent letterhack in Joe Kennedy's *Vampire*, had just sent a scathing letter gloating over Rap's shellacking from Baring-Gould in a recent *Harper's* article. Maybe he was having a bad day, but whatever the reason, Ray exploded: He fired off a personal reply to Wilson, man-to-man and "off the record." Shocked by the contents of Rap's letter, Wilson saw it as an attack on fandom. He forwarded the letter to Kennedy, who reprinted both Wilson's and Rap's letters in tandem. Kennedy titled it "In Caverns Below" for the December 1946 *Vampire*.

Of most interest is Rap's reply to Wilson, of which excerpts follow. Rap's spelling and grammar are left intact. It should be noted that normally the word "fen" is the plural of "fan," but Rap uses it in a vaguely derogatory way. Rap also used the term "scientifiction" (stf) that has since been rejected by modern fandom and replaced with "SF."

Dear Don,
When you mention "science fiction fans" you refer to the WHOLE readership of science fiction. Therefore when Baring-Gould says MOST FANS place *Amazing* at the bottom of the list, he is willfully misinterpreting. It's cheap rottenness, and part of the *fen* campaign to smear honest stfandom....

Who started the "smear" campaign? Wasn't it the "fen." Yes, that's the word you SHOULD use in describing your particular group of FANS. Be specific, as BG wasn't. All I intend to do is set my FANS straight — those who join your club as eager science fiction fans — as to what they are joining ... a small, narrow-opinioned group who spend much of their time "smearing" the biggest magazine in science fiction (and from my own viewpoint the only one which lives up to its title).

Do you think an stf mag is defenseless? We can't hit back? Well, watch AS and see. Who the hell do you bastards think you are? 192 or less crackpots who climb lampposts to see if a bus is coming. Yeah, I saw a *lady* fen *do* that in Chicago at the Chicon. The *scientific* thing to do is to step out into the street and look! As long as you boys insist on the *proper* scientific way to do it.

Is everybody who is not a technician a crackpot? You say so. Are you a technician? Let's have the dope about you. What do YOU do? Shaver is a technician. He is a *top* technician in the creating of a pulp magazine story. He's the best damn author who ever hit the science fiction field. Nobody can top his fan mail, nobody can claim his rates, nobody can claim his power at getting new readers. Those are facts. An Edgar Rice Burroughs yarn raised our circulation 4,000. Shaver raised it 80,000! More than the TOTAL circulation of *Astounding*. Facts, my boy, and scientific facts. They have to do with numbers from one to ten. Do you know about those numbers?

Do you fellows think it's going to help your club to incur the enmity of the biggest if not the best *stf* magazine? Well, you've got it. You slap at me in your mags, I'll slap at you. I'll tell my readers not to join you because you hate *Amazing*. I'll tell my readers who hate *Amazing* to join you. Fair enough?

...Science says nothing exists that can't be proved. With five meager senses, if you please. What about the invisible? You can't SEE that? So, ergo, there is no invisible. You can't prove God in a laboratory, ergo there isn't one, and so, because a lot of people are religious "fanatics" science will just shrug its shoulders and say sanctimoniously "we don't know." They DON'T KNOW! ... what poor, blind, dumb bastards....

Science — a cult. Scientists — priests. Fen — kneeling, trembling, adoring, befuddled, unthinking, stupid worshippers. Go ahead, take somebody's word for it. And HOPE they're right — if you're *lucky*. Don't question a thing. Never use your brain for DOUBTING. Doubt only what you're TOLD to doubt. Be a follower.

But for Crissakes, don't FOLLOW *Amazing Stories*. You'll get all PO'ed.

Rap /Raymond A. Palmer/

P.S. we have a few more convictions. WHEN IN ROME, DO AS THE ROMANS DO.

Also, FIGHT FIRE WITH FIRE.

P.S. Again: Shaver's caves are real.

Once more: Stay outta the caves, the dero would love you!

And: Nuts to you....

The letter revealed Ray's true feelings: that science was a cult and scientists were its priests. Like mindless religious followers, these fans were "befuddled worshippers" of their god. A psychologist might pose that the Catholic Church and Rap's authoritarian father just got a thrashing.

The antipathy still roils beneath the surface of fandom, and has kept Rap from entering the First Fandom Hall of Fame. Bill Hamling, inducted into those hollowed halls in 2004, knows first hand of fandom's vendetta against Rap. One can still hear disdain in his voice as he recalls Rap's fen of fandom: "They didn't like Ray Palmer; never did. But Ray catered to anybody who read the magazines he edited. And [the fen] always resented the fact that he was boss man at Ziff-Davis. It was the fan element. And in science fiction, those fans could be brutal. Oh, I tell ya, those fan magazines could be personally vicious...!"[1]

Fan agnostics did exist. They were less inclined to jump on the anti–Shaver Mystery bandwagon, but were few and far between. Fan-turned-pro Gerald W. Page was one of them. He grew up as an SF fan, attended conventions, and eventually became an editor at *TV Guide*. Now in his 70s, Page remains convinced Rap and Shaver got a bum deal from fandom:

> Palmer thought fandom was unfair in its attitude and attacks on him, and he certainly had a point. But ... Palmer did exaggerate and reinvent his versions of what happened.... Sometimes he seemed to like argument more than debate, and he seems to have had a perverse desire to keep some of his points as obscure as he could.
>
> Of course, most fans weren't reading his editorials, and they certainly weren't following the arguments closely, so it didn't matter what Palmer said. They paid more attention to the handful of Palmer's vocal opponents in fandom, and they quickly seconded their versions. There is a certain degree of herd mentality in SF fandom, as in every such group, and Palmer ran right up against it. There are and have been fans who think things through but they tend to be a minority, and a lot of them seem to be regarded by other fans as controversial or eccentric. If fans have cosmic minds, as some have claimed, the cosmos is in big trouble.[2]

Far more enamored with Rap and Shaver were the *true* fans of Shaverism. No census was ever taken, but they likely numbered as few as active SF fandom. Some went off in search of cavern entrances to confront the dero. Others attempted to confirm Shaver's science by building a telaug to listen in on others' thoughts. We hear little of these fans today because writers like Gardner marginalized them. Nevertheless, they were the driving force behind the popularity of the Shaver Mystery and were an eclectic, if not entertaining lot.

2414 Lawrence Ave., Chicago, Illinois

> *"Chester and I were completely compatible. And he read lips very well."*—William L. Hamling

Bill Hamling and Chester Geier's writing studio became the destination of an odd assortment of Shaver Mystery fans. These were dyed-in-the-wool Shaver fans steeped in astrology, metaphysics, Oahspe, and other occult lore. Geier became the focus of their admiration after his appointment as president of the Shaver Mystery Club in 1946. They ate up Geier's valuable writing time, but he played the congenial host nonetheless. He recalled the visits with some trepidation as he continued his story in *Re: Richard S. Shaver*:

> With my office address being the address of the Shaver Mystery Club, various Shaver fans came to visit, expecting to find themselves in an enchanted world of Titans and alluring goddesses. They found an ordinary writing office with a couple of desks, a big bookcase filled with SF magazines and framed paintings that had been covers for *Amazing Stories* and *Fantastic Adventures*, occupied by an unusually tall and preoccupied chap who required that they converse on his typewriter.
>
> Among visitors was the shrewd-faced, ferret-eyed, hobo-like chap who had hitchhiked from "Washington"—whether the state or the capitol was not clear—to ask how come the dero did not torment me. It seemed that only an answer as unusual as his question would satisfy him, so I told him I wrapped my aura around myself to deflect the rays. I could see the rays bounce off, be attracted to the radiator near my desk and disappear down the pipe. His sharp, searching eyes grew wary of me and he had little more to say before he left, moving his ragged sneakers in a strange, bouncing walk. I think I saw him bouncing along near the office one evening a few days later on my way back from a cafeteria supper and was glad I was outside where I could avoid him.
>
> There was the sharp-featured, rather sallow young woman (actually about half a dozen years older than I at the time) who admitted to having an old husband, being bored with him, and attending clay modeling classes for amusement. She thought I lived an exciting life: "How wonderful to know Richard Shaver and be a writer and have such a lovely office!" I did not tell her she was an interruption in my daily agonies of hacking out fiction and soft soaping exasperated SM Club members. When she appeared a third time and grew intimately confiding, I forestalled further visits by keeping my office door closed at the time she usually appeared.
>
> And there was the lean, elderly, and infinitely garrulous occultist who worked as a motion picture projectionist a mile or so down the street from my office and who popped in at least three times a week. Among other esoteric matters, he had studied the measurements of the Great Pyramid of Gizeh for some 30 years of his life and could relate the figures to the stock market, the day's temperature, or the distance a particular fly crawled. He possessed an amazing amount of occult lore and could ramble endlessly from one subject to another. He wanted to talk to Dick Shaver and kept offering to drive me out to McHenry. Finally I wrote DS and told him, and DS said to come on out.
>
> The old pyramidologist and I arrived at DS's cottage in McHenry about 11:00 on a fine summer morning. DS did not often have visitors and was glad to see us. The O.P. had brought with him several of his Great Pyramid drawings, all on huge sheets of drafting paper, with significant features indicated by letters and numbers. At the bottom of each drawing the numbered and lettered features were explained in mathematical terms and related to geographical or astronomical distances, or to dates and events in history. Everything was neatly and exactingly done, a labor of love....
>
> As the O.P. expounded on the meanings he attributed to pyramid measurements and then on

his theories of such matters as how the flying saucer operated (by negative electricity), DS grew wearily resigned to just listening. He got little or no chance to expound on the Shaver Mystery. Dot had fled to a neighbor's house where she remained all the while. About one o'clock DS produced coffee and just enough doughnuts to go around; all he had in the larder, I suspect, as then he was financially at a low ebb.

Along about two o'clock I told the O.P. I had to get back to the office (sensitive about DS's boredom), but the old boy was just getting warmed up and hung onto DS's ears for an hour more. DS and I were being kind to an SM fan and the fan was entirely preoccupied with his own ideas, which is the strange way such fan matters seem to go. I had not got a chance to say more than half a dozen words to DS and he had been unable to do more than grin at me and pump my hand — coming and going — which is how our contacts went.[3]

The Progress of Man

> *"The day will come when there is no more Amazing Stories, but the day will never come when its effect is not written on the pages of man's history."*— Ray Palmer

Each issue of *Amazing Stories* was prepared three months in advance of its release, so Rap wrote his February 1946 editorial in November 1945. Two atom bombs had ended the war three months earlier. It was *Amazing*'s 20th anniversary issue, and Rap reached new heights of idealism, ego, and suspicion in his editorial.

"*Amazing Stories* IS science fiction," he said. "But it is also something more — it is the untrammeled mind of Man; it is the signpost pointing the way to his mental development; it is the slide-rule of his physical progress; and lastly, it is the growth of that most important thing, his soul.... The progress of Man toward his mysterious goal has been influenced enormously by this magazine — may the future carry on this work a hundred fold; for in its pages is the seed of all true knowledge."[4]

Shaver's cover story "Invasion of the Micro Men" continued the saga of his alter ego Mutan Mion, along with the towering nude Princess Vanue and her saucy, satyr-like variform, Arl. Rap was still mourning the loss of David Wright O'Brien, one of his top writers, shot down over Germany a year earlier.

Shaver always suspected that Rap brought him on board at *Amazing* as a replacement for O'Brien. True or not, Rap lovingly doled out O'Brien's unpublished manuscripts in the months following his death. Other writers were wounded but survived, like Hamling and O'Brien's longtime buddy William P. McGivern.

By the time the Japanese formally surrendered aboard the USS *Missouri* on September 2, 1945, *Amazing Stories* had already featured three Shaver cover stories. Even the casual Ziff-Davis SF reader could see that something had changed radically. The Shaver Mystery and *Amazing Stories* had merged.

A new crop of writers stepped up to meet Rap's new editorial needs. One husband-and-wife team named de Courcy began to write cave stories *à la* Shaver. They claimed to be firm believers, even down to tribulations caused by deros. In an editorial, Rap explained that the de Courcys told him of "the hardships of writing each manuscript for us; which included, among other things, plagues of insects which departed only when the manuscript was finished; voices; acts of violence; mysterious rappings, and so on."[5]

In 1945 Rap launched "What Man Can Imagine," a feature where readers were encouraged to "present new theories, new science, new ideas that are not yet accepted by the world as fact...."⁶ Conspiracy was also becoming an important part of the Shaver Mystery. Rap warned his readers that unseen forces were trying to silence him. It added a new sense of urgency to Shaver's message.

Rog Phillips appeared for the first time (under his real name Roger Phillips Graham) in the February 1946 *Amazing*. Graham, a self-styled mathematician and avowed atheist, burst on the scene with some incredible claims, one of which was his discovery of "the solution to the fundamental nature of the universe in explicit and demonstrable form which ... will put all science on the same foundation of logical perfection and exactness as is mathematics and geometry itself."⁷

He explained that his mathematical revelations were coming to him from somewhere beyond his own mind. He was convinced that his parents were not really his parents, and said he arrived on Earth via Halley's comet. As a boy he possessed the ability to see "creatures around the house that stood silently, watching, with enormous eyes."⁸ His first article recounted the influence of the Oahspe bible on his life.

As Rap had done with so many other writers, he took Graham under his wing. He claimed that Graham's first letter inspired him to send $500 with instructions to buy a ticket for the next train to Chicago, which he did. Rap met a tall, slender 35 year old who impressed him as something of a "dreamer and idealist." Chester Geier was also there to witness Graham's arrival:

> [H]e was a bachelor while in Chicago, occasionally dated Bea Mahaffey, gal editor of Ray Palmer's own mags, a tallish strongly built fellow, solemn and serious, with a cigarette always in the corner of his mouth and curling smoke into one eye, which eye later developed problems. In an issue of one of his mags, Rap told a curious story of how Graham reacted to the Shaver Mystery; he claimed he was a Titan, one of Shaver's Elder Races, and threatened to kill Rap for revealing forbidden secrets....⁹

Rap talked Graham out of homicide and encouraged him to write for *Amazing Stories*. His first story, Rap said, was terrible, but eventually Graham developed into an exceptional writer, with popular stories like "So Shall Ye Reap." Said Geier, "Graham had a deep, slogging sort of mind and was not mercurial, like Hamling. He married a girl he met at an SF convention and then died."

In Graham, as with Shaver, Rap found a fellow traveler who clicked with his ideas about the inner workings of the universe. Graham went on to become a popular writer of non–Shaver Mystery science fiction, and was even nominated for a Hugo award for Best Novelette in 1959. But the mercurial Bill Hamling was not impressed:

> Roger Graham was a loony toon. He was a kind of a phony guy. He wanted to make a living at doing nothing, and was very diligent in doing that. He wrote anything that Ray asked him to. He was a hack. I liked him, and actually he was a good gin player. He was one of the best gin partners.... Roger was a hunkered-over fella, and very casual; I never saw him with a tie. In those days, you sometimes wore a tie. Today you don't very often. At Ziff-Davis you always wore a tie. Oh yes, you never came down without a tie on. You could take your jacket off, but you always had the tie.¹⁰

The Shaver Mystery added a few subtler changes to *Amazing*, like Rap's choice of science fillers. His "Science Quiz," a straightforward science feature, disappeared entirely, as had the question mark on his Shaver Mystery feature "Report from the Forgotten Past?" A new crop of filler writers emerged: Vincent Gaddis, John McCabe Moore, and the readers' favorite, L. Taylor Hansen, whose adventurous tales of lost civilizations, petroglyphs, Aztec calendars, and exotic native rites were a good fit for the new *Amazing Stories*. Hansen, as it turned out, was a woman, but hid the fact from readers.

Rap's predilection for occult subjects had taken a front seat. It was all too obvious in *Amazing*'s June 1946 issue, where Rap confronted his newest group of readers — the spiritualists. They were lured to *Amazing* by Rap's new slant. A metaphysical group from San Diego, California, Borderland Sciences Research Foundation (Meade Layne was their director), advised that taunting the dero set Rap on a dangerous path. If he valued his life, Layne said, he should drop the Shaver Mystery pronto. Layne's information came from Mark Probert, a trance medium in daily contact with a group of spirits that knew about such things.

The feisty Rap countered that spirits using mediums as a mouthpiece were more than likely deros trying to throw him off track. No one, human or inhuman, was capable of threatening *Amazing*'s editor, he said. To prove it, he revealed a blockbuster: that he and his family had recently been the target of kidnappers.

The kidnappings were meant to put an end to the Shaver Mystery once and for all. Rap learned of the plot from a friend named Joe, who advised him to go public. Corroborating Rap's source was Richard Shaver himself, who said he was in touch with a cave ally that told of clandestine dero meetings under London and Berlin. His informant said the meetings "had been held to determine what to do about us.... And to cover up the kidnapping, trained doubles for all of us were to be substituted and the world would never know that we had been kidnapped and that the people in our place were dero...."[11] All ended well when Rap learned that the deros realized their plan was unfeasible. Rap noted in his report, "All these bits of info come to Mr. Shaver by means of telaug ray operated by tero in the caves...."[12]

Insider Bill Hamling observed Shaver at times when the tero's information came through. "The guy never denied — in fact he bragged that he heard voices — and he did hear voices! I'm telling you, over the years, I was a witness to it. He'd almost go into a trance ... listening to something. [He would say,] 'Well, Bill, the teros told me this, and or the deros.' The two groups, teros, t-e-r-o were the good guys. But he had a lot of bad guys, like the dero: d-e-r-o. All of that is true stuff."[13]

It was a strange, confusing, and exciting time for the Ziff-Davis fiction group. Rap had not only become a scholar of the arcane Oahspe bible, he was also experimenting with a vegetarian diet. At age 36, he was enjoying an experimental stage of life.

Riders on the Storm

"Ray Palmer wanted me to replace him some day."—William L. Hamling

William L. Hamling was a steady contract writer for the Ziff-Davis fiction group, but what he really wanted was a salaried editorial position. Ray was editing *Amazing Stories*, *Fantastic Adventures*, *Mammoth Adventures*, and *Mammoth Western*, not to mention spending substantial amounts of his time rewriting Shaver's manuscripts. Fandom's ongoing siege at the castle walls was merciless. Besides Shaver, Rap was tutoring other new writers to replace those who had died or moved on.

In January 1946, Rap informed Hamling that he would ask Mr. Davis to hire him as an assistant editor. Hamling was elated, but his meeting with Davis was far from what he expected. "I failed the first interview with him," Hamling said. "Ray came with me to see him, because Ray wanted me on his staff as his personal assistant.... Then I was hired a little later, and I stayed with them for five years until they moved the company to New York."[14]

Hamling now shared an office with Rap, his dream come true. He attended poker games at Rap's Evanston home (as did Browne, William McGivern, Robert Bloch, Rog Phillips, and others), bowled with Rap on the Ziff-Davis team and generally learned the ropes from Rap working at a big-name publishing company. "I simply *loved* my work," Hamling said.[15]

When the clock on the wall struck 12 noon, Rap and his inner circle walked to Eitel's Old Heidelberg Rathskeller on Randolph near State for a martini lunch. Eitel's was air conditioned and featured Herr Louie and the Weasel and their Hungry Five, who played nightly. Hamling saw to it their "club" got preferential treatment. Hamling recalled in a 2009 interview:

> Yeah, terrific place, right down town in Chicago. We always walked from our building to any place in the Loop. Ray didn't drink. Once in a while he might have a sip of wine, but he was not a drinker. In those days, I might have a martini. That was our headquarters for lunch. Yeah, we had a table that I tipped the maitre d' five dollars a week [to reserve for us]. Can you believe what they'd do for five bucks? And we had our own table five days a week Monday thru Friday for lunch.

Jubilation accompanied the end of wartime paper shortages with *Amazing*'s May 1946 issue. It also meant the return of advertising, which had been removed during the war's paper shortage. William B. Ziff agreed to counter the shortage by removing all ads, thus allowing more reading enjoyment for the fighting men overseas.

Eitel's Old Heidelberg Rathskeller as it looked in the 1940s when Rap, Bill Hamling and Howard Browne met there for lunch nearly every weekday.

From now on, *Amazing Stories* was back to its monthly publishing schedule, with every issue selling out at newsstands. The Shaver Mystery was a phenomenal success for sales. Still, the stately Ziff, known to presidents, senators, and those in positions of power, was doubtful of Rap's approach.

Word began wafting up to Ziff's hideaway in New York's Chatham Hotel that unflattering hype from the likes of *Harper's* had sullied the Ziff-Davis brand, and that well-placed brickbats were being thrown at his SF and fantasy magazines. Letters from angry fans reached Ziff at his suite. The Shaver Mystery, they advised, was dangerous nonsense aimed at lunatics.

Browne was likely bending Ziff's ear with his own complaints about Rap's editorial approach. Hamling was dodging fandom's poisoned arrows due to his proximity to Rap. The critics claimed Rap *knew* the Shaver Mystery was a hoax, ergo, he was a con man intent on scamming his readers. Hamling disagreed, but was unable to hold back the tide. "Somebody got to Bill Ziff with that kind of chatter," he said. "Bill Ziff believed it, and he told Davis that he thought Palmer was a crackpot.... But that wasn't true at all. He wasn't a phony. *Astounding Science Fiction*, the Smith & Street publication in New York, had 80,000 [readers]. Ziff-Davis had three or four times that through Palmer and the Shaver Mystery. Ziff could read numbers, and they spelled *dollars*!"[16]

Ziff and Davis conferred on their next move. Was it in their best interest to censure Rap? After all, he was making the company a pile of money.

"I'll tell you what happened," Hamling continued. "After that type of conversation with the owners of the company — and this was a big company that had half a dozen major publications, and occupied two floors of a skyscraper in downtown Chicago — a big deal, you know — Ziff finally said, 'He *is* a little bit wacky,' but he never told Davis to fire him or anything, because the circulation of *Amazing Stories*, where Shaver was involved through Palmer, skyrocketed to hundreds of thousands of readers."[17]

So Ziff looked the other way. When Ziff waffled, the fans continued their anti–Palmer effort through fanzines. But Rap stood firm in his regular column, "The Observatory":

> [W]e've a few remarks to direct at nobody in particular, or everybody in particular (take your choice) which are not in any sense "editorial." First, some few readers seem to be worried about us; they ask us what we will do when we have to admit that the Shaver Mystery is really the Shaver Mystery Hoax; and how we'll like it when the boss fires us because of the tremendous drop in circulation that will come because of our sheepish admission. For those of our readers (they are in the minority!) who are *certain* the Shaver Mystery is a hoax, let it be definitely placed on the record that your editor *believes* it is a legitimate mystery, and that he *knows* it is neither a hoax on his part nor on Mr. Shaver's! Have you got it, or do we have to repeat it? [W]e predict right now that the circulation we have today will be peanuts beside the circulation when we have paper and presses to put out the number of copies *you readers are demanding that we put out.*[18]

More Proofs

"Ray Palmer kinda lived in his own fiction world!" — William L. Hamling

Ray Palmer was making far too much money for William B. Ziff to shut him down, so he assumed that as long as he kept circulation figures soaring in the six figures, his boss would let him continue. This was the devil's bargain between Ziff and Rap: They were attached at the hip not by ideology, but by the almighty dollar.

As an editor, Rap was shrewd but he had his weaknesses. He believed in the Universe of All Possibilities, and that included ancient high-tech civilizations, invisible rays, and people living 100 miles in the sky above Duluth. His very first science fiction yarn "The Time Ray of Jandra" was about time-traveling to a vanished high-tech civilization in the African jungle. Rap's boyhood imagination never left him.

Back in McHenry, Illinois, Dick Shaver was snapping photos with his Kodak in an attempt to capture evidence of dero skullduggery on film. He sent an exposed roll to Rap for developing. They were looking for concrete proof of the Mystery. But the film was inconclusive, Rap said.

"Thus we have one picture of Mr. Shaver, asleep (the camera lens having remained open into the early dawn); one picture which is just an unrecognizable blur; and one picture which seems to show a ray projecting upward directly through Mr. Shaver's bed and into the air. It has baffled the staff of *Popular Photography*; but being only one blurred photo, your editor cannot call it conclusive evidence. Mr. Shaver says that cave tero insist that they will produce something if and when they can get through the dero guard ray."[19]

Also of note in 1946 was Rap's first mention of what would become a new obsession: flying saucers. "If you don't think space ships visit the earth regularly ... then the files of Charles Fort[20] and your editor's own files are something you should see. Your editor has hundreds of reports (especially from returned soldiers) of objects that were clearly seen and tracked which could have been nothing but space ships. And if you think responsible parties in world governments are ignorant of the fact of space ships visiting Earth, you just don't think the way we do."[21]

Rap was ahead of the curve. He wrote this a year before newspaper headlines across America ballyhooed Idaho pilot Kenneth Arnold's sighting of nine silvery discs skipping over Mt. Rainier, Washington.

The Pendulum Swings

> *"More persons, on the whole, are humbugged by believing in nothing than by believing too much."*— P.T. Barnum

The turning point came in 1947. This was the zenith year for the Shaver Mystery, when Rap devoted *Amazing Stories*' entire June issue to Shaver's unique worldview. Changes were afoot much earlier, in 1946, when William B. Ziff began to change his mind about Rap's new wave in science fiction.

Still euphoric over circulation figures, Rap boasted to his readers that the Audit Bureau of Circulations reported that Ziff-Davis pulp magazines for February 1946 sold a dizzying 261,611 copies, catapulting him into the stratosphere as a pulp editor. Other publishers tried to lure him away from Ziff-Davis, he said, but his name was so thoroughly connected to *Amazing Stories* he chose to remain loyal.

But the allure of the flying saucers beckoned, and Rap began to enthuse over them as he had done with the Shaver Mystery. Nevertheless, he saw to it that Shaver fueled the juggernaut of what he touted as the "world-famous" Shaver Mystery. And he was still squabbling with fandom's insurgency.

Rap said he had a list of names amounting to 173 of these fen. They demanded that he and Shaver be relegated to the dustbin of history. Again Rap brushed them off. They hated the Shaver Mystery, he said, because "it isn't dogmatic science out of outmoded textbooks!"[22]

Rap reconfirmed his belief in Shaver and the Shaver Mystery, stating it was *not* a hoax. "I believe in the 'mystery' for what it is. Every word uttered editorially in *Amazing Stories* is my *firm conviction,* not any attempt at a hoax...."[23] The Mantong alphabet, he said, was the best proof to date of the reality of the Shaver Mystery.

"More and more of our readers are beginning to 'prove' the Shaver Mystery to their *own* satisfaction. Now that we think about it, isn't proof a personal matter?"[24]

Rap's rejection of accepted science was emphatic as far as it concerned the Shaver Mystery. He trumpeted Shaver as "the new Merritt," one of the finest fiction writers of his day. He ran Shaver stories in other Ziff-Davis magazines, like *Mammoth Adventures* and *Fantastic Adventures*. He ran 15 Shaver Mystery stories for 1947, published under Shaver's name or his pen names. Rap said that Shaver infused vivid insights into ancient history due to his access to the Atlan thought records.

Back in his suite at the Chatham Hotel, Ziff was fretting over a letter signed by a number of BNFs. This one carried enough clout to make him wonder if Rap might not be treading on thin ice. Not only had the Shaver Mystery become a national controversy, it was indelibly linked to the Ziff-Davis brand.

This particular letter became as important as the one Howard Browne tossed into the wastebasket years earlier. But unlike Shaver's letter, saved in the nick of time, this new letter vanished, its contents and signatories lost forever. Rumors about it do exist. Some say it stated that Shaver's Lemurian science contradicted Einstein's Theory of Relativity. That was enough for Ziff. He called Bernard G. Davis and set up a meeting.

Davis had kept a watchful eye on the swirling controversy around Rap, but let it ride. Finally, in the winter of 1946, events coming from within and without the Ziff-Davis Publishing Company forced Rap to change course. Under continuing pressure from BNFs and the negative media coverage, Davis finally agreed with Ziff that the hyperbole surrounding the Shaver Mystery should go. Davis met with Rap, telling him it was fine to publish Shaver yarns as long as he promoted them as *fiction*.

Rap's problem with this new directive was that "hidden truth" had been the selling point of his promotion. It was the wellspring of Rap's magic. Without the Mystery's "fact," reader curiosity would plummet, and Rap knew it. How to comply with this new order and not look like he was recanting or caving in to critics was the challenge.

And so it was that Rap devised a strategy to solve the Shaver Mystery while making it appear as if it was the plan all along. As much as he hated to do it, it would mean eviscerating the Mystery. He advised Davis of his plan, then announced that the Mystery was on the verge of being solved, and the controversy, as well as any further research, was being turned over to a fan club devoted entirely to Shaver. He called it the Shaver Mystery Club. But instead of taking charge of the club as the Mystery's number one cheerleader, Rap gave the job to Ziff-Davis writer Chester S. Geier. Historians have since depicted Geier as a willing, starry-eyed Shaver Mystery devotee.

Geier repudiated the claim, stating it was a shotgun wedding from the start, with Rap holding the shotgun. The first hint of Rap's plan to shake off his responsibility for the Shaver Mystery came in the February 1947 *Amazing* in an open letter signed, "Chester S. Geier." In truth, Rap wrote the letter in the autumn of 1946, outlining the club's scope and purpose and signing Geier's name: "This club will not be commercial, no dues, no staff of officers, no swank. Just earnest seekers after the truth, like myself and Mr. Shaver. I am preparing (with the kind assistance of Mr. Shaver as editor) a club magazine of 64 pages, intended to appear every month, containing original material such as appears in 'Discussions'.... How about it, Shaver Mystery fans? Let's do more than just *talk* about the mystery. After all, we all know it's no fake by now!"[25] Fast-forwarding 35 years into his future, Chester Geier was ready to set the record straight.

The Shaver Mystery Club
By Chester S. Geier

> *"Rap kept the Shaver Mystery perking for years by playing on suspense."*— Chester Geier

If my recollections are not entirely off the beam, a group of prominent SF fans wrote to Bernard G. Davis, then president of the Ziff-Davis Publishing Company ... and complained about Rap's huckstering of the Shaver Mystery. Shaver, they said in effect if not in actual words, was demeaning SF with unscientific and illogical claims, was prostituting *Amazing Stories*, and was warping the minds of unsophisticated and uncritical readers. Davis was aware of the tumult in *Amazing* but had tolerated it as it was selling some 90,000 copies of the magazine per month [this figure is by Geier's reckoning] where a SF magazine was doing well to sell 50,000 copies and very well to sell 70,000 per month. But it seems the SF fan letter — with quite a number of signatures, I think — gave him second thoughts. He decided enough was enough and told Rap to cease and desist. It was okay to present Shaver stories, it seemed, as long as they were presented as fiction and not as a factual sun around which *Amazing Stories* revolved.

Not long after this, Bill Hamling told me Rap was starting the Shaver Mystery Club and wanted me to serve as president. The Club was to publish a monthly magazine to provide the forum for the Shaver Mystery no longer available in *Amazing Stories*. I was knocking myself out trying to build a reputation as an SF writer and did not see that being directly associated with the SM was going to help me.

But in being so much alone as a writer, in fumbling for new directions, for more mature ideas and conflicts, in having a family to support, in being pressured to do bread-and-butter hack writing and having no time to relax and reflect, I had, like too many writers before me, slipped into a quagmire. I hated the hack stuff, which I hid under pseudonyms, wrote it like slogging through mud, and my production was way down. I was getting story advances from Rap to keep me going and what with owing him money I was in no position to refuse the honor of serving as president of the Shaver Mystery Club. Besides, Bill told me, the club was a great idea that could make money for all concerned. He was quite enthusiastic himself.

Rap had acquired a long list of names of people who over the years — from about 1945 to 1947 — had expressed interest in the Shaver Mystery. We sent a letter to these names announcing the formation of the Shaver Mystery Club and inviting membership, which included the *Shaver Mystery Club Magazine* at $1 per copy, a huge sum in those days. Subscriptions-memberships poured into my writing office (the address of the club) and shortly we had about 3,000 names. Publication of the first issue of the club magazine was late and came just in time to keep hundreds of irate members from coming to Chicago to assault me physically. The magazine was small but handsome, professionally printed and bound, and illustrated with drawings in an oddly Oriental style by Shaver himself. It made club members happy and for a while the heat was off me.

Despite a further boost for the Shaver Mystery Club in the form of a letter with my name to the approximately 90,000 readers of *Amazing Stories*, the 3,000 members we obtained did not mark an auspicious start. Perhaps not so many people were interested in the SM after all; perhaps the $1 per copy for the club magazine was too high. Apparently Rap lost interest, or had his interest diluted by another enterprise: *FATE* magazine, the first issue of which appeared in the spring of 1948.

The second issue of the *Shaver Mystery Club Magazine* also was late and following issues even later. I had to plead with Bill to get Rap to move. About all that was being done in the magazine was to run unpublished stories by Dick Shaver, with his drawings, and some letters from club members. It seemed Rap had no time or interest for the sort of editorials and comments on the Mystery that he did for *Amazing Stories*.

Shaver was anxious about the club and magazine and wrote to offer his help and suggest things we should do editorially. I did not have editorial control of the magazine. I had ideas, too, inspired by things club members wanted to read in the magazine, such as a picture and biography of Shaver, and a history of the Shaver Mystery and the Mantong alphabet. I could only pass on suggestions to Rap and Bill and stress that club members were getting angry about delays in publication of the magazine. But time wore on and still little or nothing was done. Shaver seemed to lapse into a despairing silence, evidently under the impression that much of the situation was my fault because I was not interested in him or the Shaver Mystery.

One Sunday afternoon, not long after the Shaver Mystery Club was started, I accompanied Rap, Browne, and Bill Hamling on a visit to see Shaver in McHenry, where we had Sunday dinner with him and Dot. I found Shaver — this was my first meeting with him — a husky and well-built man in his middle 30s, ruggedly good-looking, quiet and subdued, with sort of an artistic sensitivity about him. It seems that in his youth he had studied art and had been interested in earning a living as an artist. He had a unique drawing style.

He kept looking at me in a sort of anxious and appealing way as if he had things on his mind that he felt he could not communicate then and there. Dot was a matronly woman, sort of Junoesque, and I sensed she was the dominant force in the Shaver household. They were living in a small wood summer cottage and the group of us crowded the small room we sat in.

Shortly after that visit, Shaver wrote me that he wanted to come to the office in Chicago to help with Shaver Mystery Club work. I told him my end was well in hand and that the only important things had to be done by Rap. Shaver wanted to come anyway and asked me to write a letter he could show Dot saying I needed him at the office. It appeared he needed a good excuse in order to be able to get away. I sent him a letter saying that imminent doom could be staved off only by a prompt visit from Dick Shaver.

A few days later, about 10 in the morning, Dick Shaver showed up at my office. He was wearing heavy boots, a flannel shirt, a leather jacket, and a Homburg hat, this last apparently for deference to city culture. He communicated with me on my typewriter. He was worried about the handling of the Shaver Mystery Club. He was generally unhappy. He had writing problems and told me I had writing problems because I did not let myself go and let the wordage pour out. I briefed him on the Shaver Mystery Club situation. By then it was around 11 o'clock and Shaver suggested we go to a burlesque show. I was rather dumbfounded and told him that the theater did not open until 1:30 in the afternoon. We had lunch at a nearby cafeteria and he returned home.

The Club involved me in a very considerable amount of work and I handled my end punctually and honorably. I did all I could do, but my end was mainly clerical: I kept record cards of members with addresses and address changes, dates of membership, amount of membership fees paid, typed address labels, mailed out copies of the magazine, answered a large correspondence consisting of questions and complaints.

I tried to keep up with my writing, too, and got into the habit of coming to the office on Saturdays and Sundays and of staying late weekday evenings. I got frazzled emotionally. Club members were writing to denounce me as a crook and a cheat who had taken their money without any honest intention of delivering the magazine as promised. I kept soothing them and each late issue of the magazine stilled complaints for a while, then they began again. (Correction: reading back over the last few pages, I realize the magazine was published quarterly instead of monthly; monthly publication would have been even more of a disaster.)

By about the fourth issue of the magazine, membership in the Club dwindled to about half of what it was at the start. Around a year had passed [that would put it in mid–1948]. One evening Bill came to the office and told me Rap had decided to turn the Shaver Mystery Club over to Shaver, all the club records and the magazine printing, paper, and engraving bills, postage and part of the rent on the office. Dick Shaver, who had been wanting a hand in the club, suddenly had everything dumped into his lap and I think he hardly knew what to do.

It was a rough way to treat him; I feel he was used and abused. I think he got out a couple of issues of the *Shaver Mystery Club Magazine* on his own and then some fans came to his rescue and put out a mimeographed fanzine version of the magazine, much less professional and attractive than the original.

Get Lost, Mr. Shaver!

"Roll on, Shaver Mystery!"—Ray Palmer

Shaver Mystery fans began to notice fewer Shaver yarns on *Amazing*'s contents page. Rap blamed that on the Chicago printers' strike. Though Rap's role in the Mystery was waning, it appeared just the opposite in print. He continued his role as a firebrand besieged by doubting fandom. To affirm his commitment to supporters, he planned an entire issue devoted to Shaver Mystery stories, Shaver Mystery trivia, and Shaver Mystery science features. Rap was about to reverse his stand on the Shaver Mystery, but the average reader would have been hard-pressed to see it at first.

The all–Shaver issue became a monumental undertaking, full of snafus that hinted at a dero conspiracy. He told readers of bizarre problems getting the issue to press. Galleys went missing, then mysteriously turned up at the print shop: "When they *were* delivered, they were almost entirely useless," Rap explained, "because ranging from just a few dozen typographical errors, to as many as 92 in four inches of type, they required complete resetting of all vital passages! Even more mysterious than otherwise letter-perfect typographers should set so atrociously, the proofreaders who received that copy for checking *found no errors!*"[26]

Rap and Bill Hamling jumped into the breach in a mad dash to proofread and clean up the mess. The problems arose, Rap said, from Shaver's deros subverting their effort to expose them. "We only mention what we have as just one more proof (?) that Shaver isn't the only one who has what he calls 'tamper.'"[27]

The question mark after the word "proof" was an insider clue. It was one of Rap's subtle changes, a nod to William B. Ziff to let him know the plan was moving forward.

Still, the June 1947 issue was exactly what Shaver fans had been begging for: a list of proofs and a recap of the Shaver Mystery from Day One. Rap even dug into his ironclad memory to describe his first encounter with Dick Shaver:

> Deluged by thousands of letters, and faced with such evidence that here we had something that was definitely not a fraud, your editor made a special trip to Barto to investigate. While there we heard Mr. Shaver's "voices," but to our vexation, the gist of them was that we were "a dope." Later Shaver confided he had requested them to "lay off" while your editor was there. However, we did determine that the "voices" were not due to microphones, hidden on the premises, but were either real, or in our own mind. Self-hypnosis the experts would call it. Let's say that's what it was, and save the experts more postage.[28]

Rap's self-hypnosis explanation and use of quotation and question marks whenever he came close to calling the Shaver Mystery factual was undoubtedly at the urging of Ziff. Proof had become "proof (?)" and voices were "voices," leaving the door wide open for the reader to decide. As a parting shot for his Shaver Mystery edition, Rap dropped a bombshell that suggested an imminent invasion of the United States was about to happen:

> We can do no more than hint at the amazing "fifth column from hell" that we have begun to uncover and which will be presented in the future ... the incredible way in which a foreign government(s) may have obtained cavern mech, set them up in this country, and is using them to set up a fifth column to end all fifth columns in a future invasion! No, we have no proof, but we intend to present a consecutive narration of what we suspect, and maybe it will be reasonable enough to follow to its bitter end.[29]

The "bitter end" was unfolding in his office at the Ziff-Davis Publishing Company. This is where Richard Shaver's mystery was about to become *persona non grata*.

Goodbye, Howard, Adieu!

> *"This morning I wrote eight pages eulogizing Ray Palmer. It's now in the wastebasket."— Howard Browne, 1977*

Ray Palmer's inner circle discovered a defector in its ranks when Howard Browne handed his resignation to William B. Ziff in the spring of 1947. Without fanfare, Browne's name disappeared from *Amazing*'s staff page with the December 1947 issue. One of Rap's most strident critics, Browne said (years later) that he was fed up with Rap's editorial policy, specifically, the Shaver Mystery. He emptied his desk and moved to California where he worked on screenplays for TV shows and continued writing his series of Chandler-inspired novels already begun in Chicago.

Browne had his own ideas about the Ziff-Davis pulp fiction group, specifically, that *Amazing Stories* should target a more mature audience. As long as Rap was in charge, Browne knew he was doomed to play second fiddle to the Milwaukee wunderkind. Their stormy relationship was hinted at in Browne's 1977 Ray Palmer eulogy: "Besides teaching me to be something more than a journeyman editor, he set out to drill in me the basics of dramatic writing. He was patient with me, although he tried to cloak it with an acid wit that raised blisters on my ego."[30]

Browne's ego prevailed. He found another job. Though Rap trumpeted Browne as one of his greatest discoveries, his departure made nary a ripple on the surface of the fiction group. There was deafening silence at Ziff-Davis. Rap said nothing about the resignation in *Amazing*, only a cryptic blurb in the September 1947 issue that Ziff made a decision to "suspend" Browne's detective magazines in order to shift valuable paper to the sizzling hot *Amazing Stories*. Browne would not return until 1949, after Rap's resignation.

Browne disliked his role as Rap's assistant, and since Bill Hamling was allied with Rap, Browne had little patience for him, too. "Bill Hamling was never one of my favorite characters," Browne quipped in a letter to Chester Geier.[31] Geier suspected that his dislike stemmed from Hamling's cocky, in-your-face personality. It all went back to the day in 1946, when Hamling learned that novelist John Evans was really Howard Browne. Geier recalled, "I don't think Browne liked Bill's reaction to the John Evans revelation and I suspect now that Hamling's other traits and qualities did not set well with Browne."[32]

Geier occasionally allowed Browne use the Lawrence Avenue writing office whenever Browne needed privacy for his work. Geier later had second thoughts after an incident he recalled in 1982:

> For a while, before he left Chicago for L.A., he used a room in the writing offices I shared with Bill Hamling while working on a mystery novel. One evening he brought a young woman there who was trying to break into mystery writing. In the process of "educating" her, he had sexual relations with her. I happened to be there, not knowing of the assignation until later. I thought they were just talking ... presently Browne told me they were going out for ice cream.
>
> About this time he got a divorce from his wife, a nice, simple lady, who once complained to me that he never told her about his activities and particularly about how much money he made. Probably he was planning ahead. He was a member of a hard-nosed (and hard-hearted) bunch, all taking care of No. 1, which about sums up the "glamour" of the old days. Hold no illusions about the Ziff-Davis group as a bunch of rollicking geniuses; they were ordinary human beings with a certain amount of talent and a generous amount of luck.[33]

Flying Saucer Conspiracy

"Your editor has kept secrets from his readers...."— Ray Palmer

Browne's departure from the fiction group did nothing to change the direction of the Shaver Mystery, but anyone who knew Ray knew a sea change was coming. It would affect Rap's career and the careers of others who depended on him for a living—especially Richard Shaver.

A rumor circulating at the time suggested that pressure from the government made Ziff cancel Ray's promotion of flying saucers and the Shaver Mystery. Hamling confirmed that government agents often stopped by the Ziff-Davis offices during the World War II and post–World War II years.

Pressure on Ziff increased in 1947 when Rap became a key player in a flying saucer investigation that led to the deaths of two Air Force intelligence officers—not that it was Rap's fault. It all had to do with two Tacoma, Washington, "loggers" named Dahl and Crisman. The story was as strange as anything that came out the Shaver Mystery, and it all started with an Idaho pilot.

On a routine flight on June 24, 1947, Boise pilot Kenneth Arnold spotted nine silvery discs unlike any flying objects he had seen. There was no name for flying saucers in those days, though American bomber pilots brought home stories of "foo fighters," luminous flying objects seen during bombing raids over Europe.

News of Arnold's sighting found its way into scores of daily papers across America.

Huge headlines screamed about a new postwar phenomenon: flying saucers. This proved to Rap that science fiction had again proven itself as prophetic literature. Throughout his career he had written of these spaceships, and now they were making real headlines. He began collecting newspaper clippings of saucer sightings and informed his fans that Shaver had written of the flying discs in his Shaver Mystery stories. Shaver's Lemurian "rollat," an anti-gravity flying machine used in the caverns, became another of Rap's proofs (?) of the Shaver Mystery.

Flying saucers were the lead for Rap's *Amazing Stories* editorial in October 1947, and for a time, flying saucers nearly eclipsed Shaver:

> A portion of the now world-famous Shaver Mystery has now been proved! On June 25th [sic] (and subsequent confirmations included earlier dates) mysterious supersonic vessels, either space ships or ships from the caves, were sighted in this country.... During the past few years, your editor has kept secrets from his readers, for the single reason that duplication of reports *after* publication of the first report would lead to a flood of such reports from those pranksters who have bothered us in the past with fakes. Now we can reveal that we have had numerous reports of these disc-ships and that each one has agreed in all essential details with the reports now made public in so sensational a manner.[34]

Shaver added his two cents in the same issue: "The discs can be a space invasion, a secret new army plane ... *or* they can be Shaver's space ships, taking off and landing regularly on Earth for centuries past, and seen today as they have always been — as a mystery."[35]

Shaver seemed less enthusiastic than Rap, realizing (if only subconsciously) that his Mystery was being usurped by a newer sensation. "I predict that nothing more will be seen," Shaver said, "and the truth of what the strange disc ships really are will never be disclosed to the common people."[36]

Rap's saucer excitement grew. He reported that within two months of Arnold's sighting he had received nearly 400 clippings about the saucers from readers. He encouraged them to continue. "*Amazing Stories* ... takes exclusive credit for telling you about the visitors in a truthful manner. We not only have imagined them in our stories, as have other science fiction magazines, thereby proving prophetic — but we have been the only ones with courage to point out that they have already been *seen*. So, if you want to get the straight dope from now on, read this magazine. It has guts as well as imagination."[37]

Rap planned an all–flying saucer issue, similar to his special Shaver Mystery issue earlier that year. But the FBI took note of Rap's flying disc fervor and in September 1947, agents interviewed Rap and Shaver. The reports, filed at the FBI's Chicago office, concluded that Rap and Shaver conspired to create the "flying disc hysteria" gripping the nation. The agents asserted that Rap's constant chatter about flying saucers in *Amazing Stories* was making people see things in the sky: "[I]t should be noted that Raymond Palmer, Shaver's employer, was from the start 'exploiting' the appearance of the flying discs, possibly to enhance the appeal of Shaver's stories. It is possible, therefore, that the entire flying disc theory was conceived by Palmer and Shaver."[38]

As early as December 1944 Rap learned of a meeting between Ziff and two Secret Service agents who came calling at Ziff's office. Rap mentioned it to Shaver, but Shaver was not surprised: "One way a dero can hurt you," Shaver advised, "is by tamper. They are very accustomed to fooling people — such as that they are the Secret Service — and once the impression is conveyed into a mind that they are Secret Service, the victim is apt to believe anything they tell him. If they have so convinced Ziff, you will have a hard time getting certain things done, for he will veto it every time...."[39]

Rumors had it that Ziff was about to shut down the Shaver Mystery due to arm-twisting from the Air Force. Rap, too, felt that Air Force "brass hats" and "shave-tail lieutenants" threw cold water on his special flying saucer issue. Rap, like Shaver, knew something was going on behind closed doors, and that government agents were turning up the heat on Ziff.

"The United States government, in the form of various operatives, frequented our editorial offices at Ziff-Davis during the 1940s," Hamling confirmed. "They felt that the Ziff-Davis company, through *Amazing Stories* and Ray Palmer's staff, was responsible for all this shit. Can you believe it? They kept a very close contact with us people. That is all true."[40]

All hell broke loose when Rap became directly involved in the bizarre Maury Island saucer incident in Tacoma, Washington, further tarnishing his image with Ziff. It became known as "The Maury Island Hoax," and Rap unknowingly was the patsy of an alleged government operative named Fred L. Crisman. The story is so complex it deserves a book of its own, which it got some years ago with Kenn Thomas' *Maury Island UFO: The Crisman Conspiracy* (1999). Ray co-authored his own version of the story with Kenneth Arnold, *The Coming of the Saucers* (1952).

What made the incident worthy of a military presence at Rap's office was that two Air Force Intelligence officers sent to investigate the sighting died. On returning to their home base at Hamilton Field in California, their B-25 crashed near Kelso, Washington. Newspaper headlines called it "Sabotage!" when reporters learned the plane was carrying debris from one of the flying saucers.

Rap was left holding the bag, fingered as the instigator behind the whole affair. Ziff was likely contacted by military intelligence, informing him of his editor's part in the melodrama. This, coupled with the ensuing hoopla over the Shaver Mystery, did not endear Rap to the Ziff-Davis Company.

Rap knew of the government's interest in his work, explaining it to New Orleans District Attorney Jim Garrison in 1968. Garrison had learned of Rap's run-in with the shadowy Fred L. Crisman and the Maury Island saucer incident. Garrison (played by Kevin Costner in Irving Stone's film *JFK*) was heading up an investigation into the John F. Kennedy assassination. Crisman had apparently moved on from crashed flying saucers to turn up as one of the so-called "three tramps" on the grassy knoll in Dallas at the moment of JFK's assassination. Rap gladly told Garrison of his dealings with Crisman, as well as his promotion of the Shaver Mystery and subsequent scrutiny by federal agents:

> Obviously you would imagine the reaction to [the Shaver Mystery] would be to consider it fiction, so you can imagine my surprise to find that many government agencies felt called upon to investigate it, and to pry very vigorously into my own life and background. As an example, the FBI, the various military secret service agencies, and the CIA were constant callers ... this puzzled me. And interested me![41]

The Tacoma incident added to Rap's reputation as a hoaxer; now he was the "Chicago publisher" behind a deadly scam involving Air Force Intelligence. The dirty laundry was hung out to dry in Captain Edward J. Ruppelt's book *The Report on Unidentified Flying Objects* (1956), which summed up the Air Force's *Project Blue Book* investigation into flying saucers. Though Rap was innocent, Ruppelt's accusations in an official publication of the U.S. Air Force made it hard for Rap to wash off the slander. If Fred L. Crisman's (and the government's?) intent was to publicly discredit Rap, it seems to have worked.

1948

> *"And one last blast at those critics who 'note we are soft-pedaling the Shaver Mystery.' Ever hear of the knockout punch? It takes a big wind-up."*—Ray Palmer

The "big wind-up" actually came *after* the knockout punch had hit its target. William B. Ziff delivered the K.O. when he told Rap to stop promoting the Shaver Mystery. Rap was attempting to fulfill Ziff's mandate without appearing to capitulate in public. He had already founded the Shaver Mystery Club, which would handle the Shaver controversy outside the parameters of *Amazing Stories*. But he still had important details to work out. His solution was as brilliant as it was obvious, and with the October 1947 issue, Rap set it in motion.

At first it was hard to see *any* change in editorial policy. January 1948 found Rap still defending the Mystery and Dick Shaver, predicting the proofs he had promised from the very beginning would come within a few months. There were subtle hints that something was about to happen. Something big.

Printed in full in the January issue was a declaration of opposition to the Shaver Mystery hammered out by angry fans at the 1947 Philadelphia Worldcon (the Philcon). The "Resolution Concerning the Lemurian Policy of *Amazing Stories*" was a scathing line-by-line repudiation of the Mystery's basic tenets, followed by dire mental health warnings to Rap's readers and a list of fandom-approved SF magazines.

Rap saw this as a declaration of war, meant to banish all Ziff-Davis publications from fandom. A new fanfeud seemed inevitable. Rap was livid: "Well, readers of *Amazing Stories*, here's the official stand of 'fandom,' our honorable opponents of the Shaver Mystery. We present it as they wrote and voted on it in their convention. We don't know the results of the voting, but we'll wager *Amazing Stories* wasn't on the list!"[42]

No Shaver Mystery yarns appeared in the January 1948 issue. Instead, Rap threw in two slush-pile Shaver essays on the futility of life and the hidden power brokers who keep it that way.

Further distancing himself from the Mystery, Rap included a debate feature titled "The Shaverian Hypothesis." Its purpose was to apply the acid test to Shaver. A new writer to *Amazing*, Robert Paul Kidwell, took the opposing view of the pro-and-con debate. The name "Kidwell" is suspicious, suggesting Rap was, in fact, both debaters. Mr. Kidwell was far from critical. However, a letter purporting to be from Kidwell surfaced in the April 1948 "Discussions," possibly a shill to confirm Kidwell's existence.

The letter discussed topics that coincided strangely with Rap's pet themes: the threat of the atom bomb, the prescience of science fiction, and looking to the past for answers to questions posed in the present. Since Rap had been writing Chester Geier's letters, it takes no stretch of the imagination to assume another Rap spoof. In any case, Kidwell confirmed at least some of Shaver's mystery.

"As for the possibility of the Shaver Mystery's being factual, I admit this much," said Kidwell. "[I]t offers one (so far excellent) explanation for the occurrence of Fortean phenomena—that which cannot at present be explained in scientific terms and proved as possibly occurring."[43]

After his mysterious debut, Kidwell promptly vanished. It was becoming clear that Rap's plan was nearing resolution. The upcoming April 1948 issue, he said, would reveal solid proof of the Shaver Mystery, thus ending the controversy. Once solved, the Mystery would no longer be grist for the magazine.

Meanwhile, fan activists were stepping up their efforts to blacklist Shaver, and one SF club in particular began circulating a petition. A sympathetic Shaver fan, a G.I. stationed at Ft. George Meade, Maryland, sent a letter to Shaver warning him of "a powerful anti–Shaver Mystery club ... trying to outlaw your work. They asked my support ... and asked me to sign a petition, which they would use to force the editors to refuse all your work.... They called you everything from a moron to a jerk with a money-making idea."[44]

The March 1948 issue arrived right on schedule. Rap pointed out that Shaver's latest story "Gods of Venus" was straight fiction: "For those of you who object to us calling our stories true (whether they are or not!) let's call this one fiction, and let those who can recognize the true portions (if any) dig them out for themselves."[45]

Instead of the usual complimentary fan letters, "Discussions" had turned to rants against the Shaver Mystery. One reader, Russell A. Bauer of Milwaukee, wrote a searing swipe at Shaverism, summing up with, "One more thing I'd like to add. To my dear friends who thrive on Shaver, and who will no doubt cut my throat verbally, I draw my trusty forty-four and make the following comment: BANG, BANG, BANG."[46]

Finally, Rap gave the big wind-up, as promised, and let it fly. "Next month we are going to do it! Do what? Prove the Shaver Mystery, of course. Yes, we now have a portion of the proof. We still can't produce a dero, or a cave, but dammit, we have something that you can sink your teeth into!"[47]

At the very moment Rap poised himself to give the Mystery the bum's rush, he was in the midst of a plan to free himself from William B. Ziff's short leash. Bill Hamling knew what it was, and so did Frank M. Robinson, the former Ziff-Davis office boy who became one of Rap's SF writers. Everyone seemed to know about the plan except Ziff. Rap called his new exit strategy *FATE* magazine. Robinson, who went on to co-author *The Towering Inferno* and write campaign speeches for San Francisco city supervisor Harvey Milk, noted, "He started *FATE* a few years after the war, and the long lunch hours at Ziff-Davis turned into work sessions at another office close by."[48]

FATE was everything Ziff did *not* want Rap to do with *Amazing*. He featured all the flying saucer reports and occult goosebumps that obsessed him throughout the Shaver Mystery years. Rap began working with Curtis Fuller, Ziff-Davis editor for *Flying* magazine, and in 1948 the first issue of *FATE* hit newsstands. Ziff-Davis execs may have been left in the dark, but Hamling, the most loyal member of Rap's inner circle, was fully briefed: "Ray said to me privately like, 'I want to go out and make my own money. Why should I keep feeding it into the Ziff-Davis company?' *FATE* magazine was first; numero uno. Curt Fuller was also on the staff of *FATE*, because he was a helluva good editor."[49]

Terror in the Ivory Tower

> *"Even if we say something is founded on fact, that doesn't make it true...."*—Ray Palmer, 1948

One spring day in 1948, William B. Ziff left his swank Chatham Hotel suite to make a call on his Chicago publishing office. Whenever word reached the Wabash Avenue office of an impending Ziff visit, staff rolled out the red carpet. Hamling recalled how editor Lila Shaffer would spring into action: "When Bill Ziff came to town, she would instantly drop everything and be his Girl Friday. When he wasn't in town, if Davis [needed] anything, she'd be his secretary. Davis had two secretaries. A steady one, day to day, and a casual one, Lila, and she was also a member of the fiction group, part of our team."[50]

Besides checking with Ray to ensure his edict to dismantle the Shaver Mystery was moving forward, Ziff had also scheduled a meeting with FBI agents. This was very hush-hush. Ziff sat behind the desk of his ultra-plush office, waiting for the G-men summoned by his attorney. Strange things had been happening to Ziff, and he was nervous, unsettled. He feared for his life.

Ziff's beauty pageant secretary ushered in the FBI agents. After seating themselves in front of an expansive mahogany desk, the G-men listened in silence as Ziff explained why they were there. One of the agents took notes, acquired through the Freedom of Information Act in 2009.

According to the agent, "In March 1948 Agents of the Chicago Office interviewed William B. Ziff at the request of his attorney, Thurman Arnold. Ziff rather melodramatically told them of his belief that British agents or Russian agents, as a result of his pro–Zionist activities, were endeavoring to do away with him. He described strange happenings since 1945, including burglary of his apartment, tapping his telephone, surveillances, attempts to poison him, and the sticking of him with sharp instruments which he surmised was being done to inject germs into his system."

The timing of Ziff's misfortunes, between 1945 and 1948, coincided perfectly with Rap's publication of the controversial Shaver Mystery, though Ziff did not believe in dero skullduggery. Nevertheless, it appeared the Ziff-Davis Publishing Company was awash in conspiracies. Something had to give, and the Shaver Mystery would take the fall.

Chester Geier was still handling the Shaver Mystery Club, and Bill Hamling was assisting Rap with the workload at the office. With Howard Browne now living in Hollywood, Hamling was promoted to managing editor of *Fantastic Adventures*. Hamling's first editorial appeared in the November 1947 issue and he continued as editor of *Fantastic Adventures* until the company moved in 1950.

Amazing's "Discussions" letter section, thanks to Rap's new enthusiasm for flying saucers and Fortean phenomena, had transformed from a watering hole for Shaver Mystery buffs to a Fortean bulletin board of saucer sightings and scientific anomalies. There was very little discussion of science fiction. Rap's familiar editorials of three or more chatty, upbeat pages had dwindled to one-page introductions of stories. There was no talk of saucers, caves, rays, or Shaver.

April 1948 rolled around and the Shaver Mystery proof Rap promised was nowhere to be found. Apparently, it had been shelved to allow a mysterious "respectable citizen" to explain them; at least, this was Rap's new storyline:

> This is the month we were going to offer a partial proof of the Shaver Mystery. Well, we've made several interesting discoveries that made us change our plans. One was that someone else was going to publish our "proof," and what could be better than that! ... [W]hen we found out there was another angle, to appear soon under the byline of a respectable citizen of this big country of ours, and one who does not even read *Amazing Stories*, we felt anything we'd say on the same subject would only serve to cast doubt on what he'd say without prompting from us — and after all, *Amazing Stories* is a *fiction* magazine. Even if we say something is founded on fact, that doesn't make it true — and if we insisted on something like that, we'd have people believing our *fiction*.... Now we can turn the Shaver Mystery over to the Shaver Mystery Club ... and relax.... Editorially, we have already presented Shaver's theories twice, and we'd risk our high standard of originality if we continued. Shaver has said what he has to say — and there's no sense to saying it again. We are a *fiction* magazine, and fact has no real place in it, now that the fact has been proved. *All* our

stories are based on fact. Didn't we invent almost everything, including the atom bomb? Well, it's time we went on to new fields of the future, to place them before the inventive minds of our scientists, so that they too, in years to come, will be realities.[51]

In one long, rambling paragraph Rap divested himself of the Shaver Mystery, dropped the offer of proof, and stated twice that *Amazing* was a *fiction* magazine having nothing to do with fact (other than predicting future science). And who was the respectable citizen that would reveal further proof of the Mystery? He never materialized.

19

Armistice of 1948

"I was not Dick Shaver, but a different man entirely."—"The Dream Makers"

In a breathtaking Hail Mary pass, Rap called for a truce with fandom in 1948. These were the same fans who had slandered him since 1945; the ones he called dopes and morons. Referring to the Philcon's Lemurian resolution—and the loud round of booing *Amazing Stories* got at the convention—Rap managed a "Kumbaya" moment. All was forgiven, he said. In deference to his former adversaries—the disgruntled foes of Shaverism—Rap created a new feature dedicated to their pursuits. He called it "The Club House" and he put his man Rog Phillips in charge. The fanfeud had ended.

> And, as to that [resolution] against us, we know the truth about it now. It was *not* voted upon by the convention, and was in fact, shelved forever by our friends at that convention.... Therefore, we retract any hard feelings, and realize that it was not as serious as it might have seemed.... We've discovered now that the laundry has been washed, that they're a pretty nice bunch of guys! There'll be no more of that petty stuff, we're sure. We owe our personal thanks to all the fans who worked to patch things up.[1]

Roger Graham, meanwhile, was making the rounds of the nation's fan clubs, introducing himself and "The Club House" to bring the anti–Shaver faction in from the cold. A January 29, 1948, meeting of the Los Angeles Science Fiction Society documented Graham's presence and a statement he made to the fans in attendance:

> There isn't going to be any more Shaver Mystery two issues from now. On March 10, the April issue of *Amazing* will be on the stands and it will contain the summation of the Shaver Mystery, the proof of the Shaver Mystery, complete with photographs, letters, and so forth. Palmer's editorial will go something like this: "We have definitely proved that the Shaver Mystery is the truth and since this magazine is devoted to fiction, rather than fact, we must discontinue it." ... My fan column will have nothing to do with Shaver.[2]

Amazing's May issue rolled around and news of the "respectable citizen" who held the key to the hidden truths of the Shaver Mystery was never mentioned. In his place was a special feature offering three proofs, with no byline. This was the final nail in the Shaver Mystery's coffin. Likely written by Rap himself, the proofs, all "scientifically substantiated," went like this:

1. All living matter on Earth is contaminated by "radioactives" in food, water, and air, and it accumulates in the body to cause the condition we call "age."
2. Space is filled with particles of disintegrated suns. Smaller than atoms, these particles are drawn together through a process that eventually creates new matter and accounts for gravity, as we know it.
3. Interstellar ships routinely visit the earth, making contact with the cave people.

Meanwhile, *FATE*'s first issue, edited by Robert N. Webster (Rap), was already on newsstands. Rap coyly plugged his new magazine in *Amazing Stories*:

> [T]hose who stated there is no evidence of this planet being visited by space ships will be forced to admit that there is evidence, and if a photo isn't proof any longer, at least a photo that is vouched for by reliable people is. However, that particular proof isn't our province. We admit we could have duplicated it, but we preferred to have it appear in another publication, where it would certainly carry more weight. We are sure this other publication isn't bent on any hoax. Nor were we. There is only one proof remaining to settle the Shaver Mystery for good, and that is actual discovery of the caves and a dero, or one of the mech. We're waiting for that. Meanwhile, we see no point in repeating the Shaver stories a third time.... So Shaver's stories, from now on, are straight science fiction, and nobody will deny that when it comes to spinning a yarn, there are few who can surpass him.[3]

Rap again encouraged Shaver fans to contact Chester Geier. The Shaver Mystery Club, he said, would present the subject "on a scale *Amazing Stories* couldn't hope to equal," adding that Rog Phillips' "The Club House" was on its way to becoming a new hit with SF fans.

Rap's master plan succeeded in separating the Shaver fans and the mainstream SF fans by giving these two warring camps their own venues. He appeased Ziff by declaring the mystery solved, while chanting his new mantra that *Amazing* was, after all, a *fiction* magazine. From then on, *Amazing Stories* would carry only Shaver *fiction*, he said.

All seemed right with the world until a shocking letter from Shaver Mystery Club president Chester S. Geier appeared in *Amazing Stories*. This time it was actually written by Geier, who announced his resignation. He wanted out from under the weight of the presidency. He made arrangements with Rap, who in turn dropped the entire operation in Shaver's lap.

This was an important step, wrote Geier, because "...the Shaver Mystery has been proved in a great number of ways during the past few months. As you may have read in this magazine, since the Shaver Mystery can no longer be disguised as fiction, it no longer can be fully presented in a fiction magazine. For this reason the Shaver Mystery Club, founded last year for the express purpose of proving, or disproving, the Shaver Mystery, is now taking the burden of presenting this startling collection of facts and data that have proved beyond any doubt that the theories of Richard Shaver are in a great sense true."[4]

Was Rap eating crow during this editorial shell game at *Amazing*? Not on your life. He was secretly paving the way to independence, and the freedom to publish whatever he wished in *FATE*.

Following his *de facto* election as president of the Shaver Mystery Club, Shaver founded Aldebaran Press, which would have been the club's publishing outlet had it gotten off the ground. He teamed up with an illustrator from Mendocino County, California, Theron Brown, and designed and printed a colorful brochure full of impressive titles, like the 800-page *The Elder World* and *The Shaver Mystery Digest*. As it turned out, the brochure was the only title Aldebaran Press managed to publish.

Becoming sole spokesman for the Shaver Mystery had always been his dream, but without a budget to pay a reliable staff, and with no training to operate the club's offset press, Shaver's dream became a nightmare. Nevertheless, a review of Aldebaran's impressive offerings appeared in the British fanzine *Fantasy Review* for October-November 1948 (page 8):

> The Aldebaran Press announces a volume "of the deepest interest to followers of the Shaver Mystery and to science fiction readers, as well as to students of the occult and prehistoric"—Richard S. Shaver's *The Elder World*, which will incorporate in its 800 pages the complete history of the enig-

Brochure from the Shaver Mystery Club, 1948. Designed by Theron C. Brown, it featured Shaver-related materials, including books on magic and sorcery (Richard Horton collection).

matic "caverns" and the "prediluvian culture," with an autobiography of the author, titled (appropriately?) "The Dream Makers." With the book, which is illustrated by Theron C. Brown, a former Paramount Pictures artist will also come a folio of "Letters to Shaver," giving "the story of American life tormented and persecuted by invisible attacks."

Also forthcoming from this new source are "Grey Lord of Death," by *Amazing*'s Guy Archette [Chester Geier]; "The Magic That Was," by "The Red Dwarf," comprising three unpublished Shaver stories, and *Forever Is Too Long*, the reprint of a Chester S. Geier novel which was highly praised, even by the severest critics of the Ziff-Davis magazines, when it appeared in *Fantastic Adventures*. Other volumes in preparation include a complete reference work on the Shaver Mystery compiled by Geier, and a Shaver Omnibus.

Geier explained in an August 11, 1981, letter to the author that the titles in Aldebaran's brochure were somewhat more than premature, having not even gone to press: "*The Shaver Mystery Digest* was another thing Dick hoped to put out; I never actually edited it as it never actually materialized, including the listed books, as far as I know. Most of the titles mentioned in the flyer seem to be imaginings on Dick's part...."

Snapshot of Dick and Dottie Shaver (left) with "former Paramount Pictures artist" Theron C. Brown and wife, 1946. Brown illustrated Shaver's Aldebaran Press ad, distributed through the Shaver Mystery Club. The shoestring publishing house planned to offer *The Elder World* and several other Shaver-related books, including some by Chester S. Geier, before it died for lack of direction and funds (Dottie Shaver collection).

Aldebaran Press, along with Shaver, were sinking into a funk that would bring back Shaver's old case of ulcers, and worse — writer's block. Rap had plucked the Shaver Mystery from the pages of *Amazing Stories* with surgical precision. Deserted by those he counted on, Shaver turned to Chester Geier, who had problems of his own.

Re: Richard S. Shaver
By Chester S. Geier

"We are all living Fords from the production line of time."— Richard Shaver

Dick Shaver and I exchanged several letters about our writing problems. He did not get mine into focus and felt I could solve them by just letting myself go. I was stymied by the awareness that the SF field was changing, that I had to get a new perspective, move in a new direction, and did not know how to accomplish this as quickly as I felt was needful. Writers improve or change by a process of gradual evolution, and gradual growth of insights that proceeds from story to story, but I was under pressure and in a hurry.

Shaver too seemed to feel he had to move in new directions and did not know how. His way of writing — usually in the evening, after a hot bath he found relaxing — was to start with characters doing something urgent and to proceed from incident to incident according to inspiration. He did not have a definite plan or plot in mind and all too often the tangle of incidents became a maze in which he was lost. He admired my ability to plot a yarn from start to finish and to do a story outline chapter by chapter. He felt that writing the outline was writing the story and I should not have trouble writing the story if I could write the outline.

He sent me stories in which he had become mired and told me, "You finish them, Chet; you know how." I studied the stories, determined how they had to end according to the conditions that had been set up, wrote outlines and sent them to Shaver. But he could not work from outlines; he sent everything back to me and pleaded, "You finish it; you've already written the story.' I finished a couple of yarns and then had to beg off because sharing the income with him took up valuable time and halved my profits. I had part of the rent to pay on my writing office, rent to pay on the apartment in which I lived, a family to feed, and had the panicky impression that I was committing professional suicide what with all the matters in which the Shaver Mystery Club had involved me.

Rap stated in one of his magazines[5] in a comment on a reader's letter that Dick Shaver could not write, could not type, that he misspelled or mistyped words and was ungrammatical. Rap had a tendency toward exaggeration and over-emphasis.

I do not recall that the stories Shaver sent me to finish were that bad. They had interest, an exotic background, realistic characters, conflict, a sense of drama and crisis. But Shaver, as I mentioned, wrote without plan or method. He wrote when "in the mood" and let incidents take shape as sentences flowed out in his mind. This is not at all a bad way to write, provided one is willing to revise and polish. Shaver seemed always impelled to move forward and rebelled against backtracking.

In the same comment about Dick Shaver mentioned above, Rap does admit that Shaver had a great imagination, a sense of the unusual and bizarre, a feeling for emotion and beauty. These are as vital a part of writing as anything else. In other comments about Shaver in his magazines, Rap (who is not noted for consistency) said that the Dick Shaver of circa 1951–1954 had improved a great deal as a writer over the Dick Shaver of 1945–1949.

I must explain at this point, belatedly, that after starting this "history" I recalled that my employer at *FATE* had a couple of cardboard boxes containing most, if not all, of Rap's magazines, *Other Worlds*, *Science Stories*, and *Universe*. I went through the magazines in the process of writing this and was able to add some accurate details.

I agree with Rap that the DS stories of the early 1950s had improved; the incidents were tighter and more coherent and the characters had more refinement.... Dick Shaver might have accomplished more as a writer had he not been so tied up with Rap, so dependent on Rap for a living. Rap had encouraged him to freelance, and Rap alternated between periods when he practically supported Shaver and periods when he practically threw him out the door and told him to go it alone.

Shaver went through some bad times, but even in the best times he probably lived on a shoestring. Rap was his main story market and Rap could not publish all of DS's production.... I estimate that while writing for Rap's own magazines, Shaver was living on $100 to $200 a month. Since he lived in low-rent rural areas and spent little on clothes, transportation, and pleasures, he seems to have managed to exist.... He would have done better to get a job, since with financial independence, he could have relaxed as a writer (if he kept writing at all) and kept submitting to other magazines until he sold them. He did sell a couple of yarns to other magazines, one of them *Planet Stories*, if I remember right, but he remained dependent on Rap....

Rap stated in *Other Worlds*, May 1955, page 131, that "much of the Shaver Mystery came out of my own head." Evidently Shaver did not like some of the elaborations and additions. In *Other Worlds* (November 1950, page 158), Rap admitted that Shaver protested against some of his insertions.

So we seem to have the strange situation that DS was not the actual father of what came to be known as his brainchild but that he was forced to adopt the little monster and drag him through story after Shaver Mystery story. All this to be a "writer," to freelance, to avoid a steady job, to keep eating and pay bills. Where does it leave a man's pride and self-respect? That question may have occurred often to Shaver, particularly late in the night when he sat at his typewriter with a story that had gone sour.

1949

"Mr. Shaver has requested, and we have given him, sole ownership of his 'mystery.'"—
Ray Palmer

William B. Ziff's new Shaver Mystery policy confused and angered Shaver fans. This gave Rap a modicum of satisfaction, and he began to include letters of complaint in "Discussions." Said one dissatisfied reader, "These guys who take such pleasure in panning the great Shaver stories make me sick! What's the matter, readers, his yarns too deep for you? I'm here to say Shaver is the best man on the staff with Geier nipping at his heels. Why drop it from *Amazing Stories*? Carol Darling, Detroit 14, Michigan."

Rap agreed with Ms. Darling. If readers want a return of the Shaver Mystery, he said, just say so. He waxed nostalgic that Richard Shaver was the one author in his experience who "achieved a record for continuous circulation rises which is above the average." Shaver stories added another 50,000 readers, he said, and even after the magazine dropped the Mystery, the readers were still there. "[W]e attracted the readers through the novelty of Mr. Shaver's material.... The real question is the Mystery. Do you want it back, readers? It's up to you. We, and Mr. Shaver, have personally continued our investigations. Which ought to scotch the rumor that the deros have gotten after your editor and are sizzling his behind with rays!"[6]

A subsequent issue revealed that 132 readers voted for a Shaver Mystery comeback. Only six declined, Rap said. This, however, was not enough to warrant a return to the glory days. "We will publish Mr. Shaver's stories as we do any good stories. But when it comes to doing it as a 'great mission' there we simply shrug our shoulders.... We absolutely cannot enter into that segment of the Mystery. That's much too close to the word fanatic. We can't take anything that seriously. Our intent is solely entertainment.... How you *believe* is your business."[7]

Rap knew the Shaver Mystery would never return to *Amazing*. It was William B. Ziff's magazine, and Rap had to toe the party line. He also knew that his days at Ziff-Davis were numbered — that in short order he would hand in his resignation. For now his involvement with *FATE* would remain a secret, at least to Ziff. Shaver fans, not privy to the office politics of 185 North Wabash Avenue, grumbled that deros were behind Rap's about-face on the Mystery. It all smacked of conspiracy.

As Rap's last surviving member of the inner circle, Bill Hamling had the final say in 2009. The last chapter of the Shaver Mystery, Hamling said, was all Ziff's doing.

> Bill Ziff didn't like it. But Bernie Davis did. Bernie Davis knew the circulation of *Amazing Stories* literally was dependant on the Shaver Mystery. I'd say about 50,000 additional readers of *Amazing* at that time, drew to the Shaver Mystery. That's simple fact.
> Ziff didn't believe in it, and he owned over 50 percent of the company stock. Bernie Davis owned about 40 percent.... But that's Bill Ziff, a crazy multi-millionaire. I never liked him. Always liked Davis. Bernie was A-OK. Bernie was one of the boys. And that's what kept the company going.[8]

Rap blamed Ziff for caving in to government pressure when he forbade *Amazing*'s flying saucer issue in 1948. "The Tacoma incident intervened," Rap said. "The owner of the magazine ordered the special issue halted, killed the Shaver Mystery, and tossed aside a bit of business that had netted him a half million dollars in four years — all the day after a man with a gold badge paid him a visit."[9]

Shaver took the brunt of Ziff's decision. It was a quick, hard fall for *Amazing*'s bestselling author. Shaver was lucky to get a mention in *Amazing* after that. "And speaking of fan activities," Rap wrote in his February 1949 editorial, "Dick Shaver writes saying he still has a few copies of his 'I Remember Lemuria!' left on hand. His address is Box 74, RT. 2, Lily Lake, McHenry, Ill."

Adding insult to injury was Ziff's announcement that he intended to move Ziff-Davis headquarters to New York City. Maybe he felt he could keep a tighter rein on the fiction group if it was on his own turf. Whatever the reason, the Chicago staff was not happy with the decision. As Bill Hamling tells it, it was the final blow to the Chicago inner circle: "Davis called a meeting of the editors and asked us what we thought of it, and we said, no way, José! Ziff wanted Ray Palmer to go [to New York City]. Well, the handwriting was on the wall. Ray was going to quit. There was no way he was going to New York. Howard was gone already, to Hollywood, out there making screenplays.... I said no, I'm going to stay here...."[10]

Ziff's plan to move the operation to New York was the last straw for many of his Midwest staff. Rap was already feeling the pressure of his boss's paranoia — about the Shaver Mystery, about flying saucers, and about Russian assassins. The leash had become too tight for the independent Rap. And so, after 11 years as editor in charge of the fiction group, Rap resigned.

Hamling knew the time had come for Rap to move on. Others may have known it, but kept their mouths shut. Rap made his first public announcement at the 1949 Worldcon in Cincinnati, the "Cinvention." It was noted by Rap's old nemesis, Harry Warner, Jr.

"The first sensation of the Cinvention occurred before its formal opening. On September 2nd, the eve of the Worldcon, Walter Coslet asked Palmer for his autograph. Palmer inquired: 'As an ex-editor or as a fan?' This was the first word for most fans that the stormy petrel of the prozines had resigned from Ziff-Davis to become his own publisher."[11]

Back at the Ziff-Davis Publishing Company, the official announcement of Rap's departure, Hamling said, came indirectly "through Howard Browne being appointed by Ziff to the editorial offices. I kept my mouth shut.... So Howard kind of took the front of the deal...."[12]

No outpouring of emotion, no farewell party, and no gold watch accompanied Rap's departure, Hamling said. "No, we didn't have anything like that. It just happened. He gave his notice to Bernie Davis and that was it."

Part IV
Diaspora

20

Reconstructing Ray Palmer

"So who's afraid to step out for still another new idea? Not us — and you'll see us soon. The name is ... Ray Palmer."— Rap, 1949

Magazines fluttered on the newsstand near 185 North Wabash Avenue as a sudden September breeze caught hats and sent them flying. The sun that day was a bloodshot eye sinking into a soupy autumn haze. It was five o'clock, time for the Loop to begin its daily exodus of office staff. They deserted their skyscrapers as fast as elevator jockeys could empty them onto terra firma. One passenger, Raymond A. Palmer, formerly of the Ziff-Davis Publishing Company, had ridden the elevator for 11 years. But this ride was different. It was his last as an employee of New York millionaire William B. Ziff.

Rap had just finished writing his farewell editorial for *Amazing Stories*. He reminisced about his career, sharing tidbits of wisdom gained throughout his journey with Ziff-Davis. He laced his goodbye with nostalgia that he made no effort to contain: "Eleven years, seven months, one week and two hours ago, your editor sat down at this typewriter and wrote his first editorial word as editor of *Amazing Stories*. Now he is seated at the same typewriter, writing his last.... A great many of our friends are worried about this editor, and how he'll eat after he quits this job, and what he'll do. They point out that he's been with *Amazing Stories* for nearly 12 years, and you don't just quit a job that pays that much money."[1]

Rap's inner circle was already down one man at the time of his resignation. Howard Browne was first to go, and now it was Rap's turn. Bill Hamling's orders were to hold the fort with Lila Shaffer until reinforcements (Howard Browne) arrived from California. Browne would then take control of the fiction group — his reward from Ziff for enduring six years of Ray Palmer. Browne had big plans, too, none of which were remotely connected to Rap and his alternate universe. Browne recalled the moment in his memoir: "With Palmer gone, Davis asked me to drop the book-writing nonsense and return to Chicago as editor of the Fiction Group. The editorial staff I inherited was made up of Bill Hamling, a capable and imaginative associate, plus being a fair-to-middling writer; and Lila Shaffer...." [2]

Browne's first order as editor was something he had only dreamed about as Rap's assistant: He threw out nearly $30,000 of Rap's unpublished manuscripts, "over the strong objections of the company treasurer." He then turned to Rap's contract writers, informing them that the old policy of buying stories sight unseen was over.

His old loves, *Mammoth Detective* and *Mammoth Mystery*, would never again see the light of day. Instead, Davis put him in charge of *Mammoth Western*, *Amazing Stories*, and *Fantastic Adventures*, with Hamling shouldering responsibility for the latter. Thus Browne moved forward with his plan to transform *Amazing* into a "mature" offering on the SF market.

Hamling kept a low profile, something that did not come naturally. Secretly he refused to accept that the Fates had put Browne in charge of the fiction group. Years passed, and still Hamling could not accept it. "I *never* worked for Howard," he said in 2010. "I always did my thing at Ziff-Davis."[3]

Hamling still feels that Browne did nothing for the fiction group that Rap had not done in bigger and better ways before. This is not how SF historians see it. They lauded Browne's takeover as a breath of fresh air, bringing in better writers and finer stories, especially when Browne merged *Fantastic Adventures* with a digest pulp called *Fantastic*. In *Fantastic*, Browne featured writers Mickey Spillane, Cornell Woolrich, Theodore Sturgeon, Raymond Chandler, and even Rap's former writers William P. McGivern and Robert Bloch. But Browne's success with *Amazing*, according to Hamling, was elusive. "He never had any," he said, while the stratospheric circulation *Amazing* enjoyed through Rap "went to hell."[4]

Rap took credit for Browne's return to the fiction group, having suggested him to Ziff and Davis as his replacement. Hamling confirmed Rap's claim, but the reason behind this suggestion was less than altruistic, according to Hamling. It harkened back to a stormy relationship during the Shaver Mystery era: "Rap felt that Browne would louse up as an editor of SF and he wanted to teach Howard a lesson. Thus he pushed him for the job. Actually, Howard hated SF and its fans and only wanted to edit, or write for, detective-mystery mags. I was out in left field during the mid-fifties and I ignored the Rap-Browne feud, *period*."[5]

Besides, Hamling was busy behind the scenes with his own plans to leave Ziff-Davis. He approached Davis with a proposal after learning of Ziff's intention to move the company to New York City. "Davis ... asked me if I would go, and I said, 'No, I'm going to stay here. And furthermore, for this last year, I want your permission to be my own publisher.' That's where *Imagination* came in. I was using Ray Palmer to initiate it...."[6]

With financial help from Ray, Hamling began work on *Imagination*. It was the new look in SF pulps: smaller, with updated art and trimmed edges. The old, large-format pulp with ragged edges was on the way out. Rap was Hamling's front man for the first four issues of *Imagination*, and his name appeared as editor. No one could have known it at the time, but Hamling was poised to become the inner circle's wealthiest member.

Exhilarating as it was, Rap's emancipation from Ziff-Davis was tinged with an aftertaste of defeat. He felt that executives had underrated his hard work and editorial acumen. His suspicions were confirmed when Ziff raised doubts about his editorial savvy concerning the Shaver Mystery. Rap left *Amazing Stories* at a difficult time, when pulp fiction, once a staple of the reading public's entertainment diet, was about to go under.

Drastic market changes emerged in the post-war years as reading habits began to change. Television was a big problem, though not the only source of the SF-fantasy market's woes. The growing popularity of paperbacks competed with the fiction magazines. Pulp fiction, as it was known for nearly 50 years, was about to vanish in the blink of an eye. SF writers scrambled to figure out ways to adapt. Should they go psychosocial or action-adventure? Rap held onto his beloved SF for another decade. Hamling was of a younger generation. He could read the handwriting on the wall.

Chicago Farewell

"The Ray Palmer he was before marrying my mom and Ray Palmer after getting married were two different people."— Linda Jane Palmer

FATE magazine was well underway in September 1949, the month Rap left *Amazing Stories*. He had eight issues under his belt, and was working out of a cavernous old wood frame building that had formerly been a laundry, according to Chester Geier, who worked in the same building. Geier was about to become *FATE*'s managing editor.

Rap started a mail-order bookstore shortly after *FATE*'s first issue, and that, too, was headquartered in the creaky laundry. Rap called his mail order business Venture Bookstore and sold books on occult, psychic, mystic, and spiritualist subjects. He even sold Ouija boards.

Geier began working in the *FATE* office in May 1952. He said it leaned slightly to one side, but the rent was cheap and there was space for half a dozen desks and for shelves to store the Venture Bookshop stock. The mailroom was in the back. Geier had actually begun working for *FATE* several months earlier, on a moonlighting basis, picking up from and delivering to Curt Fuller articles to proofread and caption.

"It seems to have been about this time that Fuller became associated with *FATE*," Geier said, "having borrowed the money from a financially well-fixed uncle who lived in Wisconsin and who later visited the *FATE* office and sort of strutted around in a possessive manner."[7]

Geier did not believe the official story, told much later, that Rap and Fuller were partnered in *FATE* from the beginning. He said it was Rap's brainchild. It appears, however, that Geier was a lone voice in the woods, since most historians, including the Fullers, disagree with him. Curtis Fuller was a journalism school grad from the University of Wisconsin. His involvement with *FATE*, Geier said, came *after* Rap began editing *FATE* under the pseudonym Robert N. Webster. "Fuller appeared to be financially strapped at the time, having just bought a big old house, paying medical and psychiatry bills for Mary Fuller (who seems to have been quite a source of woe at the time), wearing old suits and driving an old car," according to Geier.[8]

Fuller's situation began to improve about 1951, Geier said, when he became editorial director of a group of magazines published in Chicago, one of them a nudist magazine and another a man's magazine that also ran pictures of nudes. Fuller moonlighted on the side, helping Rap with *FATE* and writing articles for *Today's Science*. Geier also worked on the latter until he became a full-time staff member at *FATE*.

At *FATE*, the Shaver Mystery had all but vanished from Rap's lexicon, replaced by flying saucers. But Rap could not resist the allure of science fiction. In 1949 he hired young fan Bea Mahaffey to edit his new SF pulp *Other Worlds Science Stories*. Bill Hamling was the venture capitalist. "He started it with $10,000 of my money," Hamling said. "If we needed money, we'd say to each other, hey, have you got a thousand? I mean, that wasn't the conversation, but that's how it ended up; we supplied it to each other."[9]

"The Fall of Lemuria," a Richard Shaver yarn minus the Shaver Mystery element, appeared in Rap's debut issue of *Other Worlds*. Readers still sore over the Shaver Mystery hoopla debated whether Shaver should be included in Rap's new pulp at all. But Rap defended his old friend and eventually brought back the Shaver Mystery as a permanent feature in future magazines, including *Search, Mystic, Flying Saucers from Other Worlds,* and *Forum*. Rap's publishing career was gaining momentum, just as Bill Hamling was beginning to realize that SF was not the moneymaker he had hoped for.

The Hamling Mystery

"I could end up in an automobile crash twenty minutes from now that would look like an accident. Or maybe, I fall off a roof or maybe I'm caught as an innocent bystander in a riot or holdup in a store. It could be staged."— Bill Hamling, 1971

The simmering paranoia that rooted itself in the Shaver Mystery began to infect others. It wrapped its tentacles around former inner circle members and those who knew them. This new threat had nothing to do with Shaver's deros or torture ray; it came from FBI agents under the direction of J. Edgar Hoover. It was a gradual process, and Bill Hamling was the target.

Following Rap's lead, Hamling lived his dream by founding his own small SF publishing empire. The Rap-Hamling relationship was still tight, though a little less so as they carved out their own slice of the dwindling sci-fi pie. Both planned to secure the future of science fiction for the betterment of humanity; that, and make money.

After his December 1948 marriage to Frances Yerxa, widow of deceased pulp fiction writing machine Leroy Yerxa, Hamling moved into Frances' brick house on Fowler Avenue, a short distance from the Palmers. This was the same house Rap and Marjorie picked out for Frances during the trying months after Leroy's death. Hamling would eventually adopt Frances' four children and produced two of his own. For a time all was well with the Palmer and Hamling families, though friends noticed that Hamling became agitated whenever Leroy's name came up in polite conversation.

The house at 1426 Fowler Avenue was where Bill and Frances began *Imagination*, their first publishing effort. Some historians disagree who exactly founded *Madge* (the magazine's new nickname). The confusion arises from the fact that the first four issues were produced by Rap's Clark Publishing Company, and Rap was listed as editor. It was all a smoke screen for the benefit of William B. Ziff, who did not approve of employee moonlighting. Rap and Hamling played the game straight-faced in editorials until the February 1951 issue, when Rap relinquished his role at *Imagination*. This became known as the hand-over issue. Rap set the scene in his final editorial with a short introduction of Hamling: "You may have heard by this time the Ziff-Davis science fantasy magazines *Fantastic Adventures* and *Amazing Stories* have moved their editorial offices to New York. Howard Browne and Lila Shaffer welcomed the change, but Bill Hamling, the Managing Editor of *FA* for five years, found it impossible to go along.... We were quick to ask Bill if he would like to join us and handle *Imagination*...." Hamling, of course, accepted:

> To Ray Palmer all I can say is that whatever I know about this business, he taught me. I started out as a fan some twelve years ago, branched out into professional writing and joined him as an editor at Ziff-Davis.... I'm glad to be at the helm of *Madge*. Fact of the matter is, though Forrie Ackerman did have a fanzine of the same title years ago, it was I who suggested the title *Imagination* to Ray Palmer. Ray used to kid me that he stole it from me. Well, all kidding aside, I'm glad to have it back! And don't worry about drastic changes in the policy of the magazine. There won't be any to speak of.

Hamling likely got a laugh out of that last line, since he had been editing the magazine all along. Rog Phillips, the writer Rap put in charge of "The Club House," suggested that Hamling hire his wife Mari Wolf to write a similar column in *Madge*. Hamling agreed, and "Fandora's Box" premiered in the April 1951 issue. Wolf's name appeared on the column until she retired in April 1956, when Robert Bloch took over. "Yes, 'Fandora's Box,'" Hamling mused in 2009. "Everything in those days tied in. Everybody tied in to somebody in the inner circle."

Frances' son Richard Yerxa, in his early teens at the time, still recalls the Hamlings' early publishing years and visits to the Palmer home on Grant Street:

> I knew [the Palmers] best when they lived in Evanston. It was a really nice-looking little house, pretty close to where I went to middle school. It was near a park. We were family.
>
> We were publishing at that time, and Ray had supported us so we could get into publishing. We were doing *Imagination* and *Imaginative Tales*, digest-sized things. I was around 14, so I don't know how instrumental Ray was, but I do know that without Ray we wouldn't have been doing it.
>
> We remodeled the basement; tiled the floor and the ceiling, and built a bar. During my childhood, every major figure in science fiction was down there getting crocked. Chester Geier was part of our family, too. Howard Browne was my "uncle." He was a big guy in every way. He was Tarzan.[10]

With the completion of the basement office, Hamling pulled out of the Lawrence Avenue rooms he shared with Geier, relocating his SF cover art and pulp magazine collection to the Fowler Avenue basement. Frances Hamling, whose writing skills were honed with help from Leroy and Rap, pitched in as the other half of *Madge*'s editorial staff. The basement had desks for both of them, his and hers.

Earl Kemp, a young fan and fanzine editor who eventually became Hamling's editor and right hand man, often visited Evanston to soak up the ambience of Hamling's subterranean lair. Kemp has since recalled his years with Hamling in his online fanzine *eI*:

> I found every excuse I could to go to Evanston and to visit with Bill [he had become Bill by then] in his basement office. I would drool over his books and his pulps and the awe-inspiring cover paintings hanging on the walls. Now and then he would tell me tales of the good old days when he was at Lane Tech and some of the stunts he and Mark Reinsberg had pulled. He would show me copies of *Stardust* and let me fondle them, leaving finger marks on their perfection.[11]

The telephone exchange in Evanston at the time was GReenleaf. It became the name of Hamling's new publishing company. In September 1954, they founded their second magazine: *Imaginative Tales*. He raved about his new title in his "Meet the Author" feature in the June 1954 issue: "The little lady is the love of my life and I am as proud and fond of her as I am of my own family. This is understandable when I reflect that science fiction is not just a means of livelihood to me: science fiction is my major interest, both as a pastime and career...."

Rogue Fan

> *"Disintegrant ... mental impulses split united men into warring groups, as rocks split in the fire, and the agent of that disaster is the dero."—Richard Shaver*

Hamling's devotion to science fiction was only as strong as market demand. As darkness descended over science fiction, the paradigm shift begun in the late 1940s was decimating the 1950s market. Scores of magazines folded as old-timers desperately hung on, including Howard Browne's *Amazing Stories*.

This was the climate of SF publishing in 1955 when we find former *Stardust* editors Geier and Hamling seated at the bar in Greenleaf headquarters. They were engaged in a heated discussion in sign language. The subject was Hamling's future as an SF publisher. Geier was giving advice: "When Bill Hamling brought out *Imagination,* I often sat in Bill's basement office reading submissions. Hamling confessed he was unhappy with the stories that came to him, and felt something might be wrong with his own judgment or perceptions." Geier said that Hamling had good reason to be dissatisfied. The stories by amateurs had the usual unsophisticated qualities, but the professional yarns were self-consciously "adult," little more than slick characters or incidents set against an SF background, obviously written for and rejected by the leading SF magazines. Geier offered some direction.

> I told Bill that being a pale imitation of the major mags would not help him and that the thing to do was to appeal to the group of SF fans that the major mags were ignoring: those who enjoyed action-adventure SF, with romance and mystery — that is, the "old type" of SF. Rap seemed to have the same realization and he and Bill competed for much the same type of story.
>
> Bea Mahaffey, though, sensitive about her ties with the elite of fandom, disliked the "kid stuff" and kept agitating for "adult" stories by big-names. She enticed many of them into Rap's mags — Asimov, Sturgeon, and Fredric Brown among them — but the stories were their worst and Bea got them because they were not good enough to sell anywhere else. I believe that eventually she came around to Rap's way of thinking.[12]

21

The Unexpected Gafiation of William L. Hamling

"I just got tired of losing money publishing science fiction!"—William L. Hamling

Gafia is a fan term, an acronym for "get away from it all." Fans used it as a verb, "to gafiate," which they often did when science fiction obsessed them to the point that they finally gave it up completely. Fans have been known to gafiate for other reasons, too, like boredom, a demanding job, divorce, illness, and old age.

When Hamling gafiated from SF publishing in 1958, it shocked loyal readers and a sizable chunk of fandom. SF was losing one of its rising stars, but from a business standpoint it made perfect sense. Hamling dreamed of success, and the last thing he wanted was to stagnate in a dead-end literary genre. *Imagination* and *Imaginative Tales* may have been the loves of his life, but he had a mistress on the side. She was called *Rogue* magazine.

A few years prior to his surprising gafiation, Hamling made an announcement in *Imaginative Tales*. It was an about-face in editorial policy — a return to action-adventure yarns. In this, he was no different than Howard Browne and any number of other SF editors trying to stay alive by swapping so-called adult SF for the old two-fisted yarn. But Hamling went even further; he changed his cover art. Typing from his basement office, Hamling explained his reasoning in the November 1954 *Imagination*:

> We've been studying popular trends for some months, and have come up with an interesting fact. Calendar art is by far the most popular form with most people. We got the bright idea ... to incorporate true calendar art into a science fiction cover. What sort of calendar art? A landscape? A seascape? Nope. There's one that stands head and shoulders above all others, utilizing a word that came into prominence in the Armed Forces. Pinup!

His covers were instant classics, painted by Rap's former cover artist Paul Macauly, creator of the famous "Mac Girl." Macauly had a knack for painting sexy femmes in SF surroundings. The idea for pinup girls on *Madge* and *IT* came when Hamling learned that sex sells in a big way. So big, in fact, that within a few years he would dump science fiction like a day-old cup of coffee. It was a mind-boggling chain of events that involved former Ziff-Davis editor Curtis Fuller and an unknown editorial staffer and cartoonist named Hugh Marston Hefner.

Hamling lounged behind the desk of his Palm Springs home office as he explained the genesis of *Rogue*. He had told the story many times, but his version is at odds with Hugh Hefner's. It is more than likely Hefner has added his own embellishments (and made omissions) over time.

Hamling's story begins prior to his 1950 departure from Ziff-Davis, when Curtis Fuller, like Hamling, declined William B. Ziff's request to move to New York. Curtis had a job at George von Rosen's Publishers Development Corporation. Von Rosen published *Modern Man* and an airbrushed nudist magazine called *Modern Sunbathing & Hygiene*. "Curt ... said, would I join him at this publishing operation for six months or a year while he established a new magazine there called *Modern Man*. I said, 'Sure I'll do it as a favor to you.'"[1]

Though Hamling claimed he was doing Fuller a favor, he also needed the money to bankroll his new publishing business. It just so happened that Publishers Development Corporation employed Hugh Hefner as a promotion director, and Hefner had his own ideas about sexy magazines.

The relationship between Hamling and Hefner is a controversial one. Dueling versions of history make reality hard to pin down. However, there were enough witnesses to suggest that something was indeed going on between Hef and Hamling. At one point, even Rap made the claim that he, too, was a Hefner crony, and was offered a share in Hefner's new *Playboy* magazine. This, Hamling said, was a figment of Rap's imagination:

> Ray never even knew Hugh Hefner. He never met him. Hefner came out of my side of the equation. A couple of years before *Playboy* came out, Hefner came to me and wanted to publish. He had holes in his shoes, and was driving a 1950 Studebaker and didn't have any money. That's how I met him.
>
> He came up with the idea for a men's magazine called *Stag Party*. *Stag Party*! I told him at the time, "It's a shitty name! It's no damn good!" Anyway, it became *Playboy* and not *Stag Party*.
>
> I knew Hefner because he used to come over to my little office, which was nothing then, but I was a publisher in those days and he was not. He was a cartoonist. He'd sell me cartoons at five dollars apiece, which I never published because they weren't good enough. But I felt sorry for him. That was my relationship with Hef before *Playboy* became official. Then he came out with the first issue of *Playboy* through Jerry Rosenfield's Empire News Distribution Company that I was about to use too. And that was the birth of the relationship.[2]

It gets even better. How much of it was interpretation and how much was fact, only Hef and Hamling know for sure. In any case, the Hamlings and the Hefners got along famously in those early years (in Hamling's version). It all happened in the little brick house on Fowler Avenue:

> In my home in Evanston one night — I was still living in Evanston then — [Hef] and his wife Millie came over with their newborn kid, and Frances and the girls were there. And Hef and I were sitting at my desk; I remember this so well.
>
> He said, "You've got some available capital haven't you, Bill?" I said "Yeah, I got a few grand stashed around." He says, "I need $10,000." I said, "What do you want to do with it?" He said, "I want to publish a magazine.' I said to him, "What kind of magazine, Hef?" And he said, "Oh, a little risqué. More risqué than *Esquire*." He offered me half of his company ... for $10,000. And I told him, "You can't sell sex to the American public."
>
> *Time* magazine published that, by the way, with a photograph of me, and that was the caption. It was the most stupid remark of the century. I still kick my own ass whenever I *think* of such a stupid thought. He went to a national distributor, Jerry Rosenfield. Jerry was a buddy of mine in those days. He's dead now. Hefner went to him, and Jerry financed him. But then I made a small fortune myself, after *Playboy*. Life is so peculiar.[3]

There is more to the story, according to Hamling's stepson Richard Yerxa, who hung out in the basement office while he soaked up history in the making.

> If my recollections serve me (and you must keep in mind my tender years in those times), it was the breakup of the American News Company and its near monopoly which set in motion the scramble to find avenues of distribution and brought about the ferment which resulted in *Esquire*

dropping the Petty girls and other such risqué features. Hef and Bill got to talking about the potential offered by *Esquire*'s abandonment of controversial sex content, and the opportunity it presented.

As best I can recall, it was Hef who got the idea rolling and then Bill came on line. They brainstormed in our basement for some time, and deadlocked on the issue of whether a 50¢ slick or a 35¢ pulp would be the right path. They sort of flipped a coin and Bill thought he got the best of it with the 35¢ pulp.

The first tire I ever changed on a car was on some "fancy" car Hef had, which developed a flat while he and the family were visiting us. Hef sort of went bad himself, it seemed to me. His wife Millie was, I thought, a great woman but he dumped her. The last time I saw him he was sitting at the bar at Kelly's and looking like the loneliest man in the world. Mom and Dad went to his office one time and Hef left the door to his bedroom open so they could see the lush bunny he had stashed in there. I forgot her name, but Mom would remember. The gal told them, in a private moment, that Hef was a "looker," not a "performer."[4]

One of the great mysteries of 20th century erotic publishing is the apparent split between Hefner and Hamling. Friends suspected there was a falling-out over *something*. Richard Yerxa is still baffled. "They worked up the idea together but at some point decided to go separate paths. Maybe that was the plan from the beginning but maybe it was disagreements that split them. I remember that the two families spent time together for a while then we stopped seeing them. Then 'they' stopped being a couple and Hef was a bachelor...."[5]

And Hef? He made a statement in a letter to Earl Kemp, for the record, on September 10, 2003:

Bill Hamling and I were never close friends. We worked together at Publisher's Development Corporation in 1952, the year before I started *Playboy*.

He launched a knock-off of *Playboy* called *Rogue* and he once made an unwelcome pass at my estranged wife, but I never really had any ongoing connection with him other than that. If there are other stories out there floating around, I'm not aware of them.

In the documentary *Hugh Hefner: Playboy, Activist and Rebel*, Hef tells his *Playboy* genesis story at length, but fails to mention the von Rosen Publishing Company or Hamling. He says he worked for a children's book outfit. He admitted he was a cartoonist, and said that he was originally going to call *Playboy*, *Stag Party*. Hefner also said that he made the rounds to family and friends, raising $8,000 to start *Playboy*. Instead of laying out the prototype in Hamling's kitchen, he said he did it in his own home.

As for Hamling, after losing his shot as half-owner of *Playboy*, and with SF pulps crashing and burning all around him, he took the decisive step that changed his publishing career: "I saw the error of my ways, and published *Rogue* magazine and a few other sexy publications. *Bingo*! *Rogue* was a helluva good magazine. I competed directly with Hef, see? We had around 50 graphic art awards for that magazine. Yessiree. Then I sold the whole publishing deal to Cable News Company in New York years later...."[6]

After the successful launch of *Rogue*'s first issue in 1955, Hamling emerged victorious from his basement and rented office space in a commercial building at Sherman Avenue and Dempster, not far from Ray Palmer's Clark Publishing Company at 806 Dempster. Rap was aware of Hamling's publishing experiment—and his success—with erotica. But Rap was committed to SF and metaphysics. Hamling's success raised doubts in Rap's mind about his decision, and they lingered for decades.

Shaver Mystery Caravan

> *"It all confirmed my original discovery that mankind is a mutilated monkey with sadistic leanings...."— Richard Shaver*

With Browne in charge of the Ziff-Davis fiction group, the welcome mat, as far as Shaver was concerned, was gone. To Shaver's way of thinking, it was a callous way to treat the former star of *Amazing Stories*. This was the thanks he got for all the money he made for William B. Ziff.

He considered driving to Chicago to discuss it man-to-man with Mr. Davis, but then thought better of it. As far as Shaver was concerned, Ziff-Davis had given him the bum's rush to placate a handful of annoying fans. Rap would echo that sentiment as years went on.

Shaver tried to reinvent himself. The first clue of a plan appeared in a 1948 issue of the *Shaver Mystery Club Magazine*. An advertisement, accompanied with a photo of a country home appeared on page two:

SEVEN ROOM SWISS CHALET TYPE DWELLING — This beautiful home now available. Contains three bedrooms, a knotty pine dining room, and full bath with linen closet, glazed sun porch, modern kitchen, and basement garage with full basement. Oil heat furnace in cellar, hot and cold running water. Land consists of four lots, beautifully landscaped, situated facing Lily Lake and separated from all other property by gravel roads. Fenced yard. With the property go lake rights and a boat, one year old. Address inquiries to Box 68, Route 2, McHenry, Illinois.

Shaver had decided to pull up stakes. He scouted for land in neighboring Wisconsin. When the McHenry house finally sold, they dropped by the Palmers to say good-bye. They stayed two nights. Marjorie remembered their visit because the Shavers' two dogs left an abundance of fleas. Rap had to call an exterminator to get rid of them.

Shaver's dream of becoming a successful writer had soured. And so, like Shavers that had come before him, he chose farming. Never mind that he had zero experience as an actual farmer. The way he saw it, farm life offered the self-sufficient lifestyle he craved. He could make a living with his own two hands, and what he did not know he could learn from free informational pamphlets offered by the U.S. government. Farming was an honest living, without the stress of plotlines and character development. Farming would be his salvation. It was 1949.

22

The Stigmata of Raymond A. Palmer

"Just as a physicist will look for theorized unseen particles, Ray Palmer wanted to learn the unseen and unknown."— Raymond B. Palmer

Shaver's scouting led him to the tiny hamlet of Lanark, Wisconsin, near Amherst. He found a rundown farm and purchased it with money from the McHenry sale and help from his well-to-do sister, Catherine Claire. It encompassed 160 rock-strewn acres that had lain fallow for ten years. The sale included old wood-frame buildings in various states of disrepair and some acreage with mature timber.

Shaver's first letter to Rap on finding his new home (and career) must have sounded like a sales pitch from the Lanark Chamber of Commerce, if Lanark had one, which it did not. Come see it for yourself, Shaver enthused. It was the next best thing to Heaven on Earth, and a way to hedge their bets against the atomic war that both Shaver and Rap believed was at hand. Shaver insisted that a farm was a "kind of insurance against the probable breakdown of our country during the coming war with Russia which is trying to start."[1]

Rap was still finalizing plans to leave Ziff-Davis when Shaver moved to Wisconsin. Spending so many hours away from his family working on *FATE* and *Other Worlds*, Rap thought it would be fun to take Marjorie and the kids to see Dick and Dottie Shaver's new home. And so it was that Rap took his family to Lanark. It was a pleasant visit, and Rap and Shaver fished and talked while the children explored the farm. Rap vowed to return, and he did.

During those early visits, Rap and Shaver rekindled their friendship. They took in the local sights, ate Dottie's simple but hearty Pennsylvania Dutch meals and talked late into the night. As it happened, a farm went up for sale about a mile down the road in the town of Amherst, and Rap looked it over. It was 124 acres with a pond, a mill, an old schoolhouse, and a farmhouse. Rap convinced Marjorie the farm could be refurbished as the perfect place to raise the children. After all, Marjorie was still an Eaton Rapids farm girl at heart.

Rap signed papers for the Amherst farm on July 7, 1949. The Palmer household was abuzz with the new developments. Trips to Amherst became frequent as Rap prepared the farm for their relocation. One of his first priorities was the installation of an indoor bathroom in the farmhouse. Even as late as 1949, Amherst farms came with an outhouse as standard equipment. The Palmers' bathroom became the object of local chatter. It gave them an image of rich city folk, something that bothered Marjorie. In truth, the Palmers were not rich, but rumors among locals hinted otherwise.

Rap put a lot of miles on his red Buick convertible in the eight months that followed.

Finally, in the summer of 1950, Rap set a date to move in with the Shavers as temporary houseguests. Said Shaver, "[T]hey will be here on June 1 to stay until their house up the road ... is cleaned and ready for them, which I suspect will take a month. It is in bad shape and overrun with rats from the feed mill."[2]

But life has been known to make its own plans. As he readied the family for the big move, Rap had an accident that would change his life.

Near-Death Experience

> "There was a time when the medics said that even Old Mother Nature couldn't help us. We fooled the medics—and we're going to do it again."—Ray Palmer

On returning to Evanston in driving rain from a trip to the Amherst farm, Rap found the storm had flooded their basement. On descending the basement stairs to save what he could, Rap slipped and fell. He later claimed in one of his magazines that the fall was not an accident, but another effort by unseen forces to get rid of him. Rap explained what happened that night in the October 1950 issue of *Other Worlds Science Stories*:

> We're writing this editorial from a hospital bed in the St. Francis Hospital, Evanston, Illinois. You've all heard of the guy who braved the perils of the open highway on a long trip to reach home and breathe a big sigh of relief that he made it in one piece—only to slip and fall a few minutes later in the complete safety of his own home? Well, that's us. We eluded drunken drivers and the dangers of a driving rainstorm returning from our farm in Northern Wisconsin. Yep, we took that with no trouble at all. But a simple little thing like going downstairs and cleaning the basement (an aftermath of that rainstorm) was too big a task. We slipped—still don't know how it happened—and ended up on the floor with a complicated spinal injury.[3]

Richard Shaver, Lanark, Wisconsin. Dottie Shaver wrote on the back of this photograph: "Was down to our mailbox and I took the pic. Then, no long hair, only mustache, no whiskers. 1956" (Dottie Shaver collection).

The doctors said surgery was out of the question. They told Marjorie his prognosis was poor. At best he might not walk again; at worst, he would die. They said it was up to Mother Nature. It was a bad rerun of the

Milwaukee beer truck incident. Bill Hamling rushed to Rap's side within hours of the accident. What Rap eventually told him was so strange that Hamling never forgot it:

> Ray fell in his basement on his hump. I found out about it at two o'clock in the morning. Marjorie called me. I walked into that room and the poor bastard was lying in that bed, and he was gray, just *gray*. I went to the bed and touched his hand and it was cold. He opened his eyes. It damn near killed him. It was almost total paralysis. He was going. The doctors thought that he would not live. They told Marjorie that.
>
> A week later, when he was much better, naturally, I was sitting with him one afternoon and he said, "Bill, I'm gonna tell you a story you're not gonna believe, but it's the gospel truth!"
> "What, Ray?"
> "You remember the night you came and visited me here? Well, you weren't the only one."
> I said, "What do you mean?"
> He said, "I was visited that night by a team of doctors. I don't remember their names, but they analyzed my problem. I found out the identity of one of them."
> "What are you saying?"
> "These were men who were no longer living. One of the doctors said to another doctor in the room, 'I failed this man when he needed me most as a child, and I will not allow a failure today.' They operated on me and that's why I am alive now."
> I said, "Raymond, maybe you were just plain hallucinating. They gave you all kinds of injections."
> He said "No, Bill, this is God's truth!"
> That's the story, and I believed him. If that makes me a nut, okay, I'm a nut; but he believed it. He believed in an astral life. [The doctors] not only said he wouldn't live, but he'd never walk again. Why, shit — he walked again! That's why I really believed that maybe the story he told me that day was true — an astral operation. Who can prove it? Nobody in this dimension anyway.[4]

The familiar face in Rap's vision was Dr. Frederik P. Gaenslen, the surgeon whose failed spinal graft doomed young Ray Palmer to a life of deformity and pain. Hamling was an eyewitness to a Ray Palmer miracle, the kind that baffled doctors. Rap not only regained his mobility, but he also recovered in time to attend Rog Phillips' wedding a few months later.

Hail and Farewell

> *"The Shaver Mystery is so obscure, even the Hubble telescope can't find It."*— used bookstore owner, Marin County, California, 1996

Fans chose Portland, Oregon, as the site for the 1950 SF Worldcon. Howard Browne, Rog Phillips, Bea Mahaffey, and other Rap associates were in attendance. Due to his accident, Rap stayed home, but he heard the news of Roger Graham's proposal to Mari Wolf at the convention. Later, Graham asked Rap to be best man at his wedding.

"Rog made it a very romantic little country-church-in-the-city thing, getting married at the same church where your editor got married eight years ago," Rap said in *Other Worlds*. "So there were fond memories for yours truly as he stood at the altar listening to the great Rog repeating somebody else's lines.... Your editor had one swell job hanging onto a ring and two canes and keeping from falling flat on his face in the process.

"...[T]he wedding dinner afterward [was] attended by Howard Browne, Bill Hamling ... Bea Mahaffey, and Lila Shaffer ... Charles Recour, Mrs. Browne, Mrs. Hamling, your editor, and his wife."[5]

The wedding was a spontaneous reunion of the Chicago inner circle, the last one in its members' lifetimes. Richard Shaver, no friend of Graham's, was out of the loop by his own design. He was in Lanark, where his initial rush of optimism about farm life was beginning to fade in the harsh light of reality. At first the possibilities were endless; now he saw the many disadvantages: "[T]his land is not considered worth a lot as farm land for several reasons. One — too dry and too sandy — second, rocks — third, short season plus dry spells — fourth, you have to feed stock seven months out of the year and such projects as steer raising don't pay well on account of the work."[6]

Considering the many odd twists in throughout Shaver's life, it should come as no surprise that the second complaint on his list would become his ultimate salvation.

Hamling Disagrees

> "Ray never got out of the rut — and I don't mean that in any deleterious way, only in a complimentary way." — Bill Hamling, 2009

Shock set in when Bill Hamling learned of Ray Palmer's plan to move to the boondocks of Wisconsin. As he saw it, Rap was throwing his career out the window. Nevertheless, Rap made up his mind, and try as he might, Hamling could not convince him to remain in Evanston.

Though he did come to Amherst on occasional family visits, Hamling never warmed to Rap's decision. What Rap wanted, Hamling believed, was to be the big fish in a small pond. Linda Jane Palmer knew of Hamling's dissent, but she saw the move from her parents' point of view:

> I know it bothered Mom and Dad that Bill and Frances didn't understand. They often talked about that. Bill really pushed Dad to give up his "bad decision" of moving to Wisconsin, but obviously my parents made the right decision. No big money, but at least they had a happy, normal life in Amherst and provided a great place for us kids to grow up.
>
> Dad never expressed any remorse for not running off with Bill to California to make lots of money. He always thought that Bill was making the mistake, not him. They had different goals. It think a lot of my dad's decision to move back to Wisconsin was because he finally had a real family and wanted to live a normal life, something he hadn't been able to do in his early years and probably something he never thought he would have because of his physical disability. I suspect if he hadn't had a family he may have followed Bill to California, because the Ray Palmer he was before marrying my mom and Ray Palmer after getting married were two different people.[7]

But Hamling had more important things on his mind. After admitting his mistake of turning down Hefner and *Playboy*, he had launched *Rogue*, but did not give up on SF just yet. Chester Geier, second-tier member of Rap's inner circle, was still hovering in the wings, but gradually losing touch with the old "rat pack": "After I started working for *FATE* in 1952, I became hugely busy and increasingly lost contact with Hamling. A few years later, Hamling moved the *Rogue* editorial offices ... several buildings away from the *FATE* office.... And a few years after that *FATE* moved to modern and attractive offices in another part of Evanston and I practically saw no more of Hamling."[8]

The Palmer family moved into the partially remodeled farmhouse, where they would live for five years until a large stone house was completed. Life on Rural Route 2 in Amherst was nothing like busy Chicago. It was more like Petticoat Junction.

A mile down the road, Dottie Shaver kept track of local gossip by listening in on her telephone party line. Dottie's snooping was easy to detect. Her bleating goats came in loud and clear. Every Amherst home was equipped with an old-fashioned wall phone without a dial. A dozen or so households shared one party line, and each had a distinctive ring. The Palmers answered to one short and one long. The Shavers responded to a long short long. Seven-year-old Linda Jane Palmer realized that a huge sea change had taken place in their lives:

> We had a dial phone in Evanston so we definitely went back in time when we moved to Wisconsin. We even put a bathroom in our house before we moved in because most homes had outhouses. That might have been the first thing that happened that made my mom think that all the locals thought we were the "rich people from Chicago." My poor mom had that thought in her head until the day she died even though we were never rich.[9]

Rap's New Inner Circle

> *"Maybe my mom understood what Dad was thinking, but she's probably the only one."*— Linda Jane Palmer

Ray Palmer's need for an inner circle was part of his life. In Milwaukee he had the Fictioneers and the Riverside Theater. When he moved to Chicago he surrounded himself with a new group. When he left for Amherst, his family became the logical replacement. It had grown to an appropriate number — five. Amherst was the perfect place to raise a family and live the good life, said daughter Linda Jane.

> We were living in Wisconsin when I was between the ages of seven and 16 in the '50s. [My dad] never traveled anywhere without the family and our travels in the '50s were to Michigan to see my mom's family and to the Chicago area to see my mom's sister and to see Bill and Frances and also to Milwaukee to see his dad, sister, and nieces and nephews. I can't recall that he went anywhere without us....
>
> It was difficult for him to walk and he would be so angry at himself if he would trip and fall. He was determined to prove everyone wrong about how his life would turn out. He had an incredible determination to live a normal life with a normal family. And he was successful in that we had a pretty normal family life. He never made it financially, but we lived well enough and didn't realize that we didn't have much money.
>
> He and mom took five years building a rather large stone house on a pond, so everyone thought we were rich. But the fact was that they worked on the house when they could afford to do it. I was about seven when they started building the house and was 12 when we moved into it. It was very sparsely furnished the whole time I lived there.... [It] never had curtains nor did we ever get any new furniture. We lived pretty frugally even though we lived in a big house.[10]

Rap integrated himself into the Amherst community. He became a regular at Flemming's Café on Main Street, where he sipped coffee each morning before heading off to the post office. He joined the school board, the Fair Committee, and the Lion's Club. He hired locals to help run his print shop.

He spent untold hours at the edge of his small lake, picking up stones until he had a sandy, rock-free beach. Rap turned the lake into a wildlife refuge for birds and fish by deepening the pond, removing tons of silt and spreading it on surrounding fields. He and Marjorie offered local kids swimming lessons, teaching as many as 150 kids how to swim.

Amherst also turned Rap into an avid chef. He cooked on all the holidays, and of course his Saturday night potato pancake dinners when the Shavers dropped by. Once the

Ray Palmer standing in front of Kenneth Arnold's plane. Arnold, the pilot credited with the first flying saucer sighting in 1947, landed in a hay field next to Rap's Amherst farm, circa 1954. He took the Shavers and the Palmers for a plane ride that day (Dottie Shaver collection).

big stone house was completed, the summer months were for picnics, and Rap would invite up to 80 neighbors at a time. He hosted New Year's Eve parties that became the talk of Amherst.

Richard Yerxa remembered the Palmer farm during times when Bill and Frances took a break from their duties at *Rogue*. Rap let them laze around the farm fishing and partying, country style, Yerxa said:

> Ray threw [big barbecues and social gatherings] because he owned a local business. Local was important to him. He had a great spread for parties. I don't know how many people worked for him, but I imagine it was a large amount because he was publishing a lot of stuff. The print shop was in town in Amherst, and that was some distance from where he was. Everyone had an office everywhere they went.[11]

Amherst worked like a tonic on Rap. It smoothed the rough edges of his childhood, and even resolved the conflict with his father. "I always saw my dad take the high road," Linda Jane recalled, "especially with his forgiveness of his dad, Roy Palmer. He always welcomed his dad to our home. All I knew about my grandpa was that he had not provided my dad with a loving home and had deserted him. But the whole time I was growing up, Grandpa was welcomed into our home and always came bearing the same gifts — catfish from the Wolf River where he had his home and bags of M&Ms."[12]

Mystic

> *"We are including the Shaver Mystery in* Mystic *because we think it will help sell the magazine."*— Ray Palmer

In 1954 Ray launched *Mystic*. He was still publishing *FATE*, but appeared to be losing interest. Chester Geier believed it was due to flagging sales. So why would Rap create another psychic-type digest to compete with *FATE*? The answer was simple. Other than the fact that he enjoyed starting new magazines, *FATE* gave him a steady supply of unused manuscripts considered outside its editorial policy. Rap saw potential in those rejected manuscripts. In an editorial he explained *Mystic*'s origins:

> We print articles rejected by *FATE*, because *FATE* is dedicated to publishing only "documentary" material. It strives to print only what can, as far as is possible, be proved. When it can't, it adopts a neutral viewpoint, or carefully points out that the article lacks proof. *Mystic* will print a theory. *FATE* will not. *Mystic* is intended to round out the field filled by *FATE*, so that the two magazines form a complete coverage of the subject of the psychic.... That is why *Mystic* gives all types of material, to the exclusion of nothing...."[13]

Mystic began a bi-monthly schedule in January 1954. Rap's all-inclusive editorial policy was perfect for his eclectic tastes. He published anything that interested him, and that covered a lot of ground. *Mystic* became a soapbox to rail against U.S. atmospheric tests of atom bombs. He said they were poisoning the environment. He tracked drifting clouds of nuclear fallout as carefully as he followed flying saucer reports. He said that the bomb had put scientists in charge of life-and-death decisions that were not voted upon by the American public, ergo, U.S. citizens had lost the right of participating in their own government. "We hereby say that the A.E.C. is lying to the American public — and we want it stopped!"[14]

This kind of talk did not endear him to the government agencies observing him from afar, and his FBI file continued to grow during the 1950s. In spite of all that, his editorials became more strident. He wondered aloud in *Mystic* what Americans feared most, Joe McCarthy or the bomb? It was subversive talk in the midst of Cold War America. Rap connected mysticism with free speech and the American way of life in *Mystic*, and woe unto the man who would deny Rap's right to believe in whatever he chose to believe. "Free speech is inexorably linked with free thought.... You cannot have true mystic freedom without free speech. Free speech, the greatest gift from the Unseen (for the principle does come from mystic realms!), is worth fighting for, and must be fought for whenever it is threatened."[15]

Mystic was also the first of Rap's magazines to stop paying for articles. The reasoning behind *Mystic*'s new policy was two-fold, Rap said. If he paid for stories of true mystic experiences, he might get fabrications written for financial gain. Secondly, *Mystic*, he admitted in the August 1955 issue, was having "trouble paying its bills." This came a scant two years into its publishing run, and Rap began pleading with readers to buy subscriptions, offering details of the woes of a small publisher. This, too, became a familiar theme at Palmer Publications as time went on.

Rap's long-winded complaints and pleading increased as finances got tighter. "Ever since we started *Mystic*, we've been facing wolves at every door. Our nerves are worn to a frazzle," he wrote.[16] Starting with the October 1956 issue, *Mystic* was renamed *Search* and remained so until Rap's death in 1977. Chester Geier, still working at *FATE* and grateful for it, noticed a disturbing trend in Rap's magazines:

> In early 1980 [Curtis Fuller] asked me to go through a couple of boxes of Rap's magazines to see if a certain project would be feasible, and in reading one issue after another, Rap's decline became very evident. It was sad. Rap maintained his bluster, braggadocio, and ballyhoo but his readers had dwindled to 20,000 or less; *Search* magazine had only about 3,000 readers. Toward the end Rap was practically begging from his mailing list, asking for lifetime subscriptions and promising marvels to come. He seemed to think of himself as an institution to be subsidized and maintained.[17]

Shaver Mystery 2.0

> "What's happened to the big boom that science fiction entered on, going into the movies, radio, TV, even the big slicks...? Well, the answer is that science fiction got too big for its britches and it went bust."—Ray Palmer, 1954

A new crop of letters began to turn up in *Mystic*. Readers were again asking questions about the Shaver Mystery. It started as an organic process throughout the first seven issues. They pressed Rap for insider information, the real story. With newsstand sales of *Mystic* flagging, Rap embraced the Shaver Mystery hoping it would rekindle the same magic it had worked at Ziff-Davis ten years earlier.

And so the Shaver legend resurfaced. Rap again told the story of the thousands of letters "that when stacked on the floor in the office of W.B. Ziff ... formed a pile four feet high."[18] He recounted his amazement on hearing from hundreds if not thousands of readers who believed what Shaver was saying; how the critics could not prove the Mystery was anything less than gospel truth; and finally, the real reason for its demise, which Rap explained differently than he had as an employee of William B. Ziff.

Recall that Rap's first account, told as the editor of *Amazing Stories*, said the Shaver Mystery had been sufficiently proven, and it was beneath *Amazing*'s high publishing standards to keep repeating it. But from the inner sanctum of his Amherst office, he gave a new account, the *true* story, he said:

> Why, then was the Shaver Mystery dropped from *Amazing Stories*? The answer to that one is simple: pressure from those who felt the Mystery was an insult to their reasoning powers. Common sense told them that what Shaver said could not be true. Their fear of the unknown compelled them to persecute (yes, that's the word) the Mystery until their hue and cry caused the publishers to seek to avoid what might be bad publicity. To be accused of "deceiving the public," or worse still, "actually believing that rot," could not be tolerated....
>
> The only way the Mystery could be presented was as "fiction." And as fiction it could not carry its own weight. The necessity of making the plot conform to a pattern of "truth" weakened the plot. Only the introduction of suspense where no suspense actually existed, made for exciting reading; and therefore, expertly written fiction stories were superior. There was only one answer. The magazine had to present the best fiction obtainable, and Shaver's fiction (he wrote quite a lot at our insistence), was not superior to Merritt, Smith, Burroughs, *et al.* So the Mystery was not presented at all.[19]

Never mind that in 1947 Rap touted Shaver as the *equal* of Burroughs and Merritt, and said that Shaver was the most lyric of SF writers. Things had changed. This was Rap's new Shaver Mystery, version 2.0. What the revisionism did was reopen old wounds between Rap and Shaver.

A truculent Dick Shaver boycotted the first installment of *Mystic*'s new Shaver Mystery series by refusing to participate. This forced Rap to come up with an explanation:

> You will ask: "Why not from Shaver himself?" The answer to this is a tough one, but it is a true one: Mr. Shaver himself has been a victim of the negative type of thinking....
> It's really a case of once burned, twice shy. It takes guts to go counter to the mob. And although Shaver doesn't lack intestinal fortitude, he seems convinced that "it won't do any good, so what's the use?" Your editor doesn't lack guts either, but he does have one rule: never play the other guy's game. So, we will have to present this from our own personal viewpoint, from our own personal experience. And we have the hope that when the chips are down, Mr. Shaver will sit down to his typewriter and give us his viewpoint. And we can tell you this right now — there will be a vast contradiction....

The contradiction, of course, was that Rap had become a student of Oahspe and other schools of mystical thought. Rap had reinterpreted core principles of the Shaver Mystery. He changed Shaver's caverns full of real deros into the land of Atmospherea, populated by spirits of the dead high above Earth. This was spiritualist claptrap to Shaver, who took the role of outcast; so much so that by 1971, jaded cynicism had taken the place of adoration for Rap.

> I cannot say that out of the millions who have read Shaver there were a dozen who truly grasped what I was trying to say. Ray Palmer least of all. I am always aghast at people asking Palmer for details about me, as he never got anything quite straight in this regard since I knew him. I have, for instance, no time for the occult viewpoint ... Spiritualism and so forth.... The whole slant of everything I had to say was switched from the factual to the misty umbrella of spiritualism and reincarnation — utter hokum to me.
> Deros and Teros and Shaver's alphabet are real, actual physical blood and stink and awful flesh and nightmare in fact, but when Palmer got through with it, it was all turned around into the dream world of mystical and the real/unreal religious folderol.... Palmer was just that sort of editor and I have struggled with it from the first.[20]

Rap finally sold his interest in *FATE* to Curtis Fuller in 1955 to help pay bills and try to make *Mystic* pay. That would never come to pass. Rap was struggling, while Bill Hamling's gamble on *Rogue* was making him rich. Rap never had second thoughts about the move to Amherst, but his decision to stick with occult and science fiction magazines may have kept him awake nights. Hamling gave him updates on the fortune he was making in erotic publishing. They discussed his successes on Hamling's infrequent visits to the farm: "I went up to Wisconsin where Ray had his own little lake. Some people might call it a pond, but he had a dam, which created the pond-lake deal, and I'd go up there and Ray and I would go in a rowboat and go fishing."[21]

Hamling played devil's advocate on these visits with Rap, browbeating his former boss to leave New Age publishing behind and make real dough in skin magazines. After one of these "talks," Rap blew off steam in *Mystic*'s June 1955 issue, essentially his reply to Hamling:

> [W]e'll pound away at *Mystic* in spite of the mortgage. We're not really practical. We could publish a sex book and get rich! Science fiction fans always say "Ray Palmer's after that fast buck." Wonder how they figure? We could put out that sex book full of dirty pictures for 50¢, sell every copy

and retire in two years...! We just don't get it...! We're safe as a church! Smart cookie, that Palmer. He's out to rook you. But then, why doesn't he put out a sex book, and play a sure thing? All his friends are doing it, and getting rich! Take *Playboy*, for instance, and a certain science editor who puts out an "art" book for a dollar? (He asked us not to mention his name, but we don't know why.) But every time he says nobody'll support the junk we print, it sure stings when we realize he's right.... Maybe we'd get smart and convert *Mystic* to *Hidden Mysteries of Sex in Four Naked Colors*. We'd sell a million!"

A Farmhand for Shaver

> *"If you went to Richard Shaver's place, everything stunk."*— Richard Yerxa

About a year into Shaver's farming career, 1950, he realized what an overwhelming job he had taken on. He had no farm machinery, only a promise that Rap would share whatever farm equipment he had once it arrived. But Rap's move to Amherst kept getting postponed. Shaver's nerves began to kick up, as well as his ulcers. Writer's block clung to him like a persistent cold. Then the unexpected news of Rap's basement accident dashed Shaver's last hope of making it on the farm.

> June 14, 1950. The [deros] hit a hard blow below the belt — and Rap is in the hospital in Evanston paralyzed below the waist. As I get it, his bowels are paralyzed too, which means it's bad. He fell on his hump while hosing out his cellar. One of those "accidents" which put a crimp in all plans, and I suppose knocks my income for its last loop. The light bill ain't paid and I just got a shut-off notice. Without Rap up here where I can get at him I will probably be looking for a job selling karmel korn.[22]

Nevertheless, Shaver's reputation as the man behind the Shaver Mystery conferred a kind of celebrity. Unannounced houseguests to the Shaver farm were common. They were a constant irritation to Dottie, who had to feed them and put them up for a night or longer. According to Dottie:

> We had a lot of visitors. We always had company, even from Peru, England, Canada and just about every state. Some would come and stay for a couple of months. Some were helpful and some weren't. On one Sunday dinner my cousin from Pennsylvania was there, and her mother, my aunt, and two lady boxers on their way to Chicago to a fight.
>
> A man came one time on a motorcycle and had a robe on, and a beard; looked just like Christ. I was in the hay barn when he pulled up. It scared me. I thought He was coming back already. We had anything from housewives to college students. A lot of people would write to Richard who had troubles. He'd write back to them and set 'em straight.[23]

One of those college students, Richard Horton, came close to everything the Shavers imagined a son could be. In time they adopted him, unofficially. Whenever he could get away from his college studies, Horton drove all the way from Iowa to help Shaver on the farm. He did that, off and on, from 1950 to 1953.

It all began with an ad Horton saw in *FATE*. It ballyhooed the Shaver Mystery with a photo of Dick Shaver wearing what Horton described as "that Arab-looking white thing on his head, used when welding."[24]

The ad read, "Atlantis, Lemuria! Magic Names! Are you interested in the almost forgotten past of the Earth? If you are, here is the wonder book of all time concerning the great catastrophe which destroyed the civilization of 24,000 years ago!"

Horton was definitely interested, and yes, it had a photo of Shaver smoking a cigarette with a towel draped over his head. He looked like a Rosicrucian on a smoke break. Horton mailed the required sum to the address in the ad, and by return mail got a few issues of the *Shaver Mystery Club Magazine*.

Hooked, Horton wrote to Shaver with big plans. He suggested they organize a Shaver Mystery convention but Shaver nixed it. "I could organize one if I wanted to," Horton said, "but he assured me it would go awry, with people getting lost on the way, etc. So I dropped the idea."[25] Horton then offered to come work on the farm. Shaver sorely needed the help, but had no money to pay for it, so he did his best to discourage Horton from coming:

> I am broke, worse, I am in debt, last month I was supposed to turn in sufficient words to Rap to pay my keep and I got shorter every time I looked at the typer and no story.... I don't even have a tractor yet—but Palmer offers machinery on a share alike basis—when he gets his—a year away—he is a generous guy—meanwhile I am very broke and wondering how do I write for a living when I can not write hardly a letter? I have pains at frequent intervals which double me up and I warn you that some ill results of your facing the opposition of the Shaver Mystery will be noticed by you ... they cut your head apart with the antique needle rays.... I guess you get my drift. I am offering you a chance to help me make a living and get yourself into hot water with the worst element in our American life.... I am warning you—don't be a sucker and help me get along, it might pay. I am right up against it, and you're very welcome.[26]

After Shaver's downbeat invitation, it was surprising Horton made the trip at all, but he did and in no time the two hit it off. Their first meeting, however, was not what Horton expected:

> When I first saw Richard Shaver he was, of all things, feeding chickens. Had I expected something else? Like him tapping out a story about the Elder World? I don't know, but it wasn't feeding chickens in a hen house.
>
> Dottie, his wife, greeted me at the front door ... and sent me out back to find the man I'd driven 450 miles to see. Hearing some noise in an outbuilding I stuck my head through the doorway and there, in the dim interior, stood a well-built guy about 5'9" in old jeans, lumberjack shirt, and black stocking cap—Richard Sharpe Shaver....
>
> To me it was an unlikely beginning but typical somehow, for as I was to learn, Dick Shaver for all the fantastic things of which he wrote, could also be one down-to-earth guy.[27]

Horton, a history major (history was one of Shaver's favorite subjects), accepted the challenge of farm life with gusto, which suited Shaver just fine. Over a series of about a dozen visits, Horton and Shaver mended fences, built a silo to hold silage for the cows, fed and milked cows, and cleaned stalls. One summer they built a rock and dirt wall along one side of the barn. It was Horton's summer camp, with Shaver as camp counselor. They worked together building, repairing, and keeping the wolves from Shaver's door.

On Shaver's Farm
By Rich Horton

> *"Dorothy was brash and loud but a very nice person. Richard was very involved in collecting rocks. Other than that, and one time when I heard strange voices coming from him, everything else seemed normal."*—Linda Jane Palmer

Everything we did around the farm was accompanied by conversation about it. Dick explained the whys and hows as we went along. Really, he was teaching me what he had

Richard Horton and Billy Goat pose for Shaver's camera in 1951 on the Wisconsin farm, with the Shaver farmhouse in the background. Shaver's fans traveled great distances to stay there as guests, much to wife Dottie's dismay (Richard Horton collection).

learned. Being a greenhorn farmer himself, he had sought advice from his neighbors, who were good enough to supply the needed knowledge about cows, goats, chickens, gardening, and field crops, raising corn, hay, and cucumbers for pickles — a cash crop around there.

On my first visit he showed me around his 160 acres of rocky fields and 40 acres of timber. While we tramped, we talked, or rather he did mostly, pointing out different things. He loved his woods, the birds, squirrels, rabbits, and the occasional deer. It was a long, circling excursion with him taking the lead. After about three-quarters of the way around I noticed that he was limping. When I asked him about it he said he'd broken his ankle some years ago, and if he walked too much it stiffened up on him.

Dick was a highly intelligent guy. He once told me that there was nothing he couldn't figure out if he put his mind to it. He educated himself in whatever interested him, which was most everything. He had a strong jaw with an underbite and big, strong teeth. At the finish of a statement about evil or some other dark subject, he'd thrust his jaw out and perhaps shift it slightly to the side. It gave him a wolfish look. If what he'd said was particularly

On Shaver's farm, circa 1950, Rich Horton (left), Shaver (inside truck), and unknown helper load a milk cow into the truck (Richard Horton collection).

depressing, and hopelessness hung in the air, he'd lighten the mood with a wry smile and say, "But what do I know? I'm supposed to be crazy."

He rolled his own cigarettes, at least when he had to save money, which was most of the time. He was skillful at it, too, obviously from long practice. In the kitchen, in the dead of night, he'd sit at the table. I'd watch his cigarette smoke rising straight up, alternating to lazy curls from the movement of his arm reaching for another drag, and then the exhale. His was a thinking man's manner, long intervals between drags, ashes growing and falling off as he deliberated. Lost in his thoughts, he would suddenly remember the cigarette again.

[Author's note: At the end of his deployment in Korea, Horton was discharged, applied for the G.I. bill and earned his master's degree. Shaver tried to convince him to return to the farm, but to no avail. When Horton began to speak of marriage, Shaver advised against it. Regardless, Horton married, had two children, and got a job as a history professor. That meant the end of Horton's farm visits, much to Dick and Dottie's dismay.]

Letters from Home

"I didn't give up, I got lost in a stray now and have been lookin' for a real solid then to get out on." — Richard Shaver, 1973

22. The Stigmata of Raymond A. Palmer

The Shavers kept in touch with Rich Horton when he was at school and eventually sent to war in Korea. Following are two examples of the kind of news Horton got while away from the farm.

From Dottie, January 28, 1951:

> Richard almost died last October. Ulcers. Had to have X-rays, a doctor, and such a bill to pay. Got it paid and now Rich is doing fine. Drinks one gallon of milk a day. That's half-and-half mostly, with cream. Good old Jersey milk.
>
> The Palmers moved up November 3rd. [Ray's] doing wonderful. Walks all alone now but can't drive a car. We drive and use his, as ours clunked out. He's got a Buick convertible, a red one. Ray's right leg isn't working right to drive. Maybe in a year or so. He's been such a good guy to us.
>
> In October he came on two canes and couldn't hardly get around. In pain. He had R.P. Graham drive him and family up to see us, and get a doc and so on for Richard.
>
> They stayed a week and came back to live in November. The old house up there is getting all fixed and is nice. Ray does a lot of the work. He and Rich are cementing the cellar and it's almost done. Ray gets down on his knees and works. He will get the mill going this summer. Had it all cleaned out for re-fixing. Needs new joists and timbers underneath.
>
> Ray paid Merle to move a small house off his property for $100. You see, Ray gave him the house, land, timber to fix house up and a steady job. He was drunk so much and is now in court on three different charges. Just a naughty boy.
>
> Well, I guess Richard's mother will drive here for the summer again. She is getting close to 70 or 71 and we want her to stay here this time.

In the spring of 1952, the Shavers managed to buy a small tractor. Even with that, Shaver found it difficult to keep the farm profitable. He was still writing in his spare time, and even sold to *Amazing Stories* when Howard Browne failed to realize it was Shaver's work. Horton received the following letter in Korea.

February 15, 1952:

> Shaver Mystery stories will be coming in *Other Worlds*, will try to get a sub for you sent, unless my memory slips as usual. Had a long SM story in *Amazing* lately called "A World He Never Made." Under the name of Benson — they thought Palmer wrote it. My title was "Lords of the Flame." No sense to theirs, who could make a world but God anyway, and nobody even believes he did.
>
> I am at present bearing a black eye from boxing with Jomey Dain. Jomey is fourteen now and packs a wallop — wanted me to help him get ready for a school meet — the champions of several

Shaver posing in a sombrero next to the farmhouse front porch, circa 1951 (Dottie Shaver collection).

of these little red schoolhouses were having a sponsored meet somewhere. His old man won't box with him any more — claims he is suffering from an infection — the which claim [*sic*] I now understand. So am I, around the eye.

But I surprised myself, and probably him. I held him to one sock, the one he made on my eye I never saw coming. And I even hit him occasionally, just so he'd know I was there.

Learned later, after accompanying him to the "meet" (which he didn't expect), that it was strictly a fiction, just to get me to box with him. It was a cub scout go, all contestants were scouts under 12. Next time I'm going to drop something on him when I see him coming over.

Ordered a hundred apple and fifty peach trees, then picked up a government fruit book which advised peaches were impractical above southern Illinois and were raised in Michigan only along the lake. So changed the order to apples ... which will plant in the field on the south of the woods. Your friend, Shaver.

Grace moved in with Dick and Dottie in 1951 and lived on the farm for the next ten years. She died in 1961 at the age of 90. The family buried her next to Ziba in the Fairmount Springs Cemetery.

Ray Palmer's Amherst

> *"Ray wanted to be a man all the time, and he took a lot of chances he shouldn't have taken."*— Frances Ferris Yerxa Hamling

Ray Palmer adjusted to country life quickly, and in short order became a pillar of the community. He joined several local groups as well as the school board. The slow lifestyle acted like a tonic to help him recover from the accident in Evanston. Nevertheless, he still got unwanted attention from locals, according to his daughter, wherever he went: "I know he didn't like the stares of other people and none of us liked it either because we didn't really see him the way other people did. He was just our dad.... He had amazing will power, especially because he was in pain most of his life. He hid that well and I didn't realize that he had pain until I was grown and working for him and finally noticed it."[28]

Rap knuckled under to family demands in 1953 when he traded in his 12-year-old red Buick convertible for a red Pontiac station wagon. From that point on, he always drove wagons. Four years later it was a robin's-egg blue 1957 Chevrolet. Due to the Evanston accident, his right leg was weaker than his left. That failed to keep him from driving, adding a certain fear factor when riding with him. A couple of well-placed cushions to sit on with another propped behind his back and Rap was good to go. This combination of pillows gave the required height to see above the steering wheel.

In 1955 he moved his family into the big four-bedroom stone house, which was a wonder to behold. The expansive, light-filled living room had a built-in area for the radio-phonograph. A half wall of built-in cupboards separated the living and dining rooms.

A sunken sunroom with floor-to-ceiling windows faced the lake. Another half wall with built-in cupboards and a desk separated the sunroom from the living and dining areas, giving the entire space an airy, open feeling. Huge picture windows with window seats running the length of both rooms offered an impressive view of the lake.

The house had two fireplaces, one in the living room and one in the basement, directly below the living room. The large, 12-foot-wide stone fireplaces went from floor to ceiling. The kitchen had three large windows and a pass-through to the dining room. Next to the kitchen was the "freezer room" with food storage and a little greenhouse at the back. The

Shaver and Rap playing chess in Rap's dining room, Amherst, Wisconsin, circa 1957. They often played Saturday evenings, after one of Rap's German potato pancake dinners (Dottie Shaver collection).

house had three entries: one faced the lake, entering into a screened porch that led to the living room. Another faced the driveway, and was the entry the family used. Linda Jane recalled,

> You could walk out to the two-car garage from the basement. The garage had a flat roof that we could walk out onto from our driveway entry door. The flat roof had a railing all around. There were fieldstone terraces on two sides of the house ... a two-tiered one on the driveway side with a walkway from the driveway and garage up to the house. The lake side had four terraces that ran longer than the length of the house. My dad built them himself crawling on his hands and knees.
>
> They were planted with flowers and some garden items every year. There was also a huge garden down by the lake past the beach, which my dad (and all of the rest of us) tended. And yes, the house did have some large steel beams to support the wide expanse of the open living-dining rooms and the sunroom. You could see them in the basement.[29]

Rap developed a mellow, laid-back routine in Amherst; his weekdays began slowly. He would eat breakfast in the kitchen, drive the kids to school, then head over to Flemming's Café or the Meadow Inn for coffee. He sometimes held court at the café when fans caught him there drinking his morning Joe and reading the newspapers. Then he might reminisce about his career at Ziff-Davis, or expound upon arcane aspects of the Shaver Mystery.

After picking up his mail at the Amherst post office, he headed home to eat lunch and watch *Days of Our Lives* on TV. Rap and Marjorie were hooked on *Days of Our Lives*, and could always be found in front of the tube as they opened mail and ate lunch.

Marjorie used the sunroom as her office. Working at her desk, she managed the

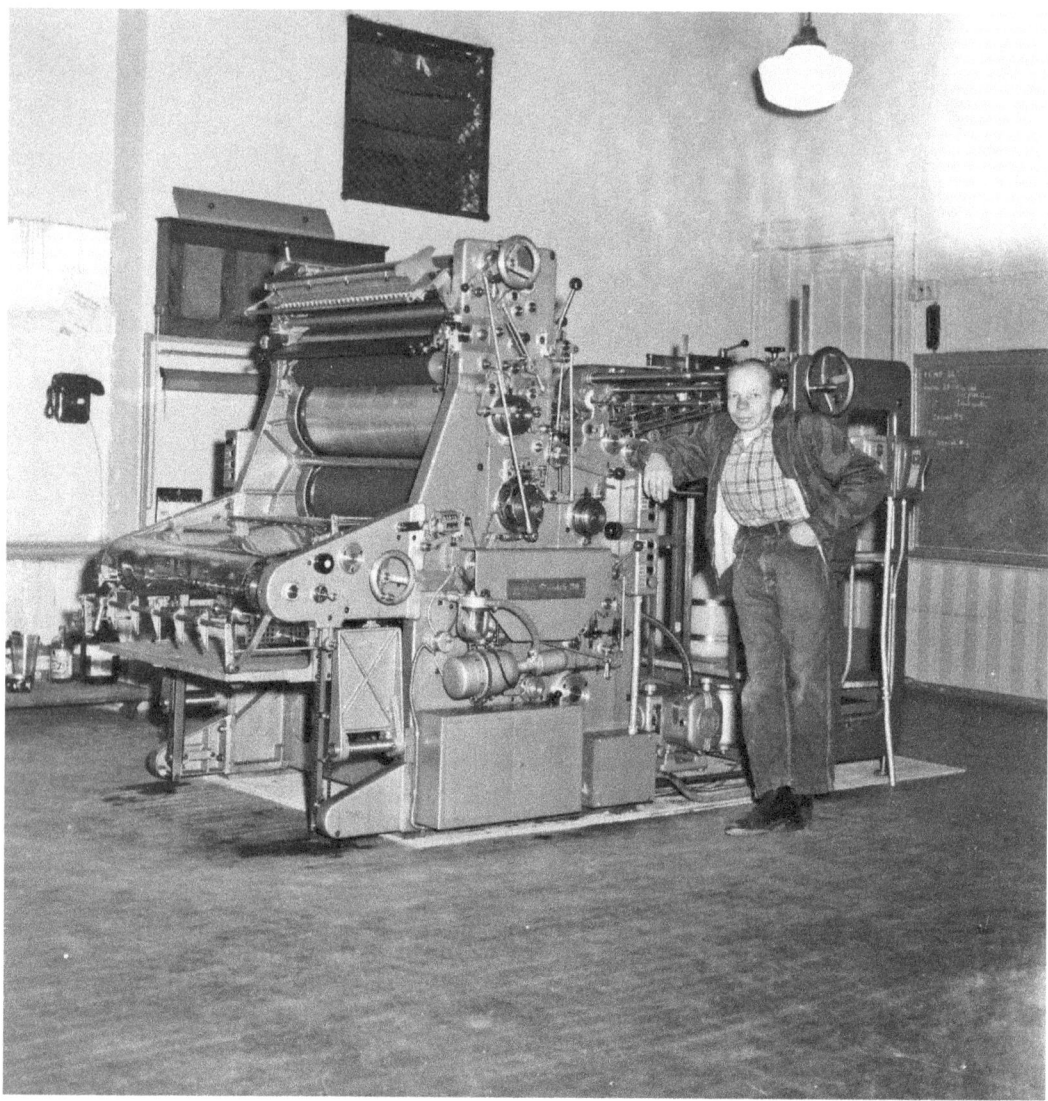

Rap posing with his new high-speed press in the old schoolhouse building he purchased to use as a print shop. Amherst, about 1963. Note the room still had a blackboard on the wall (courtesy Linda Jane Palmer).

company books and kept track of mail and subscriptions. Rap used four different offices, at one time or another, during his time in Amherst; none of them were located in the stone house. His first office was in the partially finished upstairs of the farmhouse they lived in during construction of the stone house, recalled Linda Jane. "When we moved to the stone house the old house was converted to an office and they hired some women to work on subscription services.... Dad then converted the old chicken house into an office. It was on the property next to the house and as long as he used it for an office it was called 'the chicken house.' He then rented an office on Main Street in Amherst right next to the bakery and was there for a short time along with a couple of girls doing paperwork. Then he bought the old schoolhouse where [the office] stayed the rest of his life."[30]

On Sundays, Rap piled the family into the station wagon and drove to nearby Plover for dinner at the Blue Top, where Rap ordered the Sunday chicken dinner. It came complete with bibs, and was served on tables draped with red-and-white-checkered tablecloths. "Another thing we did as a family was go to the movies on a Saturday or Sunday," said Linda Jane. "My dad, being as short as he was, had to sit in the very front row so he could sit comfortably in the seat and be able to see the screen without anyone blocking his view. That was hard on the necks for us and to this day if I go to a movie I sit in the very back row. My dad absolutely had to have candy when he went to a movie. His favorite was Milk Duds."[31]

Here Lies Science Fiction, 1890–1959

> *"A guy named Forrest J Ackerman is called 'Mr. Science Fiction' and 'Fan No. 1' but darned if I'm not 'Crazy Fan No. 1!' Simply nuts about it."*—Ray Palmer

The collapse of the 1950s science fiction market left many SF magazines in smoldering ruins. The dazed mass of refugees that were the pulp writers crawled out from under the wreckage. The watering hole that was once their oasis had all but dried up. Who or what was to blame? They all had opinions, but in 1959, fanzine editor Earl Kemp stirred the hornets' nest by asking the question no one dared ask: *Who killed science fiction?*

In a groundbreaking survey of big-name SF authors of the era, Kemp learned there was plenty of blame to go around, but two names stood out among editors of the golden age of pulp fiction: Raymond A. Palmer and John W. Campbell, Jr.

Phillip José Farmer put Campbell on the rack for his promotion of L. Ron Hubbard's *Dianetics* and, much later, his obsession with psionics. "He owes all of us science fiction readers an apology," said Farmer, "but he has never offered it. Instead, after being disillusioned, he has gone off the deep end on psi."[32]

Willy Ley, Rap's old friend from as far back as the Science Correspondence Club, grouched that the Shaver Mystery did the deed. George W. Price focused his wrath on SF *fans* for demanding so-called adult science fiction. "I believe that the largest single cause ... is the attempt to make science fiction into 'literature,'" he said.[33]

Robert Bloch, Rap's fellow Fictioneer, griped that SF was not completely dead, "although it might well be moribund." He presented a laundry list of reasons for the downfall of SF that included the public's switch from books to television. This, he said, was not just an IQ killer, it threatened "the *ability* to read, which seems to be diminishing rapidly among the adolescents."[34]

Regardless who or what killed it, pulp writers had nowhere to turn. Then, a miracle! The cavalry arrived with William L. Hamling leading the charge. He appeared out of nowhere to save his fellow SF writers from the wasteland that was pulp fiction, ushering them into the bright new world of sex paperbacks. The writers saw their future, and it was a three-letter word. They threw in their lot with Hamling.

The timing of SF's downward spiral had worked in Hamling's favor. The 1950s was a vortex of changing sexual mores on a collision course with a burgeoning new paperback industry. Thanks to the efforts of SF writers Robert Silverberg and Harlan Ellison, Hamling managed to cut a deal with the Scott Meredith Literary Agency, which represented a substantial number of SF writers. The Hamling-Meredith pact created a major source of mass-market porn by putting SF writers back to work cranking out sleazy novels, according to Earl Kemp, who witnessed history in the making: "In the beginning those books appeared under the imprint of Nightstand Books. Two titles were published every month by a company called Blake Pharmaceuticals in Evanston, Illinois. Blake Pharmaceuticals was a defunct Illinois corporation that was purchased cheaply by William Hamling."[35]

The founding officers of Hamling's newly incorporated publishing company included members of the old inner circle, specifically, Rap and Shaver. As Hamling never failed to point out, "Everyone was tied in somehow to the inner circle." For better or worse, that was how it turned out.

Deck Chairs on the Titanic

"Going broke? Boy, we went broke, but we're too stubborn to know when to quit."—
Bea Mahaffey, Other Worlds, *1955*

The dark cloud that swallowed up science fiction swelled to dust bowl proportions by 1955. It was a watershed year for gloom and doom. SF magazines were folding left and right. Editors with a will to survive had to come up with a plan. Howard Browne's plan would return *Amazing Stories* to the Ray Palmer era of action-adventure yarns, with one proviso: they would be better written, he said. Browne's dream of a mature *Amazing Stories* that would bury the Palmer years once and for all came to a grinding halt. He made an official announcement explaining his editorial about-face in a 1955 editorial, which Rap noted with unrestrained glee in *Other Worlds*: "As for Howard Browne, he's laying out old copies of Palmer *Amazing*s on his bed these days, and 'doin' what comes natural.' *Amazing* ought to improve rapidly now."[36]

Amazing was selling a lackluster 45,000 copies in 1955, about 125,000 less than Rap's Shaver Mystery heyday. *Galaxy* was hovering around 60,000 and *Astounding* at about 72,000. These big-name pulps were far above the circulation of Rap and Hamling's little independents.

Rap came up with his own plan to return SF to solvency. This time, he said, he would redefine the genre. Scientists, it seemed, had made old-style SF obsolete. "Science fiction used to say: 'What man can imagine, he can do.' Well, now he's done it! So, we've got to revise it to say: what man can't do, imagination can.... [I intend] to journey into incredible worlds, not out in space a few paltry parsecs away, but an illimitable distance into the reaches of the mind!"[37]

Rap noted with trepidation Bill Hamling's publishing success, and advice. "[H]e told us to 'forget science fiction and put your dough into sex books! We'll make a mint! Everybody loves naked pitchers!' Sadly, we looked elsewhere ... and besides, we had no dough."[38]

The sex paperback industry was about to make a lot of people very rich, but Rap clung to his SF life preserver. Browne was about to jump ship at Ziff-Davis — for good this time — and catch the next lifeboat to Hollywood. Even as late as 1956, struggling to make ends meet, Rap extolled the virtues of SF as the salvation of humanity. In the February 1956 issue of *Other Worlds* he outlined his last ditch effort to save the magazine. It would in fact, become his last SF-fantasy promotion: *Tarzan on Mars*.

Tarzan on Mars

> *"I shall never forget that fantastic leap that Tarzan made that saved the armies of La, and of Tars Tarkas, from certain death in the rising waters of the Gorge of Tarnath."—Ray Palmer*

Rap had a long and storied past as an Edgar Rice Burroughs fan. It culminated in 1940 when, as editor at *Amazing Stories*, he convinced Burroughs to continue writing the adventures of John Carter of Mars. Rap confessed to readers that the reason he worked so hard to convince Burroughs to write for *Amazing Stories* was because he craved more John Carter yarns.

But Burroughs was in ill health, and died shortly after his *Amazing Stories* comeback. Rap lamented Burroughs' death, and how he would never again read a new story with his favorite Burroughs characters. *Tarzan on Mars* was meant to change all that.

It began like most Ray Palmer promotions—when the paths of two like-minded souls crossed. In this case, it was Rap and Stuart J. Byrne, a one-time engineering writer for weapons systems. This seemed an unlikely pairing for atom age pacifist Rap, but similarities did exist between them. Like Rap, Byrne had an accident in his youth that nearly killed him; a flowerpot fell on his head at the tender age of three. Both men were science fiction fans and admired Burroughs, relishing every twist and turn in the adventures of Tarzan and John Carter.

Born in 1913, Byrne was just a Minnesotan with a career in weapons systems until another near-death experience changed his outlook. He rejected the weapons of war to become a second degree Lama Yoga in the Astarian Brotherhood. He studied scientific astrology and eventually attained a doctorate in metaphysical science. He then turned to the teachings of the Maharishi Mahesh Yogi, until he switched to the Rosicrucian Order of Mt. Ecclesia. But the mysteries of Burroughs' iconic characters equally intrigued him: "I was always drawn to the mysterious and mystical elements in fantasy fiction (Abraham Merritt, Rider Haggard, etc.) and indubitably the unresolved mystery of La of Opar and Issus of Darsoom had to be tied together," Byrne said. "I lived the fantasies and probably lived them as events developed."[39]

When not studying metaphysics, Byrne wrote fantasy fiction. His story *Prometheus II* appeared in *Amazing Stories*' February 1948 issue. Byrne steadily sold SF-fantasy yarns to Rap's *Other Worlds* from 1950 until it folded in 1957. Rumors began to circulate among fantasy fans that "someone" should pick up the Tarzan yarns where Burroughs left off. Then the Universe of Infinite Possibilities stepped in. Byrne said, "Strangely, I ended up residing 14 years in Tarzana, California, almost within walking distance of the famous Edgar Rice Burroughs landmark on Ventura Boulevard."[40]

According to Byrne, "[M]any devotees of the classical mystery-adventure-fantasy genre were starting to make some outlandish suggestions—particularly to Ray Palmer.... The growing outlandish suggestion was that I should be a successor to Edgar Rice Burroughs and continue his work and tradition!"[41]

Rap informed Byrne that he saw the potential for 20,000 immediate orders for *Tarzan on Mars*. With growing pressure from his agent to climb on board with Rap's proposal, Byrne began writing *Tarzan on Mars* in 1954 under his pen name, John Bloodstone. It was a novel in the Burroughs tradition, using Burroughs' own characters. In it, Byrne planned to resolve plotlines that the venerable Burroughs left hanging.

Byrne had reached 110,000 words when Rap read the unfinished manuscript. He was awestruck. Now it was time to generate reader interest in the new yarn. Rap planned to scoop the world by publishing Byrne's new Tarzan novel in *Other Worlds*.

The one thing Rap failed to reckon with was Burroughs' son, who controlled his father's estate. Hulbert Burroughs oversaw what was by then called Edgar Rice Burroughs Inc. and he guarded all things Burroughsian with the ferocity of a mother grizzly bear.

Rap pleaded for the estate's blessing in a manifesto titled "Tarzan Never Dies," appearing in the November 1955 issue of *Other Worlds*. It was meant as a shot across the bow of ERB, Inc., and Rap hoped the younger Burroughs would not just capitulate, but anoint Byrne as successor to his father's legacy. Rap even proposed a "Dimes for Tarzan" campaign. Fans were asked to send Rap a dime to support the new project. "I will put it into a Dimes for Tarzan fund, and use it to create the gigantic wave of public opinion which is the only possible way to convince the proper person that what I have proposed is the thing to do."[42]

Hulbert Burroughs' attorney gave Rap his answer in the form of a cease and desist order. *Tarzan on Mars* was unadulterated plagiarism, the attorney said. This meant total defeat for Rap, the kind he hated most. He planned a counter-attack: "[O]n the heels of this came the most unkind barb of all — for to read this great novel is forbidden! No man may read it. It cannot be published, for to do so is plagiarism. And this is one plagiarism that nobody could get away with. Legal action would be swift and relentless."[43]

As he had done with the Shaver Mystery, Rap played the part of firebrand. He told readers that ERB, Inc.'s denial of a new Tarzan novel as nothing less than a travesty — a cosmic scheme to deny Burroughs fans ecstasy beyond belief. With *Tarzan on Mars persona non grata* at ERB Inc., Rap shifted to Plan B. He transformed the banishment of *Tarzan on Mars* into his next crusade.

It was classic Rap, and he played it to the hilt. Fans bought *Other Worlds* to follow the controversy. They wrote letters bristling with outrage. Though *Tarzan on Mars* never did appear in *Other Worlds*, Rap sold plenty of magazines without it. The controversy became a minor hit in *Other Worlds*, but eventually, without Byrne's story, fans and even Rap lost interest. ERB fans fondly remember *Tarzan on Mars* as a quirky sidebar to the Tarzan saga, while Rap is seen to this day as a hero and a true fan of Edgar Rice Burroughs.

Curiouser and Curiouser

"I guess the Shaver Mystery has plumb died on me, and my will and wish to write anything has a sour taste in my mouth."— Richard Shaver

The unexpected death of *Tarzan on Mars* left Rap with few options. His once fertile imagination was on the ropes. He was pushing 50 and had run out of schemes to save science fiction. After devoting 30 years of his life to the SF field, he shut down his last SF pulp, *Other Worlds*. It died with a whimper in May 1957.

Shaver, too, was struggling. Desperate for cash, he sold his tractor for $250. In 1959 he went to work on the Rambler assembly line at the Nash-Kelvinator auto plant in Kenosha, Wisconsin. Instead of putting the tractor money to practical use, he gambled it on shares of Solar-X, an Idaho uranium mining company.

Kenneth Arnold was president of Solar-X and a personal friend of both Rap and Shaver. Arnold guaranteed the company would make them rich within a couple of years. So Rap bought shares too, convinced of a windfall. Shaver seemed hopeful in a letter to Rich Horton: "It should pay off sometime next year and ease the pressure somewhat. I got 2,500 shares, which should be worth around $10 a share in a couple years according to reports...."[44]

Instead, Solar-X went bust. To make matters worse, Shaver quit his job at the Rambler plant. He blamed his resignation on a sinister cocktail of dero torments called crueling:

> They chased me off the job in Kenosha three times with cutter and tamper ray until I hardly knew whether I'm coming or going, and Dottie is convinced I'm clear out of my alleged mind. I can only assure you I still have some sense, though I don't know for how long. There has been steady crueling here and throughout the state — crueling is a process of eliminating people too complicated to explain....[45]

Shaver joked to Horton a few months later that he quit his job at the Nash-Rambler plant "to preserve my sanity. Who wants to make Ramblers when I can stay home and worry?"[46]

Amazingly, every cloud that ever rained on Richard Shaver's parade had a silver lining. This time the cloud opened up an opportunity that would change his life. It happened in his darkest hour in the spring of 1960. With his farm failing, the wolf at the door, writer's block preventing pulp sales, and no job on the horizon, Shaver made a great discovery.

Actually, Dottie made the discovery, and he took it over. She was out in the cornfield one day when she noticed a small stone. Her focus was an image of the Madonna etched in glorious detail on the rock. She brought it home and showed it to Dick. "He laughed at me at first," she said, "until I found others, especially when digging, and not just laying in our cornfield.... He became interested, I think, when I found a stone mold of an infant's foot that was shaped like it was a bootie, and later found out Indians used such things."[47]

In the beginning, Shaver hoped that Dottie would find valuable gems. So he encouraged her new hobby, explaining it in a letter to Horton in May 1960: "Dottie has taken up rocks with a vengeance and I am getting interested — I got her some books on the subject and she has perused them with avidity and great profit — what I really want is one that shows how to tell a precious stone when you find one.... I am hoping she will find a large roc's egg with a diamond stuck to it."

Dottie's stones sat on Dick's writing desk for two weeks before "it" happened. Shaver explained the incident in one of his self-published brochures: "And then, like an echo, my wife's murmur soaked in to that place we all live and in that instant I found something I had been looking for many years. *The Song Stones!*"

His memory of the Song Stones came from old writings that had puzzled him for years, about ancient *jongleurs* — itinerant minstrels — who carried small stones "to sing from." Suddenly he knew: The rocks were songbooks. This was just the beginning.

While casually studying a rock formation on his farm, Shaver discovered an archeological treasure trove. His excitement fairly leaped off the page in a June 6, 1960, letter to Rich Horton. Horton received the letter just before his departure for the Shaver farm.

> Will you try and bring an archeologist and a mining student from the college. I have found a serpent temple on the place — one of the oldest archeological finds ever made and there must be some wise work [to] go on here to protect us — Palmer and I and others on whose land it lies. Please come jumping or you will miss out on the biggest find ever made on old Earth's face. I've got a jasper serpent head with a battle with the Amazons carved on it — I've dug up yellow diamonds with gem engraving finer than anything done today — the drawings are compound and complex like nothing that is done today.
>
> How could we have missed it? Come, Horto, come and marvel at your blindness. Even the

Shaver self-portrait, circa 1971. His personal caption for this photograph was: "This is me, Shaver, at my desk. I put the paintings on the desk to acquaint you with their style, which is direct photograph reconstruction from rock book pictures, projected onto sensitized canvas board. The little painting on the right is amphibious, or very early, while the big one behind me is later and is from Amazon rock."

> rocks in the barn walls have carvings ... we never noticed because we never looked.... O come, man! Your friend, Shaver

Shaver's latest discovery drew on his experience as an artist and amateur historian. The picture rocks, as he called them, would eventually become paintings as he gradually learned to transfer images from rocks to film, then to cardboard and plywood canvases. His Rogfogo Period (Shaver's name for rock book photography) is of great interest to art historians, who have since claimed Shaver's work as outsider art. Whatever else Rogfogo was, it was Shaver's final installment of the Shaver Mystery.

23

Big Trouble in Little Amherst

"I am still paying off bills two and three years old and more...."— Richard Shaver, 1959

Reading the staff page of William L. Hamling's *Rogue* magazine in 1957 was a nostalgic look back into the golden age of Ziff-Davis pulps: Editor and Publisher, William L. Hamling; Executive Editor, Curtis Fuller; Associate Editor, Henry A. Bott.

Frank M. Robinson, Rap's former Ziff-Davis office boy, eventually became *Rogue*'s editor. Chester Geier and Howard Browne became *Rogue* contributing writers.

Only Bill Hamling knows exactly when he realized the value of Rap's move to Amherst, Wisconsin. To a Chicagoan like Hamling, it was in the middle of nowhere. The population hovered around 500. It was the perfect place to incorporate a controversial new erotic paperback company.

Hamling's lawyers (he had a stable of them by now) contacted Rap and Shaver with an offer they could not refuse. For permitting their names to appear as officers on Hamling's latest dummy corporation, Hamling would make it worth their while. Other than the use of their names, their involvement in the company would be nil.

It was familiar territory to Rap. He had made Shaver his "paper president" on the *FATE* incorporation papers back in 1947. Hamling and Chester Geier lent their names to *FATE* as well, according to Dottie Shaver: "When Rich helped Rap get *FATE* going that was a good thing, but [he] never got anything ... even if he *was* president.... Hamling and Chet were in that too."[1]

Hamling gave his new company a solid, Midwest name: Freedom Publishing. He stayed as far away from the legal process as possible. "That all came up through my attorneys," he said. "I don't even remember how they handled it. The corporations were made that way. I didn't participate because it was all technical legal work."[2]

Hamling was already the clandestine owner of a long list of corporations that existed between 1959 and 1964. Greenleaf Publishing was first, begun in the basement of the Hamlings' Fowler Street home. Then came the wave of paperback companies: Blake Pharmaceuticals, Reed Enterprises, Corinth Publications, Regency Publications, Greenleaf Classics, Phenix Publications, and Freedom Publications. The imprints produced by these operations included Nightstand Books, Adult Books, Ember Library, Idle Hour Books, Late Hour Library, Candid Readers, Companion Books, Leisure Books, and Pleasure Readers — all actively sought by vintage paperback collectors today.

Whether Rap agreed to convince Shaver to join him as a signatory on Hamling's document or the other way around is not known. According to Hamling, he and Rap often exchanged favors. As his wealth increased, Hamling became Rap's silent partner and benefactor, supporting him when times got tough. Hamling was the guy in charge now, making hundreds of thousands of dollars and soon to make millions. The legal chicanery was a glory to behold, according to Earl Kemp:

> Once reincorporated, Hamling redirected Blake Pharmaceuticals into publishing pornography and Harlan Ellison was running the whole show while seemingly running *Rogue* instead. In those days, in spite of the popular acceptance of soft-core pornography in movie theaters all across the country, an operation like Blake Pharmaceuticals was at the very least frowned upon and was kept, as much as possible, completely under cover.[3]

Hamling's attorneys assured Rap and Shaver there was nothing to worry about. No one would bother to check the names on those incorporation papers. Besides, Rap and Shaver had done this kind of thing before.

Rock Books 101

> *"No, you lunkhead, any old rock won't work. Just rocks from a pre-diluvian ruin."—*
> Richard Shaver

Shaver's rock books became part of the historical record in his June 6, 1960 letter to Rich Horton, which described the remnants of a prehistoric serpent temple. The letter also contained Shaver's first mention of rocks as *books*: "[T]he stones — that is, the books — were strewn for miles." He also pointed out that "not every stone hereabout contains some picture work ... only those from pre-diluvian ruins."

The discovery imbued Shaver with a kind of euphoria, later tempered by frustration. The addition of rock books to his career was a way of reclaiming the Shaver Mystery as his own. He hailed them as "The *New* Shaver Mystery." Within a month of his finding, images hidden for eons within rocks on his farm suddenly became crystal clear. He collected his better finds and stacked them on the farmhouse porch. People began to suspect something odd going on at the Shaver farm, and Frances Hamling found out what it was during a visit there in 1961:

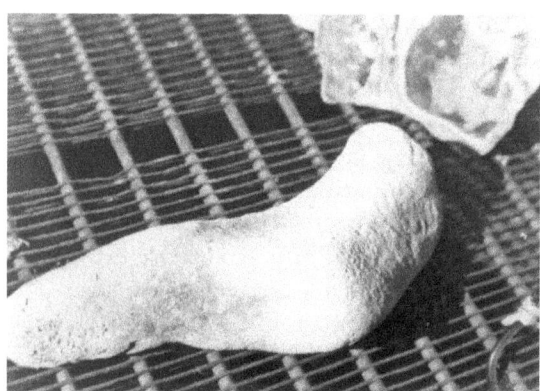

Dottie Shaver found this alleged petrified child's foot on the Wisconsin farm and gave it to Dick. This is the foot she says convinced him to begin work in earnest on rock books. Shaver then photographed it to include in one of his promotional pamphlets. His caption read in part: "This is a human child's foot, though it looks something like a flipper. When this foot was still living, it had several finny elongations now missing." Shaver took the photograph in February 1968.

> I didn't know Shaver well. I'm not sure, but I think he thought there were tribes of tiny people who lived in rocks. I didn't really know what the mystery was. We stopped [by the farm] one time. That's when my son Richard was with us, and he remembers all the goats, all over the place, and I remember lots of stones. The windowsills were lined with stones. They had a concrete porch on the side that had stones inside, and practically every stone you'd pick up, Dick would start telling a story about the people that lived in there. I thought, "Oh my goodness!" I thought he was kind of crazy.[4]

Her response was typical of most. Few shared Dick Shaver's passion for the picture stones. Nevertheless, he had plenty of enthusiasm to go around, for the rocks spoke to him of a great civilization thriving in Amherst long before Noah's flood. Strangely, this had a familiar ring to it. Picture-rock history was much like the early plots of Shaver Mystery yarns, which told of the evolution and extinction of Earth's ancient races. And yet they had so much more.

The rocks told of three major racial groups inhabiting Earth: the Giants, the Amazons, and the Mers. Interwoven throughout this pre-human rock book saga were things like deadly ape bats and multiple moon falls. Shaver learned that the moon had bounced off the Earth's surface several times, wreaking havoc in a most unpleasant way. He eventually catalogued his findings in a *Pre-history Primer*, based on his exhaustive research of the picture rocks:

> These three main races, separate and distinct from the main stream of bi-sexual humanity, had their areas and their tribes and their cities. Whole continents acknowledged the rule of the Amazon armies. Great areas were inhabited by the giant races ... and the smaller races were kept out. And the oceans were the domains of the Mer people, even in myth and legend it is acknowledged that the oceans were the realm of Poseidon or Neptune....
>
> The giant races were *not* main-stream racial strains of Earth men. Their teeth were very different, they lacked canines.... [A]lthough some of them look a lot like men of today, there were some very important differences.
>
> The Mer races seem to have been our immediate forebears and look like us except for the fact they didn't emerge from the oceans and take up land life. They stayed in the oceans.
>
> The Amazons had their own social structure, very close-knit and military, like the Spartan ... but males of the sort we call male today only entered the Amazon strongholds on certain seasonal occasions. So that Amazons of the latter time were really two sorts ... the male groups lived apart (just as some Polynesian and Malaysian tribes have their long houses for men and keep apart from the women and kids)."[5]

Two years after his discovery of the serpent temple, Shaver started a mail order business selling and renting picture rocks. Shaver's letters to Horton had changed and become fewer. Talk of farm life was replaced with long monologues about rock books. Horton, like others who knew Shaver well, was baffled by the change. Shaver tried to impress on Horton the importance of his discovery:

> May 25, 1961. There is no way to put all I have learned from them into words. These rocks are packed with tiny pictures, it takes a week to really digest one and know what they meant to say and get an inkling of what the pictures tend to delineate.... [T]he pictures are sometimes the whole story, and sometimes just the cover illustration, the rest is very tiny writing in a half dozen methods of writing.
>
> What was here was a vast museum, full of relics of a very long period of development....
>
> January 4, 1962. Will eventually get some stones to you — the slices progressively get better as I learn to distinguish my stones and know which ones will have greatest contrast after cutting — some are quite brilliant while some are faded into gray confusion. They really are ancient microfilm packs in silica — and the micro photos prove this beyond question, it is just a problem to get the right people to examine them — when you do get a VIP to look at them, he forms an opinion on one or two glances at one or two stones and decides the ladder is too high for practical climbing....

The rock books dominated Shaver's thoughts. He informed Horton that discussion of anything other than picture rocks was *verboten*: "[A]ny diversion of effort from this strict practical line is considered by me an invasion of damn foolishness."

In 1967, Shaver's rock books starred in a syndicated newspaper cartoon series similar to Ripley's "Believe It or Not!" Otto Binder, co-creator of *Amazing Stories'* celebrated robot Adam Link, was behind the feature.

Someone's Got to Take the Rap

> *"You don't seem to properly realize they are not paintings, but a form of photo done by projecting into wet glue.... [A] study of the grain would show you some remarkable things you will never see unless you really look."— Richard Shaver, 1964*

Rock books overshadowed everything in Shaver's life that had come before, including his career as a science fiction writer and farmer. Those were stepping stones to one last shot at a legacy that would outlive his allotted time on Earth. It became an all-consuming crusade that overshadowed his past failures. It gave him a reason to go on.

With his mail order business and his research well underway, it would have been an easy road to success if *they* had just left him alone; if only those Freedom Publishing papers had remained buried in the Wisconsin Secretary of State's filing cabinet. But they did not.

The *Saturday Evening Post* published an article by one Cleveland Amory, a "noted observer of morals and manners," in its April 6, 1963, issue. Amory's photo showed him smoking a pipe. It added a touch of Ivy League verisimilitude to his moral observations. This particular column was subtitled "Dirty books flourish behind the smoke screen of 'censorship.'" Amory appeared to be very ticked off.

Author's favorite Shaver self-portrait, holding a rogfogo print. Summit, Arkansas, circa 1969. Rogfogo was Shaver's name for rock book photography (Dottie Shaver collection).

> One which we should like to nominate for ... the "worst of the worst" is a publisher who operates out of Milwaukee under the good, sound American name of Freedom Publishing Company. Among this publisher's books we found *Sex Bait*—a colorful little book whose jacket showed a totally nude redhead lying on the green grass ... above the title in capital letters are the words, TWISTED PASSIONS RULED HER WANTON BODY....
>
> Again, a sampler of titles: *Sin King, Sin Teacher, Sin Damned, Sin Colony, Sin Song, Sin Monsters, Sin Devil, Sin Hellcat, Sin Time....*

The Amory exposé hit newsstands during the first week of March 1963. On March 16, 1963, Dick Shaver drove as fast as Wisconsin law allowed to the Secretary of State's office in Madison. There he filed dissolution papers for the Freedom Publishing Company. Within two weeks, the *Milwaukee Journal* ran a follow-up to the *Saturday Evening Post* article with a story of its own on page B1: "Book Printer in Smut Case Acts to Quit"—"Firm Starts Dissolution"—"State Legislator Calls for Probe; DA's to Push Inquiry."

What more could go wrong? With the lid blown clean off, the inner circle's code of silence was breached. Denials of wrongdoing began to fly, as state legislators feigned self-righteous indignation. They vowed to protect Wisconsinites from the sinister threat of smut. *The Milwaukee Journal* was unrelenting:

> Dissolution was requested by the firm's president and sole stockholder, Richard S. Shaver, who lives in the town of Lanark, near Amherst, according to the company's registered agent, Milwaukee Atty. Edward H. Snyder.

> State Senator John M. Potter said in Madison that he would introduce a bill, probably Wednesday, asking for creation of a special committee of three senators and three assemblymen to investigate pornographic literature, with power to subpoena witnesses.
>
> Raymond A. Palmer, head of Palmer Publishing Co., Amherst, announced his resignation as a director of Freedom Publishing. He said he did not know that Freedom Publishing dealt in alleged pornographic books....

Shaver and Palmer steadfastly maintained they were figureheads in the company and knew nothing of the nature of the books, which, authorities claimed, were printed in Illinois. In truth, they were printed in Sandusky, Ohio.

Shaver's willingness to dissolve the company at the first sign of trouble was not enough to satisfy Wisconsin legislators. They vowed to continue their smut crusade come hell or high water. TV news crews began setting up cameras in front of Shaver's farmhouse. It was a mess, but Hamling remained calm. He had his stable of lawyers at his beck and call.

More ominous was the possibility that the scandal would sully Rap's standing in the Amherst community. His saving grace was that he was listed as a mere "director" of Freedom Publishing. Shaver, on the other hand, was president, treasurer, *and* a director.

What transpired behind the scenes is something only Hamling, Rap, and the Shavers knew for sure, but the conversation was undoubtedly strained. Rap had much to lose. He had a family and a business that employed 17 locals. He gave the Amherst post office more business than Christmas and Mother's Day combined.

Then there was Hamling. He was on his way to the top of his game. Shaver, on the other hand, had a rocky farm with no farm equipment, a barnyard that smelled to high heaven, and a collection of pre-diluvian rock books that no one but he could interpret.

Whatever the details, it became crystal clear that Shaver would take the fall for Freedom. True to his word, he kept his mouth shut. Dottie was more outspoken, especially after Dick's death. She said it was the beginning of difficult times for the Palmer-Shaver friendship:

> We were such good friends. That is, from 1945 when we moved out to Illinois, [until] we were sent away by Ray Palmer in April 1963. That seemed an awful mess at the time, but [our] friendship really began to dwindle when Ray Palmer and Bill Hamling got that new magazine going and that really was a downfall when they made Rich some kind of an officer for that. [A] scapegoat, Rich was, for a couple [of their] deals.... I was never told too much to know what was going on, until 1963 when Ray Palmer had a lawyer at his home.... After that things began to pop, and we were told to leave....[6]

Shaver's new role as fall guy came into focus in the *Stevens Point Daily Journal* on April 5, 1963.

Odd Man Out

> *"Never accept money you don't earn or know what it's really for. It can harm you."—*
> Dottie Shaver

The headline and subhead in the *Stevens Point Daily Journal* said it all:

> Calls Self Unwitting Dupe in Pornography Case.

"You can print one great headline — 'Fool.'"

With this, Raymond A. Palmer of rural Amherst summed up his association with the Freedom

Publishing Co., an alleged printer of obscene literature. Palmer says his mistake was letting his name be used by a company he knew nothing about....

It started last October, said Palmer, when Richard Shaver, also of rural Amherst, asked him to sign articles of incorporation for a new company. Shaver has written for Palmer's science fiction publications.

"He said he had a chance to get a job, but needed a corporation and had to have three signatures," Palmer explained.

Palmer said he knew Shaver needed money and agreed to sign to help him out. He said he put his name on the last sheet of the articles of incorporation without paying much attention to what he was doing.

"I didn't think it was important because I didn't think it would come off anyway," said Palmer. "It was a stupid thing to do," he added.

Freedom had become Shaver's folly, and Rap was merely a victim of his better judgment. In an interview with a *Stevens Point Daily Journal* reporter, Shaver freely admitted his connection to Freedom, but was cautious about details like the publisher's name. He was quoted as saying he received a monthly $200 payment for lending his name to the company. The reporter listened as Shaver worried about losing his income. It supported his rock book research, he said.

Dottie was always quicker to reach the boiling point than Dick. Referring to Hamling, she told the reporter, "The other guy is taking it easy and we're doing the suffering." Asked who the real perp behind Freedom Publishing was, she replied, "If I knew, I'd tell you."

All this was rehearsed for the press. Throughout the media blitz following the scandal, Hamling's name was never mentioned. He was simply "the publisher," a shadowy figure they knew nothing about.

Thus, the inner circle's code of silence was reinstated. As part of Shaver's separation package, he continued to receive his monthly $200 stipend in perpetuity. Shaver was apparently led to believe this was Hamling's payment for an option to reprint his fiction. Six years later, Shaver explained it in a taped interview with flying saucer enthusiast Lucius "Lou" Farish of Arkansas: "Now Bill, down at Corinth, he was going to reprint the Shaver stories ... in paperback. And I sent them to him and he was all set to go and I don't know what happened. They never did it."

In truth, there never *was* an option to publish Shaver fiction at Corinth, or any other Hamling-owned company. Earl Kemp, editing under the name Jon Hanlon, worked on a series of pulp fiction reprints under the Corinth/Regency name. He unequivocally states that Shaver was never considered. Kemp, a critic of the Shaver Mystery from its inception, said, "No person in their right mind would consider publishing anything by Shaver. This specifically goes for Hamling, for Greenleaf, for me, for every person I've ever known."[7]

The Shavers remained silent throughout their Freedom ordeal, though Dottie was unhappy about that. She felt Dick had been betrayed, and she was probably right. Kemp shares Dottie's viewpoint: "You need to remember that Shaver was really a low man on a tall totem pole. He was just there to be used and abused. He was a different 'class' person, to be ignored and dismissed and blamed.... He was expendable. A few crumbs (paychecks) would keep him in line indefinitely."[8]

Rather than being abused, as Hamling sees it, Shaver was simply taking one for the team. "I retained Dick Shaver to head the company up. He worked for me, under the auspices of Ray. Whatever he got, he earned. He was taken care of, Shaver *and* Palmer. We were members of the inner circle — the little club. [Ray's] life and mine were entwined. And

I mean that in only a nice, decent sense of the meaning. These are people I respected and loved. You won't find many like us...."⁹

Shaver made a rare comment about the Freedom affair in a November 24, 1971, letter to W.G. Bliss, a Shaver correspondent and fellow rock hound. "[T]he law in Madison was after a company in which I was the paper president (I was hired by some Chicago groups to head up publishing registration companies as a 'dummy president' several times).... They have to register with the state government to publish anything, and it never backfired before *but* this one did ... and I had to get out of the state although I in fact knew nothing about it.... They had only used me to make out the papers for a fee ... a salary I needed...."

This suggests that he and Rap were involved in Hamling's operations prior to Freedom, possibly as far back as *Rogue* magazine. Illinois law in those days did not require corporations to provide a list of officers, nor the filing of annual reports. If Shaver's name appeared on "several" of Hamling's front corporations, it is likely he and Rap were officers for Blake Pharmaceuticals, which preceded Freedom by two years.

Farewell Lanark, Hello Palm Springs

> *"The menace lurking there in the darkness behind the wispy shadows somehow resembled a righteously pissed-off Richard M. Nixon ... waiting ... hungry."*—Earl Kemp

Within a few months of the dissolution of Freedom Publishing in March 1963, the Shavers packed their essentials and signed the farm over to Dick's sister, Catherine Claire, who sold it for $9,500. The apparent haste of their departure may well have been on the advice of Rap's lawyer. It may also have stemmed from Shaver's old fear of the long arm of the law, and being returned to the asylum. Since no court trial ever came out of the Freedom Publishing fiasco, it is hard to explain Shaver's willingness to leave all his worldly possessions behind. In 1964, Rich Horton received a letter from Shaver, uncharacteristically postmarked Summit, Arkansas. Their relocation, he said, was the result of a willingness to help a local friend in need.

Five years later Shaver explained the reasons behind the move in an interview with Lou Farish, who wondered at first if the cave people might not have suggested the decision. Shaver denied that.

> It's pure chance as far as I'm concerned. I come down here with a woman who lost her husband. We went to visit her up in Illinois and her husband was dying when we got there.... And we got through burying him and ... she was in such a condition from the death and everything, [that] we had to tend to everything for her.... We had to bring her down here and unload her and get her installed with relatives and so on, and here we were ... and no particular reason to go anywhere and we just cruised around and stopped at a motel down here, and really liked it.

The motel charged $20 per week, but a man named Morgan offered to let them rent a small stone house on a plot of land for $25 per week, so they moved in. Eventually, Shaver's sister Catherine Claire Haughton bought it. Again money from Shaver's well-to-do sister saved them. Claire had married into solid New England money and often found herself in the role of Shaver's financial safety net, much to her displeasure. She bought the rock cottage for $3,500. Her brother's contribution was $500.

Rich Horton and his wife Marina were the Shavers' first out-of-town visitors. Horton recalled the Shaver's new home: "On our way from Iowa to a new teaching job in New Mexico in the summer of 1964, we stopped in Summit for a few hours, and I believe he had his apparatus [rock saw] set up in his garage studio at the time.... My last letter from Dick was received on October 26, 1967, while I was teaching in California. Also enclosed was a booklet, 'Pre-Deluge Art Stones.'"[10] Still miffed that Horton married against his advice, Shaver ignored Marina for the entire visit, leaving Dottie to entertain her.

That same year, 1964, William L. Hamling discovered California—Palm Springs in particular. Though he downplays it now, his publishing business was under pressure from the Chicago mob and corrupt politicians. They wanted protection money, and stood in line for a liberal coating of grease. According to Earl Kemp, the grease went to some very big names in politics. With growing paranoia and Chicago graft weighing heavily on his soul, Hamling set out in search of the good life in Southern California.

While Shaver kept a low profile in his one-bedroom Arkansas cottage, Hamling luxuriated in the clear, crisp desert air of Palm Springs. Kemp began to notice a change in Hamling, and suspected the worst:

> The more he became addicted to California living, the less we saw of him around the porno factory in Evanston. Then, much to our dismay, he began making noises about changing the

Double-exposed self-portrait of Shaver at work in his studio, 1968 (Dottie Shaver collection).

Dick and Dottie Shaver in front of their small home in Summit, Arkansas, winter 1963. The kitchen and bathroom were each 6 × 9 feet; the living room was 18 × 15 and the bedroom 9 × 15 (Dottie Shaver collection).

whole focus of the business and moving the operation totally to California, where morals were a great deal more relaxed than in Illinois, where the really beautiful people lived, and where the sun always shined.... As those efforts became more real, Hamling picked out and rented suitable office space for the companies in an industrial complex off Mission Gorge Road in a section of San Diego known as Mission Valley.[11]

It may have been lost on Hamling at the time, but just as his former boss William B. Ziff had moved his employees lock, stock and barrel from Chicago to New York, Hamling was about to do the same thing in the opposite direction — from Chicago to California. Kemp, who had worked for Hamling since 1961, was not pleased.

Hamling bought a big, pretentious house in Palm Springs not because he liked it, or wanted it, but because it was big and pretentious. That it reflected a lifestyle totally alien to him was no consideration. That the house was built to showcase the talents of a particularly flashy gay interior decorator and was particularly flashy and gay seemed to escape him totally. No single thing about it reflected Hamling or his personal tastes except perhaps the location, ass-to-ass with Jack Warner and across the street from Kirk Douglas.[12]

Shaver, on the other hand, watched his archeological discovery of the century — the serpent temple — disappear in his rear view mirror. Gone was his 160-acre Wisconsin farm and his old pal Rap. Shaver was living in exile in a house off Highway 14 in Summit, Arkansas, where he would make his last stand.

24

Artful Obsession

"I don't know a lot of things about them, except I wish I had never found them to begin it all."—Dottie Shaver, speaking of the rock books in 1982

Once settled into his new home, Dick Shaver began cleaning up the workshop in the backyard. It had belonged to a woodworker who sold cedar-wood posts and novelties to passersby. Shaver painted a sign that read *Shaver's Shack* and hung it on the door. For the next decade this was world headquarters for rock book research and development. It was also where Dottie kept a small kiln for her new hobby, ceramics. When Dick took over the rocks, she lost interest in them.

Shaver's Shack also became his painting studio. His yen to pick up brush and paints, never realized in Wisconsin, became reality once the drudgery of farm life had ended. Now in retirement, he had time for it. He was always the utilitarian; there were no landscapes or flower arrangements in his work. Shaver's paintings explored the vast imagery of rock books.

He began painting what he saw inside slices of rock cut with his 12-inch diamond-blade saw set up in the lean-to next to the shack. Rich Horton began to lose track of Shaver when the painting began. It was all Shaver talked about — that, and the rock books. Shaver's letters were filled with updates on his crusade to legitimize rock books through art. In 1965, Shaver informed Horton that an Arizona gallery represented him, and that he was planning exhibits of his work. He explained the intricacies of his process to Horton in a letter dated May 1965:

> They look finished long before they are and the difficult part is the picture itself when finished apparently is only just begun, as it changes as you dry brush it.... I try to accent the ladies nose and learn I had mistaken the bulge of the emboss and it is really someone's elbow.... This is because they are "see-throughs" like x-rays of a crowd.... No way to explain what it has taken me years to learn ... you will have to have one of the see through pictures for many months of observation before you even begin to grasp the intricacies of 3-di x-ray design ... they used optical devices not in any way like ours.

Over time, Shaver refined his painting technique. He settled on a system utilizing simple household materials: glue, varnish, wax, paint, and cardboard or plywood as canvas. Actual canvas was either too expensive or unavailable to him. He described his complex system in his one and only book on rock art: *This Ancient Earth — Its Story in Stone.*

First, he prepared the surface "with wet glue or wet varnish, or just sprayed with water. In the case of the surface of a stone, I use an overhead opaque projector, which operates by reflected light.... I sift dry glue flakes on wet canvas, allowing the light to drive the flakes and glue powder by its 'pressure.' Light does have pressure, you know...."[1]

Inside "Shaver's Shack," his Summit, Arkansas workshop, early 1970s. This was his writing studio, darkroom, library, and Dottie's ceramics workshop.

The pressure, of course, came from exd, the source of gravity as outlined in the Shaver Mystery years ago. Shaver did paint originals, that is, scenes not specifically taken from picture rocks. He would go into a kind of trance during these spontaneous paint sessions, apparently getting help from his tero allies in the caves.

Tal Levesque and Mary Martin were wandering hippie kids in the early 1970s, much like Shaver had been in his youth. They were drawn to Shaver's legend and gradually befriended him. On a 1970 visit, they found that Shaver was about to start a painting. Levesque described Shaver's process in 2003.

> While I was there he demonstrated how he did what later became the artwork with various images in it. He did not use a projector.... I think he could have, if he wanted. This might be hard to categorize.
>
> If something was going wrong ... he would take his shoe off and pound three times on the floor while cursing the dero, blaming them for messing with him. And his speaking (rap) would change. At times he was a slow country boy type; then he would switch to a hyper intellectual genius.
>
> The sifting thing ... was more like invoking. He wanted the tero ray to guide the falling of the powder (about two and a half feet) to aid in the formation of the images. As I watched, I saw that the powder was not falling evenly as you might normally expect. It really looked like a ray or something was happening when he sifted. The powder didn't act right. Instead of falling straight down it swirled and separated into little piles all over the board on the floor, making the images appear ... 3-D, and easy to see the outline of the faces and things that appeared. I was really impressed. It was clear. All he would do was take a pencil and outline the images that were already

Richard Shaver painting of a rock book scene, late 1960s. He used common household materials, including soap flakes, glue, wax and various paints. Since his death his work has appeared in New York and California galleries (Dottie Shaver collection).

"Three-Legged Stool," 1984, mixed media by Shaver's daughter Evelyn Ann Bryant. Evelyn notes that she began her art career with no knowledge of her father's work, though they shared a similar process. While her father painted images found within rock slices, Evelyn got hers from inkblots. "Both of us pulled out images we saw which were meaningful to us," she said. "The results were very different, as our interests were, but we began the same way" (courtesy Evelyn Ann Bryant).

Richard Shaver self-portrait in his studio, with darkroom enlarger, circa 1971. He liked to be photographed with the tools of his trade (Dottie Shaver collection).

there to see. I think anyone there would have seen the same images. Later he would color them in....

Before I met Shaver I thought he was a hick-kook. After talking with him in person I came to realize he was a true *genius*. I have met "Bucky" Fuller, and he was a mega-genius. Yet, of all the humans I have ever met, Richard Shaver is in the top few whom I think are genius people. I really think Shaver was a normal guy that had data downloaded into his brain. He would not know how to spell a simple word correctly, then, the next minute would be quoting page and verse from Homer or some rare book or poem. He did this many times and blew me away.[2]

Chester Geier said he became aware of Shaver's rock books when he worked as ad editor at *FATE*:

About 1965 Dick Shaver materialized like a ghost from the past and submitted an ad to me at *FATE*. He was living in Arkansas and it appears he had become a "rock hound." ... He thought he saw pictures in the sawn surfaces of rocks and called them "the picture books of the Atlanteans." He sent me some rock slices with drawings he had made of what he saw in them and had the idea of renting rock slices so that people could see the pictures his ad copy claimed were present.

I [replied] that renting rocks was not a sound commercial venture, as it was likely to get him entangled with people who failed to return rocks. In handling advertising one quickly learns to avoid offers that may create bad feelings between advertisers and readers, with loss of good will toward the magazine itself. I suggested to Shaver that he sell a "package"—a rock slice with a drawing of what he saw in it, and a couple of pages of mimeographed background information on his claims about the rocks being Atlantean picture books. I told him he could sell the package for $10 instead of renting rocks for the $5 he had in mind. I think he felt this involved too much work and that he was disgusted with me for complicating a beautifully simple idea. This was the last I ever heard from him.[3]

Shaver Takes a Vacation: Houston, 1966

"The work I am doing may not be understood for centuries..."—Richard Shaver, 1965

The 1960s was a difficult decade for the inner circle. Two of its members would find themselves involuntarily transported to a hostile planet called Texas. The Mantong alphabet translates Texas as a "place where beneficial energy collides with negative energy." Even in English, Texas spells trouble.

And so we find the great dero overlord himself— J. Edgar Hoover — summoning Richard S. Shaver and William L. Hamling to appear in the courtroom Thunderdome of Houston's Bible belt. Here they would fight to the death in gladiatorial combat with the feds over Hamling's sex books.

Hamling planned his defense as a guardian of free speech. Hamling survived the Freedom Publishing scandal but Hoover had not finished with him yet, not by a long shot.

Shaver's one-way ticket to Arkansas (his reward as the president of Freedom Publishing) was still smarting. True, his enthusiasm for farming had waned long before the Freedom scandal sent him packing. To fans and friends alike, Shaver had simply disappeared. Ray Palmer finally addressed his disappearance in 1966, after the smoke had cleared:

> "[H]e vanished several years ago, having been forced to flee from a false charge of engaging in pornography (which also got your editor into a lot of hot water because newspapers like scandal, and don't care who gets hurt).... Well, Shaver was even reported dead. He is not.... The reason we kept his whereabouts secret is because he was in very great danger of being imprisoned for something he did not do. Now he has been cleared."[4]

Exactly how Shaver had been cleared when no charges had been brought against him is a mystery. The feds, now spying on Hamling's operation in earnest, were brainstorming ways to bring the hammer down on porn publishers. Their plan was to cripple Hamling's operation by declaring seven of his campy sex novels obscene, then summon him to Texas in July 1966. Not only was Hamling expected to pay exorbitant fees to his attorney Stanley Fleishman, he also paid for the lodging, meals, and incidental expenses of all of his

Evelyn Ann Bryant's "Self Portrait," oil, 1966. Her father was living in Arkansas, Evelyn in Michigan; the two never met. She was not aware of his work with rock book painting (courtesy Evelyn Ann Bryant).

witnesses. Houston was about to become ground zero for Hamling's federal comeuppance.

And so it was that one year before San Francisco's psychedelic Summer of Love, the sheriff of Boone County, Arkansas, showed up on Shaver's doorstep with a summons. Shaver was going to Houston, but not as a witness for the defense. The feds wanted him as a prosecution witness. They wanted to know about his presidency at Freedom Publishing.

Names from Hamling's past and present received subpoenas too. Earl Kemp was also summoned as a prosecution witness. Kemp has written long and bitterly of the judicial system's disdain for civil rights and of government harassment. He has spoken at length about the Houston trial in his online fanzine *eI*.

Kemp unwittingly became a sidebar in the Shaver Mystery saga when Hamling made him Shaver's guardian in Houston. Kemp was not pleased, but followed orders. Like it or not, he was now Shaver's chaperone *and* social director.

Long Hot Summer

> *"You'd be shocked to know that there are, today, powerful organizations devoted to the suppression of knowledge and of truth...."*— Ray Palmer

Shaver found himself among interesting company, though he never got to swim with the big fish of Hamling's Greenleaf posse. Other witnesses on the docket for July 1966 were Dr. Wardell E. Pomeroy of the Kinsey Institute; Dwight V. Swain, journalism professor and pulp fiction writer for both Rap and Hamling at Ziff-Davis; Dr. Roger D. Chittick, a minister; Arthur Knight of *Playboy*; Ian and Betty Ballantine of Ballantine Books; Greenleaf cover artist Robert Bonfils; Hamling's stepson Richard Yerxa; Tom Ramirez, a Hamling porno author; and two real-life swingers who agreed to talk about open marriage and the fabric of America's changing sexual mores.

This was of great interest to Shaver, who had never been to Houston, or was ever involved in a federal trial that had everything to do with sex, one of his favorite subjects (next to rock books). One name that was absent from the summons list was Raymond A. Palmer. Somehow Rap got overlooked, or purposely left out, said Kemp, who is baffled to this day about Rap's absence: "I seem to remember everyone else of significance. Ian and Betty Ballantine, Thomas Ramirez, Shaver ... but not one iota of Rap. Also I don't believe Rap turns up in any of the data I collected from that event ... curiouser and curiouser."[5]

Thomas Ramirez, one of Hamling's more prolific porn writers, was impressed with the opulence spread before him in Houston. On his arrival, Ramirez and his wife were whisked from the airport to the plush Rice Hotel, "one of the city's finest," he said. "We went to dinner in the hotel's Flag Room, about the fanciest restaurant I'd eaten in during my short life.... As I parted after dinner, Fleishman gave me a card admitting me to the Press Room, a private club within the hotel where I could get a drink 'or,' he said, 'go buy what you want in the hotel shops. Sign for it. All expenses on Bill Hamling. Don't skimp.'"[6]

Meanwhile, as Hamling entertained top-shelf witnesses in air-conditioned comfort in the Flag Room, Kemp and Shaver wandered aimlessly amid the humid cityscape. "There was a definite class structure separating the truly important witnesses and the peasants," Kemp explained.[7] (Apparently, Shaver was one of the serfs.) "The Greenleaf crowd, including William L. Hamling, all stayed in a downtown hotel occupying all the rooms surrounding

A group portrait of the main characters of William Hamling's Houston trial, July 1966. Hamling (second from right) looks cool and calm, but he had yet to be acquitted in the Federal porno witch hunt. (Left to right) unidentified bystander, Stanley Fleishman, Percy Foreman (Hamling's attorneys), Shirley Wright (Hamling's corporate secretary and bookkeeper), Hamling, and Richard Yerxa (Leroy Yerxa's son) (courtesy of the Richard Yerxa collection).

the swimming pool. It was nonstop room service pork-out time. For some reason unremembered, I was allowed to stay with the Greenleaf crowd. I was a witness for the *prosecution*, as was Shaver, and kept separately by the feds with no intermingling to 'confuse' stories and testimony."[8]

As Hamling sweated bullets in the courtroom, Shaver was having the time of his life. As president of Freedom Publishing he had taken the brunt of the witch hunt. Now it was Hamling's turn, and Shaver kicked back and enjoyed an all-expenses-paid vacation on Hamling's dime. Yes, Bill Hamling, the same publisher Shaver knew nothing about, according to the Wisconsin newspapers. Unlike others scheduled to testify, Shaver was cool, calm, collected. He spent most of his time sightseeing and dining out — under the watchful eye of Earl Kemp.

> Hamling was spending his time with more important players in the court game, so I was stuck as his second; it happened to me frequently. Shaver was in town for a certain number of days.... It was difficult keeping him mentally occupied because I didn't know much about him and what little I did know really turned me off big-time. Deros, indeed.
>
> I never touched upon the subjects of science fiction, Palmer, Ziff-Davis or pictures in rocks in any conversation I had with him. That limited our reach considerably. I remember we walked around a lot, went in and out of stores, ate often and lavishly. I wound up sort of liking him, in a hokey backwoodsy sort of way. He struck me as being a good old boy with not too much ... knowledge of the real world. At some levels we had much in common. He seemed almost detached from the trial, as if it didn't apply to him at all....[9]

Meanwhile, Dottie sat at home waiting for Dick's return. Years after his death she recalled that July in 1966. "[Bill Hamling] was a millionaire, but [I] knew nothing about him.... Rich had to go to Texas to a court trial.... He did not have to go on the witness stand, he said when he came home. He had all expenses paid to go. Never found out much about it."[10]

Long story short (it was indeed a long story; the trial lasted two months), Hamling was acquitted, Greenleaf rejoiced, and the judge sent the feds back to their overlord Hoover with a message: never bring a lame case like this before him again. Still, the feds came away with a partial victory. The Houston trial soaked Hamling for a cool $300,000 in 1966 dollars, a monumental sum. In a final flourish of sweet revenge, Hamling gave his editorial staff a direct order.

"The federal prosecutor was named Morton Susman. Displaying a rare sense of humor ... William Hamling directed the editorial department to undertake a special project. In every book produced, they were to exchange the name of all the more reprehensible characters, the prostitutes, low lifes, and criminal types to Susman."[11]

Think Hats and Porn

> *"The truly momentous decisions of our lives are those formed quite suddenly, in a flashing moment of inspiration."— Chester S. Geier*

As Hamling defended himself in Houston, Rap was lying low in Amherst, staying out of trouble and keeping his publishing business above water. He was making just enough money to support his magazines, his family, and his employees. By this time he had dropped *FATE*, *Mystic*, *Other Worlds*, and *Universe*. *Search*, *Flying Saucers*, and *Space World* were still in print, though *Search* and *Flying Saucers* had devolved into small, stapled formats.

This was the same year, 1966, when Rap came out with *Forum*, a small, stapled magazine sold by subscription only. *Forum* functioned like an Internet discussion group. Rap would propose an idea in his editorial and readers responded via letter. Rap published the letters, rebutted the arguments and made comments. Much of the content was one long letter column. Letters were free and plentiful. He began publishing donated contributions, too, some of them from Richard Shaver.

Forum had no paid ads at first. The purpose was to connect with Rap's hardcore fan base, which, by this time numbered around 2,200. Those who enjoyed Rap's feisty editorial style subscribed to *Forum*, and in *Forum* he kicked out all the stops. He became more outspoken, brazen, challenging, on topics like sex in Heaven (Do angels do it? Of course they do!), the Bilderbergers, the Federal Reserve Bank, the JFK assassination, and an old favorite, reincarnation. That was a heated topic of debate ever since Rap declared it non-existent. Many of his readers believed it did and he kept the argument going year after year.

Meanwhile, Shaver was in far-off Arkansas. He knew his writing career was finished, but Rap's promotion of the Shaver Mystery in *Mystic* and *Search* brought back old disagreements, and further strained their relationship. The strain increased when Rap produced 16 volumes of Shaver Mystery material taken from Rap's personal files. They went all the way back to the very beginning. He called it *The Hidden World*. Three of the volumes contained Shaver's personal correspondence to Rap. Shaver was infuriated. They were for Rap's eyes only, he said, and complained bitterly to Lucius Farish in 1969.

> It's that damn telaug business! For instance, when he put out *Hidden World*, it was mostly my stuff, and I said to him, well, you ought to pay me something out of that.... He's getting a dollar and a half ... pay me, send me a copy. Well ... that'd be ten or fifteen dollars, and that'd be my payment [for] the whole damn thing....
>
> When I first met Palmer I understood him and I believed him and knew just what was what, I thought. But as the years went by ... he fell more and more under this ... I don't know what to say. But I think he professes some things out of an idea that it gives him a defense. That is, he's going to fool dero into thinking he's on their side.... And that's why he says some things and does something [else].[12]

Fallout from the Freedom Publishing scandal in 1963 put a sizable dent in their relationship. Still sore from the raw deal he got, Shaver spent the next few years painting and writing about rock books. He entertained visitors and befriended a few Summit locals, like his next-door neighbor, the Reverend Dunn; he was a good friend to Dick and Dottie and eventually delivered the eulogy at Shaver's funeral.

It was hard at first, life without Rap, but if Shaver ever waxed nostalgic about it, Dottie was quick to remind him how they ended up in Summit. "Never accept money you don't earn or know what it's really for," she said. "That was Rich's one fault he did there. Found out years later it was one of those girlie publications...."[13]

Dottie stayed angry at Rap and Hamling long after Freedom; she called them "two peas in a pod." Shaver tried to make a go of it on Social Security, Hamling's monthly check, and what he could make off his artwork.

"Rich had so much he wanted to write about and finally he didn't do as many stories when he was fired from Ziff-Davis," Dottie recalled in 1981. "Had oodles of ready-to-mail manuscripts. He sold to *Weird* and several others, but Ray Palmer got the most for his new mags.... Did get a few bucks now and then, mostly with long periods between. [Richard] never went to welfare until about 1966 or 1967, and remained on food stamps and SSI [until] he died."[14]

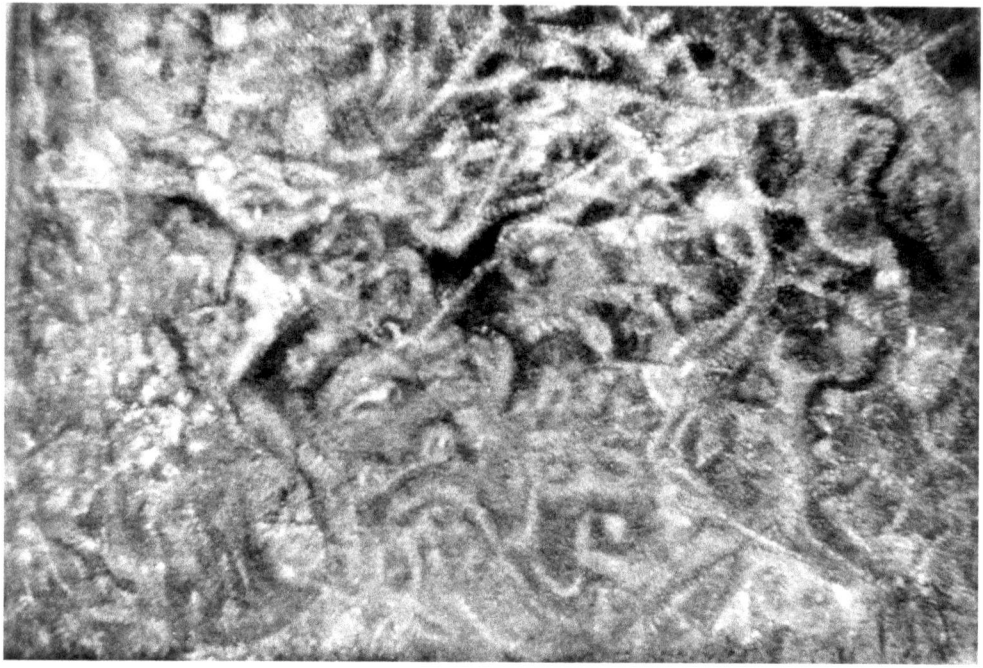

A Shaver painting, possibly one of his "inspired" works done while in trance, rather than taken from a rock book. Circa 1967.

Sometimes fans would send food or money. He never gave up on the dream that money would begin to flow as soon people saw value in the rock books. He tried to interest everyone who wrote to him. That went nowhere fast until he hooked up with a like-minded soul, an inventor and radio–TV repairman named W.G. Bliss.

Bliss was from Chillicothe, Illinois, a Navy vet of Yankee extraction. He took to Shaver's Rogfogo like a duck to Wonder Bread. This, for Shaver, was encouraging, and a long and lively correspondence progressed from 1971 until Shaver's death in 1975.

Shaver taught Bliss everything he knew, and before long, Bliss was replicating Shaver's rock photography. He branched out into slide transparencies that finally brought color to the rock books (Shaver could only afford to work in black and white).

Bliss ran a small repair shop and was fluent in electronics and physics, so Shaver sent ideas to him to turn into cold hard cash. Most of Shaver's schemes had to do with marketing the rock books, but some were inventions, like the Think Hat. Shaver was so enthused about the Think Hat that he wrote the ad copy for it, which he presented to Bliss as encouragement in 1973:

> Want to out-think the smartest ones? You can!!!! THE THINK HAT decreases resistance in neuron conductors! A harmless magnetic field decreases resistance, lets you think quicker — better — more! THE THINK HAT is a tiny battery-powered field generator that attaches to the inside of your hat. NOW ... does someone want to dicker with you about the price of a horse? OR — does the new lawnmower need fixing and you can't think what the mechanic told you? ANY problem gets easier—finds a solution quickly — when you put on THE THINK HAT. Only $8.95 plus tax. Deluxe model, $52.50. Money back guarantee if not elated, circumcised, and generally bemused with its total effectiveness in increasing the amount of thought going on in your mind.

The Think Hat died on the drawing board. Shaver said it was due to Bliss' negative thought processes. He explained the problem to Bliss in a 1973 letter.

> Yours negatively received of April 18, '73, describing the lack of enthusiasm in selling smart hats.... Who am I to argue? It's just an idea that would sell and there are several gadgets that have been sold. One I recall was a large copper wire you slipped on your head like a wreath that was supposed to do it.... They are even now constructing and using them in California hippie camps, not for thinking, but to induce a high similar to euphoric drugs. Did you know life is sabotaged by space people using the telaug? They make everybody think negatively and they ... never get anywhere. Some nut like Shaver says so.

Back in Evanston, Chester Geier was still at *FATE* magazine. He was far removed from the drama of the inner circle. Rather than galloping off to greener pastures with his former sidekicks, he chose to stick it out at *FATE* with Curtis Fuller, and a steady paycheck. This gave him less access to insider news, but now and again he got an occasional update through the grapevine.

> After the early '50s my knowledge of Hamling's activities came from other people.... Hamling had quite a traumatic experience with the government, some details of which were furnished me by a chap who had been an artist for *Rogue* and who I kept encountering at Chicago art fairs. This chap had served as a character witness for Hamling at his trial.
> In 1976 I almost made contact with Hamling.... My oldest son was living in Los Angeles, having been sent there by his company to manage a warehouse. He and my oldest daughter gave my wife and me tickets as an Xmas present to fly out and see my son and his wife and also the Southern California scenery.... One morning we drove to San Diego to visit the zoo and ... we tried to contact Hamling by phone but could not reach him. Time passed all too swiftly and when we did finally reach him it was too late to get together. He said the next time we came out he would take us on a cruise in his yacht....
> As for Browne, last I heard he was living in Burbank, California, and had been a writer for Warner Brothers Studios. Did scripts for a Clint Walker TV western series, and then wrote the script for the movie *The St. Valentine's Day Massacre*, which seems to have made hardly a ripple in the pool.... I visited Los Angeles in 1956 to make a speech at a sort of celebration held by a *FATE* advertiser and had a brief visit with Browne at the Warner Brothers writing offices, small rooms with desks and typewriters in a long, low building. He and I were never very palsy, but he was cordial enough.[15]

25

Martian Diary

"You will never know how much enjoyment you have lost until you get to dictating your autobiography."—Mark Twain

Having reached the age of 56, Ray Palmer thought it was high time to begin writing his autobiography. Thus began a period of personal torment and soul-searching that went on for nearly five years. In time, it began to resemble one of Rap's classic SF promotions.

He fretted over what the book should contain and how much of his life he would reveal. He shared every angst-filled moment and tribulation in *Forum*. He was using his readership as a sounding board, though it may not have been obvious at the time. He went over it in such detail, that much of what finally went into his autobiography had already appeared in *Forum*.

The title of his life opus was *Martian Diary*. The name likely came from the sense of alienation that haunted him throughout his life, harkening back to the childhood trauma that made him something less than "normal." The book would reflect his outlook on life, he said, and use the allegorical device of "one lonely and unaccepted Martian cast into an alien environment, an alien visitor to a strange planet. It is the story of his complete failure to be anything but alien, anything but acceptable, anything but 'each to his own kind.'"[1]

And so Rap began the difficult task of baring his soul, something he had never done before. He had hidden his childhood, just as he had hidden the truth about his ninth-grade education and his first marriage. His life was one of secrets, and yet the passage of time compelled him to tell the story. He did it the only way he knew how, through metaphor and fictional plot lines. A blending of fact and fiction in his life was Rap's trademark from the beginning, and it would not fail him now. Of this so-called Martian's report, he wrote:

> It certainly cannot be presented as fact — because we all know Ray Palmer is not *really* a Martian! Nor does he believe a word he says in his books, because even he presents it in a fictional form....
>
> [Ray Palmer] is not that wonderful, lofty personality he thinks he is; he is not that charming, gifted, three ring circus, brilliant, exciting performer *others* think he is; he is a man who has spent his life traveling down the *wrong* road, only to wind up with a minority report that nobody will read and *accept*!"[2]

Rap was using his most agile mental gymnastics to tell his story. Like an octopus frightened by his own image in the mirror, he vanished in a cloud of black ink every time he thought about it. Revealing his true story was going to be tougher than he originally thought.

Readers lined up in eager anticipation to reserve their copy of *Martian Diary*, wherein all of Rap's secrets would be revealed. But this was only 1968. Rap continued to anguish over *Martian Diary* for another five years. This required a steady stream of explanations why the book languished in limbo.

Martian Diary would reach new heights of legerdemain, he said, claiming it could stretch into hundreds of thousands of words within a vast series of volumes. His original plan was a large, hardbound edition at $10 per copy. His readers panned that idea. They suggested three smaller paperbacks at $3.50 each. Rap was only too happy to oblige. Little did these readers know that next to nothing was being written. He claimed the first section was nearly completed when a problem arose: "[I]t has been delayed by something that never delayed me before — the will to write it! At about 58 years, I thought I had enough to go on and also felt that it was time to do the actual writing, because it is a fact we don't live forever, and it is unwise to wait too long. Then, all at once, I made the most stunning discovery of my life — everything I wanted to say was *false*!"[3]

Readers had come to expect this kind of explanation from Rap, so their enthusiasm continued, as did their advance payments for the book. They received occasional updates as Rap wrestled with his inner demons. But now he was having second thoughts; was everything he had already written untrue? Maybe yes, maybe no.

> Oh yes, it was factual, up to the present. But tomorrow it will be false.... We all know that before Galileo, the sun went around the Earth. Today that is false knowledge. Actually, what we know is predicated on experience, and our experience is never complete.... *Martian Diary* will have to say to you "Don't believe a word of it...." I don't want to hang around for a couple thousand years trying to unteach what the book(s) will inevitably teach. So, should I write it at all?[4]

After telling his readers the first book was nearly finished, he confessed that he had yet to begin writing it. The mental anguish Rap revealed in *Forum* was either his way of staving off angry, paid-up customers, or an inability to bare his life story. Of course, it was both, and it became very confusing.

He admitted that he had a tendency to become too erudite, and "to forget that there are 800 basic words that are all that are necessary to be understood."[5] One angry subscriber, Genevieve Larson of Carmichael, California, had pre-paid for her copy of *Martian Diary* and was getting ticked off with Rap's stalling:

> As you have done on many occasions you got paid ahead of time for material that was still only a brain child, or to help you pay for new equipment, paper, or your current need for cash.... Now you accuse us of being so simple-minded, so incapable of separating our own truths from yours, and even imply we'll set you up as a sort of "Divine Authority," so you back down and refuse to go all out as you promised many, many times. You cannot weasel out of your promise so easily.

Rap explained that he feared he might lead his loyal fans down a dangerous path, and he could not live with himself having done that:

> What I have found out in my life concerns only me. It affects only me. It is useful only to me.... I am reminded of the day a young man walked into my office in Chicago, when I was editor of *Amazing Stories* and we were running the Shaver Mystery. He was very interested, and seemed to be one of those who had actual experiences that bolstered Shaver's account. I told him all I had discovered, and my theories concerning it. How the dero had all these powerful rays and machines of the ancient Titans and Atlans, and could even cause train wrecks, drive men mad, torture them, and cause wars. I must have been very convincing, and apparently hopeless of his future ... he went out and jumped into the Chicago River and drowned himself. After that, I was more cautious.[6]

Yes, Rap was reticent about writing his life story because it might send his more susceptible readers running to the nearest bridge. Nevertheless, he had good news: He had wrapped up the first section of the promised three volumes, but, "I rather feel it will be the last," he confessed. "It will be complete insofar as it will tell you the story of my life and of my discoveries. But you will have to figure out the answers for yourself! All of which adds up to more delay, because there will have to be certain revisions, and there will have to be certain omissions. The omissions are that awful thing named 'truth.'"[7]

The Martian Looks to Summit

> "[I have] been labeled a myriad of things ... I am schizoid, I am paranoiac, I suffer from delusions, I am a sexual aberrant, I am communist, I am obsessed, inspired, deluded, and when I publish my book ... it may well be that I will be committed for 'observation.'"— Ray Palmer

Ray Palmer was a long way off from *Martian Diary*'s eventual publishing date of June 1975. It had taken him a year to write 800 words — hardly the formidable volume promised to his readers. Rap knew he would never generate enough copy to make *Martian Diary* the shelf-crushing epic he had hoped. Then he got an idea.

He contacted his former (still a sore subject) Amherst neighbor Dick Shaver, and offered to publish an illustrated book about the rock books. This had been Shaver's dream for years, of course. There is some doubt, however, that Shaver knew the details of the book — that it would become part of *Martian Diary*.

Shaver self-portrait, circa 1970.

Rap's offer coincided with Shaver's sudden appearance as a contributing writer in *Forum*'s July 1972 issue, with the debut of "Two Dead Flies," an essay on the coming eco-war. Shaver had become something of an environmentalist during the years after Amherst.

Shaver described his end of the book deal to W.G. Bliss in 1973: "Palmer is supposed to be sending me a contract for 50 percent of [the] take on [the] book ... has not done so ... so I expect the usual runaround on money."

Not only would Shaver add sorely needed length to Rap's anemic *Martian Diary*, but it would also draw upon Shaver's fan base, as small as it was by then, to increase overall sales. And as much as Shaver said he distrusted Rap, he knew it was his best shot at a professionally printed book about the picture stones — his chance to spread the word about rock books beyond an occasional fanzine article.

Rap sent a $100 advance to prove his sincerity, which was enough to salve

Shaver's sore feelings, at least for the time being. He accepted the offer and gave his new book a title: *The Ancient Earth — Its Story in Stone.*

Bliss began collaborating with Shaver on the color photographs that would appear in the book. Bliss' enthusiasm for rock books has never flagged. Now in his 80s, he feels Shaver was too far ahead of the curve for rock books to achieve maximum acceptance in his lifetime. Bliss contributed a substantial amount of his own work to *The Ancient Earth — Its Story in Stone,* but received no credit, nor did he or Shaver get a comp copy when it published. "Palmer didn't send Shaver a complimentary copy, so I bought a copy for him," Bliss said. "The book was a dud for any sizable market. It was supposed to be entirely of the art type of rock pix with scant, if any, rock pix technical data. Why did Palmer do such a number on it??"[8]

March 1973. Still no *Martian Diary*, and the readers were getting restless. There was a problem, Rap said, a sinister one this time: "I got into trouble halfway through the first book because I discovered something new and the whole thing sort of caved in on me.... Why am I not writing *Martian Diary* at this very moment? Because 'something' doesn't want me to! ... [T]here is a force in the world that immediately sets up a strange kind of resistance when any man or woman decides something is true and important, and ought to be told! The very act of deciding to 'tell' brings such things as obstacles to telling!"[9]

The forces working to suppress *Martian Diary* were the same that would rail against the book when it was finally published, he said. "The IRS, the CIA, the Anti-Defamation League, the FBI, the Air Force, and just plain insane Joe Blow who has a gun and won't ever know why he wants to use it on me! But I intend to say it anyway!"[10]

In other words, Rap had a bad case of writer's block, and it crawled up from the cellar of his tortured past whenever he tried to write *Martian Diary*. He was simply not used to talking about his personal life in print. There were things he did not want to discuss, and he believed he was not alone in that. In fact, he encouraged others to remain silent about their pasts as well: "The fact is, that where the truth is concerned, we have to think deeply about relating it, and there is only one safe course — either neglect to tell it, or *lie about it*! Think of your family and friends who depend on your word. Don't destroy their confidence. A little white lie right here is a very smart course to pursue, and you might even get a nod of approval from the God who apparently didn't make the seventh commandment sufficiently clear."[11]

The inner circle's code was absolute and immutable. It penetrated Rap's very bones. Meanwhile, as he fretted over what truths to leave out of his autobiography, Shaver was compiling his contribution with great alacrity. He had a lot to draw on. His research had grown to epic proportions, encompassing paintings, essays, historical monologues, and photography. He had spent endless hours in his backyard lean-to, running the rock saw full tilt with enough kerosene to cut an entire library.

Reconnecting with Shaver was more than a way for Rap to solve his *Martian Diary* dilemma; it was a nostalgic nod to the past. Neither of them knew it would be the final installment of the Palmer-Shaver team. But with the addition of Shaver's *The Ancient Earth — Its Story in Stone*, the book now had two titles. To solve the problem, Rap gave the book a third title: *The Secret World.*

About this time, Rap's pursuits became darker, heavily weighted to conspiracy theory. His anger focused on the Warren Commission, the Bilderbergers, and the CIA. He had replaced the deros with government agencies and one-world secret societies.

Gradually, talk of *The Secret World* faded until, in the spring of 1975, it suddenly appeared out of nowhere. After hurriedly shipping out his prepaid orders, nothing more was said about its long-awaited debut.

His first mention was buried on the next-to-last page of *Forum* in response to a reader's letter asking if it ever got published. Rap replied, "To those who have written to find out if the first book has been published, here is the answer I've been too busy to send. It's available at $8.50 per copy."[12]

Rap's final contribution to the book was 36 pages. True, the format was 9 × 11 inches, so the pages contained more copy, but it was far from the prodigious work he promised. The other two-thirds of the book was Shaver's *The Ancient Earth — Its Story in Stone*, heavily illustrated. Though Rap had agreed to make it a paperback, he changed his mind. The baby-blue hardbound cover read "Volume One" in the lower left-hand corner.

All would have gone well except for one thing: There was only one name on the cover—Ray Palmer's—in a florid script. No Richard Shaver. No Richard Shaver on the title page either. Buried on page seven in the contents was *The Ancient Earth — Its Story in Stone* by Richard S. Shaver. Front and back covers featured Shaver's rock book paintings, while inside covers were resplendent full color Rogfogo images bled to the edge. It *looked* like Shaver's book, just without his name on it.

Shaver Farewell

> *"I never got round to remaking the world to suit me but I keep trying and I bet I made a dent in it."— Richard Shaver*

It is hard to say what Shaver believed the outcome of his book on ancient picture rocks would be, but when it was finally published in 1975, he felt he had been taken. A fan sent him a letter saying that she received her copy of *The Secret World* but his name was not on the cover. She loaned him her copy so he could see for himself. Shaver was floored.

"Did you see my book Palmer put out under his name?" he asked a correspondent. "Geez he gets me irritated!" Shaver took note of the insult in another letter in July 1975: "He lives on my ancient dying popularity and nibbles at it constantly ... chews on it with derogatory wool ... as in this book he 'rewrites' what didn't need rewriting and inserts his worn-out wool in front and puts his name on the cover as if it were all his. So I can't much help what I can't help but it's a shame somebody don't ... put out a Shaver omnibus and undersell him."

The book may have done nothing for Shaver's finances, but it finally gave exposure to the rock books. No one knew it at the time, but when *The Secret World* appeared in June 1975, Shaver had less than five months to live.

He spent most of that time doing what he usually did — corresponding with fans, photographing rock books, and working in the vegetable patch next to the alley. He was busy with cement work around the house, too, when not staring up at the night sky, cigarette in hand.

It was early October 1975, time for the annual Turkey Trot in nearby Harrison. It was a familiar event to Summit locals, but Shaver felt things had changed since he and Dottie moved there in 1963. It got him thinking about moving to the country again:

> It has become terribly over run in just a few years here lately. They built a shirt factory across a ravine behind me, and traffic is driving me nuts with the racket and fumes.
> Four or five years ago I saw maybe 20 cars a day.... This country was as empty of progress when I came here as you would want ... and you could drive north from here for nearly twenty miles before you even saw a house ... now it's overrun and getting peopled to death. They are mostly California escapees.
> I hang out in this remodeled lumber shed, about 20 by 10 with all sorts of shelves I built, full of rocks and what not ... such as two microscopes and two cameras and an enlarger and chemicals in jars. It stinks of hypo and developer ... some people can't stand the smell, but I don't even notice it. I have a ground squirrel leaves me a peeled acorn regularly on my desk for the privilege of living in the loft ....[13]

Shaver still regretted that he failed his civil service exams, unlike his brother Tate. He occasionally thought about his years with Ziff-Davis and the shellacking he took at the hands of fandom. "I often think that sci-fic-fen are the worst of all people socially, with almost no appreciation or understanding of others," he said.

He knew that his rock books would likely amount to nothing in the public eye, denying him the legacy he had hoped for. "How you get through this wool with the facts of rock books is too much for me ... my work has seen the insides of waste baskets so often I don't even send any more...."[14]

Here I Lie My Weary Feet Redux

"It burns me ... one of those idiots at Title *fanzine asked 'Is Shaver still alive?' Honestly, if a body lives beyond fifty, these youngsters wonder why."*— Richard Shaver, 1973

On or about October 10, the Reverend Dunn drove Shaver to the Boone County Hospital in Harrison, about 28 miles west of Summit. Shaver told Dottie about the pain in his abdomen, saying his old case of ulcers was kicking up. He told her he was going in for a checkup. Harrison is the center of Boone County government, with the only real hospital in the vicinity. It looked a bit like Ypsilanti State Hospital — rectangular, utilitarian, and made of red brick. Doctors decided to keep him when they found cancer.

Brother Dunn drove Dottie to the hospital during visiting hours for the next 18 days. Shaver died on November 5, 1975, after a heart attack brought on by complications of his pancreatic cancer. Dottie wanted to be sure about the cause of his death and ordered an autopsy, just in case his fans started in with talk about deros. What transpired during those last 18 days is lost to history, except for one thing Dottie wanted put into the record:

> He never was against religion. Always told it was good, and [the] best place to go is church. He believed in only one God, 18 days before [his] death. Used to say there must have been more than one God because there was too many to take care of and be loved. Felt sorry for Jesus.
> I do not believe and never have [in the Shaver Mystery]. I'm so thankful Richard got over all that stuff.[15]

After a lifetime writing about the Elder Race, deros, naked goddesses, space pirates, moon falls, and rock books, Shaver's last-minute conversion to Christianity seemed somehow out of place. Stranger things have happened, but one month before his hospitalization he was talking like his old self, full of piss and vinegar, ranting against God — if indeed, there was one — the government, and the priests.

News of Shaver's illness reached the Palmer farm in Wisconsin. Dottie thought Rap should know, so she telephoned. Rap sent her $200 to help with hospital expenses. "[Another] $50 came after I called [to tell] him he died," Dottie said.[16]

Shaver was buried after a short ceremony in the Layton Cemetery in Yellville, Arkansas. Dottie had to save up her money to put a headstone on his grave, and that took a while.

26

The Inner Circle's Last Stand: 1975–1977

"I have never been accurately quoted by anyone!"—Ray Palmer

Richard Shaver may have been dead and buried, but for the survivors of Rap's inner circle, life went on. A year before Shaver's death, Hamling was convicted on pornography charges after a legal battle that went all the way to the U.S. Supreme Court. This time the indictment was for sending porn through the U.S. Postal Service. Hamling and his editor Earl Kemp were sentenced to four years in federal prison. J. Edgar Hoover had prevailed. This came after Hamling's lawyers filed several appeals while he and Kemp were out on bail.

It all began in 1969, when President Nixon's Commission on Pornography released its final report describing all manner of American sexual practices. Hamling the rebel, encouraged by his victory in Houston three years earlier, decided to publish an illustrated version of Nixon's report. Greenleaf sent a fully illustrated advertisement to its mailing list for the new book, hence the charge and eventual conviction.

The 1974 Supreme Court ruling is still referenced by law students as Hamling v. United States, 418 U.S. 87. The case was argued on April 15, 1974, and decided on June 24 of the same year: "Petitioners were convicted of mailing and conspiring to mail an obscene advertising brochure with sexually explicit photographic material relating to their illustrated version (hereafter Illustrated Report) of an official report on obscenity, in violation of 18 U.S.C. 2, 371, and 1461."[1]

Hamling's lawyers managed to drag out the inevitable for two years, until he and Kemp were finally shackled and marched off to Terminal Island Penitentiary in Long Beach, California. The judge decreed that Hamling could never publish and sell porn again. Not that Hamling paid much attention to that.

The two spent only three months behind prison walls. Kemp was put in charge of the prison newspaper, the *Terminal Island News*. Terminal Island, as Kemp put it, was "only a short nightmare trip from Hollywood," and had its advantages. It was frequently used by movie studios for prison scenes in TV shows and films. As editor of the *Terminal Island News*, Kemp hobnobbed with TV stars Tony Franciosa and Lynda Carter. (Carter was starring in a *Wonder Woman* episode, much to Kemp's delight.)

Hamling was nowhere near Kemp's section of the prison. He was far removed from the hoi polloi. "From the day I went into the penitentiary, my counselor put me on their staff, and [I was] like a staff sergeant," said Hamling. "I spent the 120 days in their offices doing work with them. Can you believe that? I was not a prisoner in the ordinary sense. I was only there for freedom of speech. What the hell."[2]

Kemp had a different view from where he sat on his dormitory upper bunk. "Bill Hamling and I were separated from the time we first arrived in Terminal Island. It turned out there just happened to be a special pampered millionaire section in the prison and wouldn't you know it, they had room for Bill there. I drew the buttfucking and cocksucking contingent.... William Hamling was given a cushy office job clerking for some minor official ... and passes giving him access to many things and areas.... He could eat in the mess hall at any time he wanted to, for instance, but I had to eat only during rigid hours."[3]

Hamling would sometimes wait for Kemp's dinner hour so they could eat together. Then they would take a walk in the exercise yard. There, they solved the problems of the world, Kemp said. But he and Hamling were drifting apart even before the roof caved in at Greenleaf. After their release from Terminal Island three months later, they drifted to different parts of the world, physically and mentally.

Rap kept track of their predicament. He probably got down on his knees and thanked the Lord he had cut his ties with Hamling's business deals back in 1963, when the lid blew off Freedom Publishing. Nevertheless, it angered him that sexual free speech was being trampled on by the likes of J. Edgar Hoover, and worse, that his old pal Bill Hamling was going to prison for something as natural as a book about sex.

Upon their release in 1976, Hamling and Kemp sank into a deep funk. It lasted nearly ten years. Disillusioned and angered by the actions of Hoover and the U.S. government, they became embittered men. Kemp moved to Mexico as an expatriate. Hamling retreated to his Arthur Elrod–designed, mid-century modern Palm Springs home and kept a low profile. He continued to publish porn on the QT, opening a bookstore in Palm Springs. Greenleaf Publishing was the first national erotic publishing outfit to recognize the demand for gay porn, and soon other publishers followed his lead.

When asked if he would ever write his memoir, Hamling replied, "I'm not interested, to hell with the whole damn thing. I said that many years ago, in 1976 after the government incident. I was just plain pissed off at them, and I still am. Although I hope the instigators of all that crap are now dead. I think they probably are, too! I've outlived the sons of bitches!"[4]

Rap, in the meantime, was fending off harassment from other government agencies. His denunciation of government secrecy and the trampling of U.S. citizens' Constitutional rights grew more strident.

His bowling days had dwindled down to occasional visits. After his fall, his partial paralysis forced him to forgo the normal bowler's approach. Now he walked up to the line, stood there, and rolled the ball. His scores suffered. By now, the kids had grown and graduated and were off on their own. His daughters married; Linda Jane had twin daughters. Her sister Jennifer moved to Florida and started a family. That left Rap, Marjorie and son Raymond to care for the 124 acres and keep Palmer Publications going.

Rap claimed his troubles with government agencies began as far back as 1941. He said that, while on a driving trip to Canada, he was mistakenly arrested and detained for a week as a spy. That incident put his name on The List. No one, not even Hamling or Rap's family, recalls the incident.

Then came the Shaver Mystery, the Maury Island–Tacoma affair, flying saucers and, certainly not least, the Freedom Publishing scandal. Agents occasionally turned up unannounced in Amherst. In 1962 he printed the likeness of a $100 bill on the cover of *Search*. Rap had researched the legal aspect of it, and found that he was within his rights to do so. It brought swift retribution when a Secret Service agent dropped in on his Amherst printing

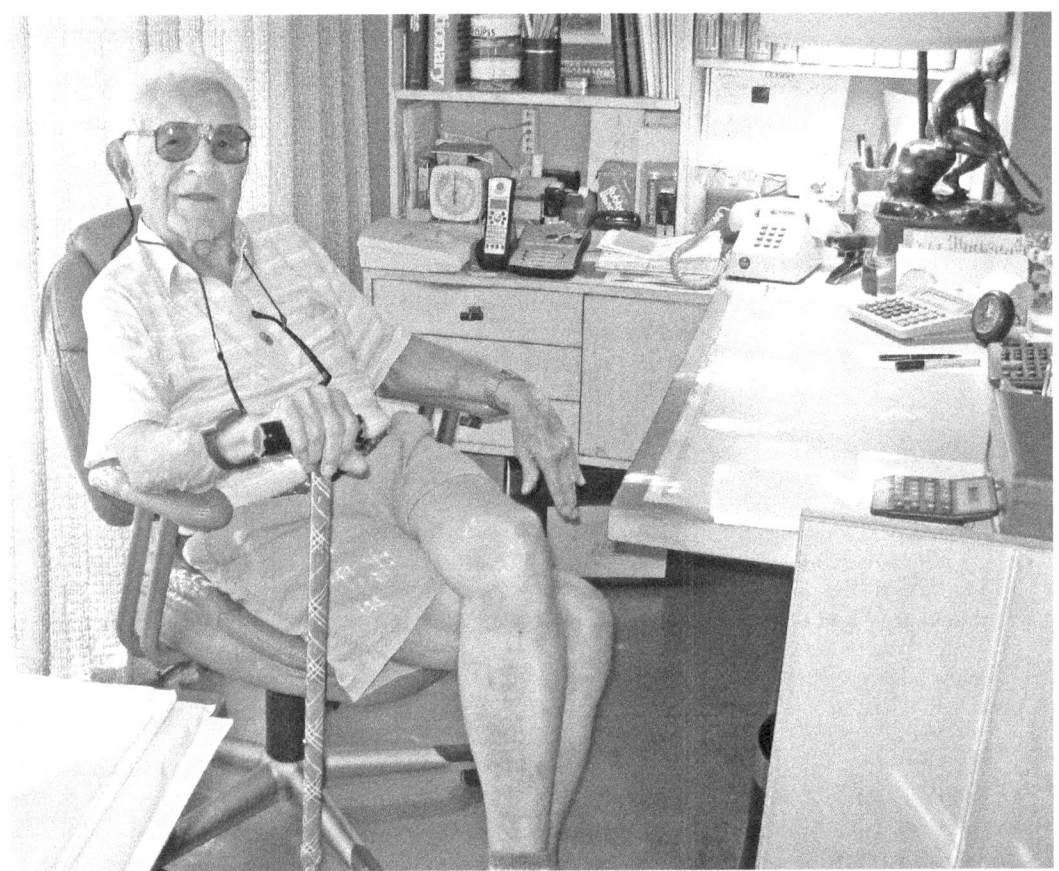

William Lawrence Hamling, 88, at his desk. Palm Springs, California, October 20, 2009. Hamling sold his first SF yarn to Ray Palmer in 1939. Rap will always be his mentor. Said Hamling, "Rap was at heart a true science fiction fan, as I always have been!"

plant making threats of $5,000 fines and 15 years' imprisonment. Nineteen sixty-two was the same year an SS agent, with help from local police, raided Rap's Illinois office. Rap was livid.

"Everything done by these SS men was contrary to justice and to Constitutional rights," he said in *Search*. Rap claimed the unwanted attention came from his outspoken attitude about flying saucers. The intrusions were so commonplace they became the butt of Palmer family humor, according to Rap's son, Raymond Bradley.

He said there was an inside joke at the shop about G-men. To find out if it was, indeed a government agent, all you had to do was look at his shoes. Whenever someone showed up at the front counter asking questions, the staff would lean over and check shoes. According to Ray Palmer the younger, they came many times: to check Rap's rocket launching base and radar (he had none) and to audit his taxes. Once they showed up as postal inspectors and wasted three days going over the books and checking every name on Rap's mailing list, then returned about 38 cents they said Rap had overpaid them.

The late sixties saw Rap publishing *Flying Saucers*, *Forum*, *Search*, and *Space World*, a serious trade journal dedicated to space flight. His print shop had just produced another serious book, *Space Law* by William C. Hyman, but Rap was a New Age publisher at heart.

In the early 1970s, he began merging his magazines to cut down on mailing costs. He combined *Search* with *Flying Saucers*, and *Forum* with *Ray Palmer's Newsletter*. It was all about saving money, he said. "*Newsletter* ... cost nearly 7¢ per copy to mail, [but] *Forum* ... cost only 2¢ to mail because of its second class privilege as a magazine...."

Ray Palmer's Newsletter began to look more like a catalog for his mail order bookstore than the feisty, ad-free *Forum*. Rap's essays on the tribulations of small-time publishing grew more frequent. He wrote an entire article about the skyrocketing cost of paper. Paper mills, he said, had discontinued his favorite lightweight paper, replacing it with heavier stock. That meant increased mailing costs. All this was affecting his business, pushing him out. Linda Jane Palmer worked in the family business. She got to know her dad better during that time, and learned how Palmer Publishing made ends meet:

> We published and printed my dad's magazines and also ... printed three state Assembly of God magazines and an AAUW magazine. We also published and printed various books, some by local authors, and some by readers of my dad's magazines. My mom and dad started a small local newspaper, the *Tomorrow River Times*, in 1975, in commemoration of the upcoming bicentennial year of America....
>
> My mother formed a cooperative group of volunteers to bring in the news and we then printed and distributed the newspaper. I typeset and helped edit the paper and also sold ads for it. The paper continued a few years after my dad died but the new owner sold it a few years after I left Palmer Publications. After my dad died I continued working for the company, typesetting, doing the bookkeeping, and selling ads.[5]

Rap said that he and Marjorie had "mortgaged themselves to the hilt" to keep things going, but he had said this before, in 1962 when he purchased equipment to start his own print shop, and probably at other times too. He vowed to keep fighting attempts to shut him down. His conspiracy fans warned him to watch out. They said he might be the next victim of an inopportune accident.

Rap and Marjorie began planning a trip to Florida for the forthcoming birth of a new grandchild in August 1977. In late July, they filled the family wagon with gas and started driving. All seemed well, until Rap's energy began to flag. Frances Hamling described what happened next:

> "I knew they were going to Tallahassee because their youngest daughter Jennifer was having her third child and they wanted to be there for that. They drove. Marjorie told me that while they were driving he said that he felt so tired, and it wasn't like him to say anything like that. He didn't feel well. When they got there, because he'd been driving so long, it was hard for him to stand and walk. It was time for Jennifer to go into labor, but she said he better go to the doctor. But the doctor, because of his blood pressure, put him in the hospital. Marjorie stayed with him. They tried to stabilize him, but found that the carotid artery was blocked.
>
> Anyway, that's why he died.... His heart was on the wrong side, and they didn't know how to test him. Most of his lungs were gone, but he didn't smoke. He was just scrambled up inside. They didn't know just where to begin.[6]

Linda Jane learned of her father's condition the day he went into the hospital; she and her brother Raymond took the next plane to Tallahassee, where doctors briefed them. She said:

> He had a stroke at my sister's house and was put in the hospital. My brother and I flew down and were able to communicate a little with him but then he had another stroke and couldn't communicate at all. I still think he could hear us until the end. When I had to fly back home to be with my then 12-year-old twin daughters, I talked to Dad and told him I had to fly home for the

girls, and that he needed to fight. He actually squeezed my hand so I know he was saying goodbye. When he died a few days later, his body was flown back to Amherst where the funeral was held. He and my mother and Dad's father, Roy Palmer, are all buried at Greenwood Cemetery in Amherst, Wisconsin.

As with Shaver's funeral, only locals and family came to mourn. Ray Palmer, crazy science fiction fan number one, the man who knocked science fiction on its ear for so many years at *Amazing Stories*, had no Big Name Fans, editors, or members of the inner circle to send him off. Linda Jane found it odd: "I am surprised that Bill and Frances didn't attend my dad's funeral. I'm pretty sure that none of the old-timers attended either. It was a small funeral held in the funeral home in Amherst and was well attended by many local people. I'm sure there was a big turnout because of all the local activities he was involved in ... the school board, Lions Club, Fair Board, and he also provided jobs for several people. There wasn't really a service, just a gathering of family and friends."[7]

Eulogies began to trickle into the SF fanzines. *FATE* magazine ran a full-page obit with Rap's familiar portrait, taken during the 1950s; it was Curt Fuller's farewell to his former partner. Even Howard Browne expressed regret over Rap's passing, though brickbats would follow, now that the shadow of his old boss was gone.

"My mother and brother ran the company from my dad's death until it was sold," said Linda Jane. "Unfortunately a few years after I quit and moved away, the new owner failed at the business and Palmer Publications no longer existed. The schoolhouse that housed Palmer Publications burned down a few years ago after it was converted to a house. Currently a newly built house stands on the property."[8]

End of an Archetype

"There are some professions that get into the blood and bones of a man, so that he does all his thinking and dreaming in its terms. Fantasy writing seems to be even more applicable to this condition."— Chester S. Geier

Chester Geier died in 1990, less than ten years after his retirement at *FATE* magazine. Howard Browne died in 1999, still blind as a bat, puffing more than a pack a day, and on his second marriage. Frances and Bill Hamling are still here, though they are rarely in touch with one another after their 1967 divorce.

In August 2011 Hamling celebrated his 90th birthday, then decided it was time to give up Palm Springs and live closer to his daughter in, as he put it, "his waning years." It was hard to imagine the feisty, in-your-face Hamling living under someone's watchful eye. He was preparing, he said, for his next gafiation.

Now an expatriate in Mexico, Earl Kemp is writing his memoir and still makes the rounds at vintage book fairs and fan gatherings.

Chester Geier wrote down his memories long ago, though they are only now coming to light. He attempted to answer tough questions, like what made Rap tick, who was behind the Shaver Mystery, and who *were* those people in Chicago?

Geier was the only member of the Ziff-Davis inner circle to give serious thought to any of those questions. As a student of Carl Jung and ancient mythology, he thus analyzed Rap and Shaver's Mystery in his memoir *Re: Richard S. Shaver*, ending with a flourish, *à la* Chester S. Geier for *Shavertron*:

The fact seems to be that human beings love mystery in general, including mystery stories, and they love a mystery that seems to have roots in the real world, in real people and events. They seek magic ... to give charm and a sense of wonder to an otherwise drab and humdrum existence.

Perhaps the Shaver Mystery touched on something deep-buried, dark and elemental in human nature, something akin to Jung's "collective unconscious," in which archetypes and symbol figures loom gigantic like shadows thrown by fire on the walls of a vast cavern....

The Shaver Mystery feature of underground caverns is a significant and primordial one. Primordial human ancestors sheltered in caves in which lurked fearsome denizens, bears, lions, snakes. In the shadows beyond the first fires hid even worse things, the evil demons and ghostly powers conjured up by early man to explain the mysterious phenomena of nature. Demons and devils have lurked in the underworld ever since.

In Egyptian, Greek, and Oriental mythology, Osiris, Adonis, Attis, and Persephone descend into — and are rescued from — an underworld inhabited by sinister gods and beings. In Gnosticism evil and "hell" result from the descent of the godhead into matter. In Christianity the devil and his demon cohorts await the sinner in vaguely underground torture chambers, while "heaven" is an etherealized place above our world, an echo of Gnosticism which itself was an echo of Persian thought in the few centuries before Christianity.

The times change, and with them, mythological figures, names, scenes, and trappings change — but the essential human nature that responds to them with chills or with delight remains the same. The child, with his dreams, hopes, fears, and fantasies, lives on in the adult. Something like the Shaver Mystery can seem significant and hauntingly evocative because the child responds to it, recognizes the gods, heroes, and demons and feels their characters, drives and deeds in his own drives, hungers, and instincts.

So what the Shaver Mystery may boil down to is that Dick Shaver, from the foundation of his own childhood dreams, awoke the eternal child in the psyches of his fans. In providing an escape from adult worries and woes, a return to a world of wonder, he may have accomplished not a little.[9]

Chapter Notes

Introduction

1. Dorothy Shaver, Interview by author, Telephone, Summit, AK, 1981.
2. Ray Palmer, "Editorial," *Forum,* January 1968. 6.
3. Bea Mahaffey, Interview by Lloyd Biggle, Audio recording, Mahaffey's Cincinnati, OH, home, April 11, 1980, archived at The Science Fiction Oral History Association, www.sfoha.org.
4. Ray Palmer, "Editorial," *Forum,* April 15, 1966, 5.
5. Ray Palmer, letter to Long John Nebel, February 4, 1957. Reprinted in *Gray Barker's Newsletter,* Number 11, July 1980.
6. William L. Hamling, Interview by author, audio recording, Palm Springs, CA, October 20, 2009.
7. Bea Mahaffey, Interview, April 11, 1980.
8. Martin Gardner, *The New Age, Notes of a Fringe Watcher* (New York: Prometheus, 1988), 219.
9. Ibid.
10. Howard Browne, "A Profit Without Honor." *Amazing Stories,* January 1984. 74.

Chapter 1

1. Ray Palmer and Richard Shaver, *The Secret World* (Amherst: Amherst Press, 1975), 13.
2. Ibid., 16.
3. Ibid., 15.
4. Ibid.
5. Ibid., 14.
6. Though Forrest J Ackerman is also known by the nickname "Forry," he signed himself "Forrie" in letters to Palmer. Thus, he is Forrie in this book.
7. Palmer and Shaver, *The Secret World,* 15.
8. Ibid., 16.
9. Raymond Bradley Palmer, Email to author, September 17, 2008.
10. Her age in November 2008.
11. Frances Hamling, Interview by author, Telephone, November 2008.
12. Harry Warner, Jr., *All Our Yesterdays* (Chicago: Advent, 1970). 76.
13. Ibid.
14. Palmer and Shaver, *The Secret World,* 29.
15. Raymond Bradley Palmer, Email to author, September 17, 2008.
16. Palmer and Shaver, *The Secret World,* 29.
17. Raymond Bradley Palmer, Email to author, September 17, 2008.
18. Palmer and Shaver, *The Secret World,* 29.
19. WhereInCity.com, Astrology, "Leo Health," www.WhereInCity.com/astrology/leo-health.php.
20. Ray Palmer, "Editorial," *Forum,* April 1, 1966, 4.
21. Ibid.
22. Ibid.
23. Palmer and Shaver, *The Secret World,* 30.
24. Ibid, 28.
25. Ray Palmer, "Editorial," *Forum,* January 1, 1966, 6.
26. Howard Browne, "A Prophet Without Honor," 74.
27. Robert Bloch, "Fantastic Adventures with Amazing," *Amazing Stories,* January 1984, 94–95.

Chapter 2

1. Warner, *All Our Yesterdays*, 75.
2. Palmer and Shaver, *The Secret World,* 26.
3. Gernsback is considered the father of popular science fiction. He founded *Amazing Stories,* the first all SF pulp magazine, in 1926.
4. Hugo Gernsback, "Prize-Winning Letters of the Second Contest," *Science Wonder Quarterly,* June 1930, 422.
5. Palmer and Shaver, *The Secret World,* 26.
6. Ibid., 27.
7. Ibid.
8. Ibid., 28.
9. Ibid.
10. Ibid.
11. Ibid.
12. Ibid., 27.

Chapter 3

1. Judith Lewis Herman, *Trauma and Recovery* (New York: Basic Books, 1992), 58.

2. Palmer and Shaver, *The Secret World*, 27.
3. Herman, *Trauma and Recovery*, 60.
4. Ray Palmer, "Ideations about Editor Palmer," *Forum*, October 1, 1966. 13.
5. Ray Palmer, "Editorial," *Forum*, January 1, 1966, 6.
6. Palmer and Shaver, *The Secret World*, 19–20.
7. Ray Palmer, "Editorial," *Search*, August 1961, 7.
8. Ray Palmer, "Editorial," *Universe Science Fiction*, January 1955, 7.
9. Palmer and Shaver, *The Secret World*, 11.
10. Sam Moskowitz, *The Immortal Storm: A History of Science Fiction* (Westport, CT: Hyperion, 1974), 8.
11. Ibid.
12. Ibid.
13. Ibid.
14. Ibid., 9.
15. Robert Bloch, *Once Around the Bloch* (New York: Tor books, 1993), 76.
16. Ibid.
17. Sam Moskowitz, *Explorers of the Infinite* (Westport, CT: Hyperion, 1974), 298.
18. Ray Palmer, "Spilling the Atoms," *Fantasy Magazine*, September 1936, 28.
19. Ibid., January 1936, 29.
20. Ibid., 35.
21. Ibid., 30.

Chapter 4

1. Ibid., May 1934, 25.
2. Linda Jane Palmer, Email to author, February 23, 2010.
3. Palmer, Ray. Letter to Forrest J Ackerman, June 26, 1936, Linda Jane Palmer Archives.
4. Ray Palmer, Letter to Forrest J Ackerman, September 14, 1935, Linda Jane Palmer Archives.
5. Ibid. March 28, 1935.
6. Moskowitz, *Explorers of the Infinite*, 308.
7. Julius Schwartz, "The Editor Broadcasts," *Fantasy Magazine*, January 1936, 29.
8. Warner, *All Our Yesterdays*, 77.
9. Ray Palmer, Letter to Forrest J Ackerman, July 24, 1935, Linda Jane Palmer Archives.
10. Moskowitz, *The Immortal Storm*, 74.
11. Ibid.
12. Ibid., 94.
13. Ray Palmer, Letter to Forrest J Ackerman, March 22, 1937, Linda Jane Palmer Archives.
14. Palmer and Shaver, *The Secret World*, 26.
15. Ibid.
16. Bloch, *Once Around the Bloch*, 100.
17. Warner, *All Our Yesterdays*, 76.
18. Palmer and Shaver, *The Secret World*, 27.
19. Ibid.
20. Ibid.

21. Bloch, *Once Around the Bloch*, 100–101.
22. Ibid., 101.
23. Ray Palmer, "The Observatory," *Amazing Stories*, August 1938, 4.
24. Warner, *All Our Yesterdays*, 76.
25. Ibid.
26. Moskowitz, *The Immortal Storm*, 194.
27. Palmer and Shaver, *The Secret World*, 27.
28. Ray Palmer, "The Observatory," *Amazing Stories*, January 1940, 97.
29. William L. Hamling, Interview, October 20, 2009.
30. William L. Hamling, Letter to author, November 26, 2010, Richard Toronto Archives.

Chapter 5

1. William L. Hamling, Interview, October 20, 2009.
2. "Chicon I Program," Fancyclopedia 3, last modified January 8, 2012, http://fancyclopedia.wikidot.com/chicon-i-program.
3. Frank M. Robinson, "Raymond, I Hardly Knew Ye," *Locus*, September 1977, 14.
4. William L. Hamling, Interview, October 20, 2009.
5. Warner, *All Our Yesterdays*, 77.
6. Harry Warner, Jr., "Guest Editorial," *Flying Saucers From Other Worlds*, October 1957, 8.
7. Ibid., 9.
8. Bea Mahaffey, Interview, April 11, 1980.
9. Ray Palmer, "The Observatory," *Amazing Stories*, March 1942, 6.
10. Ibid., September 1942, 7.
11. Ibid., May 1942, 7.
12. Ibid., 8.
13. Ibid., January 1943, 96.

Chapter 6

1. Howard Browne, "Meet the Authors," *Amazing Stories*, December 1942, 239.
2. Moskowitz, *The Immortal Storm*, 239.
3. Chester Geier, Letter to Jim Pobst, 1982, Jim Pobst Archives.
4. Ibid.
5. William L. Hamling, Interview, October 20, 2009.
6. Ibid.
7. Ibid.
8. Berkeley Livingston was one of Ray Palmer's Ziff-Davis writers.
9. William L. Hamling, Interview, October 20, 2009.
10. Chester. Geier, Letter to Jim Pobst, 1982.
11. Alexander Blade, Frank Patton, G. H. Irwin, Henry Gade, Lee Francis, Morris J. Steele, Richard Casey.

12. Leroy Yerxa, "Meet the Authors," *Amazing Stories*, August 1942, 232.
13. Some of the more famous Hollywood adoptive parents included Bob Hope, Al Jolson, George Burns and Gracie Allen, and Donna Reed.
14. Frances Hamling, Interview by author, Telephone, October 2008.
15. Linda Jane Palmer, Email to author, August 13, 2010.
16. The Shangri-La Restaurant was located at 222 North State Street in Chicago.
17. Frances Hamling, Interview, October 2008.
18. Linda Jane Palmer, Email to author, August 13, 2010.
19. Frances Hamling, Interview, October 2008.
20. Howard Browne, Letter to Chester Geier, 1988, Jim Pobst Archives.
21. Browne, "Profit without Honor," 79.

Chapter 7

1. "Shavertown, Pennsylvania," Wikipedia.com, last modified on August 14, 2010, http://en.wikipedia.org/wiki/Shavertown,_Pennsylvania.
2. H.C. Bradsby, "Societies and Associations," *History of Luzerne County Pennsylvania*, ed. H.C. Bradsby, 454 (Philadelphia: S.B. Nelson & Co., 1893).
3. Katherine Pouba, and Ashley Tianen, "Lunacy in the 19th Century: Women's Admission to Asylums in United States of America," *Oshkosh Scholar* 1 (April 2006): 99.
4. W.J. Dougherty, "Report of First Vice President," *The Blacksmiths Journal* 9 (May 24, 1908): 18.
5. Richard Shaver, "The Dream Makers," *Fantastic*, July 1958, 16.
6. Richard Shaver, Letter to W.G. Bliss, No date, Richard Toronto Archives.
7. Jim Pobst, *Richard Shaver: The Early Years* (Stone Mountain, GA: Arcturus Book Service, 1989), 1.

Chapter 8

1. Shaver, "The Dream Makers," 14–15.
2. Ibid., 17.
3. Ibid., 16.
4. Ibid., 16–17.
5. Ibid., 17.
6. Ibid., 18.
7. Ibid., 18–19.
8. Shaver's listing in the 1925 Bloomsburg High School Yearbook.
9. E. Keller, Letter to Richard Horton, 1991, Richard Toronto Archives.
10. Shaver, "*The Dream Makers,*" 23.
11. Ibid.
12. Ibid.
13. Ibid., 36.
14. Ibid., 37.
15. Ibid., 45.
16. Ibid.
17. Ibid., 45.
18. Ibid., 47.
19. Ibid., 48.
20. Ibid.

Chapter 9

1. Jim Pobst, *Richard Shaver: The Early Years*, 5.
2. Shaver, "*The Dream Makers,*" 48.
3. Ibid.
4. Evelyn Shaver Gurvitch Bryant, Interview by author, Telephone, 2009.
5. Ibid.
6. Martha Grevatt, "The Ford Hunger March of 1932," *Workers World*, March 25, 2009, www.workers.org.
7. "4 Die in Riot at Ford Plant," *Detroit Free Press*, March 8, 1932.
8. Richard Shaver, Letter to author, July 28, 1973, Richard Toronto Archives.
9. Pobst, *Richard Shaver: The Early Years*, 9.
10. Ibid., 10.
11. Ibid., 8.

Chapter 10

1. *The Detroit News*, February 26, 1934.
2. Richard Shaver, "A Witch in the Night," *The Hidden World*, Spring 1961, 17.
3. Ibid.
4. Richard Shaver, Letter to Ray Palmer, *The Hidden World*, Fall 1964, 2520.
5. Ibid., Spring 1964, 2249.
6. Shaver, "A Witch in the Night," 18.
7. Ibid.
8. Richard Shaver, "Flight Into Futility," *The Hidden World*, Spring 1961, 30–31.
9. Dr. H.E. Harris, Wayne County, Michigan, Probate Court document, July 30, 1934.
10. Grace Shaver, Letter to Sophie Shaver, June 12, 1936, Evelyn Bryant Archives.
11. Dr. Jack Agis, Wayne County, Michigan, Probate Court document, August 5, 1934.
12. Wayne County Probate Court document, August 30, 1934.
13. "Ypsilanti State Hospital," AsylumProjects.org, last modified August 15, 2011, asylumprojects.org/index.php?title=Ypsilanti_State_Hospital.
14. Ibid.
15. Richard Shaver, Letter to Ray Palmer, *The Hidden World*, Summer 1964, 2413.
16. Evelyn Bryant, Interview, Telephone, 2009.
17. Grace Shaver, Letter to Sophie Shaver, June 12, 1936.

18. Ibid.
19. Ibid.

Chapter 11

1. Richard Shaver, Letter to unknown correspondent, February 1967, Richard Toronto Archives.
2. Richard Shaver, Letter to W. G. Bliss, November 4, 1974, Richard Toronto Archives.
3. Lucius Farish, Richard Shaver interview, Audio recording, Summit, AK, 1969.
4. Richard Shaver, Letter to Ray Palmer, *The Hidden World*, Fall 1964, 2250.
5. Richard Shaver, Letter to unknown correspondent, February 20, 1967, Richard Toronto Archives.
6. Pobst, *Richard Shaver: The Early Years*, 17.
7. Ibid.
8. Evelyn Bryant, Interview, 2009.
9. Richard Shaver, Letter to Ray Palmer, *The Hidden World*, Fall 1964, 2645.
10. Ibid., 2251.
11. Ibid., 2455–56.
12. Richard Shaver, "A Witch in the Night," 32.
13. Ibid., 34.
14. Richard Shaver, Letter to Ray Palmer, *The Hidden World*, Fall 1964, 2645.

Chapter 12

1. Jonathan Metzl, *The Protest Psychosis* (Boston: Beacon Press, 2009), 53–54.
2. Ibid., 12.
3. Evelyn Bryant, Interview, 2009.
4. Richard Shaver, Letter to Ray Palmer, *The Hidden World*, Fall 1964, 2533.
5. Richard Shaver, "A Taste of Heaven," *The Hidden World*, Spring 1961, 45.
6. Richard Shaver, Letter to Ray Palmer, *The Hidden World*, Winter 1964, 2843.
7. Ibid.
8. Shaver, "A Witch in the Night," 37.
9. Richard Shaver, "The Mind Rovers," *Amazing Stories*, January 1947, 121.
10. Ibid., 115.
11. Jonathan Metzl, *The Protest Psychosis*, 88.
12. Mike Jay, *The Air Loom Gang* (New York: Four Walls Eight Windows, 2003), 18.
13. Ibid., 173.
14. Ibid., 174.
15. Ibid.
16. Ibid., 195.
17. Richard Shaver, "*The Dream Makers*," 11.
18. Richard Shaver, Letter to Ray Palmer, *The Hidden World*, Summer 1964, 2362.
19. Richard Shaver, "I Remember Lemuria!" *Amazing Stories*, March 1945, 37.
20. Richard Shaver, Letter to Ray Palmer, *The Hidden World*, Summer 1964, 2364.
21. Ibid., 2365.
22. Raymond Pearl, *Biology of Death* (Philadelphia: J.B. Lippincott, 1922), 67.
23. Dorothy Shaver, Interview by author, Telephone, 1979, Richard Toronto Archives.
24. Ibid.
25. Ibid., January 17, 1981.
26. Ibid., May 9, 1981.
27. Richard Shaver, Letter to Ray Palmer, *The Hidden World*, Summer 1964, 2325.
28. Evelyn Bryant, Interview, 2009.

Chapter 13

1. Browne, "A Prophet Without Honor," 71.
2. Ibid.
3. Ibid., 73.
4. Ibid., 72.
5. Chester Geier, Letter to Jim Pobst, 1982.
6. William L. Hamling, Interview, October 20, 2009.
7. Browne, "A Prophet Without Honor," 80.
8. Ibid.
9. Ibid.
10. William L. Hamling, Interview, October 20, 2009.
11. Ibid.
12. Ibid.
13. Ray Palmer, *Flying Saucers Magazine*, November 1963, 8.
14. Ibid.
15. Ibid., 9.
16. Ray Palmer, Letter to Richard Shaver, *The Hidden World*, Spring 1964, 2245.
17. Ibid., 2257.

Chapter 14

1. Ray Palmer, "The Observatory." *Amazing Stories*, March 1945. 6.
2. Ibid.
3. Ibid., 10.
4. Richard Shaver, Letter to Ray Palmer, *The Hidden World*, Summer 1964. 2383–2384.
5. Ibid., 2483.
6. Ibid., Fall 1964. 2605.
7. Ibid., 2607.
8. Ray Palmer, Letter to Richard Shaver, *The Hidden World*, Winter 1964, 2767.
9. Richard Shaver, Letter to Ray Palmer, *The Hidden World*, Summer 1964, 2356.
10. Ray Palmer, Letter to Richard Shaver, *The Hidden World*, Winter 1964, 2768.
11. Ibid.
12. Richard Shaver, Letter to Ray Palmer, *The Hidden World*, Fall 1964, 2558.
13. Ibid., 2565.

14. Ibid., Summer 1964, 2355.
15. Ibid.
16. Ibid., Fall 1964, 2567.
17. Ibid., 2586.
18. Ibid., 2608.
19. Ray Palmer, Letter to Richard Shaver, *The Hidden World*, Winter 1964, 2792.
20. Ray Palmer, "Editorial." *Search,* December 1962, 7.
21. Ibid., 4–5.
22. Ray Palmer, Letter to Richard Shaver, *The Hidden World*, Spring 1964, 2294.
23. William L. Hamling, Interview, October 20, 2009.

Chapter 15

1. Richard Shaver, *Amazing Stories*, March 1945, 15.
2. Ray Palmer, "The Observatory," *Amazing Stories*, June 1945, 6.
3. Richard Shaver, Letter to Ray Palmer, *The Hidden World, Fall 1964*, 2549.

Chapter 16

1. Warner, *All Our Yesterdays*, 182.
2. Ray Palmer, "The Observatory," *Amazing Stories*, September 1945, 6.
3. William L. Hamling, Interview, October 20, 2009.
4. Warner, *All Our Yesterdays*, 183.

Chapter 17

1. Ray Palmer, "The Observatory," *Amazing Stories*, December 1945, 6.
2. Ibid.
3. Warner, *All Our Yesterdays*, 184.
4. William L. Hamling, Letter to author, April 24, 2010, Richard Toronto Archives.
5. Linda Jane Palmer, Email to author, April 8, 2012.
6. Charles Metchette, "Michigan Memories," *Spacewarp* 42. September 1950, Last modified October 6, 2012, The Fanac Fan History Project, Fanac.org.
7. Norman S. Kossuth, "Discussions," *Amazing Stories*, January 1947, 176–177.
8. Ray Palmer, "Discussions," *Amazing Stories*, January 1947, 177.
9. Vaughn M. Greene, Interview by author, Telephone, 2008.
10. Steve Volto Dero, Postcard, date unknown, author unknown, Jim Pobst Archives.
11. Letter sent to Frank Brownley, April 5, 1951, Jim Pobst Archives
12. Vaughn M. Greene, Interview, 2008.
13. Norman S. Kossuth, Letter to Vaughn M. Greene, November 30, 1947, Jim Pobst Archives.
14. William S. Baring-Gould, "Little Superman, What Now?" *Harper's,* September 1946.
15. William L. Hamling, Interview, October 20, 2009.
16. Ibid.
17. Richard Shaver, Letter to Ray Palmer, *The Hidden World*, Winter 1964, 2782–2783.
18. Ray Palmer, Letter to Richard Shaver, *The Hidden World*, Winter 1964, 2795.
19. Richard Shaver, Letter to Ray Palmer, *The Hidden World*, Winter 1964, 2787.
20. Ibid., 2785.
21. Ray Palmer, Letter to Richard Shaver, *The Hidden World*, Winter 1964, 2803.

Chapter 18

1. William L. Hamling, Interview, October 20, 2009.
2. G.W. Page, Email to author, April 24, 2010.
3. Geier, *Re: Richard S. Shaver*, 8.
4. Ray Palmer, "The Observatory." *Amazing Stories*, February 1946. 3.
5. Ibid., May 1946, 3.
6. Ibid.
7. Roger P. Graham, "The Shaver Mystery," *Amazing Stories*, February 1946, 174.
8. Ibid.
9. Chester Geier, Letter to Jim Pobst, 1988, Jim Pobst Archives.
10. William L. Hamling, Interview, October 20, 2009.
11. Ray Palmer, "The Shaver Mystery," *Amazing Stories*, June 1946, 97.
12. Ibid.
13. William L. Hamling, Interview, October 20, 2009.
14. Ibid.
15. William L. Hamling, Letter to author, December 11, 2010, Richard Toronto Archives.
16. William L. Hamling, Interview, October 20, 2009.
17. Ibid.
18. Ray Palmer, "The Observatory." *Amazing Stories*, June 1946. 69.
19. Ibid.
20. Charles Fort collected newspaper clippings of strange anomalies, encompassing everything from sky falls of frogs and red rain, to kangaroo sightings in the eastern United States. He wrote three books detailing his theories about the origins of these anomalous events. His work fit perfectly with Shaver's claims of dero tampering with surface life.
21. Ray Palmer, "The Observatory," *Amazing Stories*, June 1946, 6.

22. Ibid., March 1947, 8.
23. Ibid., 6.
24. Ibid., 9.
25. Ray Palmer, (writing as Chester Geier), "Discussions," *Amazing Stories*, February 1947, 176–177.
26. Ray Palmer, "The Observatory," *Amazing Stories*, June 1947, 6.
27. Ibid.
28. Ibid., 9.
29. Ibid., 176.
30. Howard Browne, Letter to Charles Brown, Editor, *Locus*, December 1977, 12.
31. Howard Browne, Letter to Chester Geier, June 20, 1988, Jim Pobst Archives.
32. Chester Geier, Letter to Jim Pobst, 1988, Jim Pobst Archives.
33. Ibid.
34. Ray Palmer, "The Observatory," *Amazing Stories*, October 1947, 6.
35. Richard Shaver, "Discussions," *Amazing Stories*, October 1947, 178.
36. Ibid.
37. Ray Palmer, "The Observatory," *Amazing Stories*, October 1947, 7.
38. FBI Office Memorandum, "Flying Discs, Richard Shaver," SAC Chicago, September 20, 1947.
39. Richard Shaver, Letter to Ray Palmer, *The Hidden World*, Fall 1964, 2550.
40. William L. Hamling, Interview, October 20, 2009.
41. Ray Palmer, Letter to Jim Garrison, Nov. 27, 1968, The Jim Pobst Archives.
42. Ray Palmer, "Discussions," *Amazing Stories*, January 1948, 175.
43. Robert Paul Kidwell, "The Shaverian Hypothesis," *Amazing Stories*, January 1948, 150.
44. R.A. Garskof, "Discussions," *Amazing Stories*, March 1948, 177.
45. Ray Palmer. "The Observatory," *Amazing Stories*, March 1948, 9.
46. Russell Bauer, "Discussions," *Amazing Stories*, January 1948, 166.
47. Ray Palmer, "The Observatory," *Amazing Stories*, March 1948, 6.
48. Frank M. Robinson, "Raymond, I Hardly Knew Ye," *Locus*, September 1977, 15.
49. William L. Hamling, Interview, October 20, 2009.
50. Ibid.
51. Ray Palmer, "The Observatory," *Amazing Stories*, April 1948, 6.

Chapter 19

1. Ray Palmer, "Discussions," *Amazing Stories*, April 1948, 170–171.
2. Jean Cox, "Just a Minute," *Shangri-La*, March–April 1948, 9.
3. Ray Palmer, "The Observatory," *Amazing Stories*, May 1948, 6.
4. Chester Geier, "Discussions," *Amazing Stories*, May 1948, 173.
5. Ray Palmer, "Editorial," *Other Worlds Science Stories*, February 1953, 155.
6. Ray Palmer, "The Observatory," *Amazing Stories*, February 1949, 6.
7. Ray Palmer, "Discussions," *Amazing Stories*, April 1949, 141.
8. William L. Hamling, Interview, October 20, 2009.
9. Kenneth Arnold and Ray Palmer, *The Coming of the Saucers*, Amherst, WI: Privately printed, 1952, 9.
10. William L. Hamling, Interview, October 20, 2009.
11. Warner, *All Our Yesterdays*, 274.
12. William L. Hamling, Interview, October 20, 2009.

Chapter 20

1. Ray Palmer, "The Observatory," *Amazing Stories*, December 1949, 6.
2. Howard Browne, "A Profit Without Honor," 75.
3. William L. Hamling, Letter to author, September 13, 2010, Richard Toronto Archives.
4. Ibid.
5. William L. Hamling, Letter to author, February 11, 2011, Richard Toronto Archives.
6. William L. Hamling, Interview, October 20, 2009.
7. Chester Geier, Letter to Jim Pobst, February 1989, Jim Pobst Archives.
8. Ibid.
9. Hamling, William L. Interview, October 20, 2009.
10. Richard Yerxa, Interview by author, Telephone, 2008.
11. Earl Kemp, "Tales of *Imagination* and Space Travel: A Capricious Chronology," *eI*, Volume 1, Number 5, December 2002, http://www.efanzines.com/EK/eI5/index.htm.
12. Chester Geier, "Re: Richard S. Shaver," *Shavertron*, Number 29, 1992, 8.

Chapter 21

1. William L. Hamling, Interview by Christopher M. O'Brien, Telephone, March 2009, *eI*, Volume 10, Number 2, April 2011, http://www.efanzines.com/EK/eI55/eI55.pdf
2. William L. Hamling, Interview, October 20, 2009.
3. Ibid.
4. Richard Yerxa, "Some Notes in Search of an

Article," *eI*, Volume 2, Number 6, 2003, http://efanzines.com/EK/eI11/index.htm.
  5. Ibid.
  6. William L. Hamling, Interview, October 20, 2009.

Chapter 22

  1. Richard Shaver, Letter to Richard Horton, May (?) 1950, Richard Toronto Archives.
  2. Richard Shaver, Letter to Richard Horton, May 3, 1950, Richard Toronto Archives.
  3. Ray Palmer, "Editorial," *Other Worlds Science Stories*, October 1950, 4.
  4. William L. Hamling, Interview, October 20, 2009.
  5. Ray Palmer, "Editorial," *Other Worlds Science Stories*, January 1951, 5.
  6. Richard Shaver, Letter to Richard Horton, 1950, Richard Toronto Archives.
  7. Linda Jane Palmer, Email to author, October 15, 2010.
  8. Chester Geier, Letter to Jim Pobst, March 1982, Jim Pobst Archives.
  9. Linda Jane Palmer, Email to author, May 30, 2011.
  10. Ibid.
  11. Richard Yerxa, Interview by author, Telephone, 2008.
  12. Linda Jane Palmer, Email to author, October 20, 2010.
  13. Ray Palmer, "Editorial," *Mystic,* August 1955, 117.
  14. Ray Palmer, "The Liars in the A.E.C.," *Mystic,* October 1955, 20.
  15. Ray Palmer, "Editorial," *Mystic,* August 1955, 15.
  16. Ibid., 117.
  17. Chester Geier, Letter to Jim Pobst, March 26, 1982, Jim Pobst Archives.
  18. Ray Palmer, "Editorial," *Mystic,* October 1955, 4.
  19. Ibid., 78.
  20. Richard Shaver, "The Mystery of Shaver," *Shavertron,* Summer 2006, http://www.softcom.net/users/falconkam/shavindex3.html.
  21. William L. Hamling, Interview, October 20, 2009.
  22. Richard Shaver, Letter to Richard Horton, June 14, 1950, Richard Toronto Archives.
  23. Dorothy Shaver, Interview by author, Telephone, 1979.
  24. Richard Horton, Letter to author, 2007, Richard Toronto Archives.
  25. Richard Horton, Letter to author, 2004, Richard Toronto Archives.
  26. Richard Shaver, Letter to Richard Horton, April 3, 1950, Richard Toronto Archives.
  27. Richard Horton, Letter to author, 2005, Richard Toronto Archives.
  28. Linda Jane Palmer, Email to author, April 18, 2010.
  29. Ibid., August 16, 2012.
  30. Ibid.
  31. Ibid., April 18, 2010.
  32. Earl Kemp, ed., *The Compleat and Unexpurgated Who Killed Science Fiction? eI 29* (Kingman, AZ: Earl Kemp, 2006).
  33. Ibid.
  34. Ibid.
  35. Earl Kemp, "Have Typewriter; Will Whore For Food," *eI*, Volume 1, Number 2, April 2002, http://efanzines.com/EK/eI2/index.htm.
  36. Palmer, Ray. "Editorial." *Other Worlds Science Stories,* May 1955. 121.
  37. Ibid., 5, 127.
  38. Ibid., 4.
  39. Stuart J. Byrne, "Who Is S. J. Byrne AKA John Bloodstone? An Autobiography by Stu Byrne. From the booklet, 'Tarzan on Mars — Genesis and More,'" *ERBzine*, http://www.erbzine.com/mag19/1967.html.
  40. Ibid.
  41. Ibid.
  42. Ray Palmer, "Tarzan Never Dies." *Other Worlds Science Stories,* November 1955, Reprinted on ER Bzine, http://www.erbzine.com/mag3/0313.html.
  43. Ibid.
  44. Richard Shaver, Letter to Richard Horton, December 8, 1959, Richard Toronto Archives.
  45. Ibid., January 23, 1960.
  46. Ibid., March 1960.
  47. Dorothy Shaver, Interview by author, Telephone, March 25, 1982.

Chapter 23

  1. Ibid., August 17, 1983.
  2. William L. Hamling, Interview, October 20, 2009.
  3. Earl Kemp, "Blood and Sand," *eI,* Volume 1, Number 2, April 2002, http://efanzines.com/EK/eI2/index.htm.
  4. Frances Hamling, Interview by author, Telephone, November 2008.
  5. Richard Shaver, "Shaver's Pre-History Primer," *Shavertron,* 2006, http://www.softcom.net/users/falconkam/primer.html.
  6. Dorothy Shaver, Letter to Jim Pobst, 1981, Jim Pobst Archives.
  7. Earl Kemp, Email to author, December 2011.
  8. Earl Kemp, Email to author, November 30, 2012.
  9. William L. Hamling, Interview, October 20, 2009.
  10. Richard Horton, Letter to author, 2003, Richard Toronto Archives.

Chapter 24

1. Ray Palmer and Richard Shaver, *The Secret World*, 89.
2. Tal Levesque, Email to author, April 17, 2003.
3. Chester Geier, "Re: Richard S. Shaver," *Shavertron*, Number 29, 1992, 9.
4. Ray Palmer, "Editorial," *Forum*, March 1, 1966, 3.
5. Earl Kemp, Email to author, July 3, 2008.
6. Thomas Ramirez, "Into the Abyss," *eI*, Volume 4, Number 4, August 2005, http://efanzines.com/EK/eI21/.
7. Earl Kemp, Email to author, July 3, 2008.
8. Ibid.
9. Ibid.
10. Dorothy Shaver, Letter to Jim Pobst, June 17, 1981, Jim Pobst Archives.
11. Earl Kemp. "Beauty and the Beast Otra Vez," *eI*, Volume 1, Number 4, October 2002, http://pdf.textfiles.com/efanzines/EK/eI4/index.htm.
12. Lucius Farish, Richard Shaver interview, Audio recording, Summit, AK, 1969.
13. Dorothy Shaver, Letter to Jim Pobst, 1981, Jim Pobst Archives.
14. Ibid.
15. Chester Geier, Letter to Jim Pobst, March 1982, Jim Pobst Archives.

Chapter 25

1. Ray Palmer, "Editorial," *Forum,* July 1971, 4.
2. Ibid., 5.
3. Ibid., September 1971. 4.
4. Ibid., 5.
5. Ray Palmer, "Letters." *Forum,* January 1972, 24.
6. Ibid., 5–6.
7. Ibid.
8. W.G. Bliss, Letter to author, 2001, Richard Toronto Archives.
9. Ray Palmer, "Letters," *Forum,* March 1973, 28–29.
10. Ibid.
11. Ray Palmer, "Editorial," *Forum*, October 15, 1966, 6–7.
12. Ray Palmer, "Letters," *Forum,* June 1975, 14.
13. Richard Shaver, Letter to a correspondent, November 11, 1974, Richard Toronto Archives.
14. Ibid., September 1975.
15. Dorothy Shaver, Letters to author, January 21 and July 11, 1980, Richard Toronto Archives.
16. Dorothy Shaver, Letter to Jim Pobst, March 16, 1981, Jim Pobst Archives.

Chapter 26

1. *Hamling V. United States, 418 U.S. 87,* 1.
2. William L. Hamling, Interview, October 20, 2009.
3. Earl Kemp, "In a World I Never Made," *eI,* Volume 2, Number 4, August 2003, http://www.efanzines.com/EK/eI9/index.htm.
4. William L. Hamling, Interview, October 20, 2009.
5. Linda Jane Palmer, Email to author, March 2, 2010.
6. Frances Hamling, Interview by author, Telephone, November 2008.
7. Linda Jane Palmer, Email to author, March 2, 2010.
8. Ibid.
9. Chester Geier, "Re: Richard S. Shaver," *Shavertron,* Number 29, 1992, 11–12.

Bibliography

Books

Arnold, Kenneth, and Ray Palmer. *The Coming of the Saucers*. Amherst, WI: Privately printed, 1952.

Bloch, Robert. *Once Around the Bloch*. New York: Tor books, 1993.

Bradsby, H.C. "Societies and Associations." In *History of Luzerne County Pennsylvania*. Ed. H.C. Bradsby. Philadelphia: S.B. Nelson & Co., 1893.

Gardner, Martin. *The New Age, Notes of a Fringe Watcher*. New York: Prometheus, 1988.

Herman, Judith Lewis. *Trauma and Recovery*. New York: Basic Books, 1992.

Jay, Mike. *The Air Loom Gang*. New York: Four Walls Eight Windows, 2003.

Metzl, Jonathan. *The Protest Psychosis*. Boston: Beacon Press, 2009.

Moskowitz, Sam. *Explorers of the Infinite*. Westport, CT: Hyperion, 1974.

_____. *The Immortal Storm: A History of Science Fiction*. Westport, CT: Hyperion, 1974.

Palmer, Ray, and Richard Shaver. *The Secret World*. Amherst: Amherst Press, 1975.

Pearl, Raymond. *Biology of Death*. Philadelphia: J.B. Lippincott, 1922.

Pobst, Jim. *Richard Shaver: The Early Years*. Stone Mountain, GA: Arcturus Book Service, 1989.

Warner, Harry, Jr. *All Our Yesterdays*. Chicago: Advent, 1970.

Magazines

Baring-Gould, William S. "Little Superman, What Now?" *Harper's*, September 1946.

Bauer, Russell. "Discussions." *Amazing Stories*, January 1948.

Bloch, Robert. "Fantastic Adventures with Amazing." *Amazing Stories*, January 1984.

Browne, Howard. "Meet the Authors." *Amazing Stories*, December 1942.

_____. "A Profit Without Honor." *Amazing Stories*, January 1984.

Cox, Jean. "Just a Minute." *Shangri-La*, March–April 1948.

Garskof, R.A. "Discussions." *Amazing Stories*, March 1948.

Geier, Chester. "Discussions." *Amazing Stories*, May 1948.

Gernsback, Hugo. "Prize-Winning Letters of the Second Contest." *Science Wonder Quarterly*, June 1930.

Graham, Roger P. "The Shaver Mystery." *Amazing Stories*, February 1946.

Grevatt, Martha. "The Ford Hunger March of 1932." *Workers World*, March 25, 2009. www.workers.org.

Kidwell, Robert Paul. "The Shaverian Hypothesis." *Amazing Stories*, January 1948.

Kossuth, Norman S. "Discussions." *Amazing Stories*, January 1947.

Palmer, Ray. "Discussions." *Amazing Stories*, January 1947.

_____. (writing as Chester Geier). "Discussions." *Amazing Stories*, February 1947.

_____. "Discussions." *Amazing Stories*, January 1948.

_____. "Discussions." *Amazing Stories*, April 1948.

_____. "Discussions." *Amazing Stories*, April 1949.

_____. "Editorial." *Forum*, January 1, 1966.

_____. "Editorial." *Forum*, March 1, 1966.

_____. "Editorial." *Forum*, April 1, 1966.

_____. "Editorial." *Forum*, April 15, 1966.

_____. "Editorial." *Forum*, October 15, 1966.

_____. "Editorial." *Forum*, January 1968.

_____. "Editorial." *Forum*, July 1971.

_____. "Editorial." *Forum*, September 1971.

_____. "Editorial." *Mystic*, August 1955.

_____. "Editorial." *Mystic*, October 1955.

_____. "Editorial." *Other Worlds Science Stories*, October 1950.

_____. "Editorial." *Other Worlds Science Stories*, January 1951.

_____. "Editorial." *Other Worlds Science Stories*, February 1953.

_____. "Editorial." *Other Worlds Science Stories*, May 1955.

_____. "Editorial." *Search*, August 1961.

_____. "Editorial." *Search*, December 1962.

_____. "Editorial." *Universe Science Fiction*, January 1955.

_____. *Flying Saucers Magazine*, November 1963.

_____. "Ideations about Editor Palmer." *Forum,* October 1, 1966.
_____. "Letters." *Forum,* January 1972.
_____. "The Liars in the A.E.C." *Mystic,* October 1955.
_____. "The Observatory," *Amazing Stories,* August 1938.
_____. "The Observatory." *Amazing Stories,* January 1940.
_____. "The Observatory." *Amazing Stories,* March 1942.
_____. "The Observatory." *Amazing Stories,* May 1942.
_____. "The Observatory." *Amazing Stories,* September 1942.
_____. "The Observatory." *Amazing Stories,* January 1943.
_____. "The Observatory." *Amazing Stories,* March 1945.
_____. "The Observatory." *Amazing Stories,* June 1945.
_____. "The Observatory." *Amazing Stories,* September 1945.
_____. "The Observatory." *Amazing Stories,* December 1945.
_____. "The Observatory." *Amazing Stories,* February 1946.
_____. "The Observatory." *Amazing Stories.* May 1946.
_____. "The Observatory." *Amazing Stories,* June 1946.
_____. "The Observatory." *Amazing Stories,* March 1947.
_____. "The Observatory." *Amazing Stories,* June 1947.
_____. "The Observatory." *Amazing Stories,* October 1947.
_____. "The Observatory." *Amazing Stories,* March 1948.
_____. "The Observatory." *Amazing Stories,* April 1948.
_____. "The Observatory." *Amazing Stories,* May 1948.
_____. "The Observatory." *Amazing Stories,* February 1949.
_____. "The Observatory." *Amazing Stories,* December 1949.
_____. "The Shaver Mystery." *Amazing Stories,* June 1946. 97.
_____. "Spilling the Atoms." *Fantasy Magazine,* May 1934.
_____. "Spilling the Atoms." *Fantasy Magazine,* January 1936.
_____. "Spilling the Atoms." *Fantasy Magazine,* September 1936.
Robinson, Frank M. "Raymond, I Hardly Knew Ye." *Locus,* September 1977.
Schwartz, Julius. "The Editor Broadcasts." *Fantasy Magazine,* January 1936.
Shaver, Richard. *Amazing Stories,* March 1945.
_____. "Discussions." *Amazing Stories,* October 1947.
_____. "The Dream Makers." *Fantastic,* July 1958.
_____. "I Remember Lemuria!" *Amazing Stories,* March 1945.
_____. Letter to Ray Palmer, *The Hidden World,* Summer 1964.
_____. Letter to Ray Palmer. *The Hidden World,* Fall 1964.
_____. "The Mind Rovers." *Amazing Stories,* January 1947.
_____. "A Taste of Heaven." *The Hidden World,* Spring 1961.
_____. "A Witch in the Night." *The Hidden World,* Spring 1961.
Warner, Harry Jr. "Guest Editorial." *Flying Saucers From Other Worlds,* October 1957.
Yerxa, Leroy. "Meet the Authors." *Amazing Stories,* August 1942.

Journals

Dougherty, W.J. "Report of First Vice President." *The Blacksmiths Journal* 9 (May 24, 1908): 18.

Interviews

Bryant, Evelyn Shaver Gurvitch. Interview by author. Telephone. 2009.
Farish, Lucius. Richard Shaver interview. Audio recording. Summit, AK, 1969.
Greene, Vaughn M. Interview by author. Telephone. 2008.
Hamling, Frances. Interview by author. Telephone. October 2008.
_____. Interview by author. Telephone. November 2008.
Hamling, William L. Interview by Christopher M. O'Brien. Telephone. March 2009. *eI,* Volume 10, Number 2, April 2011. http://www.efanzines.com/EK/eI55/eI55.pdf.
_____. Interview by author. Audio recording. Palm Springs, CA, October 20, 2009.
Mahaffey, Bea. Interview by Lloyd Biggle. Audio recording. Mahaffey's, Cincinnati, OH, home, April 11, 1980. Archived at The Science Fiction Oral History Association, www.sfoha.org.
Shaver, Dorothy. Interview by author. Telephone. 1979. Richard Toronto Archives.
_____. Interview by author. Telephone. Summit, AK, 1981.
_____. Interview by author. Telephone. Summit, AK, January 17, 1981.
_____. Interview by author. Telephone. Summit, AK, May 9, 1981.
_____. Interview by author. Telephone. March 25, 1982.

_____. Interview by author. Telephone. August 17, 1983.
Yerxa, Richard. Interview by author. Telephone. 2008.

Letters

Ackerman, Forrest J. Letter to Ray Palmer. May 17, 1935. Linda Jane Palmer Archives.
_____. Letter to Ray Palmer. October 11, 1935. Linda Jane Palmer Archives.
Bliss, W.G. Letter to author. 2001. Richard Toronto Archives.
Browne, Howard. Letter to Chester Geier. 1988. Jim Pobst Archives.
_____. Letter to Chester Geier. June 20, 1988. Jim Pobst Archives.
Collins, Kyra, Letter to Frank Brownley. April 5, 1951. Jim Pobst Archives.
Hamling, William L. Letter to author. April 24, 2010. Richard Toronto Archives.
_____. Letter to author. September 13, 2010. Richard Toronto Archives.
_____. Letter to author. November 26, 2010. Richard Toronto Archives.
_____. Letter to author. December 11, 2010. Richard Toronto Archives.
_____. Letter to author. February 11, 2011. Richard Toronto Archives.
Geier, Chester. Letter to Jim Pobst. 1982. Jim Pobst Archives.
_____. Letter to Jim Pobst. March 1982. Jim Pobst Archives.
_____. Letter to Jim Pobst. March 26, 1982. Jim Pobst Archives.
_____. Letter to Jim Pobst. 1988. Jim Pobst Archives.
_____. Letter to Jim Pobst. February 1989. Jim Pobst Archives.
Horton, Richard. Letter to author. 2003. Richard Toronto Archives.
_____. Letter to author. 2004. Richard Toronto Archives.
_____. Letter to author. 2005. Richard Toronto Archives.
_____. Letter to author. 2007. Richard Toronto Archives.
Keller, E. Letter to Richard Horton. 1991. Richard Toronto Archives.
Kossuth, Norman S. Letter to Vaughn M. Greene. November 30, 1947. Jim Pobst Archives.
Palmer, Ray. Letter to Forrest J Ackerman. March 28, 1935. Linda Jane Palmer Archives.
_____. Letter to Forrest J Ackerman. July 24, 1935. Linda Jane Palmer Archives.
_____. Letter to Forrest J Ackerman. September 14, 1935. Linda Jane Palmer Archives.
_____. Letter to Forrest J Ackerman. June 26, 1936. Linda Jane Palmer Archives.
_____. Letter to Forrest J Ackerman. March 22, 1937. Linda Jane Palmer Archives.
_____. Letter to Jim Garrison, Nov. 27, 1968. The Jim Pobst Archives.
Shaver, Dorothy. Letters to author. January 21 and July 11, 1980. Richard Toronto Archives.
_____. Letter to Jim Pobst. 1981. Jim Pobst Archives.
_____. Letter to Jim Pobst. March 16, 1981. Jim Pobst Archives.
_____. Letter to Jim Pobst. June 17, 1981. Jim Pobst Archives.
Shaver, Grace. Letter to Sophie Shaver. June 12, 1936. Evelyn Bryant Archives.
Shaver, Richard. Letter to author. July 28, 1973. Richard Toronto Archives.
_____. Letter to a correspondent. November 11, 1974. Richard Toronto Archives.
_____. Letter to Richard Horton. 1950. Richard Toronto Archives.
_____. Letter to Richard Horton. April 3, 1950. Richard Toronto Archives.
_____. Letter to Richard Horton. May (?) 1950. Richard Toronto Archives.
_____. Letter to Richard Horton. May 3, 1950. Richard Toronto Archives.
_____. Letter to Richard Horton. June 14, 1950. Richard Toronto Archives.
_____. Letter to Richard Horton. December 8, 1959. Richard Toronto Archives.
_____. Letter to Richard Horton. January 23, 1960.
_____. Letter to Richard Horton. March 1960.
_____. Letter to unknown correspondent. February 1967. Richard Toronto Archives.
_____. Letter to unknown correspondent. February 20, 1967. Richard Toronto Archives.
_____. Letter to unknown correspondent. September 1975. Add Richard Toronto Archives.
_____. Letter to W.G. Bliss. Date missing. Richard Toronto Archives.

Letters in Magazines

Browne, Howard. Letter to Charles Brown, Editor. *Locus*, December 1977.
Palmer, Ray. Letter to Richard Shaver. *The Hidden World*, Spring 1964.
_____. "Letters." *Forum,* March 1973.
_____. "Letters." *Forum,* June 1975.
Shaver, Richard. Letter to Ray Palmer. *The Hidden World*, Fall 1964.
_____. Letter to Ray Palmer. *The Hidden World*, Summer 1964.
_____. Letter to Ray Palmer. *The Hidden World*, Winter 1964.

Emails

Kemp, Earl. Email to author. July 3, 2008.

___. Email to author. December 2011.
___. Email to author. November 30, 2012.
Levesque, Tal. Email to author. April 17, 2003.
Page, G.W. Email to author. April 24, 2010.
Palmer, Linda Jane. Email to author. February 23, 2010.
___. Email to author. March 2, 2010.
___. Email to author. April 18, 2010.
___. Email to author. August 13, 2010.
___. Email to author. October 15, 2010.
___. Email to author. October 20, 2010.
___. Email to author. May 30, 2011.
___. Email to author. April 8, 2012.
___. Email to author. August 16, 2012.
Palmer, Raymond Bradley. Email to author. September 17, 2008.
___. Email to author. October 15, 2008.

Websites

"Chicon I Program." Fancyclopedia 3. Last modified January 8, 2012. http://fancyclopedia.wikidot.com/chicon-i-program.
"Shavertown, Pennsylvania." Wikipedia.com. Last modified on August 14, 2010. http://en.wikipedia.org/wiki/Shavertown,_Pennsylvania.
WhereInCity.com. Astrology. "Leo Health." www.WhereInCity.com/astrology/leo-health.php.
"Ypsilanti State Hospital." AsylumProjects.org, last modified August 15, 2011. asylumprojects.org/index.php?title=Ypsilanti_State_Hospital.

Newspapers

"4 Die in Riot at Ford Plant." *Detroit Free Press*, March 8, 1932.
The Detroit News. February 26, 1934.

Newsletters

Palmer, Ray. Letter to Long John Nebel. February 4, 1957. Reprinted in *Gray Barker's Newsletter*, Number 11, July 1980.
Pouba, Katherine, and Ashley Tianen. "Lunacy in the 19th Century: Women's Admission to Asylums in United States of America." *Oshkosh Scholar* 1 (April 2006). 99.

Ezines

Byrne, Stuart J. "Who Is S.J. Byrne AKA John Bloodstone? An Autobiography by Stu Byrne. From the booklet, 'Tarzan on Mars— Genesis and More.'" *ERBzine*. http://www.erbzine.com/mag19/1967.html.
Geier, Chester. "Re: Richard S. Shaver." *Shavertron*, Number 29, 1992.

Kemp. Earl. "Beauty and the Beast Otra Vez." *eI*, Volume 1, Number 4, October 2002. http://pdf.textfiles.com/efanzines/EK/eI4/index.htm.
___. "Blood and Sand." *eI*, Volume 1, Number 2, April 2002. http://efanzines.com/EK/eI2/index.htm.
___. "In a World I Never Made." *eI*, Volume 2, Number 4, August 2003. http://www.efanzines.com/EK/eI9/index.htm.
___. "Have Typewriter; Will Whore for Food." *eI*, Volume 1, Number 2, April 2002. http://efanzines.com/EK/eI2/index.htm.
___. "Tales of *Imagination* and Space Travel: A Capricious Chronology." *eI*, Volume 1, Number 5, December 2002. http://www.efanzines.com/EK/eI5/index.htm.
___. "Taps." *eI*, Volume 2, Number 3, June 2003. http://efanzines.com/EK/eI8/index.htm.
___, ed. *The Compleat and Unexpurgated Who Killed Science Fiction? eI 29*. Kingman, AZ: an eI ebook. *http://efanzines.com/EK/eI29/*.
Metchette, Charles. "Michigan Memories" *Spacewarp* 42. September 1950. Last modified October 6, 2012. The Fanac Fan History Project. Fanac.org.
Palmer, Ray. "Tarzan Never Dies." *Other Worlds Science Stories*, November 1955. Reprinted on ERBzine. http://www.erbzine.com/mag3/0313.html.
Ramirez, Thomas. "Into the Abyss." *eI*, Volume 4, Number 4, August 2005. http://efanzines.com/EK/eI21/.
Shaver, Richard. "The Mystery of Shaver." *Shavertron*, Summer 2006. http://www.softcom.net/users/falconkam/shavindex3.html.
___. "Shaver's Pre-History Primer." *Shavertron*, 2006. http://www.softcom.net/users/falconkam/primer.html.
Yerxa, Richard, "Some Notes in Search of an Article." *eI*, Volume 2, Number 6, 2003. http://efanzines.com/EK/eI11/index.htm.

Court Documents

Agis, Dr. Jack. Wayne County, Michigan Probate Court document. August 5, 1934.
Hamling V. United States. 418 U.S. 87. 1.
Harris, Dr. H.E. Wayne County, Michigan Probate Court document. July 30, 1934.
Wayne County Probate Court document. August 30, 1934.

Miscellaneous

Dero, Steve Volto. Postcard. Date unknown. Author unknown. Jim Pobst Archives.
FBI Office Memorandum. "Flying Discs, Richard Shaver." SAC Chicago. September 20, 1947.
Richard Shaver's listing in the 1925 Bloomsburg High School Yearbook.

Index

Numbers in ***bold italics*** indicate pages with photographs.

Ackerman, Forrest J 13, 33, 34, 36–40, 138, 177, 201
aging (prevention) 106, 107, 110, 120, 123
Aldebaran Press 166, ***167***, 168, 169
American Car & Foundry ***65***, 66, 74
Amherst, Wisconsin 49, 184, 185, 187–189, 191–193, 198–200, 207, 209, 211–213, 215, 217, 226, 232, 238, 241
Arnold, Kenneth 152, 158–160, 163, 189, 204
Asimov, Isaac 32, 46, 179

Bee Hive Café 75
Berwick, Pennsylvania ***65***, 66–68, 71, 74, 75
Binder, Eando 35, 44, 50
Binder, Otto 28, 210
Blake Pharmaceuticals 4, 202, 207, 208, 214
Bliss, W.G. 68, 214, 228, 229, 232, 233
Bloch, Robert 20, 31, 32, 41–43, 150, 175, 177, 201
Bloomsburg, Pennsylvania 73–77, 79, 80
The Blue Bowl 76
Boston, Massachusetts 97, 99–101
Bott, Henry 52, 53, 207
Bradbury, Ray 43, 137
Brown, Theron C. 166–***168***
Browne, Howard 8, 20, 45, 52–54, 58, 59, 116–119, 121, 122, 127, 131, 134, 138, 142, 150, 151, 153, 155, 157, 158, 163, 172, 174, 175, 177, 178, 180, 183, 186, 197, 202, 207, 229, 241
Burroughs, Edgar Rice 41, 140, 144, 191, 192, 203, 204

Campbell, John W., Jr. 28, 35, 41, 48, 50, 65, 201
Carrel, Alexis 110

Communist 82, 83, 84, 86, 89, 91, 232
Corinth Publications 207, 213
Cosmology 39, 128
COSMOS 34, 35
Crile, George 109, 110

Dallas Township, Pennsylvania 62–64
Danville Hospital for the Insane 64
Davey Tree Expert Company 78, ***79***
Davis, Bernard G. "Bernie" 41, 116, 125, 142, 453, 154, 171, 172
Dawn of Flame 38
Dennis, Walter 23, 29
dero 2, 4, 6, 60, 90, 92, 98, 100, 105–107, 120, 125, 128, 132, 135, 139, 140, 145, 146, 149, 152, 156, 159, 162, 163, 166, 177, 178, 205, 219, 223, 227, 231, 233
Dero, Steve Volto 139, 140
Dick, Philip K. 4, 43
The Dream Makers 66, 74, 77, 81, 163, 168

Ellison, Harlan 7, 201, 208
exd 107, 209

fandom 3, 6, 7, 10, 22, 29, 32–35, 38, 39, 43, 44, 46, 48–50, 53, 58, 118, 128, 134, 136, 137, 140, 141, 144, 145, 149, 151, 152, 156, 161, 165, 179, 180, 235
Fantasy Magazine 6, 31, 35, 36, 38, 39, 41, 42, 47, 58, 134, 141
FATE 8, 131, 155, 162, 166, 170, 171, 176, 184, 187, 190–192, 193, 207, 222, 226, 229, 241
FBI 6, 14, 159, 160, 163, 177, 190, 233
Flying Saucers (magazine) 176, 226, 239, 240
flying saucers 2, 119, 147, 152, 158–160, 162, 163, 171, 172, 176, 189, 190, 213, 238, 239
Ford Hunger March 83
Forum 138, 176, 227, 230, 231, 232, 234, 239, 240
Freedom Publishing Company 207, 211, 212–214, 223, 224, 226, 227, 238
Fuller, Curtis 8, 162, 176, 180, 181, 191, 192, 207, 229, 241
The Futurians 46

Gardner, Thomas 140
Geier, Chester S. 52, 53, 117, 118, 124, 130, 131, 138, 143, 146, 148, 153, 154, 158, 161, 163, 166, 168–170, 176, 178, 179, 187, 190, 191, 207, 222, 226, 229, 241
Gernsback, Hugo 23, 29, 34, 39, 41
Grafton State Hospital 100, 101, 103
Graham, Roger P. (Rog Phillips) 53, 141–143, 148, 150, 165, 166, 177, 186, 197
gravity 59, 106, 107, 123, 165, 219
Gurvitch, Sophie 81–84, ***86***–91, 93–96, 102, 105, 113

Halley's Comet 12, 13, 18, 19, 148
Hamling, William L. 7, 8, 44–46, 48, 51–54, 59, 117–119, 127, 130, 131, 133, 134, 137, 138, 142, 143, 145–151, 154–156, 158, 160–163, 171, 172, 174–183, 186, 187, 192, 201, 202, 207, 208, 212, 213, 215–217, 223, 224, ***225***, 226, 227–229, 237–***239***, 241
Hamling/Yerxa, Frances 15, 54–57, 177, 178, 181, 187–189, 198, 207, 240, 241
Hefner, Hugh 180–182, 187
The Hidden World 120, 135, 227

255

Hoar, Roger Sherman (aka Ralph Milne Farley) 31, 35, 41, 42, 53
"I Remember Lemuria!" 9, 10, 107, 121–124, 126, 128, 140, 171
International Scientific Association 31
Ionia State Hospital for the Criminally Insane 4, 9, 100, 102–107, 109, 110–113, 123

John Reed Society 82, 83

Keating, Lawrence A. 31, 37, 38
Kemp, Earl 178, 182, 201, 202, 208, 213–216, 224, 237, 238, 241
Kennedy, Joe 135, 144
Kossuth, Norman S. 139, 140, 247, 251, 253

Lanark, Wisconsin 184, 187, 211, 214
Life Chamber 110
Lily Lake, Illinois 123, 125, 171, 183
Link, Adam 44, 50, 210
Livingston, Berkeley 53, 131, 244
Lowndes, Robert 46
Luzerne County, Pennsylvania 62

Mahaffey, Bea 5, 8, 50, 148, 176, 179, 186, 202
Mantong 3, 4, 59, 111–113, 120, 124, 130, 153, 155, 223
Martian Diary 5, 12, 14, 25, 40, 41, 230–233, 235
A Martian Odyssey 32
Mathews, James Tilly 105, 106
McHenry, Illinois 123, 125, 131, 142, 146, 152, 155, 171, 183, 184
Michel, John 46
Milwaukee Fictioneers 31, 32, 34, 38, 39, 41, 42, 188
Moskowitz, Sam 31, 33, 35, 38, 36, 43, 46
Muir, John 23, 24
Muirdale Sanatorium 23–25, 27, 29–31
Mystic 176, 190–193, 226, 227

Newfoundland 98, 101, 109
Nydia 100, 101, 103, 104, 106

Oahspe 126, 127, 138, 146, 148, 149, 192
O'Brien, David Wright 51

Other Worlds 36, 50, 124, 170, 176, 184–186, 202, 203, 204, 226
Palmer, Helen 12–14, 20, 21
Palmer, Linda Jane 5, 35, 56, 57, 126, 138, 175, 187–189, 199–201, 238, 240, 241
Palmer, Ray (accidents) 13–17, 19, 20, 27, 28, 185, 186, 198
Palmer, Raymond B. 8, 184
Palmer, Roy C. 12–15, 20, 21–23, 35, 40, 48, 189, 241
Philadelphia, Pennsylvania 6, 74, 76, 77, 97, 112, 124, 161
P.J. Lavies Company 23, 35, 36, 40, 41
Playboy 181, 182, 187, 193, 224
Pobst, Jim 81, 85, 99
Pohl, Frederik 29, 46
pornography 208, 212, 223, 237

Ray Palmer's Newsletter 240
rays 4, 9, 89, 90, 97, 100, 103, 104–108, 110, 112, 120, 131, 135, 139, 140, 146, 152, 163, 171, 194, 231
Regency Publications 207, 213
Reinsberg, Mark 53, 178
Riverside Theater 36, 44, 188
Robinson, Frank M. 47, 162, 207
rock books 1, 208–210, 212, 218, 222, 224, 227, 228, 232–235
rock painting 86, **206**, 218, **220**, 227, **228**
Rogue 178, 180, 182, 187, 189, 192, 207, 208, 214, 229
Ruppert, Conrad 33, 39

Schwartz, Julius 13, 31, 33, 38, 39
The Science Correspondence Club 29, **30**, 201
Science Fiction Digest 32, 33, 39
Search 176, 191, 227, 238, 239, 240
The Secret World 233, 234
Shaver, Dorothy "Dottie" 1, 66, 70, 73, 79, 95, 111, 112, 123, 125, 126, 142, 143, **168**, 184, 185, 187, 193, 194, 197, 198, 205, 207, 208, 212, 213, **216**, 218, 226, 227, 234–236
Shaver (Shaeffer), Philip 62, 63
Shaver, Richard: butcher 77, 78; commitment to Ypsilanti State Hospital 90, 91; deportation 99, 100; farming 183, 193, 223; landscaping engineer 78, *79*, 80; sunstroke 89, 99, 103
Shaver/Gurvitch/Bryant, Evelyn Ann 20, 21, 82, 89, **92**, 93, 95, 96, 99, 103, 113, 221

The Shaver Mystery Club 146, 153–156, 161, 163, 166, 167–169, 183, 194
Shaver Mystery Club Magazine 154–156, 183, 194
Shavertown, Pennsylvania 62, 63, 65, 67
Shavertron 1, 130, 131, 241
Speer, Jack 6

Teck Publications 41
telaug 4, 105, 142, 145, 149, 227, 228
tero 4, 107, 149, 152, 219
Thrilling Wonder Stories 37–40, 48
Tremaine, F. Orlin 44, 48
Tucker, Bob 46

Vampire 135, 144
Venture Bookstore 176
voices 4, 6, 7, 9, 74, 84, 88–91, 95, 100, 103, 105, 111, 112, 118, 120, 121, 126, 131, 132, 134, 135, 137, 142, 147, 149, 157, 194

War with Jupiter 53
Warner, Harry, Jr. 22, 32, 38, 40, 41, 43, 49, 50, 53, 135, 172
A Warning to Future Man 120, 121
Weinbaum, Stanley G. 31, 32, 38, 39, 47
welding gun 86, 87, 89
Wicker School of Fine Art 81, 83, 85–87
Williams, Robert Moore 50, 53, 56
Wilson, Marjorie 15, 18, 55–58, 103, 177, 183–186, 188, 199, 238, 240
Wollheim, Donald 46
World War II 3, 14, 28, 50, 82, 158
Worldcon: Chicago 6, 7; Cincinnati 172; Philadelphia 161; San Francisco 186

Yerxa, Frances *see* Hamling, Frances
Yerxa, Leroy 54, 56, 57, 177
Yerxa, Richard 178, 181, 182, 189, 193, 224, **225**
Ypsilanti State Hospital 91–95, 97, 100, 102, 105, 235

Ziff, William B. 41, 52, 124, 125, 127, 141, 142, 150–153, 156–163, 166, 170–172, 174, 175, 177, 181, 183, 191, 216

www.ingramcontent.com/pod-product-compliance
Ingram Content Group UK Ltd.
Pitfield, Milton Keynes, MK11 3LW, UK
UKHW050537150426
5217IPUK00026B/1970